VROOM TOONS

Volume One
2013 - 2016

By Matt Vroom
with Samuel Clemens (Zoom Man #3)
and Michele Vroom (Candle Light)

"FOR MY QUEEN AND PRINCESS"

Vroomation Studios
www.vroomation.com

Book design by Matt Vroom.

TABLE OF CONTENTS

2013

2014

2015

2016

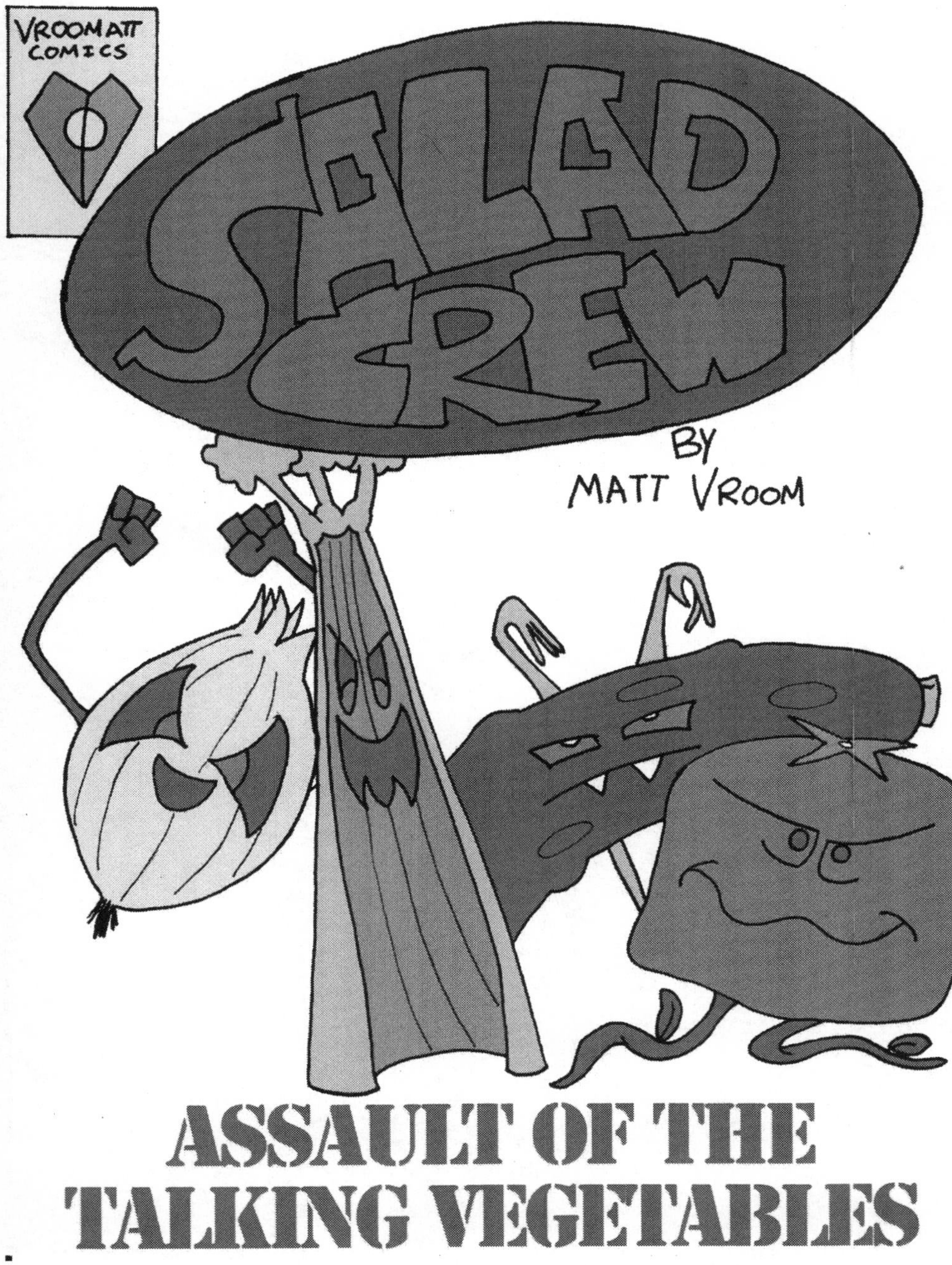
VROOMATT COMICS
SALAD CREW
BY MATT VROOM
ASSAULT OF THE TALKING VEGETABLES

MATT'S NOTES:

This comic actually has some characters in it that are based on some people that I knew as a food prep worker at Brigham Young University Idaho Food Services. I remember getting most of their approvals to publish this comic.

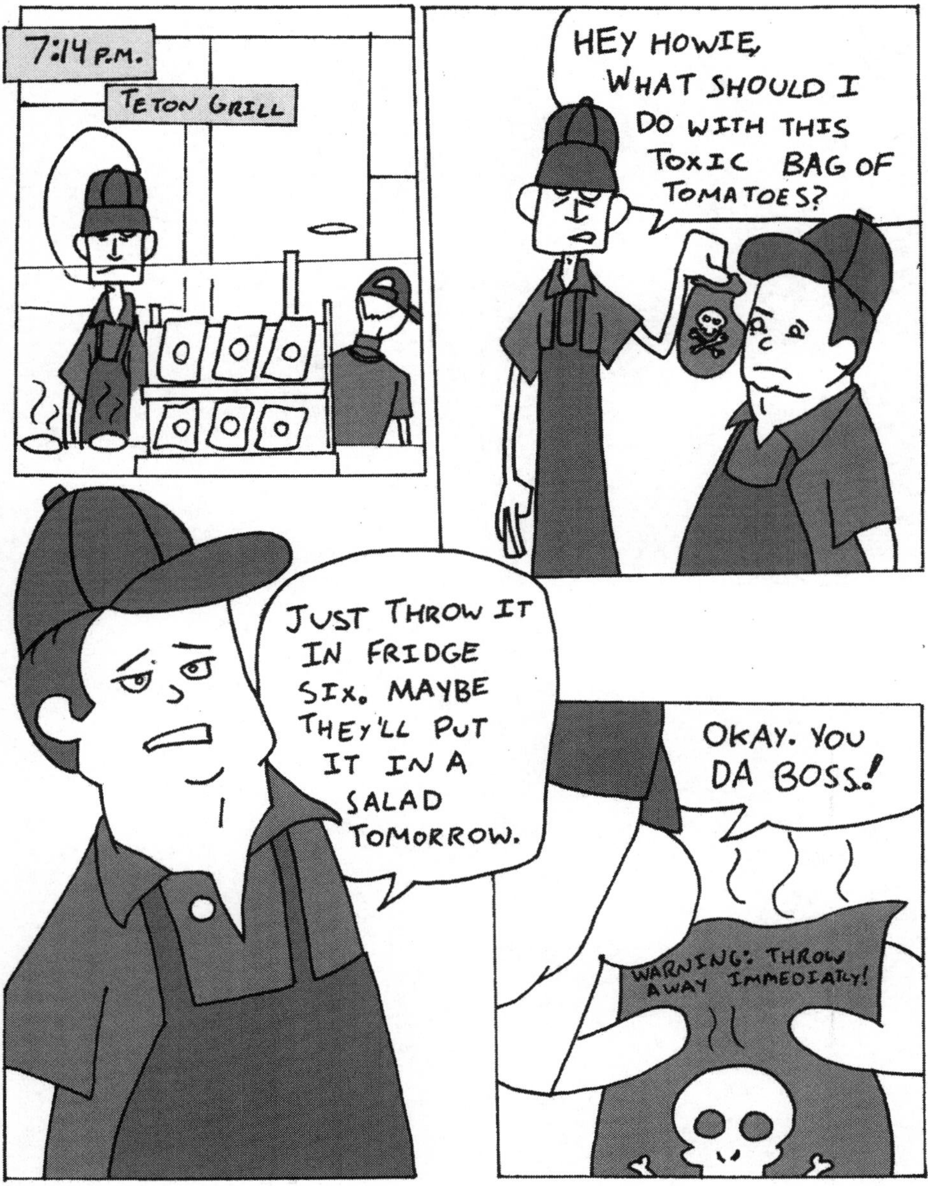
7:14 P.M.
TETON GRILL
HEY HOWIE, WHAT SHOULD I DO WITH THIS TOXIC BAG OF TOMATOES?
JUST THROW IT IN FRIDGE SIX. MAYBE THEY'LL PUT IT IN A SALAD TOMORROW.
OKAY. YOU DA BOSS!
WARNING: THROW AWAY IMMEDIATLY!

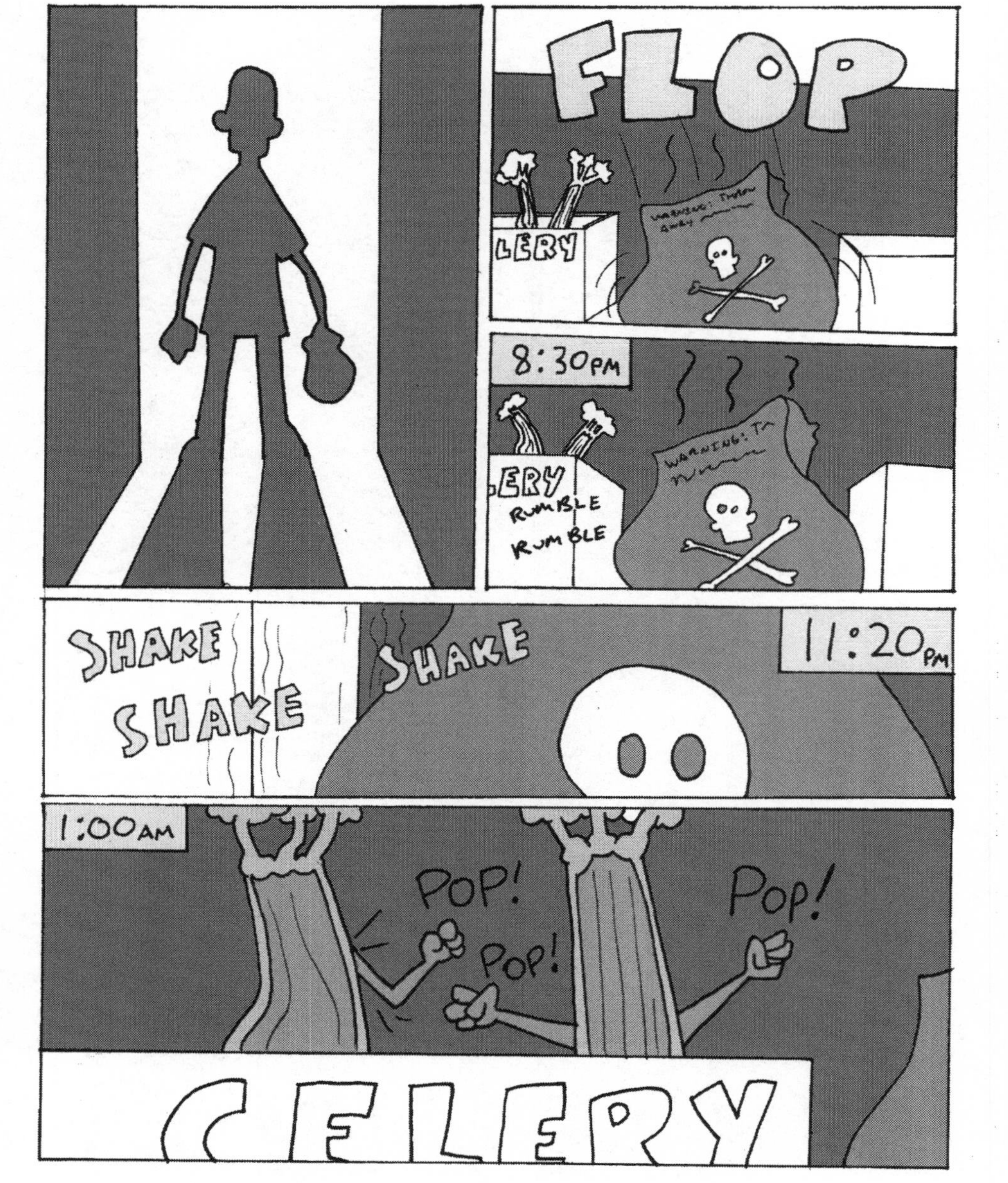
FLOP
LERY
8:30PM
ERY
RUMBLE
RUMBLE
SHAKE
SHAKE
SHAKE
11:20PM
1:00AM
POP!
POP!
Pop!
CELERY

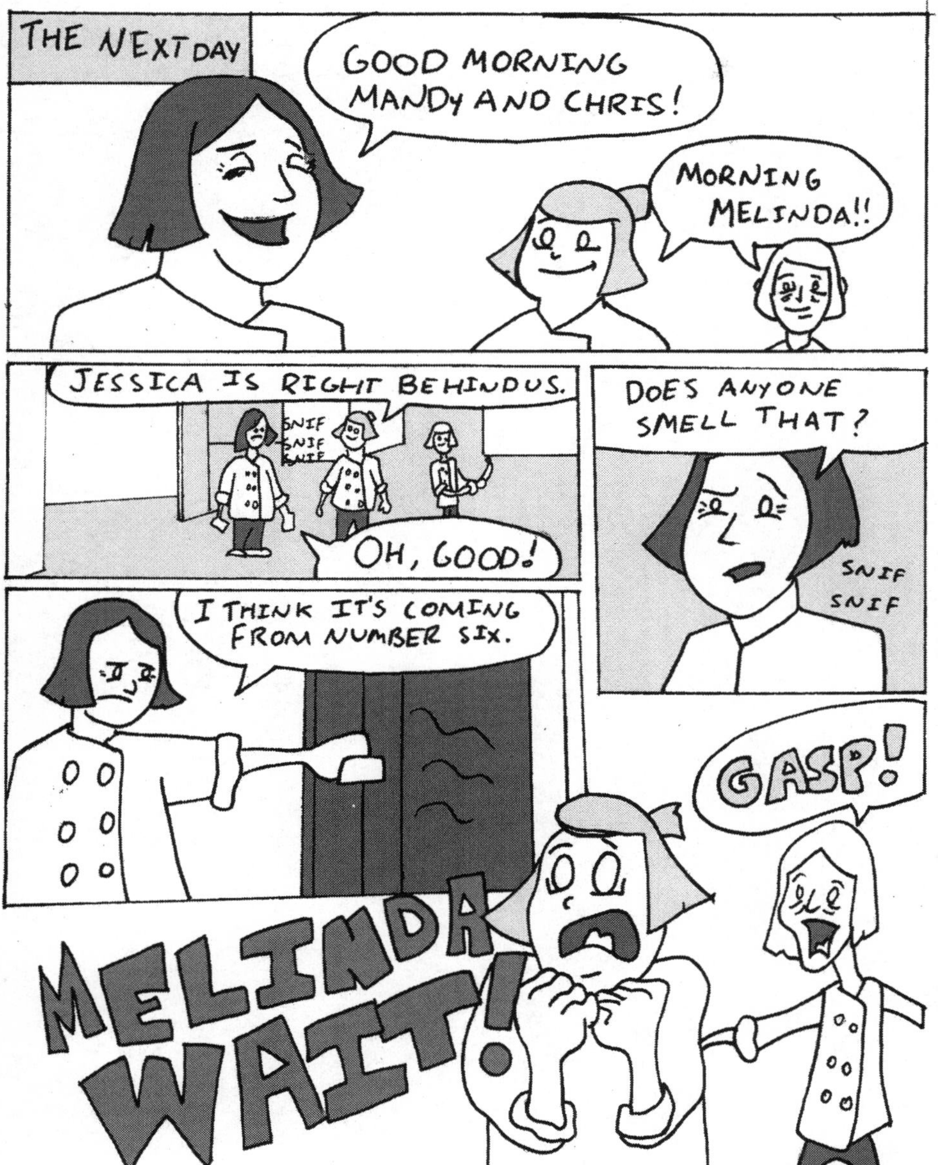
THE NEXT DAY
GOOD MORNING MANDY AND CHRIS!
MORNING MELINDA!!
JESSICA IS RIGHT BEHIND US.
SNIF SNIF
OH, GOOD!
DOES ANYONE SMELL THAT?
SNIF SNIF
I THINK IT'S COMING FROM NUMBER SIX.
GASP!
MELINDA WAIT!

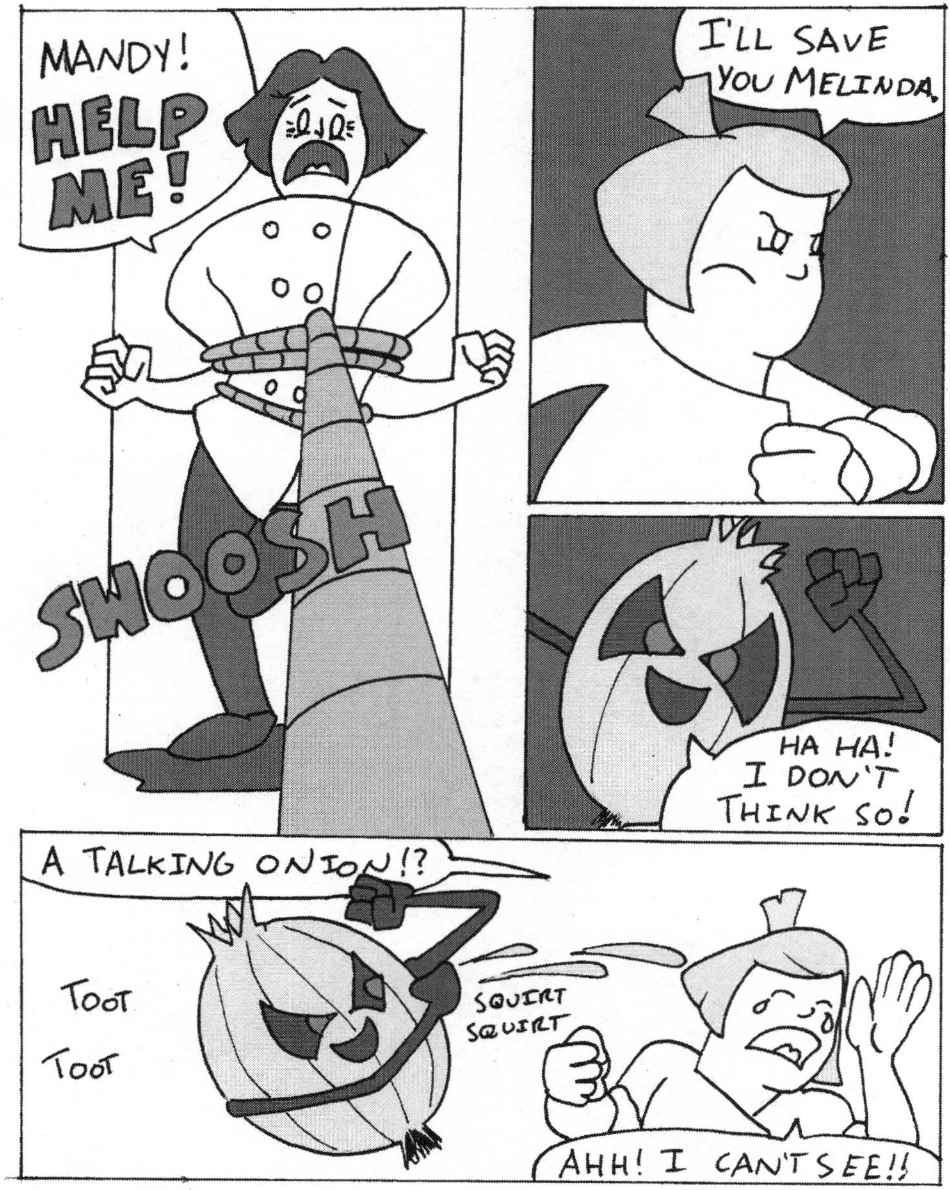
MANDY!
HELP ME!
SWOOSH
I'LL SAVE YOU MELINDA
HA HA! I DON'T THINK SO!
A TALKING ONION!?
TOOT
TOOT
SQUIRT
SQUIRT
AHH! I CAN'T SEE!!

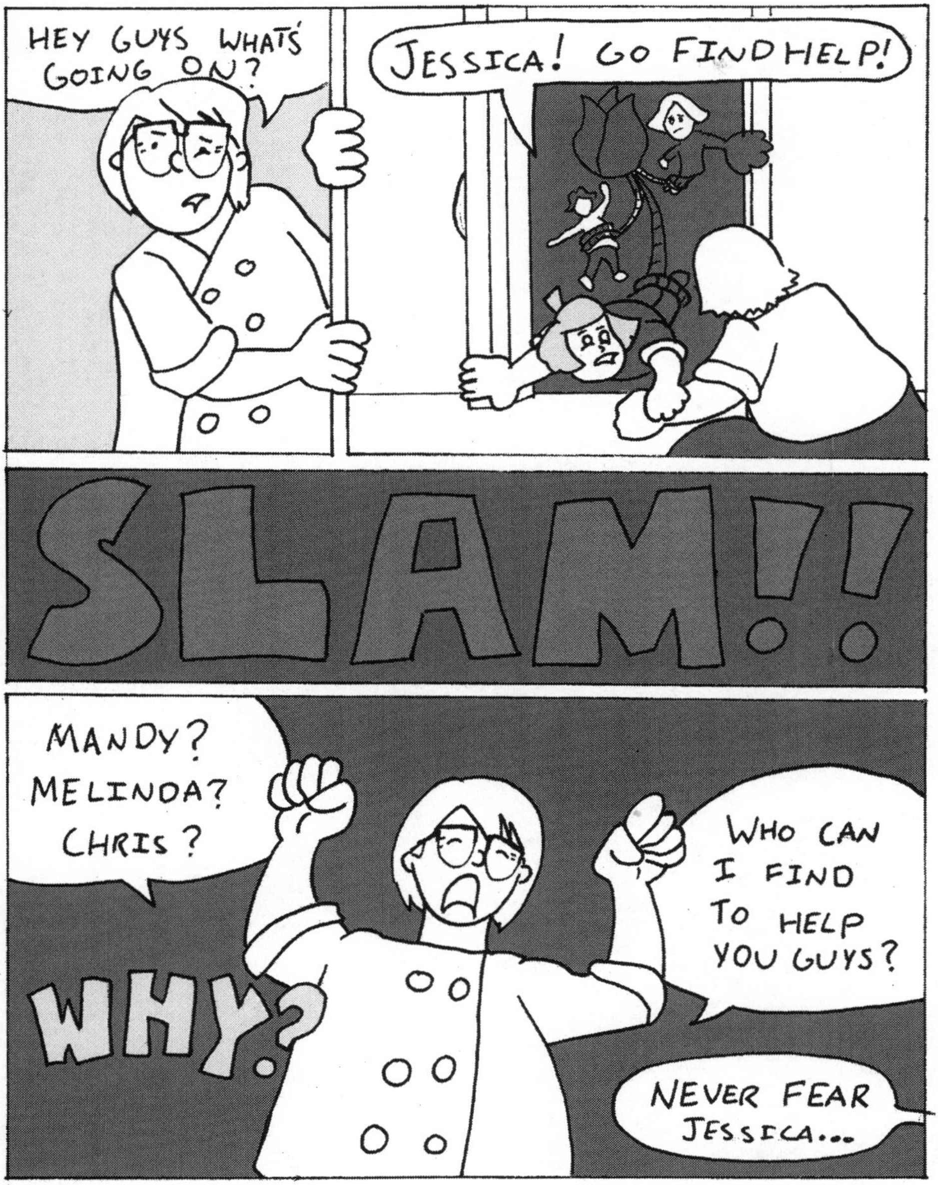
HEY GUYS WHAT'S GOING ON?
JESSICA! GO FIND HELP!
SLAM!!
MANDY? MELINDA? CHRIS?
WHY?
WHO CAN I FIND TO HELP YOU GUYS?
NEVER FEAR JESSICA...

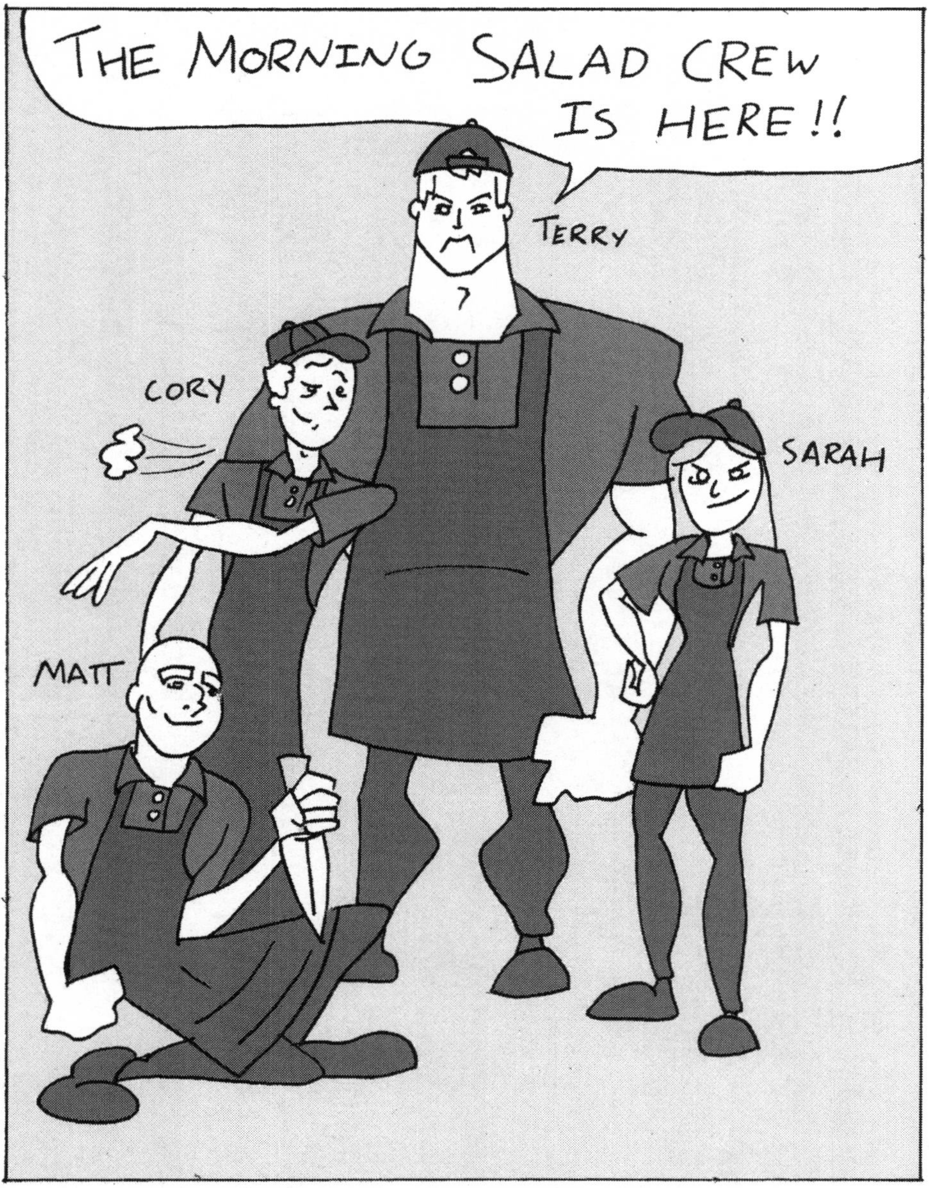
THE MORNING SALAD CREW IS HERE!!
TERRY
CORY
SARAH
MATT

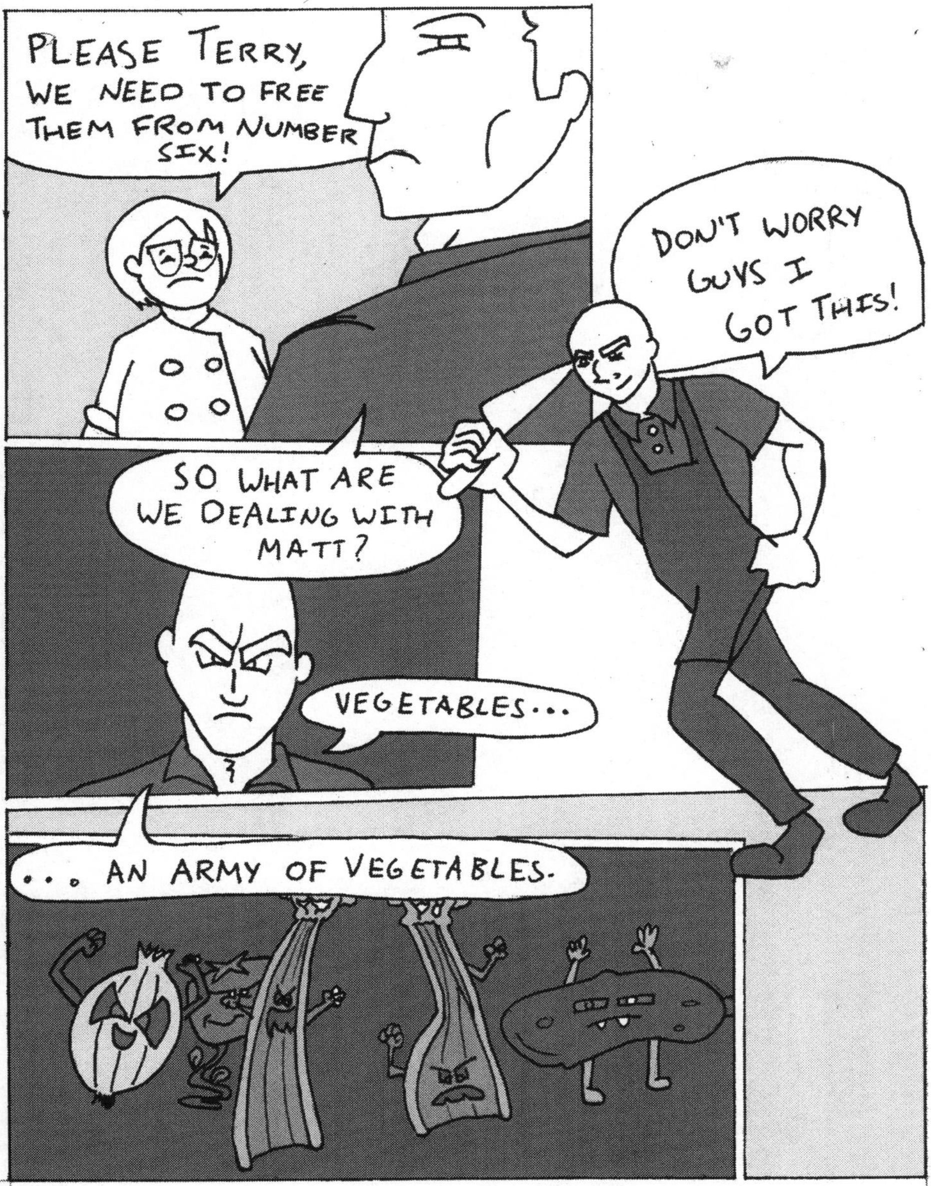
PLEASE TERRY, WE NEED TO FREE THEM FROM NUMBER SIX!
DON'T WORRY GUYS I GOT THIS!
SO WHAT ARE WE DEALING WITH MATT?
VEGETABLES...
... AN ARMY OF VEGETABLES.

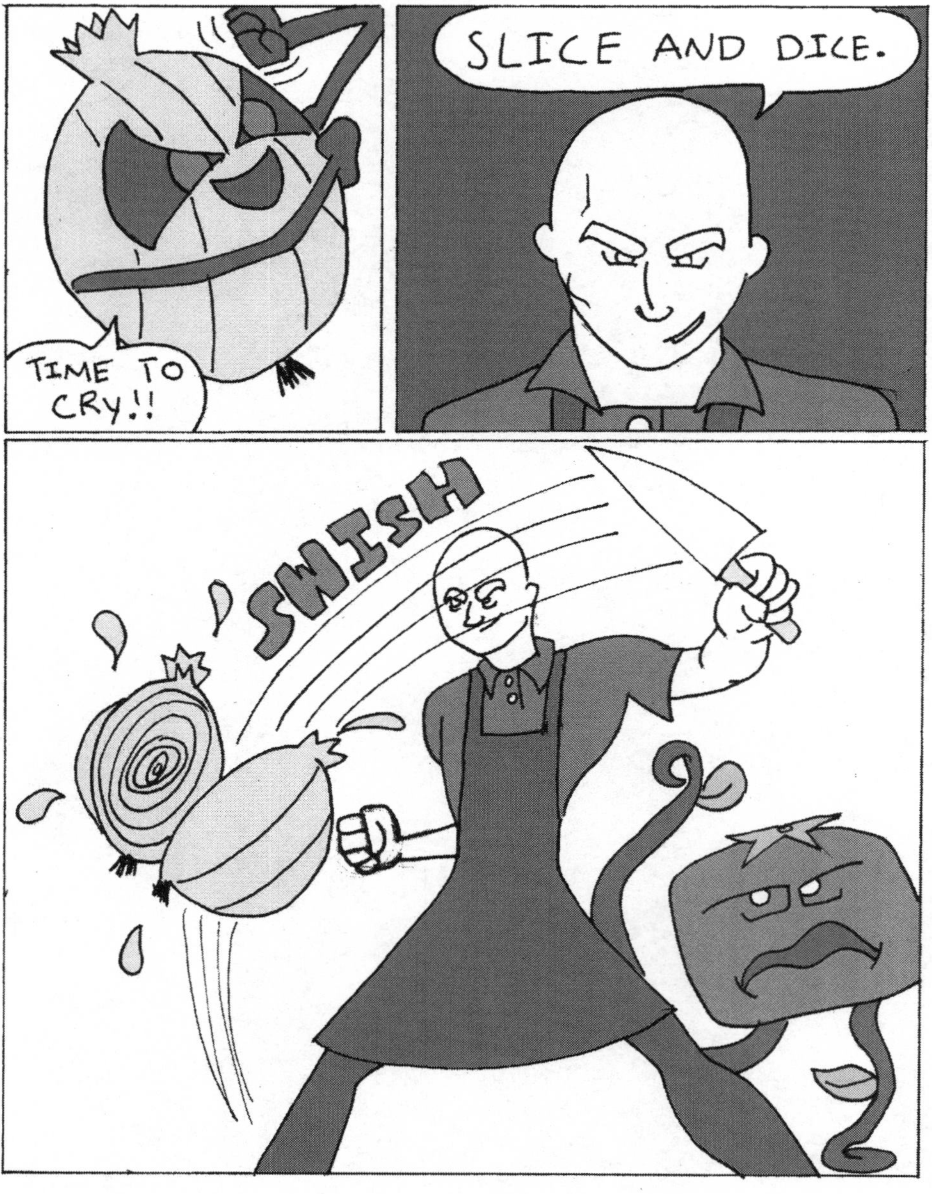
TIME TO CRY!!
SLICE AND DICE.
SWISH

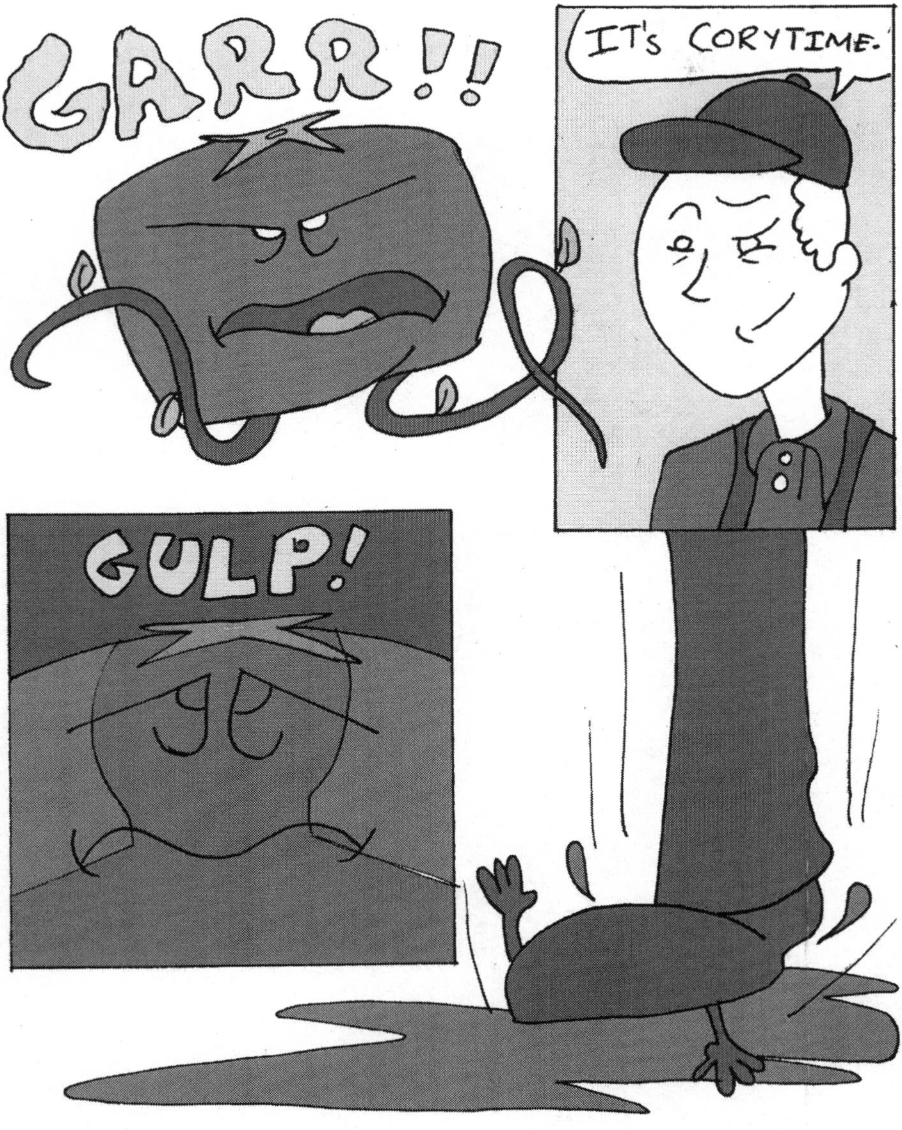
GARR!!
IT's CORYTIME.
GULP!

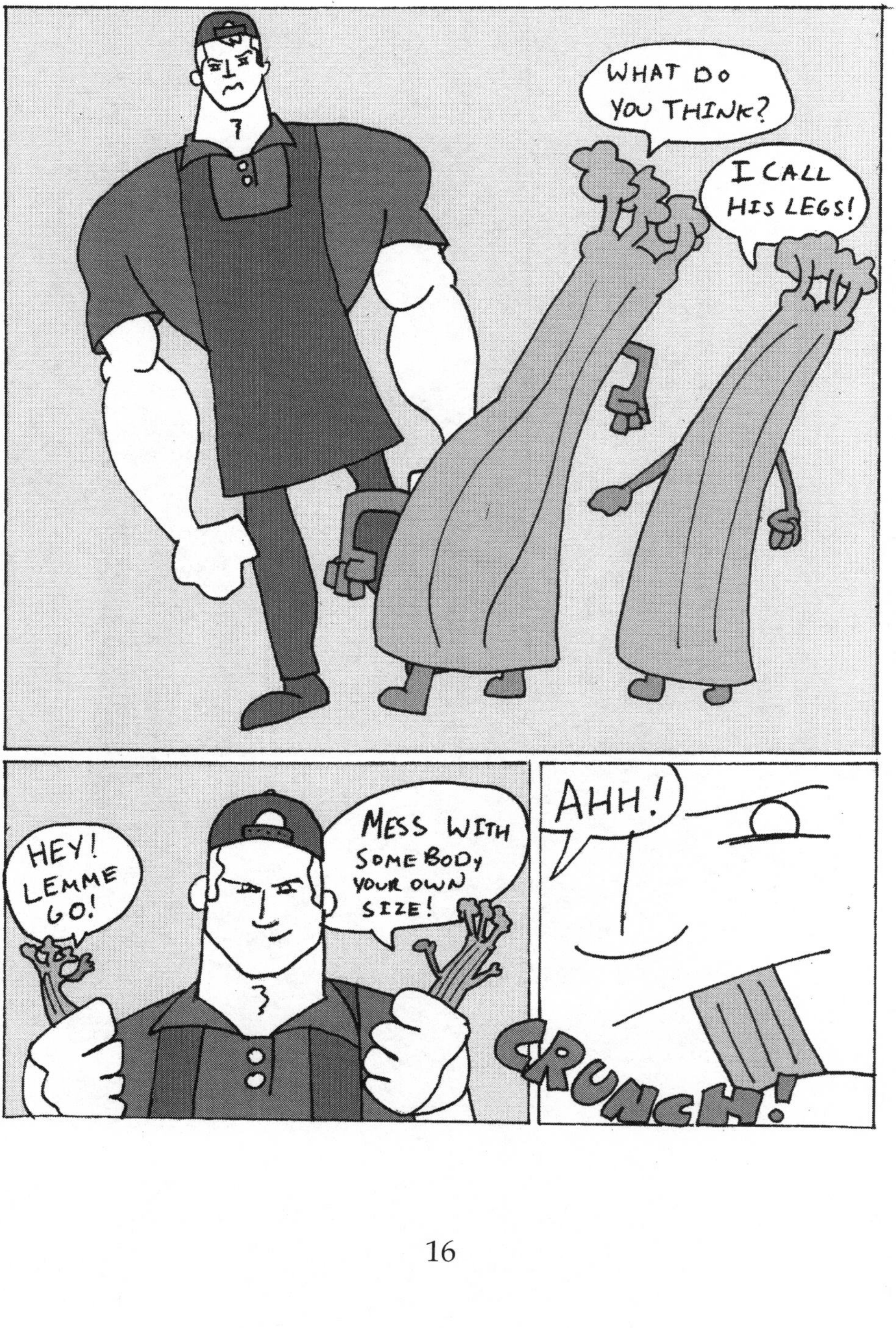
WHAT DO YOU THINK?
I CALL HIS LEGS!
HEY! LEMME GO!
MESS WITH SOMEBODY YOUR OWN SIZE!
AHH!
CRUNCH!

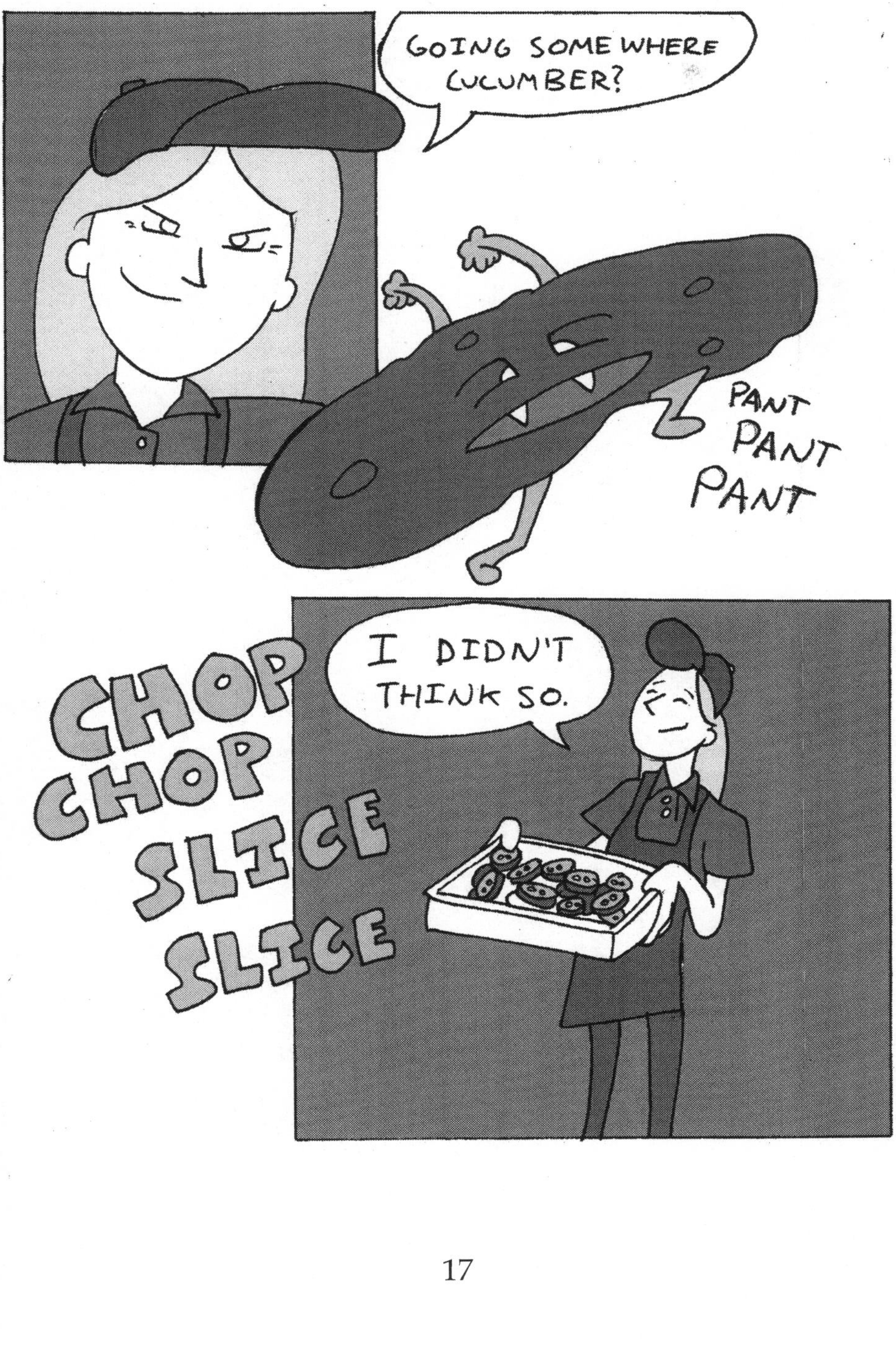
GOING SOMEWHERE CUCUMBER?
PANT
PANT
PANT
I DIDN'T THINK SO.
CHOP
CHOP
SLICE
SLICE

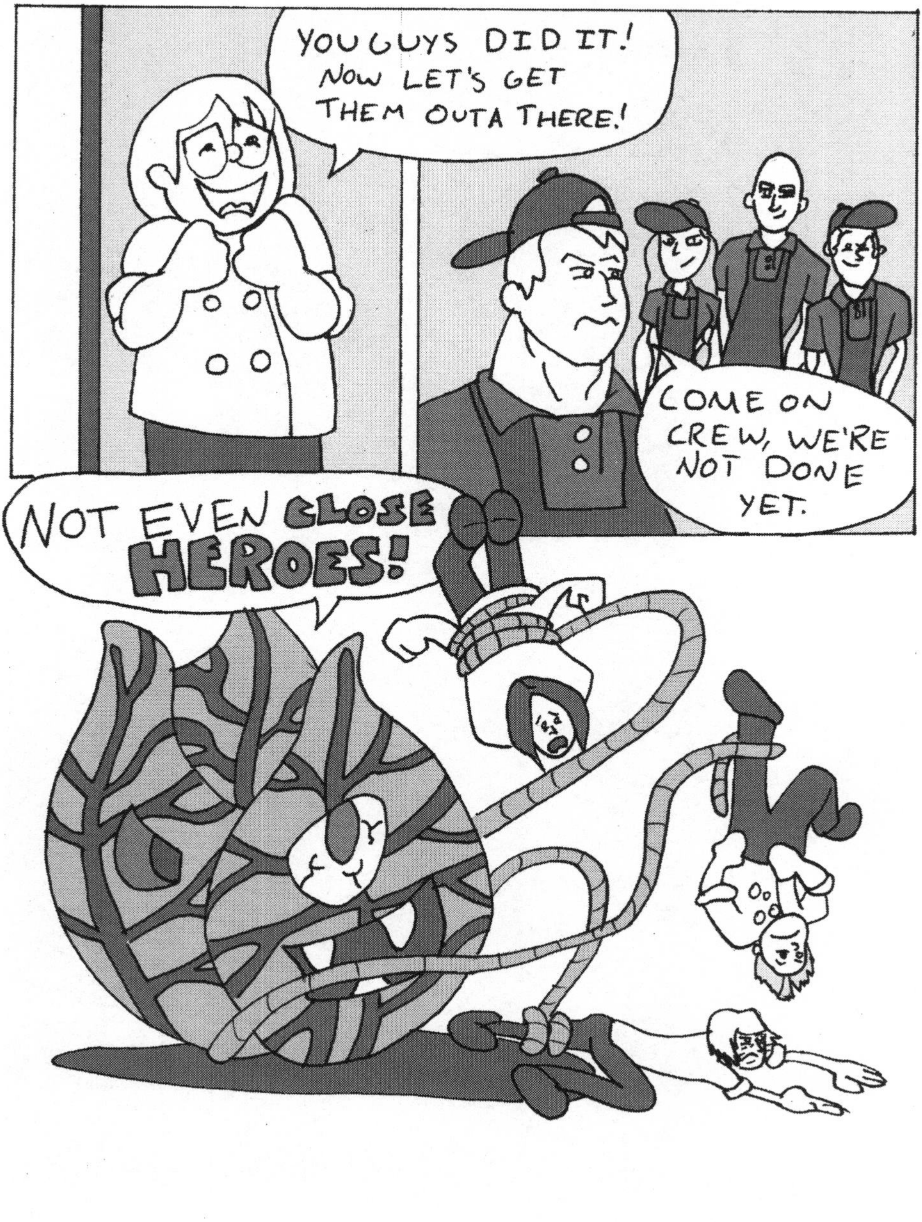
YOU GUYS DID IT! NOW LET'S GET THEM OUTA THERE!
COME ON CREW, WE'RE NOT DONE YET.
NOT EVEN CLOSE HEROES!

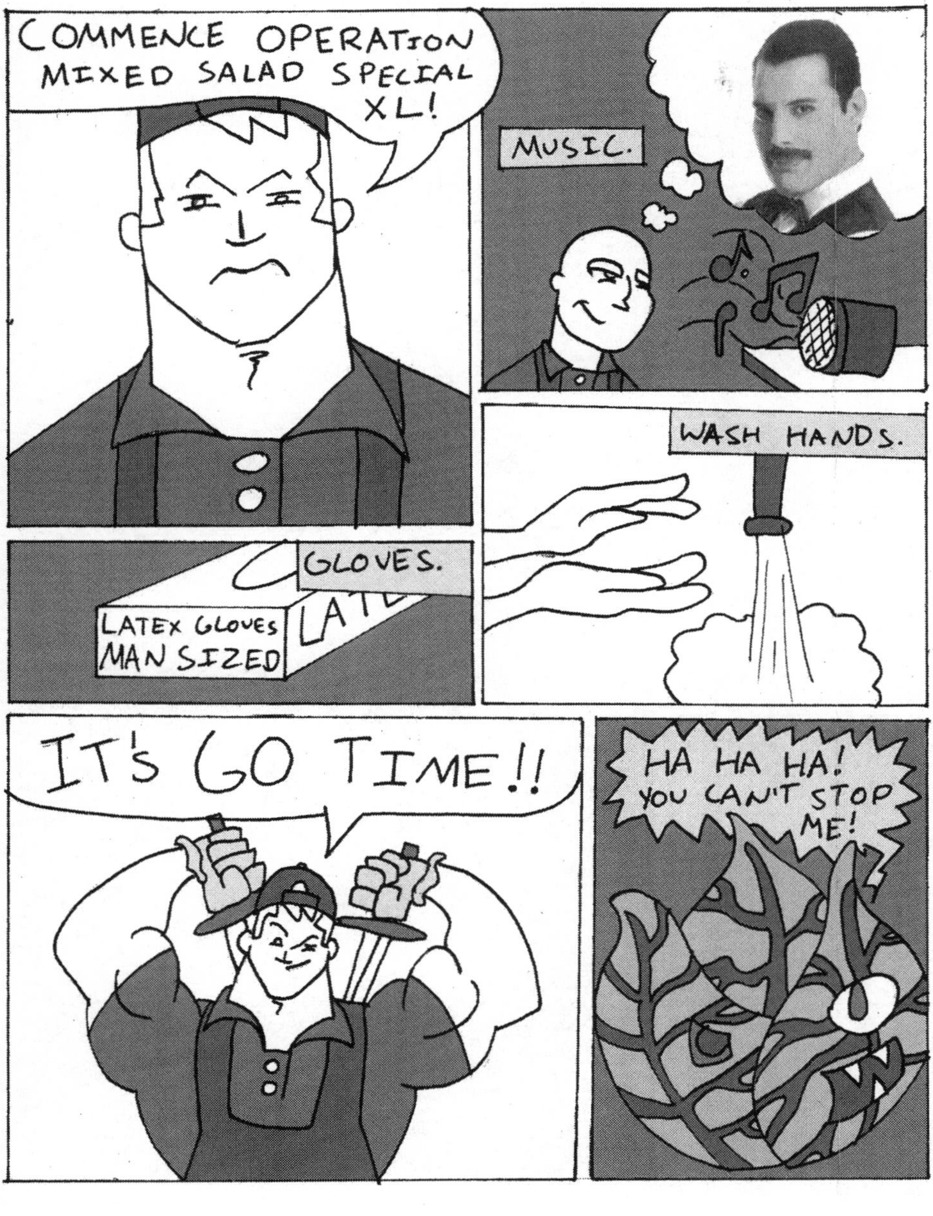
COMMENCE OPERATION MIXED SALAD SPECIAL XL!
MUSIC.
WASH HANDS.
GLOVES.
LATEX GLOVES MAN SIZED
IT'S GO TIME!!
HA HA HA! YOU CAN'T STOP ME!

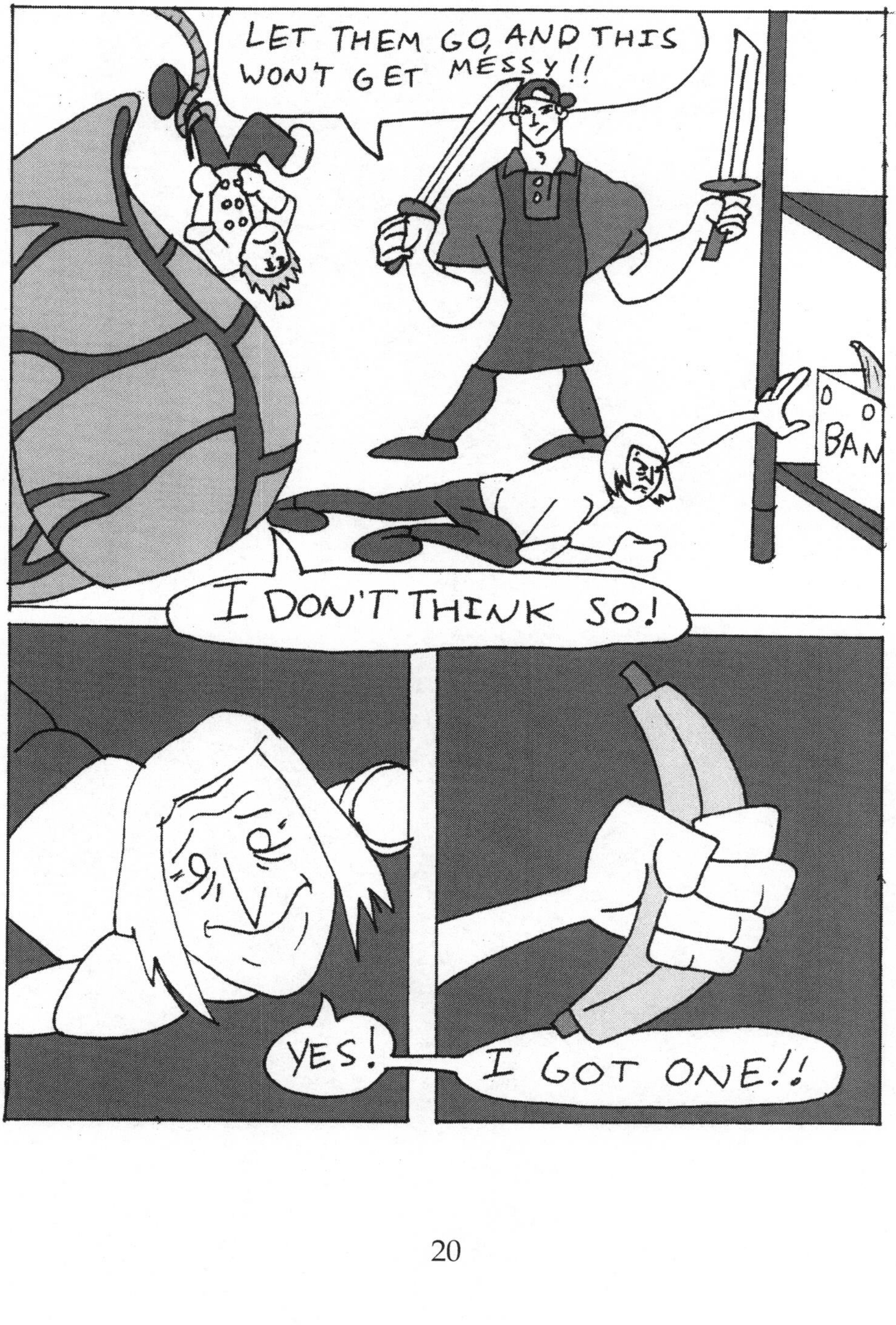
LET THEM GO, AND THIS WON'T GET MESSY!!
BAN
I DON'T THINK SO!
YES!
I GOT ONE!!

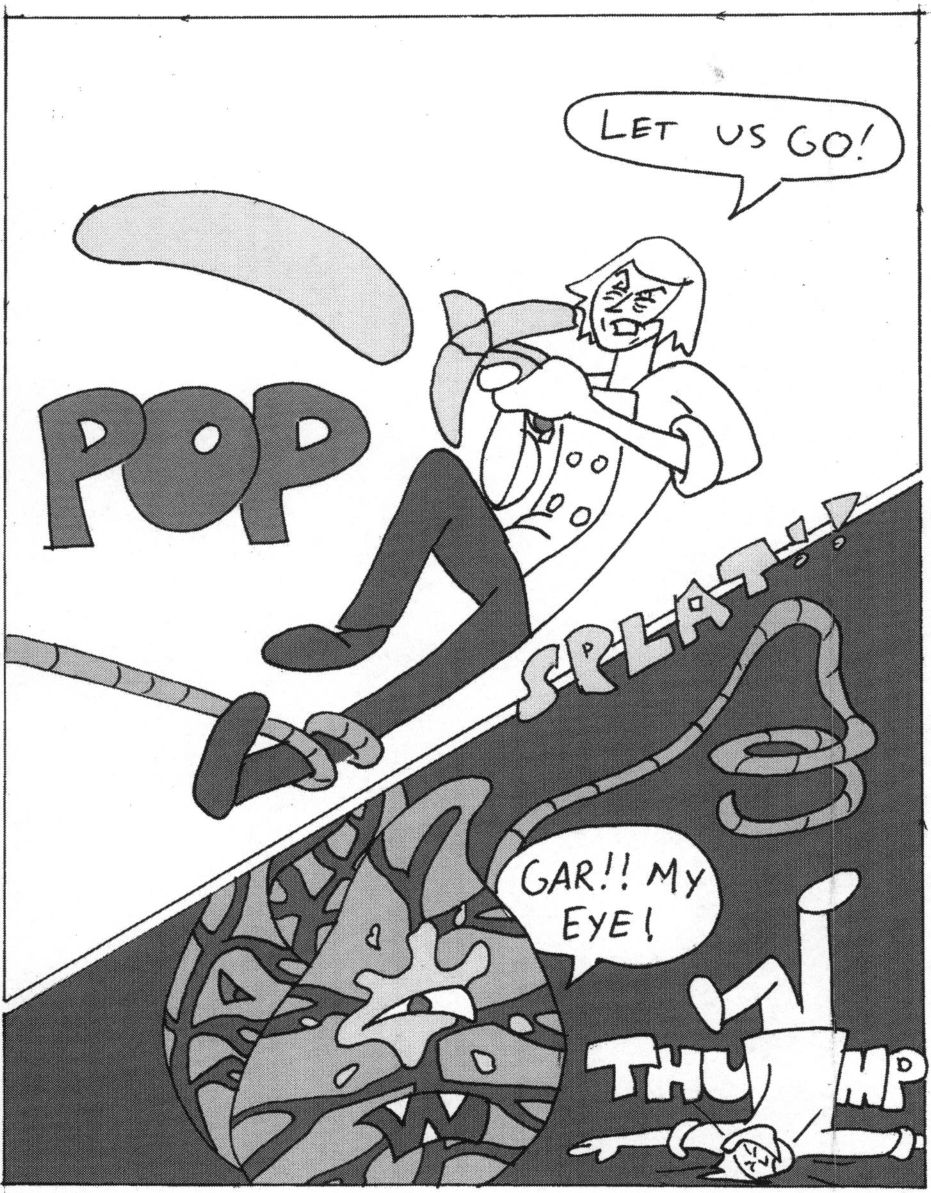
LET US GO!
POP
SPLAT!
GAR!! MY EYE!
THUMP

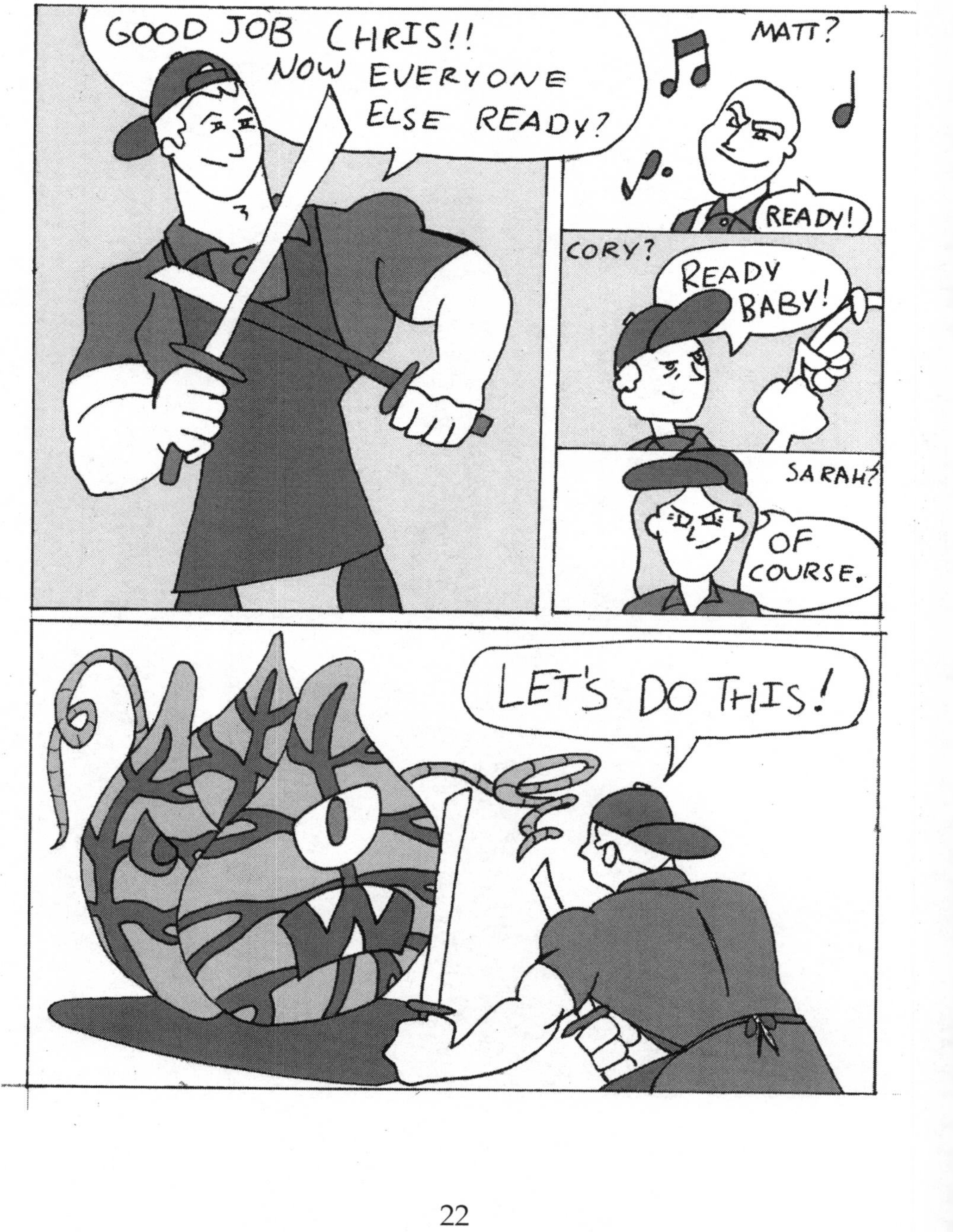
GOOD JOB CHRIS!! NOW EVERYONE ELSE READY?
MATT?
READY!
CORY?
READY BABY!
SARAH?
OF COURSE.
LET'S DO THIS!

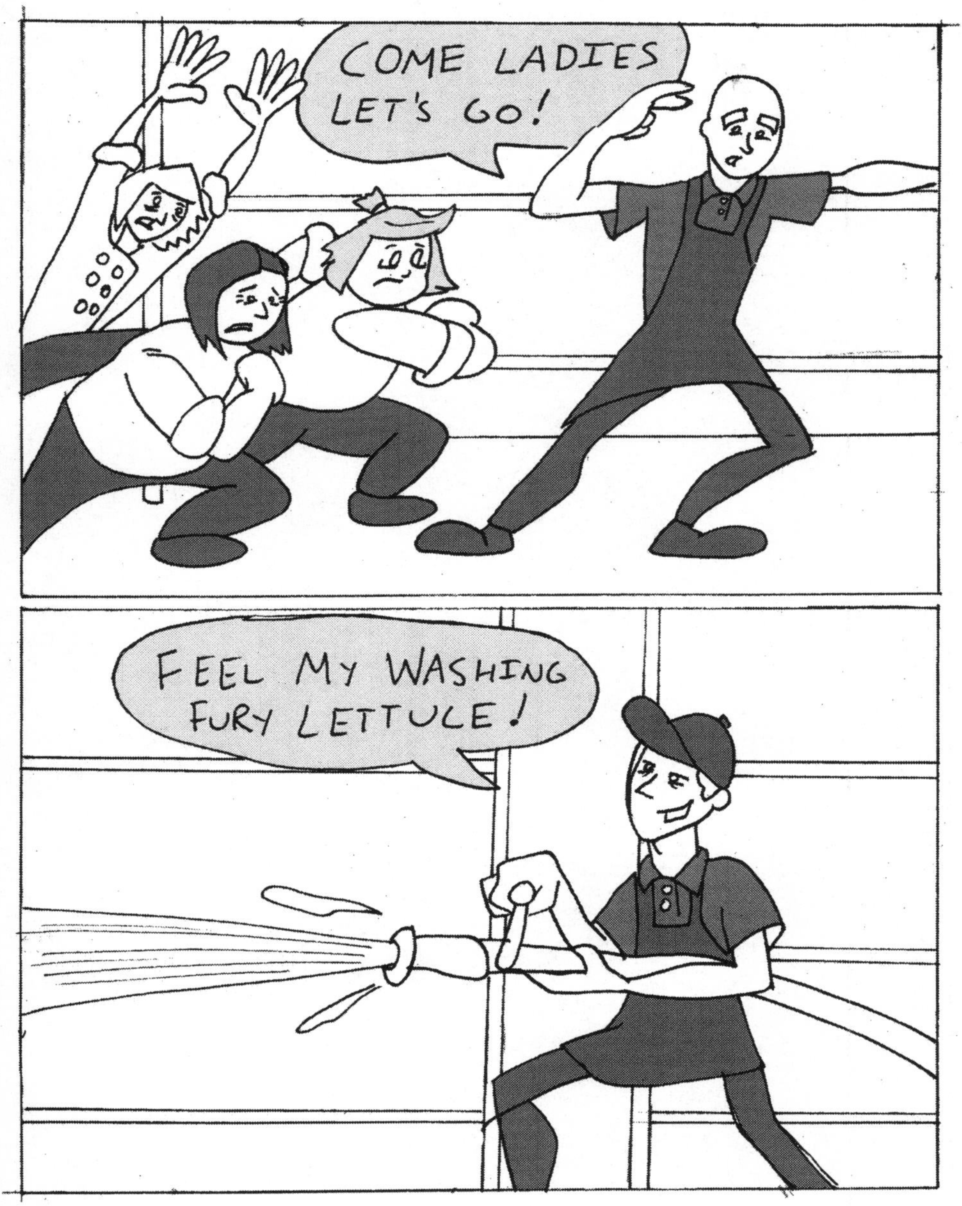
COME LADIES LET'S GO!
FEEL MY WASHING FURY LETTUCE!

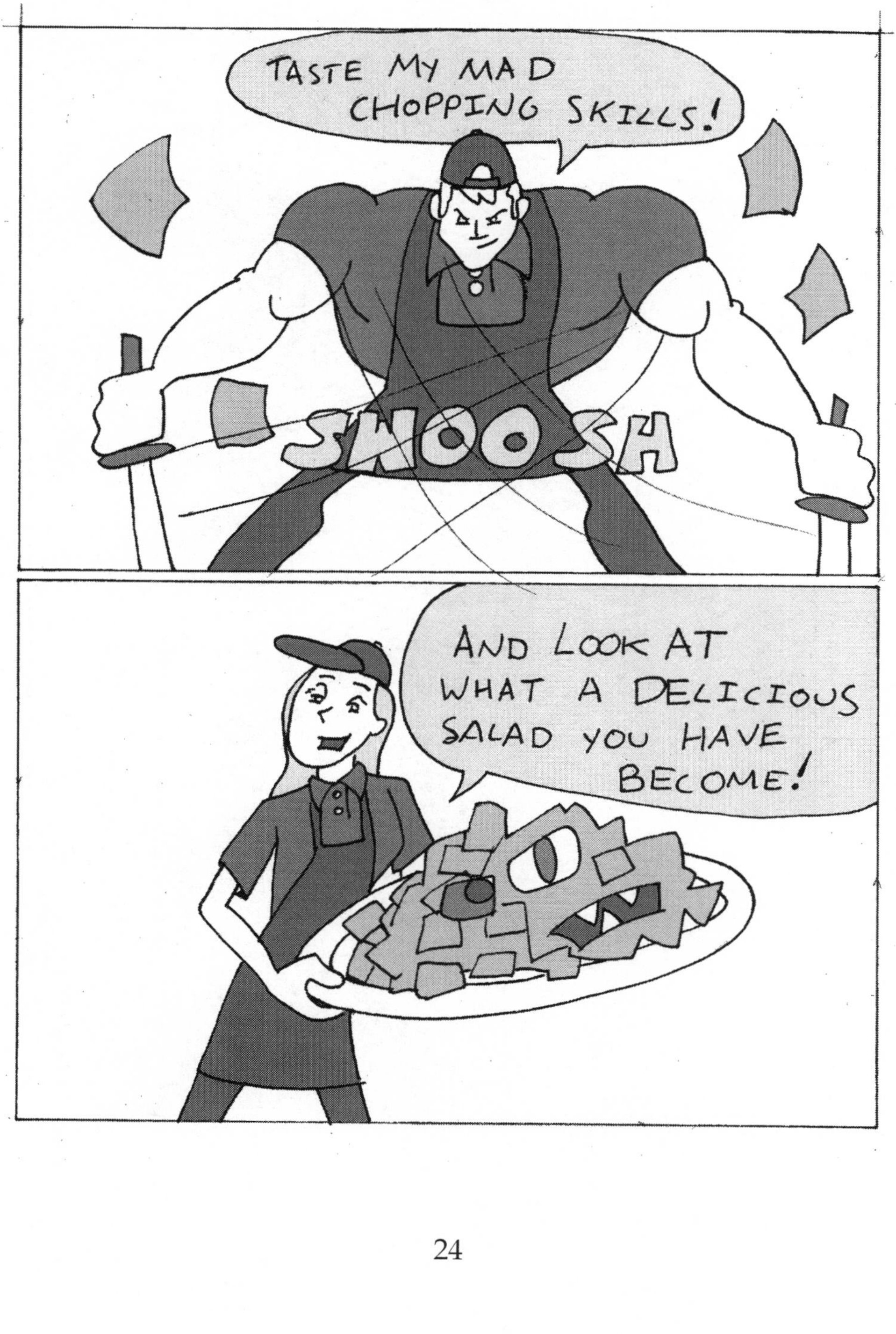
TASTE MY MAD CHOPPING SKILLS!
SWOOSH
AND LOOK AT WHAT A DELICIOUS SALAD YOU HAVE BECOME!

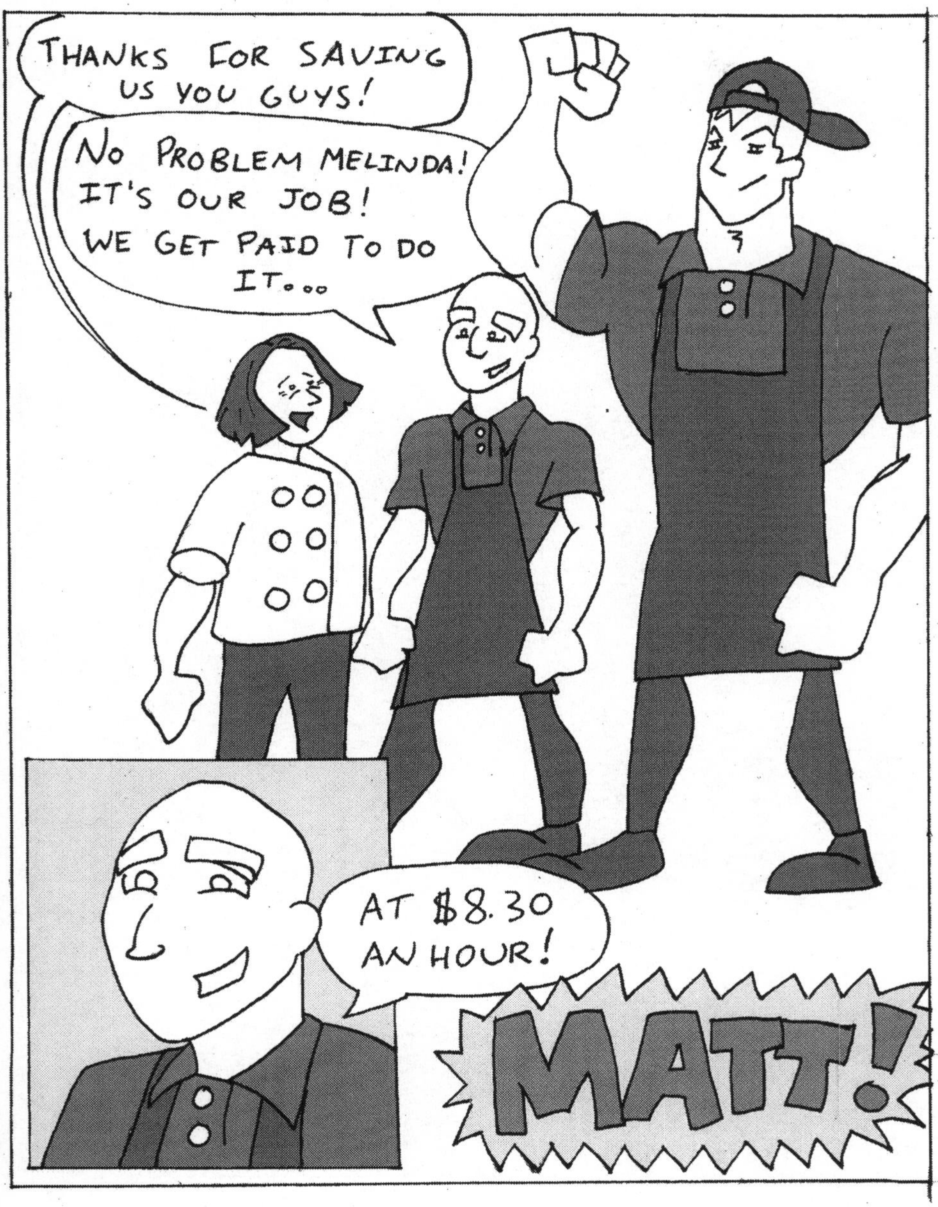
THANKS FOR SAVING US YOU GUYS!
NO PROBLEM MELINDA! IT'S OUR JOB! WE GET PAID TO DO IT...
AT $8.30 AN HOUR!
MATT!

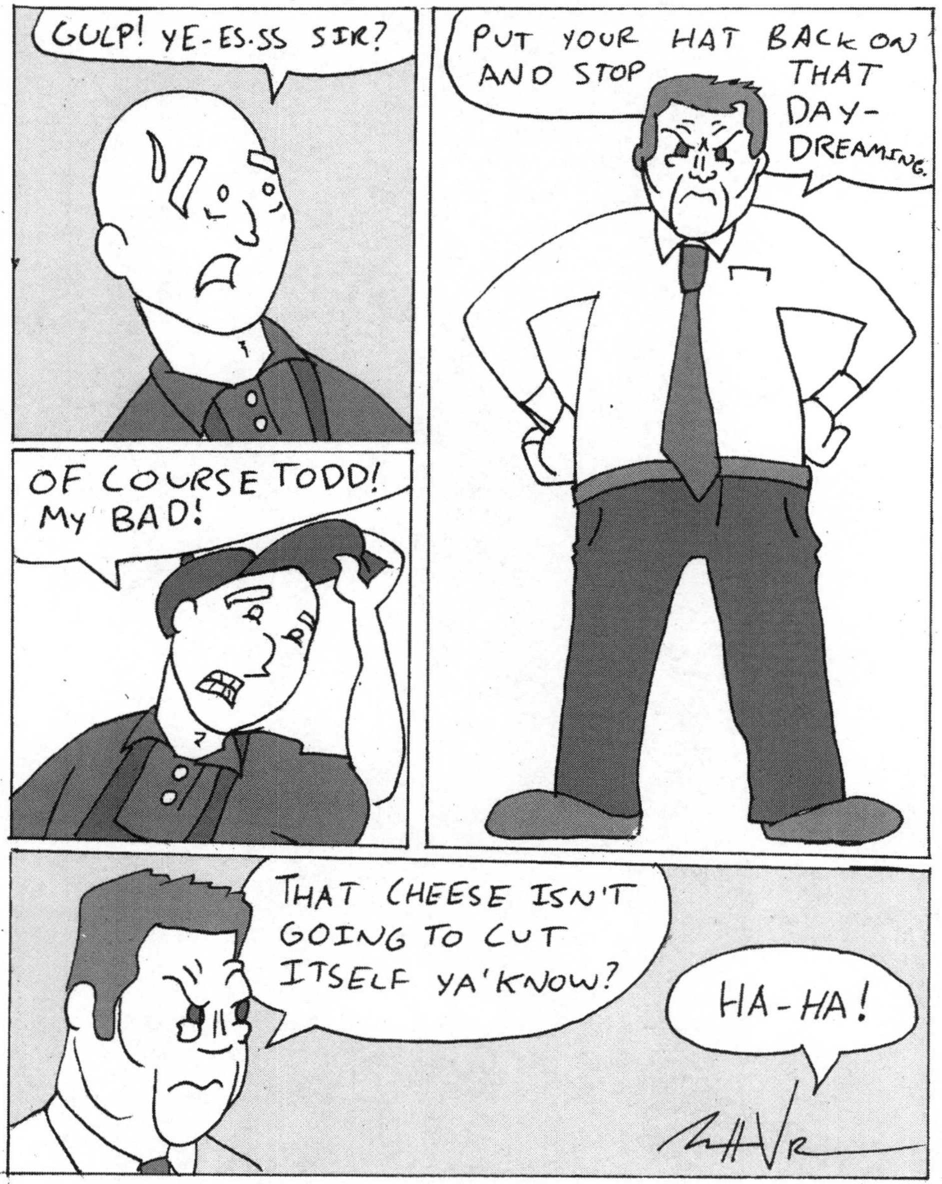
GULP! YE-ES-SS SIR?
PUT YOUR HAT BACK ON AND STOP THAT DAY-DREAMING.
OF COURSE TODD! MY BAD!
THAT CHEESE ISN'T GOING TO CUT ITSELF YA'KNOW?
HA-HA!

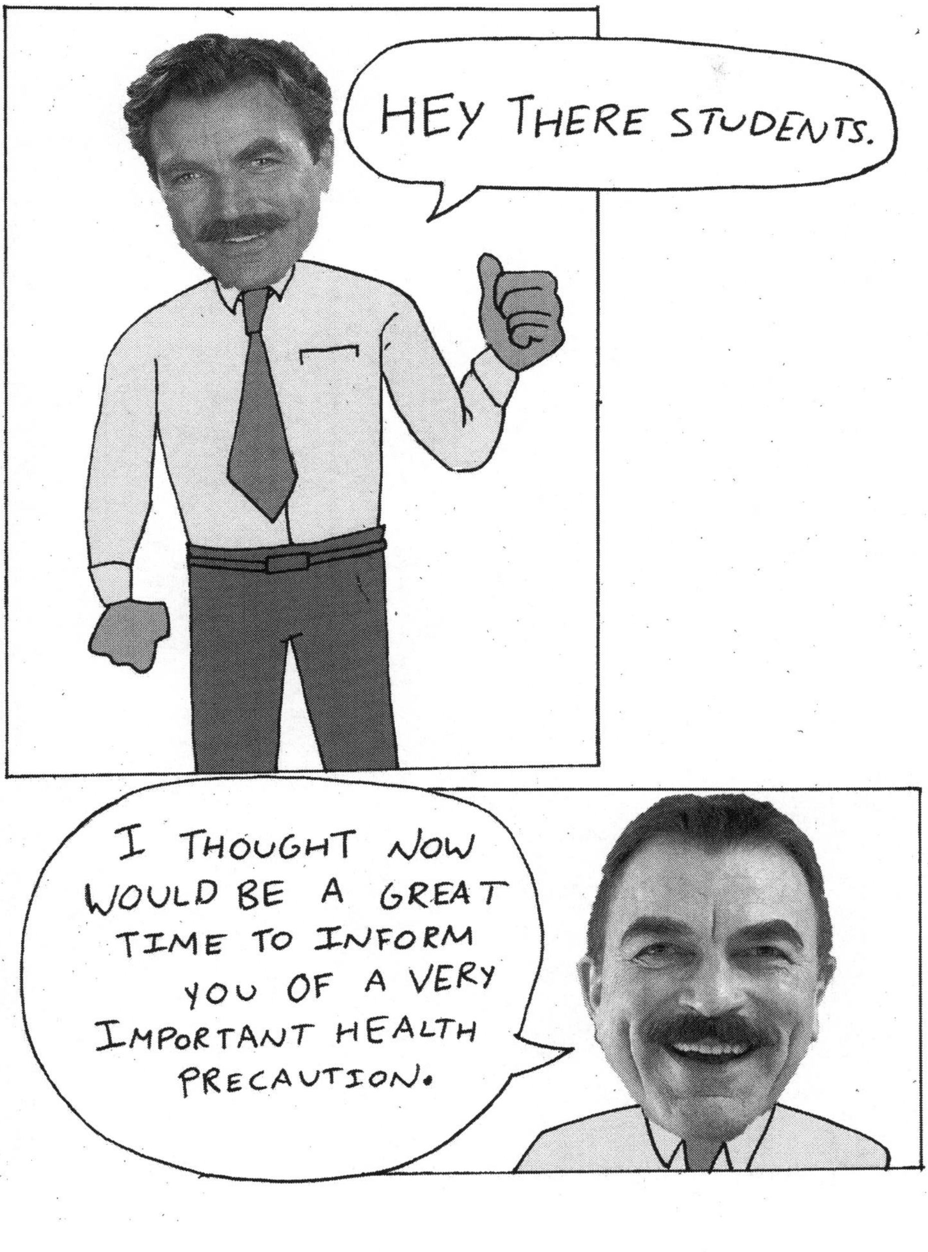
HEY THERE STUDENTS.
I THOUGHT NOW WOULD BE A GREAT TIME TO INFORM YOU OF A VERY IMPORTANT HEALTH PRECAUTION.

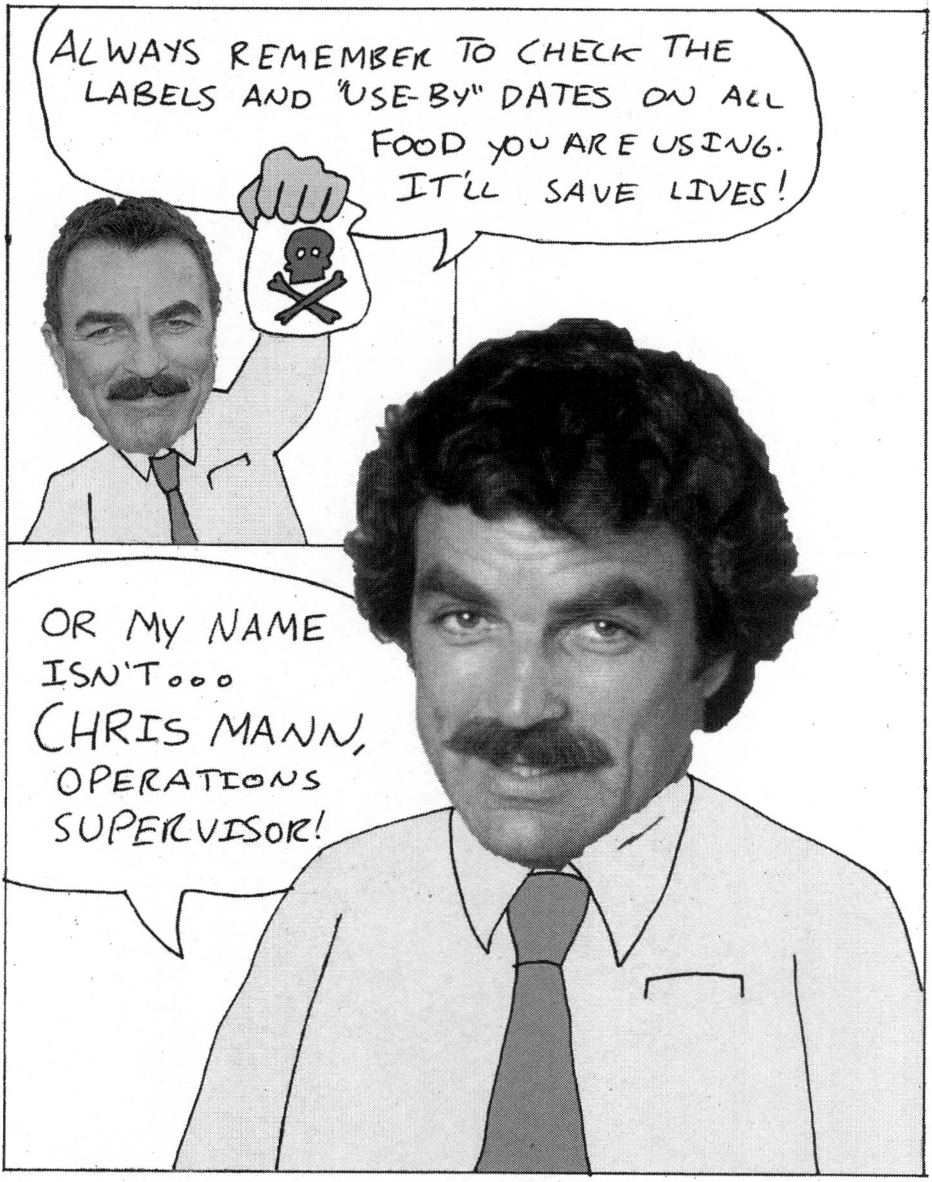
ALWAYS REMEMBER TO CHECK THE LABELS AND "USE-BY" DATES ON ALL FOOD YOU ARE USING. IT'LL SAVE LIVES!
OR MY NAME ISN'T... CHRIS MANN, OPERATIONS SUPERVISOR!

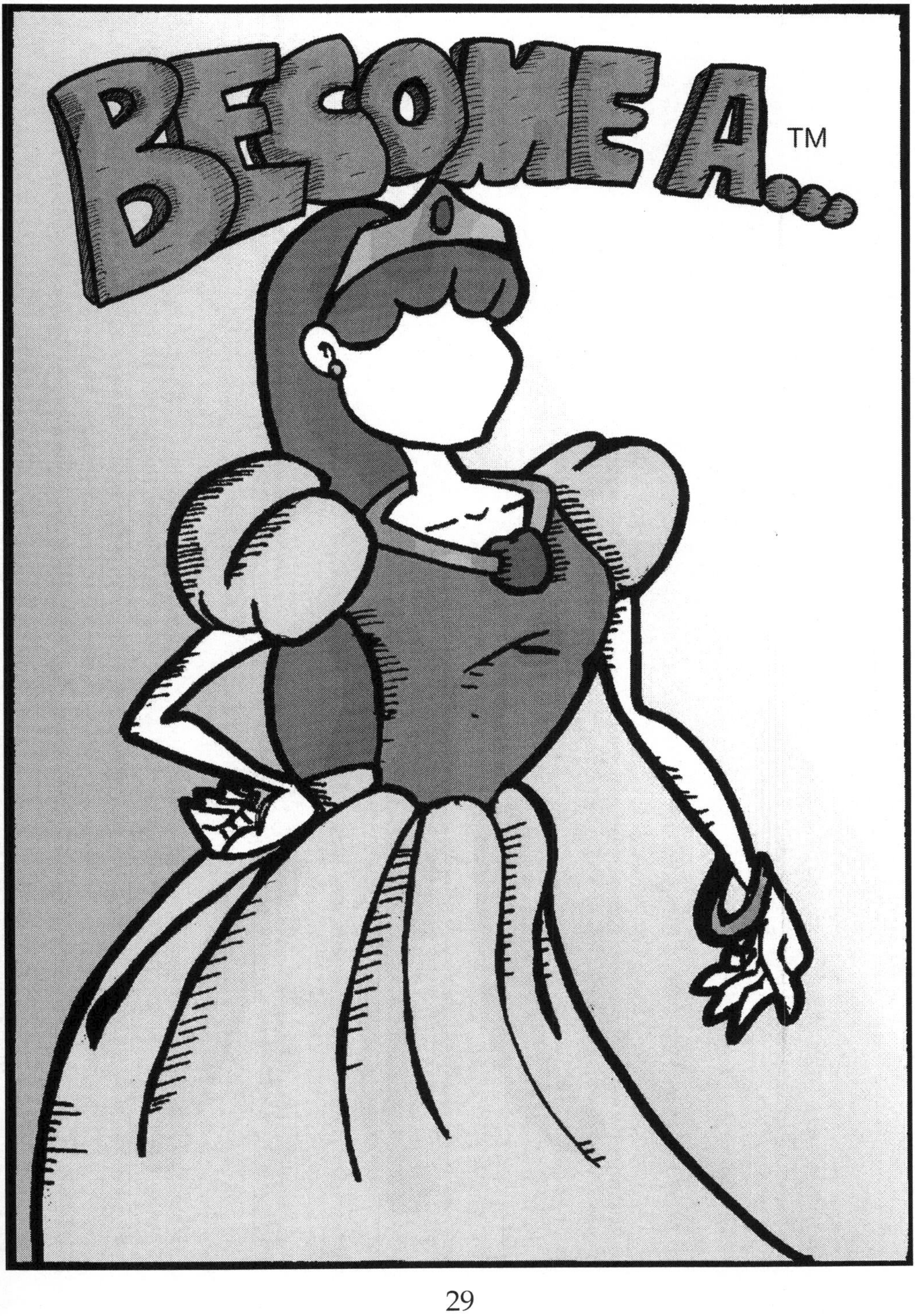
BECOME A...
TM

MATT'S NOTES:

This comic was the first of the two "Become A..." caricature books that my wife and I sold at the farmer's market in Rexburg, ID. Go ahead and draw your face if you want, and fill in the blank spaces with your princess name and villain.

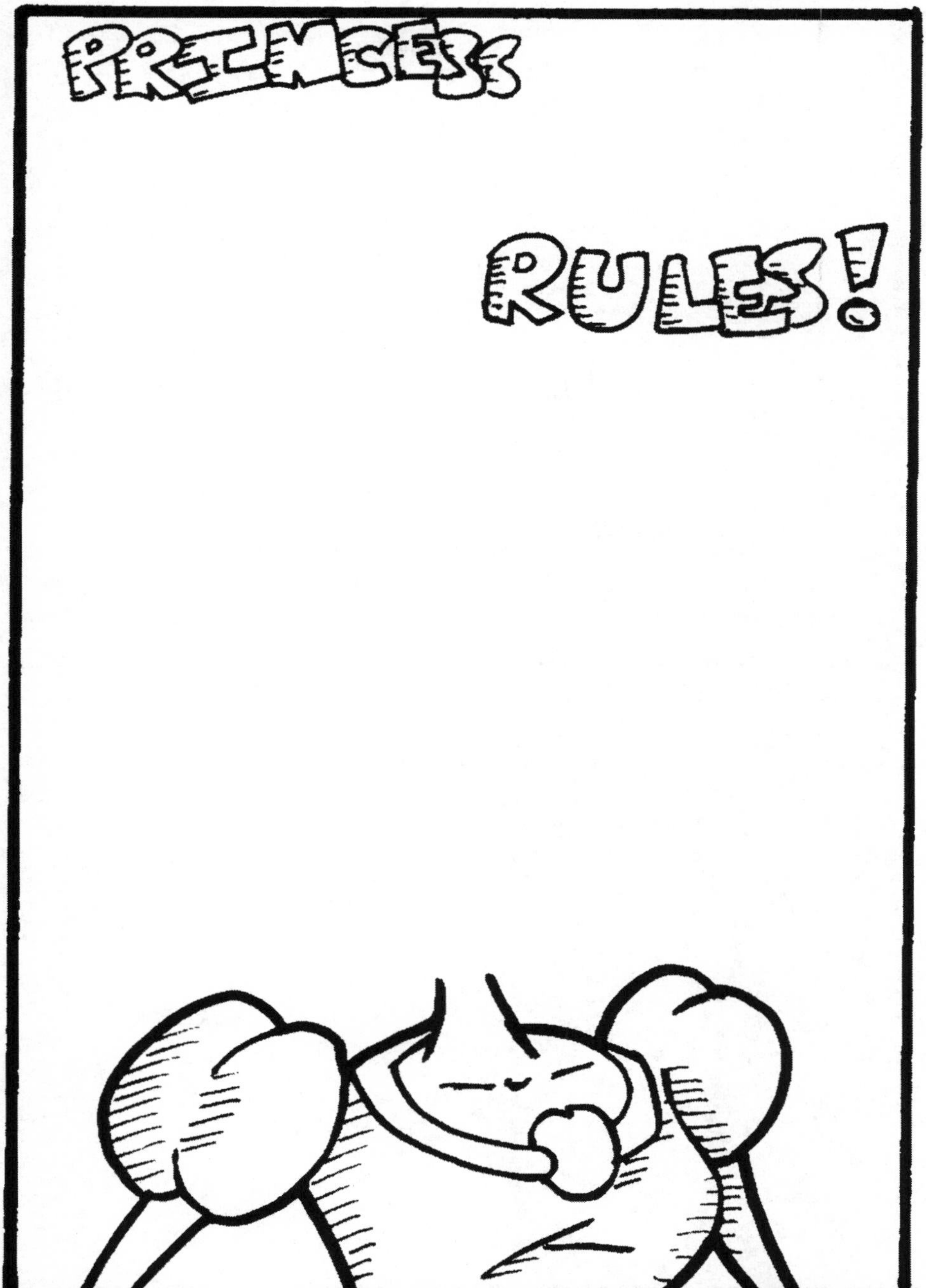
PRINCESS
RULES!

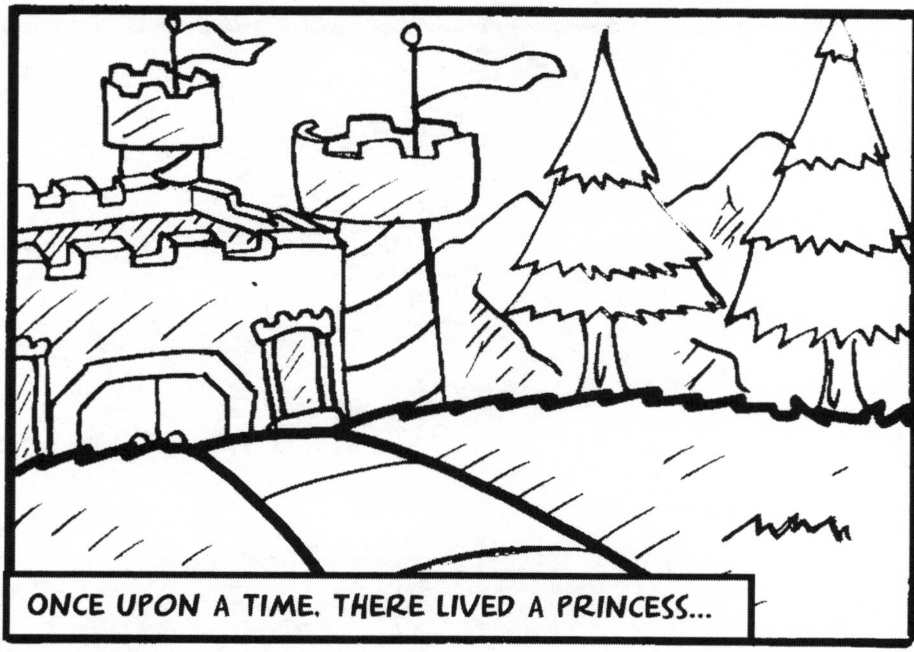
ONCE UPON A TIME, THERE LIVED A PRINCESS...

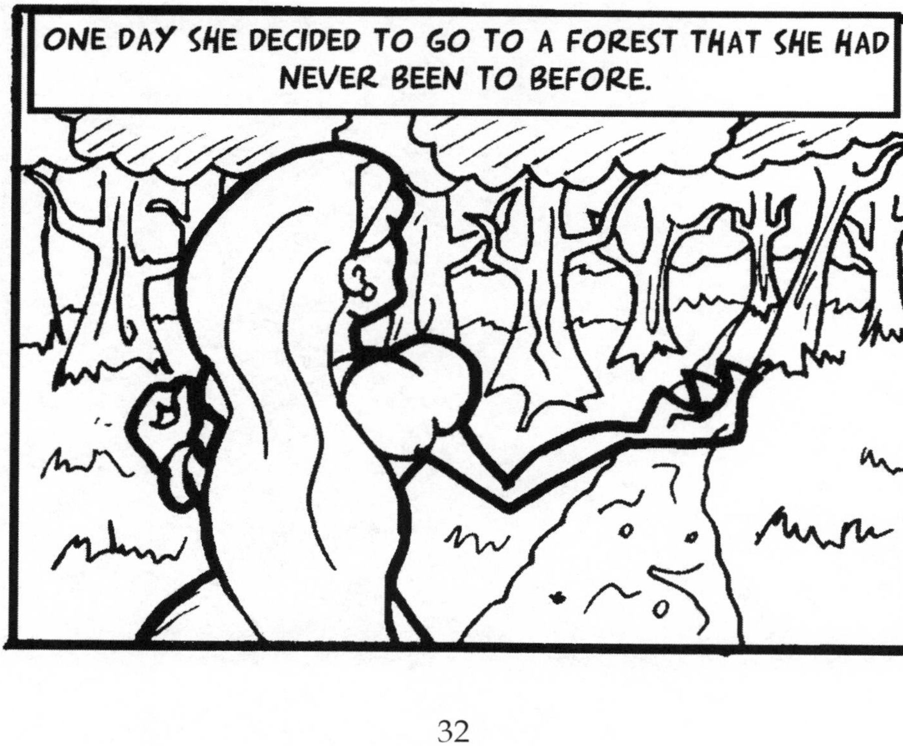
ONE DAY SHE DECIDED TO GO TO A FOREST THAT SHE HAD NEVER BEEN TO BEFORE.

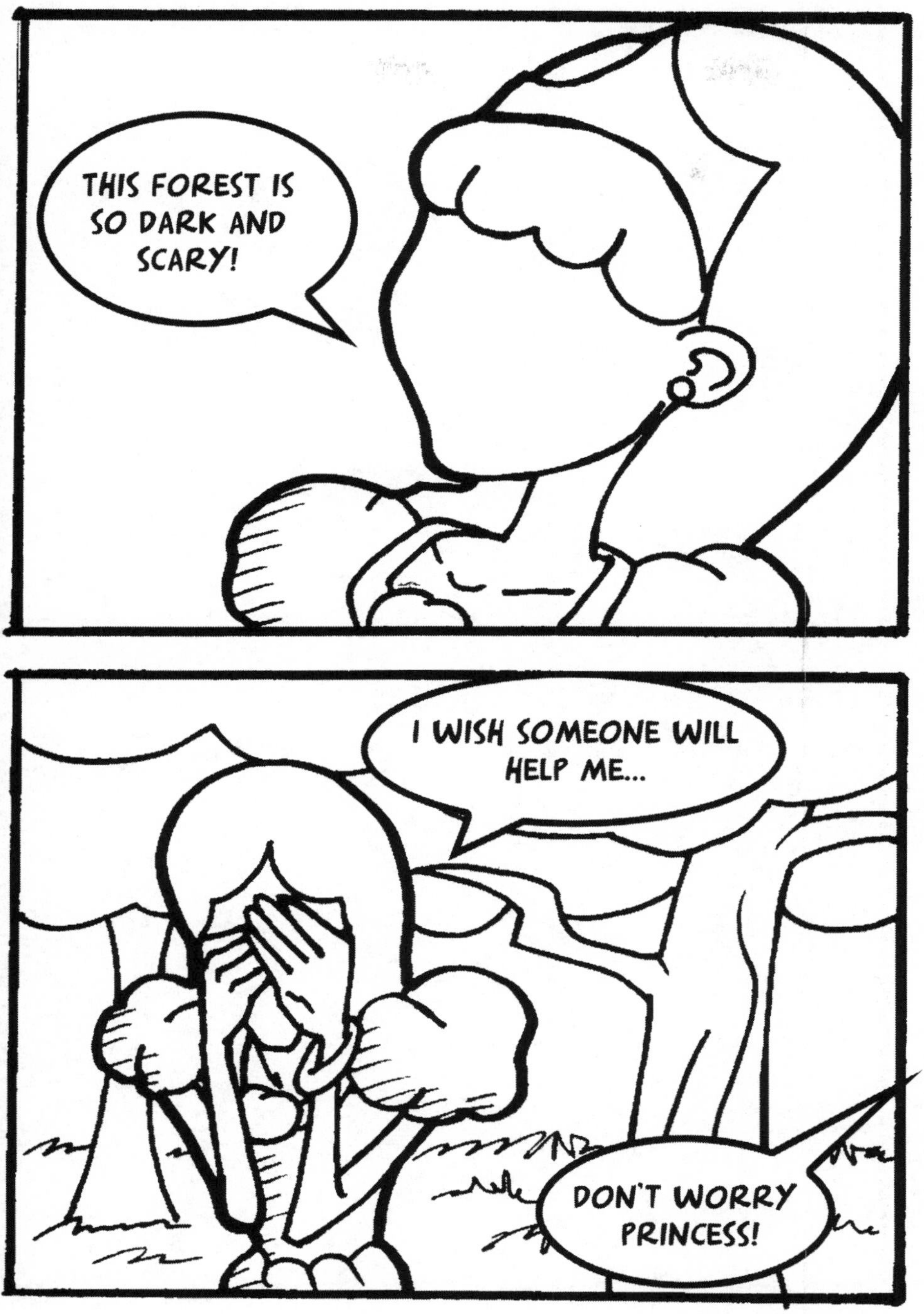
THIS FOREST IS SO DARK AND SCARY!
I WISH SOMEONE WILL HELP ME...
DON'T WORRY PRINCESS!

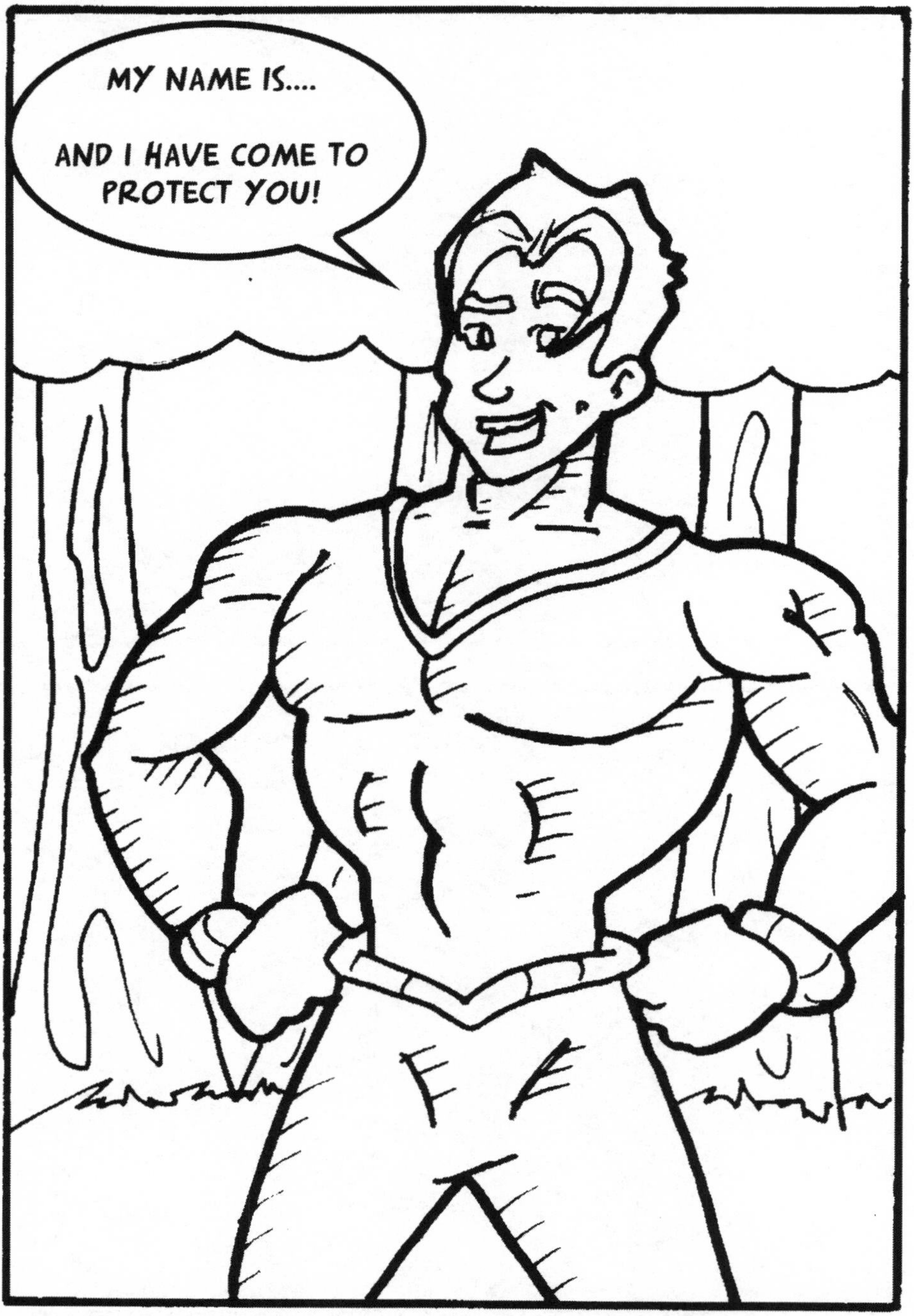
MY NAME IS....
AND I HAVE COME TO PROTECT YOU!

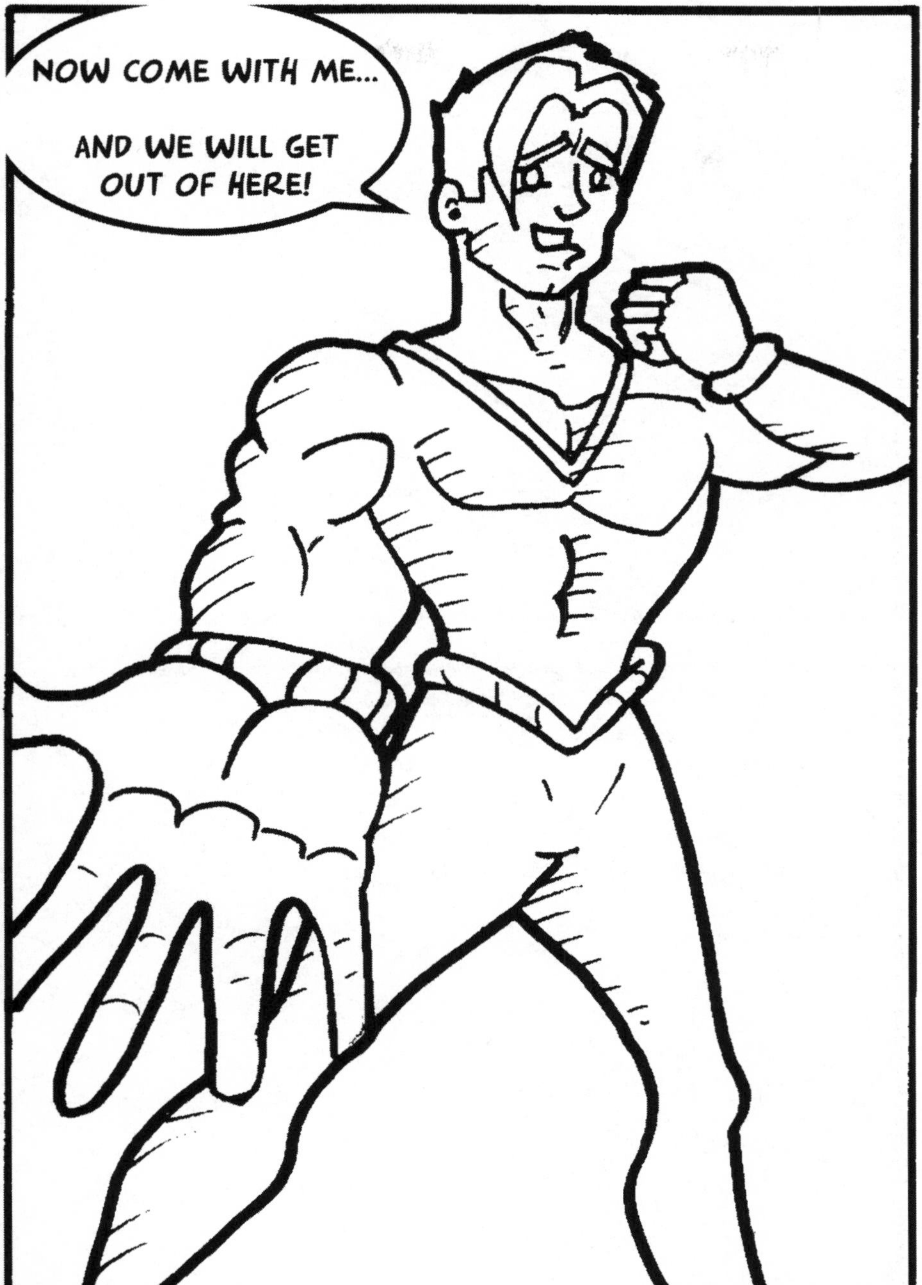
NOW COME WITH ME...
AND WE WILL GET OUT OF HERE!

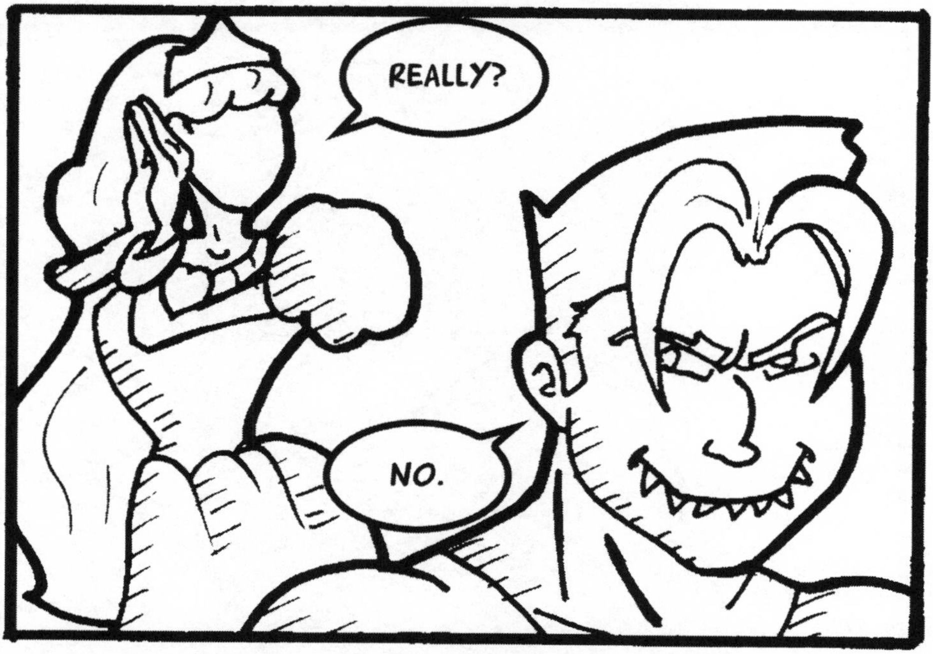
REALLY?
NO.

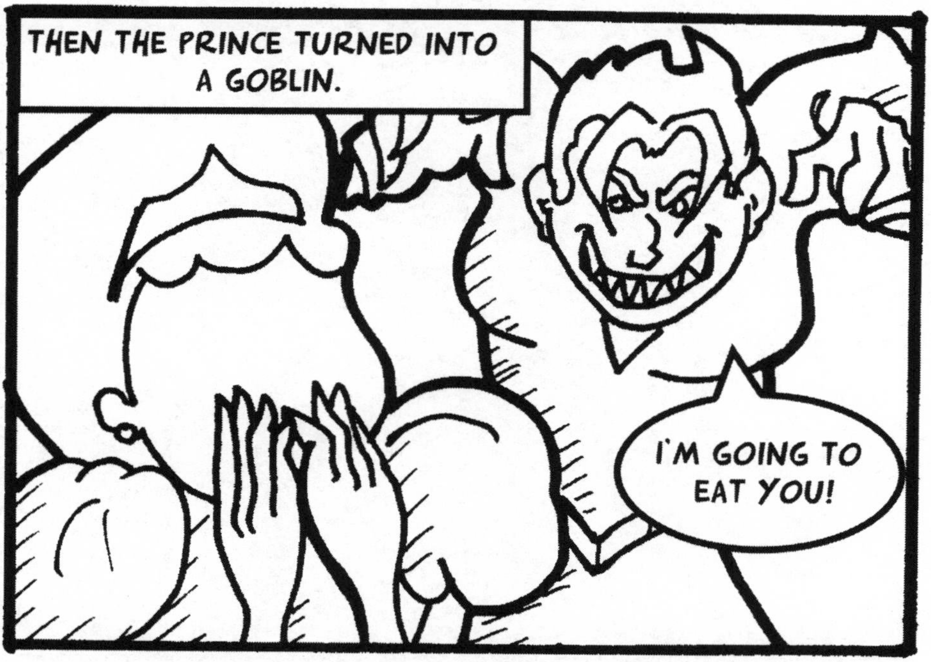
THEN THE PRINCE TURNED INTO A GOBLIN.
I'M GOING TO EAT YOU!

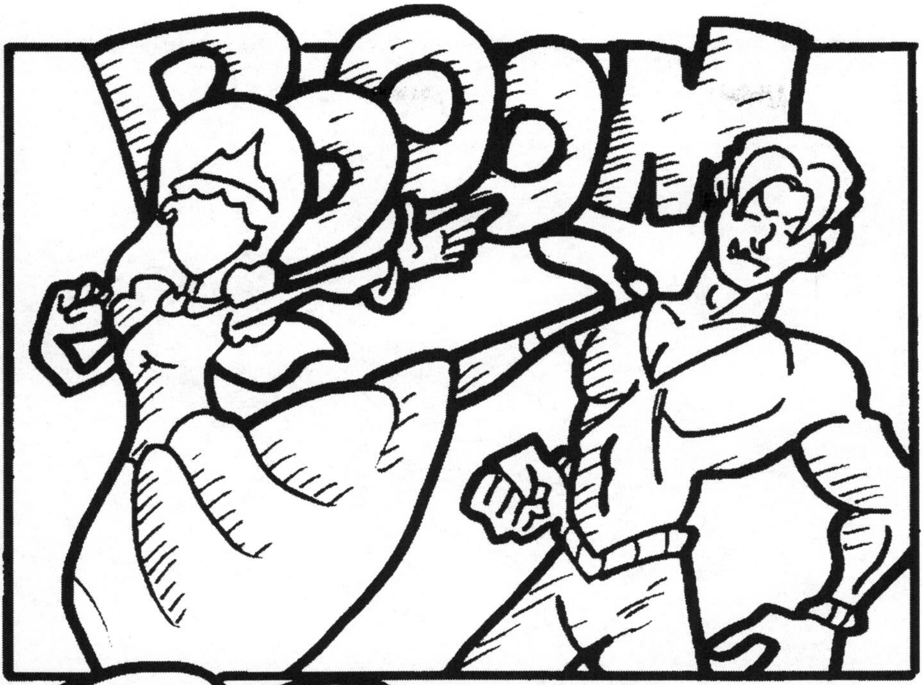
BOOOM!
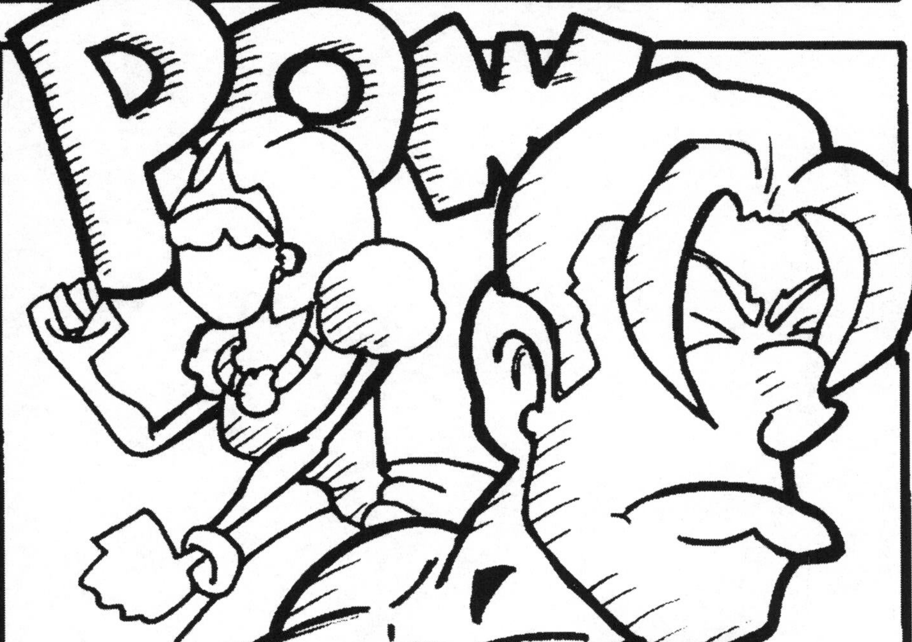
POW

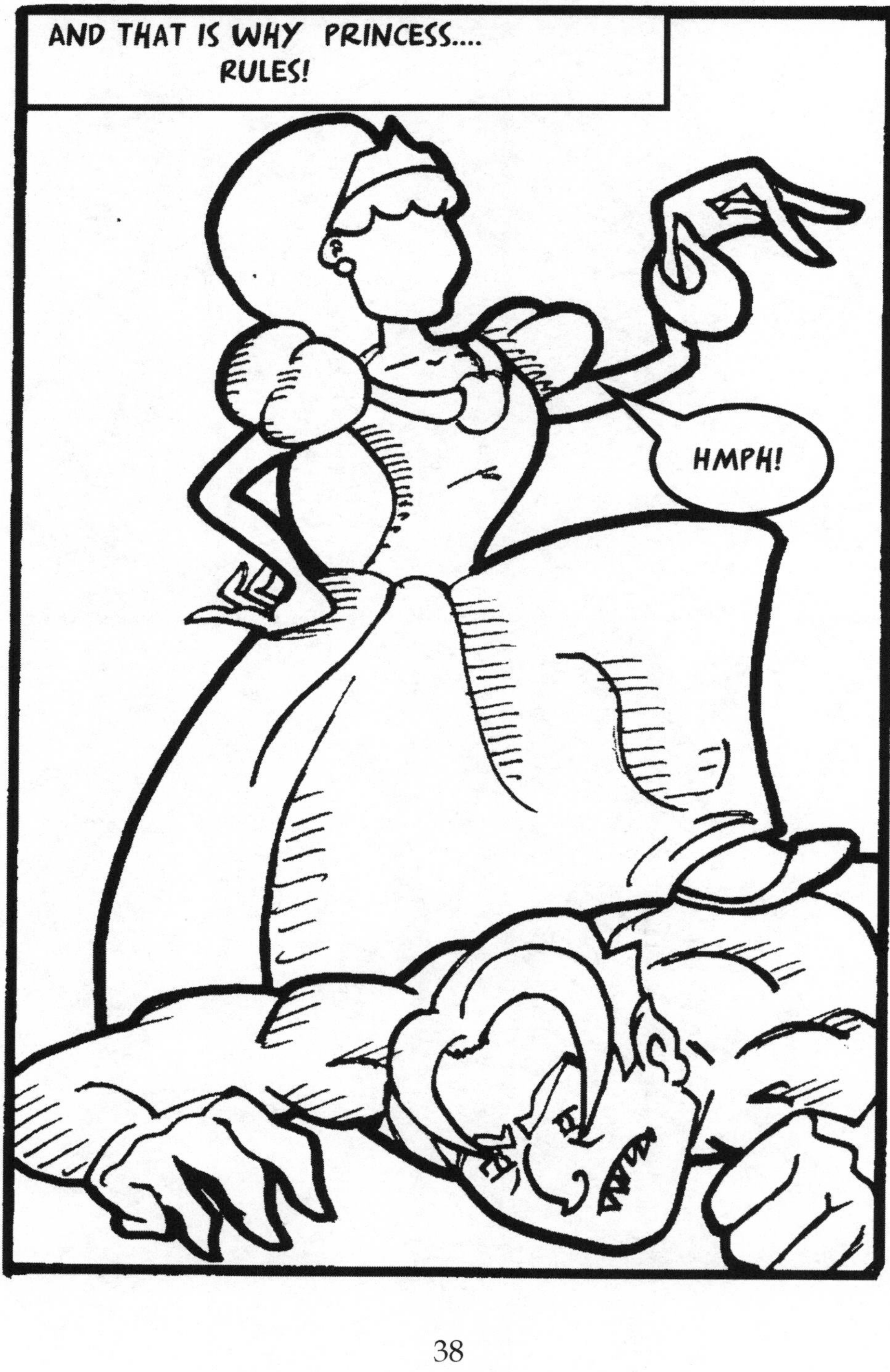
AND THAT IS WHY PRINCESS....
RULES!
HMPH!

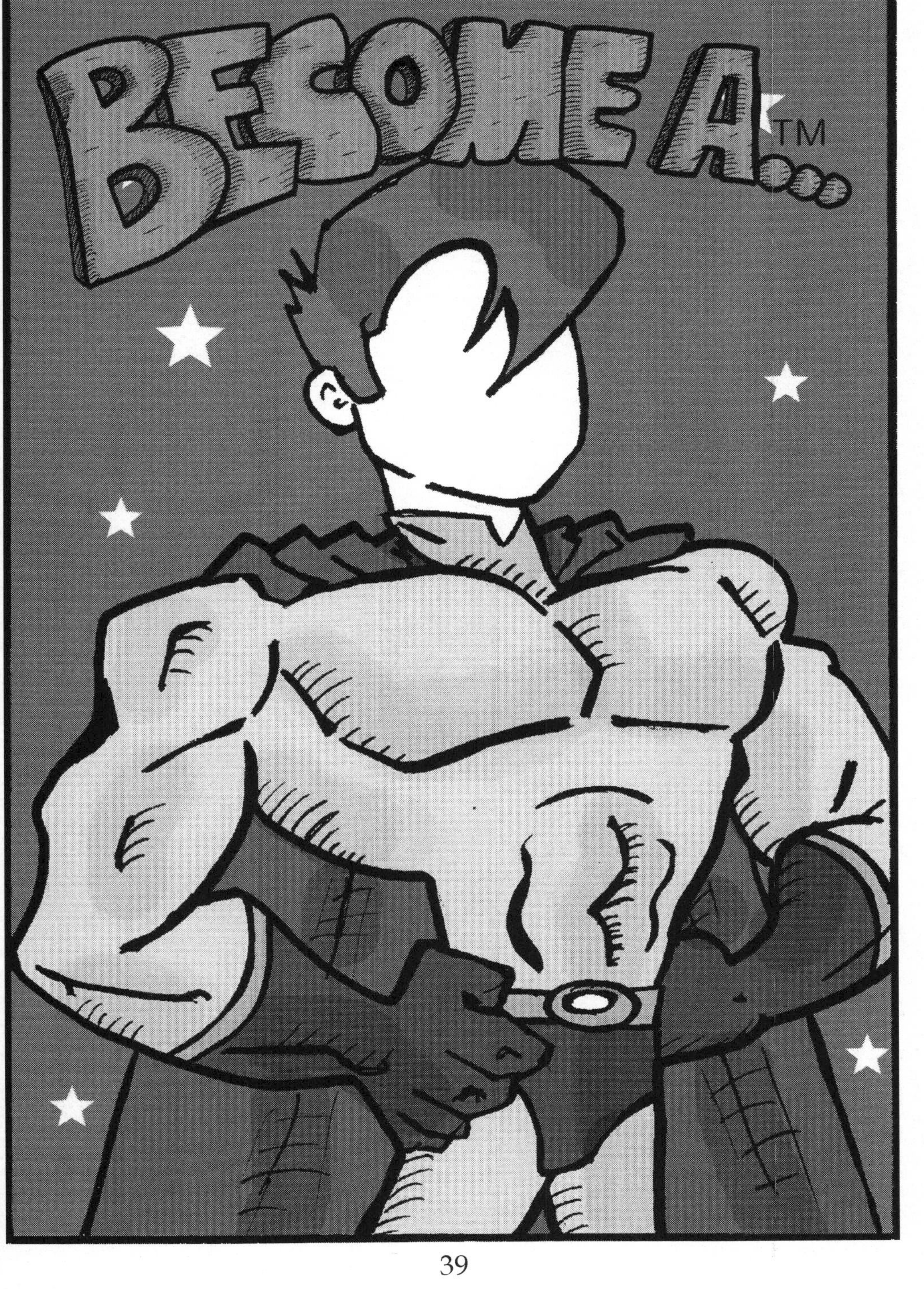
BECOME A...™

MATT'S NOTES:

This comic was the second of the two "Become A..." caricature books that my wife and I sold at the farmer's market in Rexburg, ID. Go ahead and draw your face if you want, and fill in the blank spaces with your super hero name and villain.

40

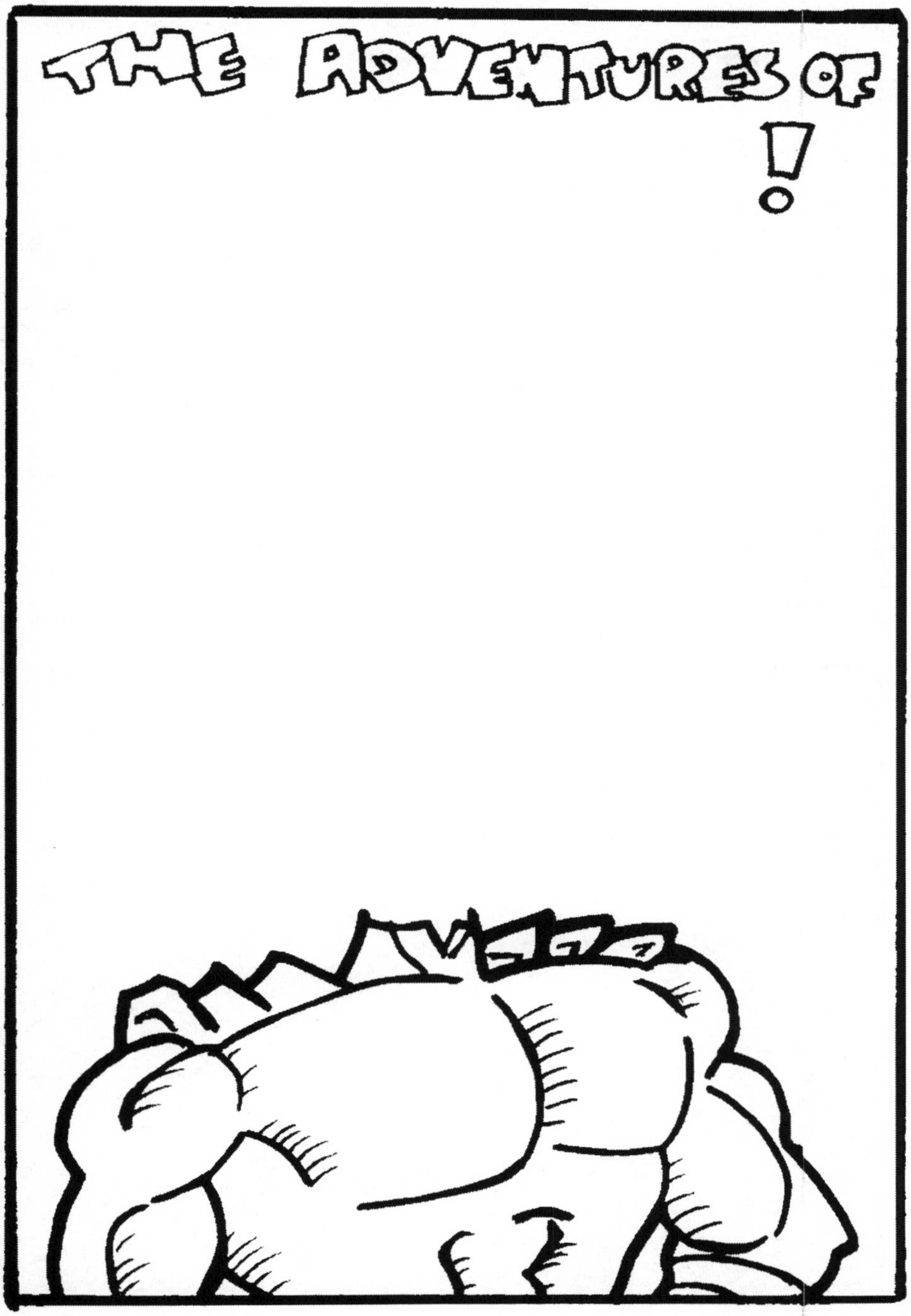
THE ADVENTURES OF
!

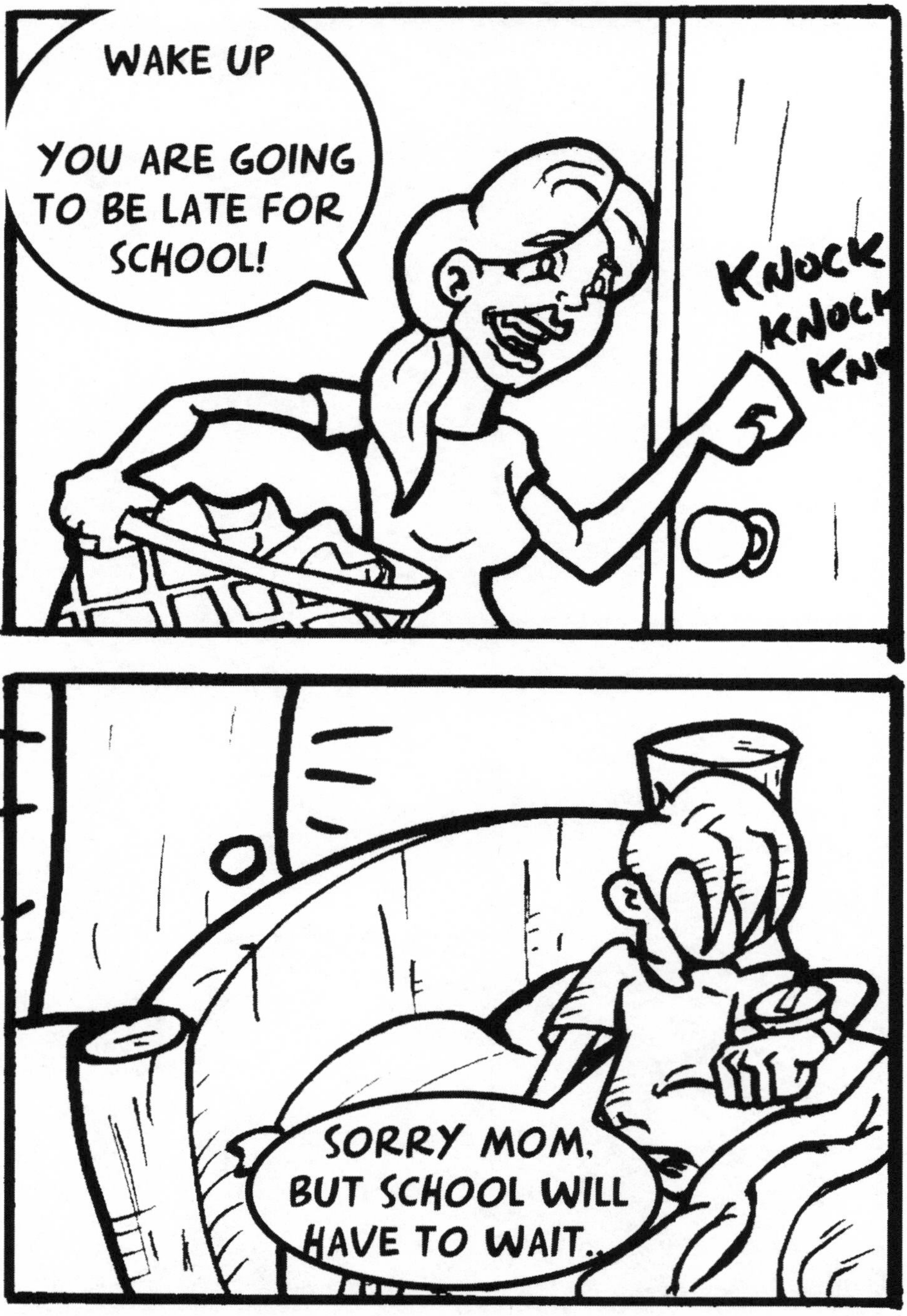
WAKE UP
YOU ARE GOING TO BE LATE FOR SCHOOL!
KNOCK KNOCK
SORRY MOM, BUT SCHOOL WILL HAVE TO WAIT..

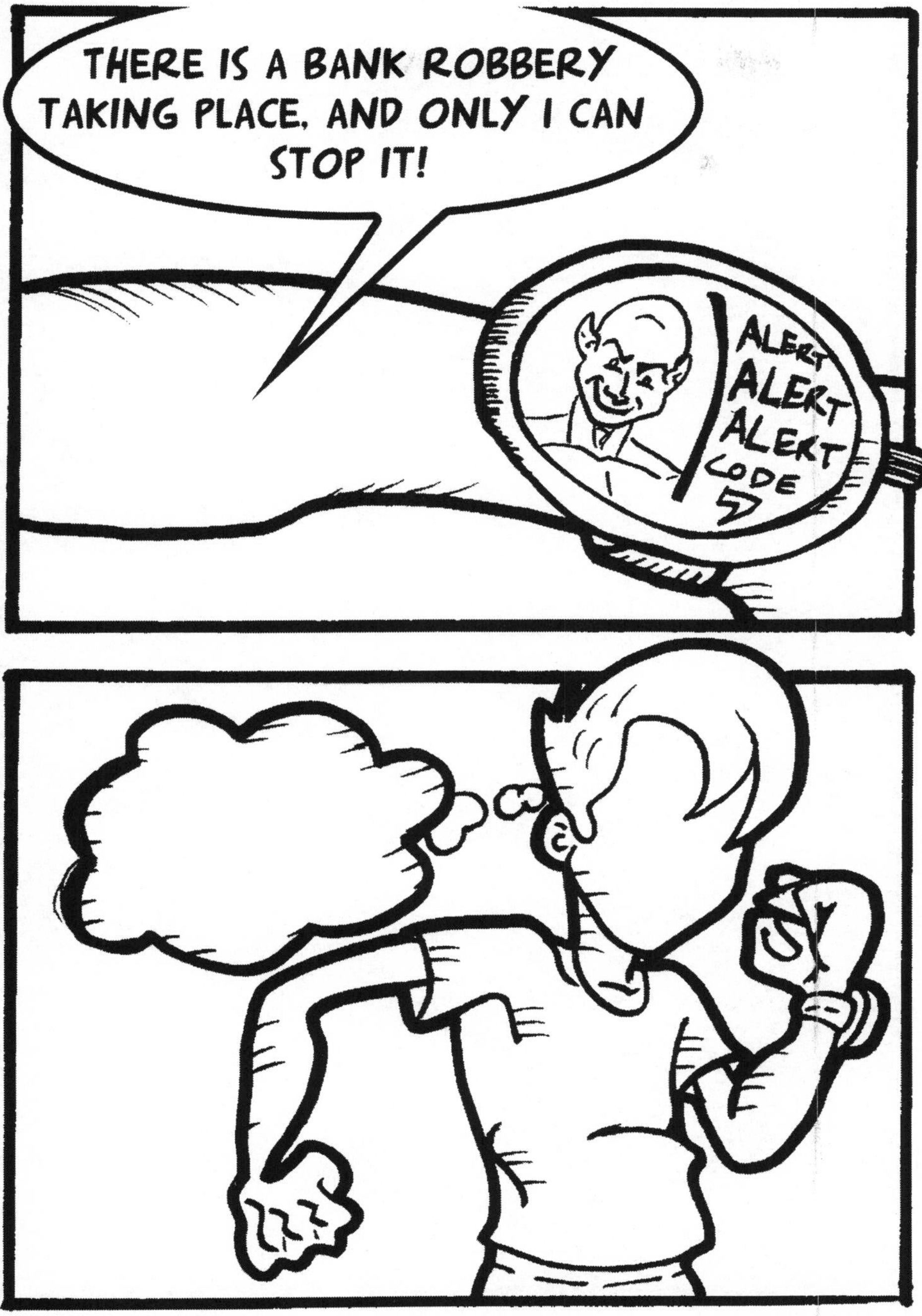
THERE IS A BANK ROBBERY TAKING PLACE, AND ONLY I CAN STOP IT!
ALERT
ALERT
ALERT
CODE
7

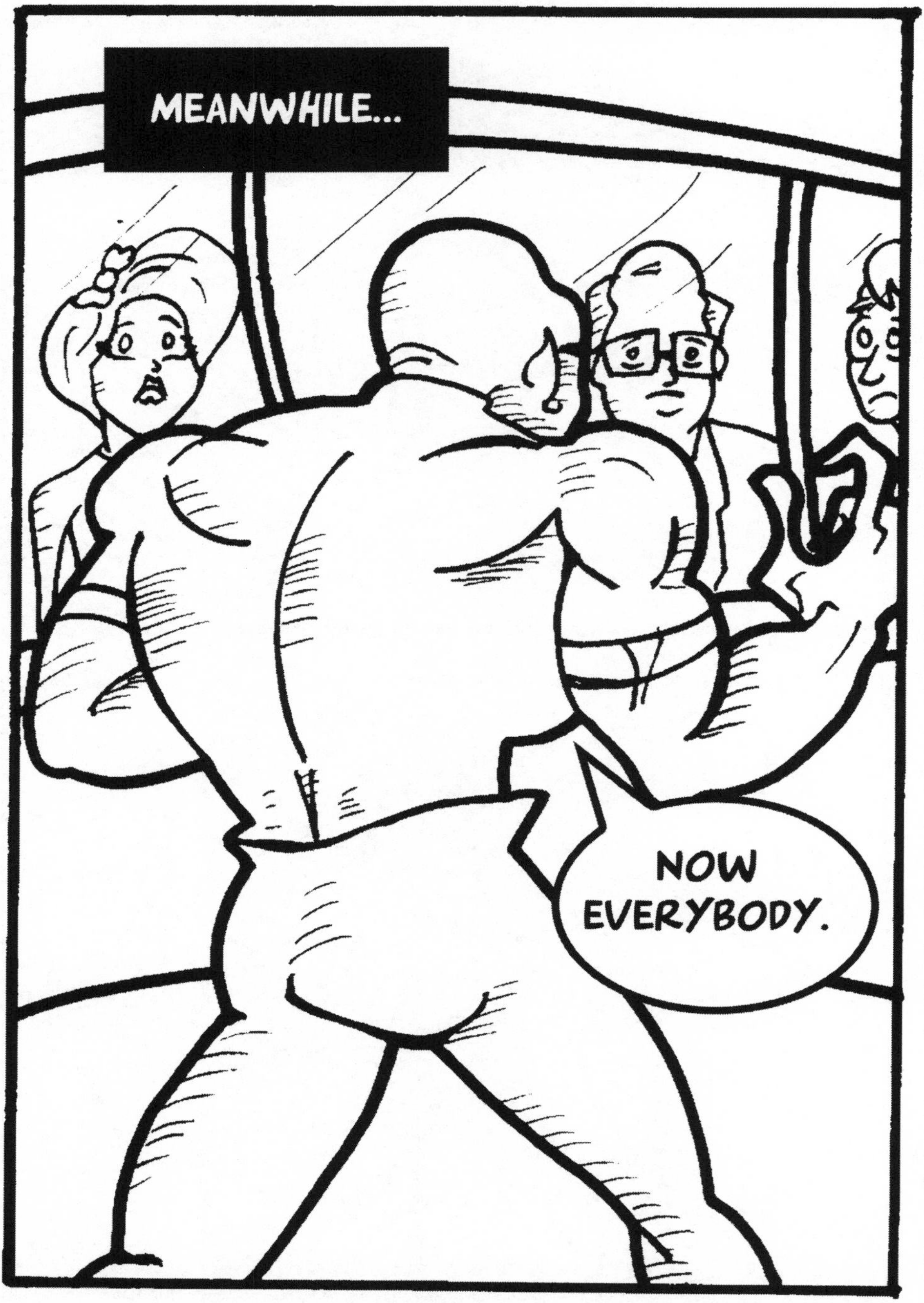
MEANWHILE...
NOW EVERYBODY.

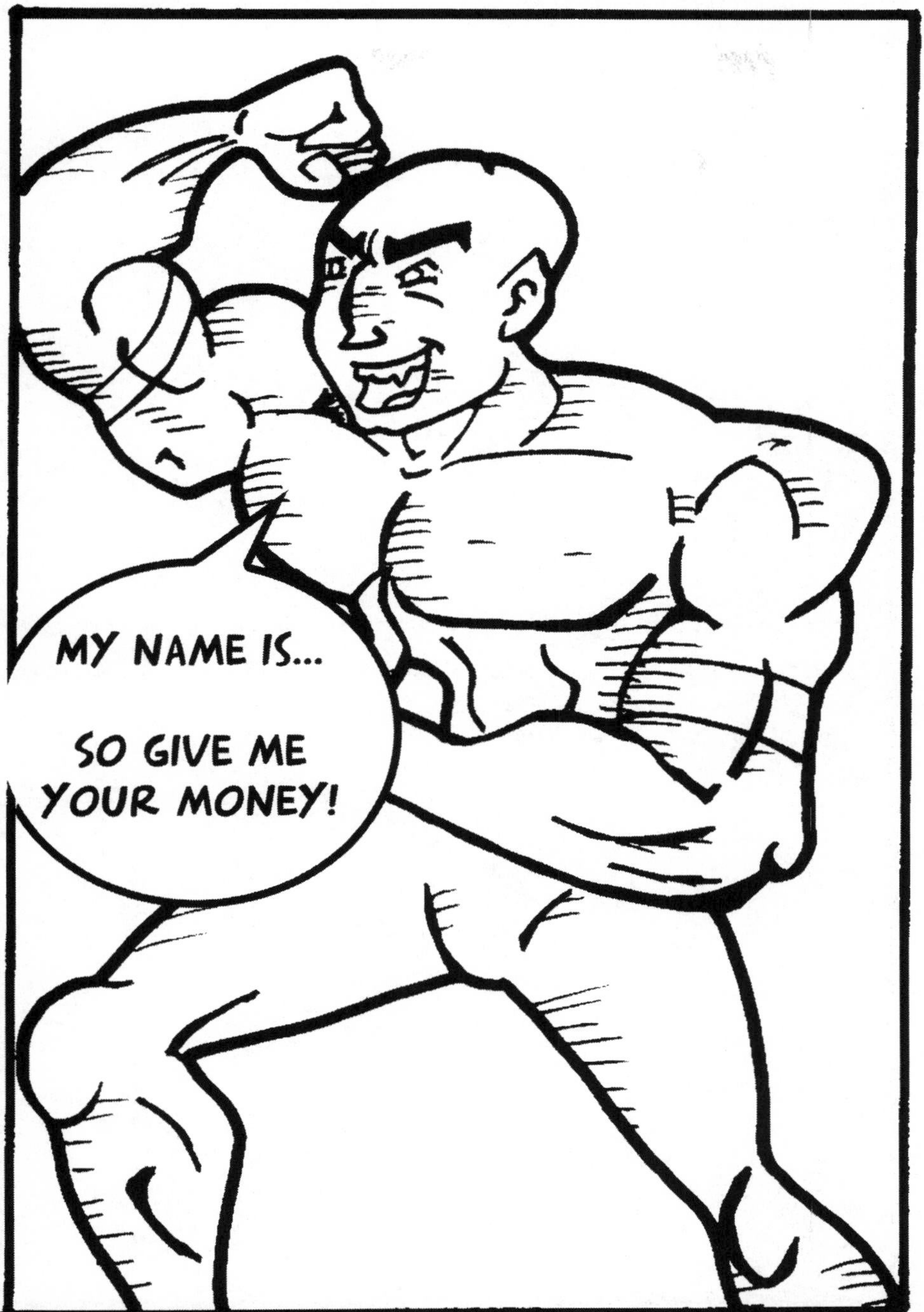
MY NAME IS...
SO GIVE ME YOUR MONEY!

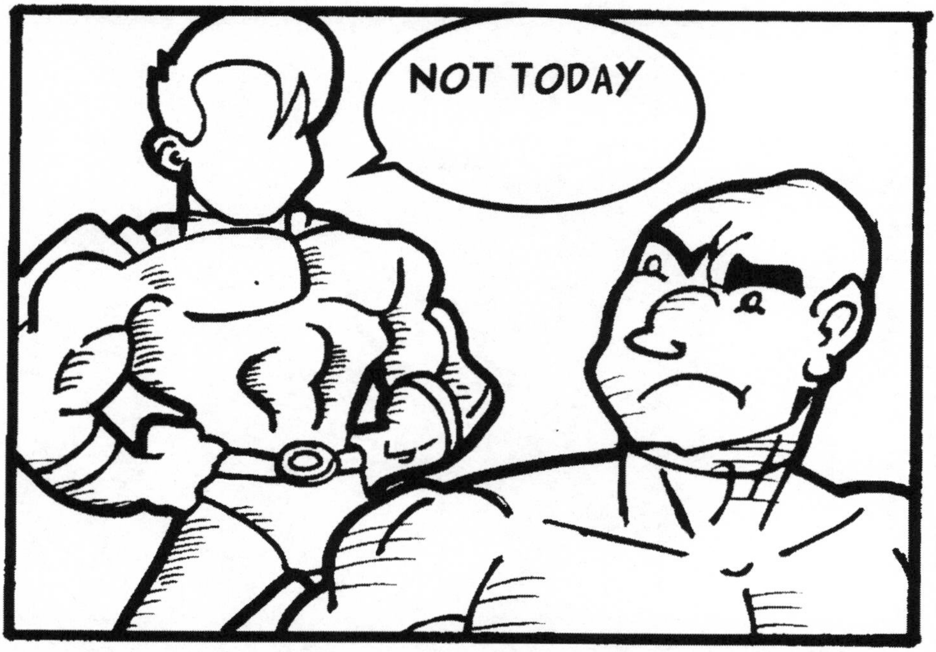
NOT TODAY

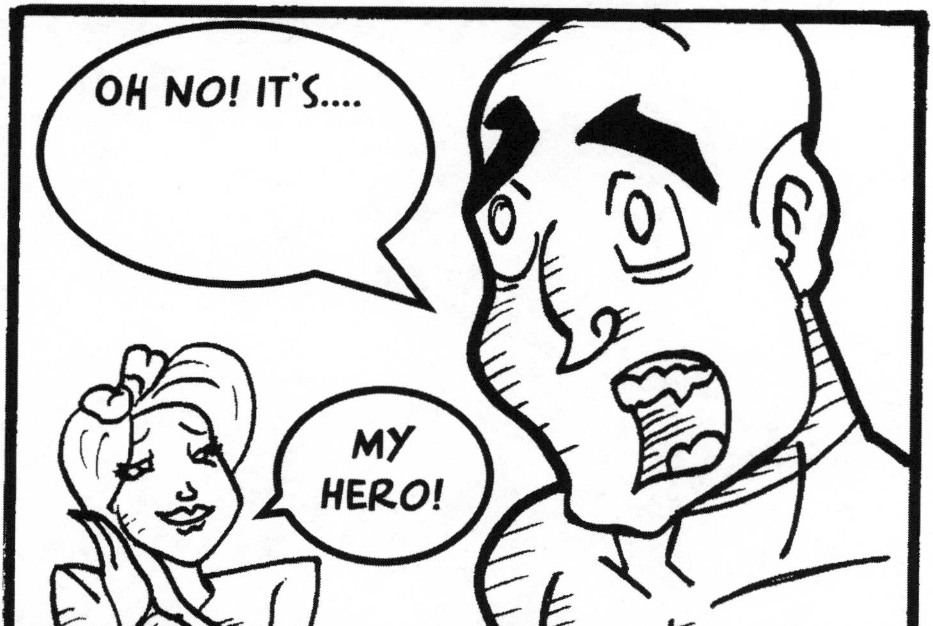
OH NO! IT'S....
MY HERO!

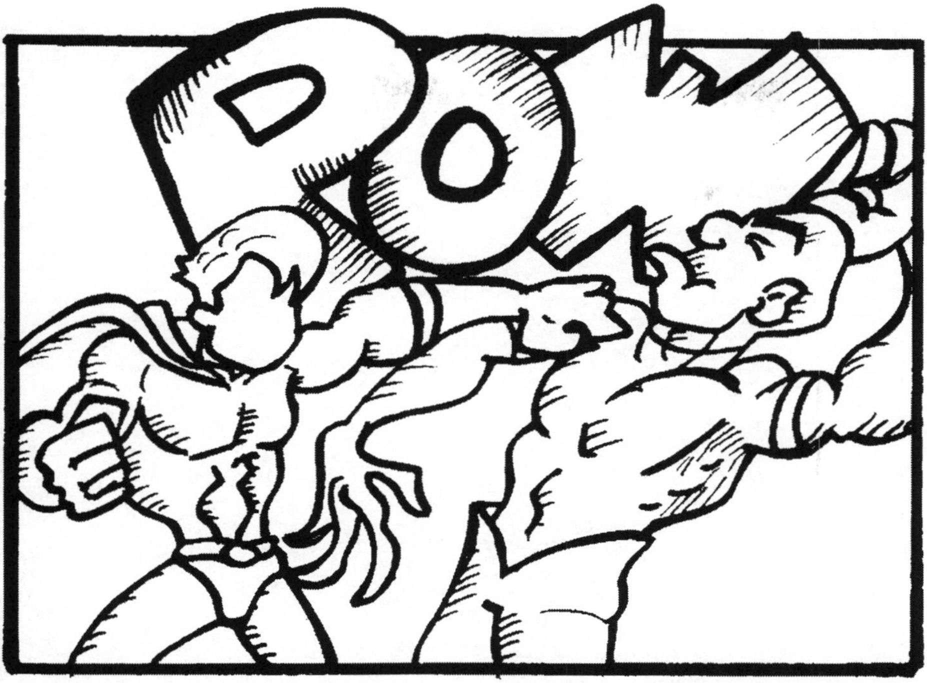
POW

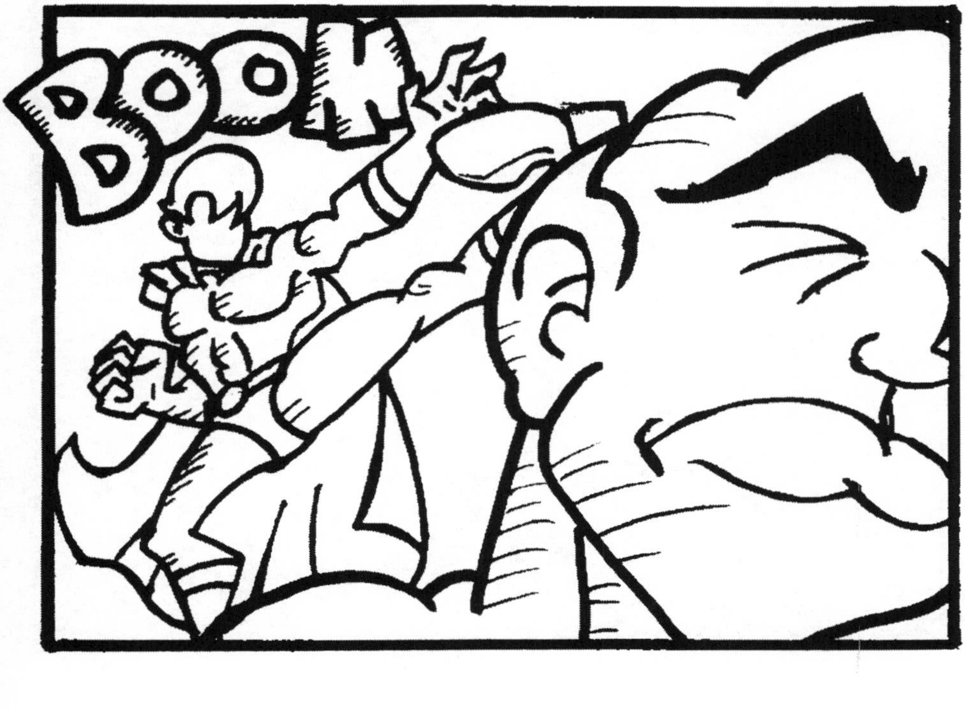
BOOM

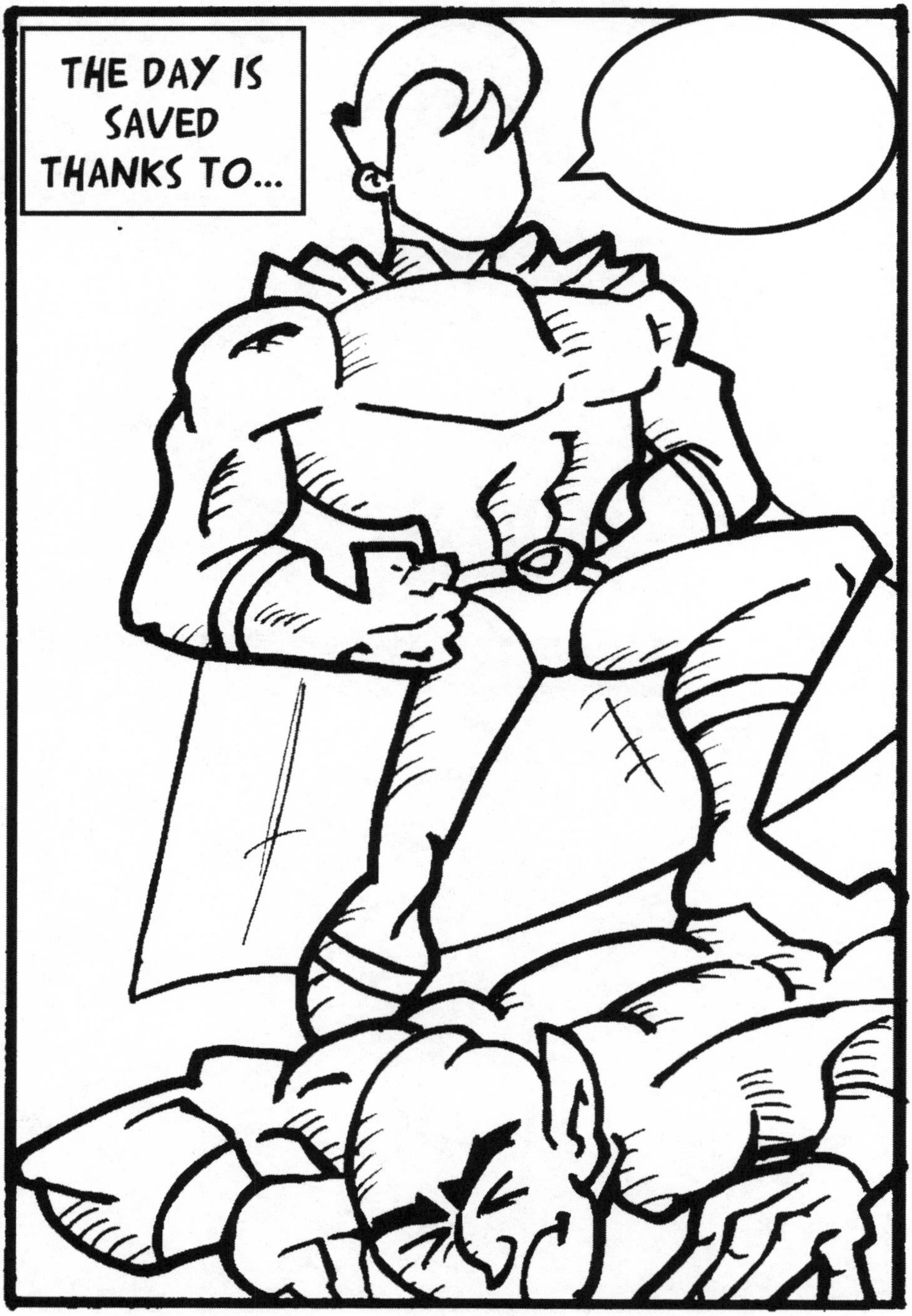
THE DAY IS SAVED THANKS TO...

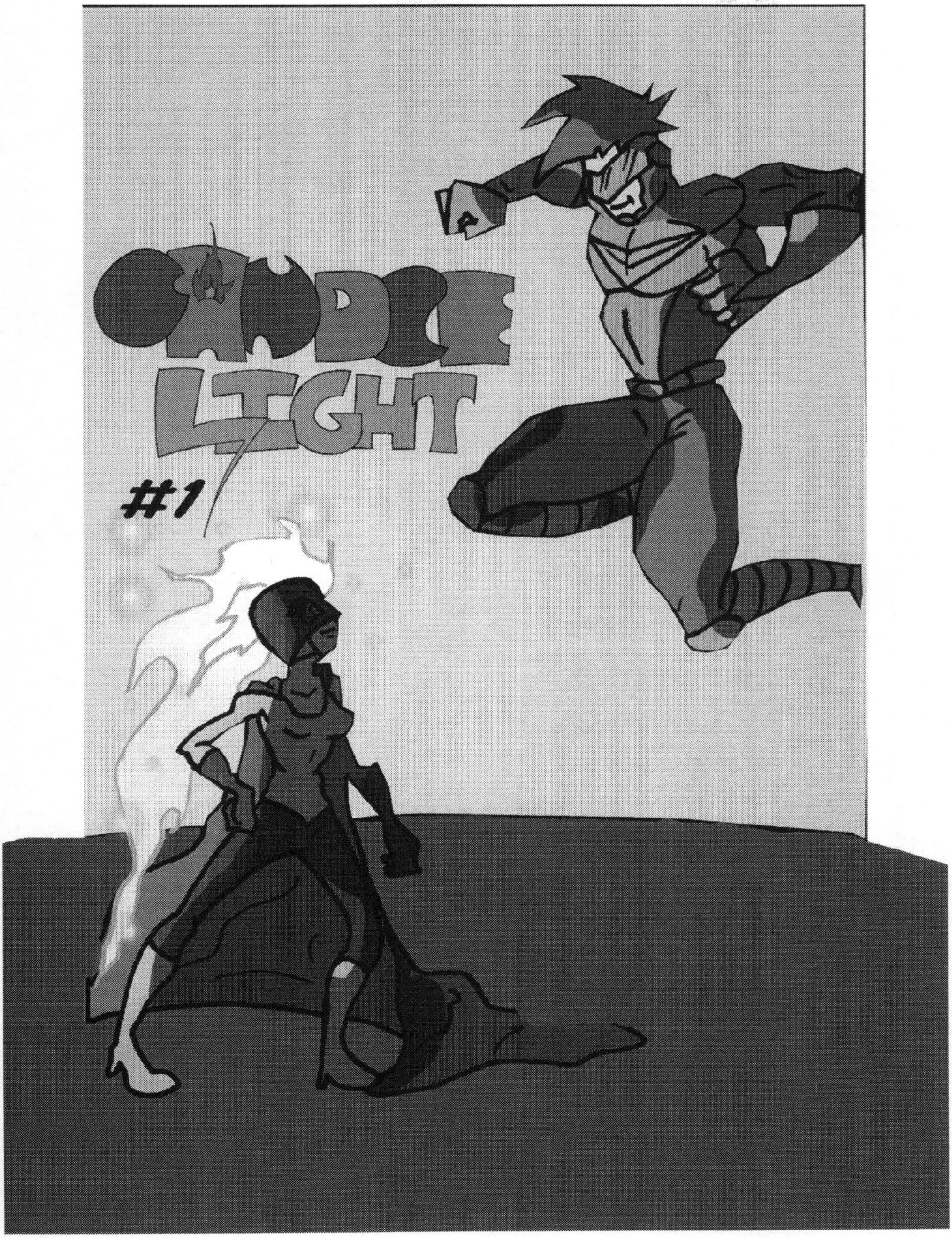
CANDLE
LIGHT
#1

Candlight character Illustrated by
Michele Vroom

Storyboard by MnM Vroom

MATT'S NOTES:

Candle Light is based on my wife,
and the Vroomster is a character
that I created to be based on myself.
This comic was too short lived, but
I definitely have plans someday to
continue the story.

BOOM
CRAK
OW. THAT HURT.

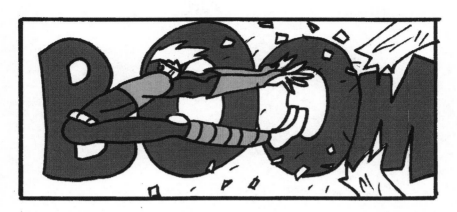

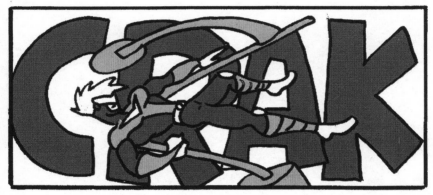

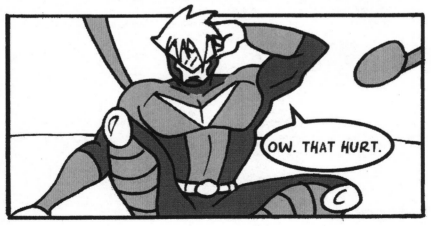

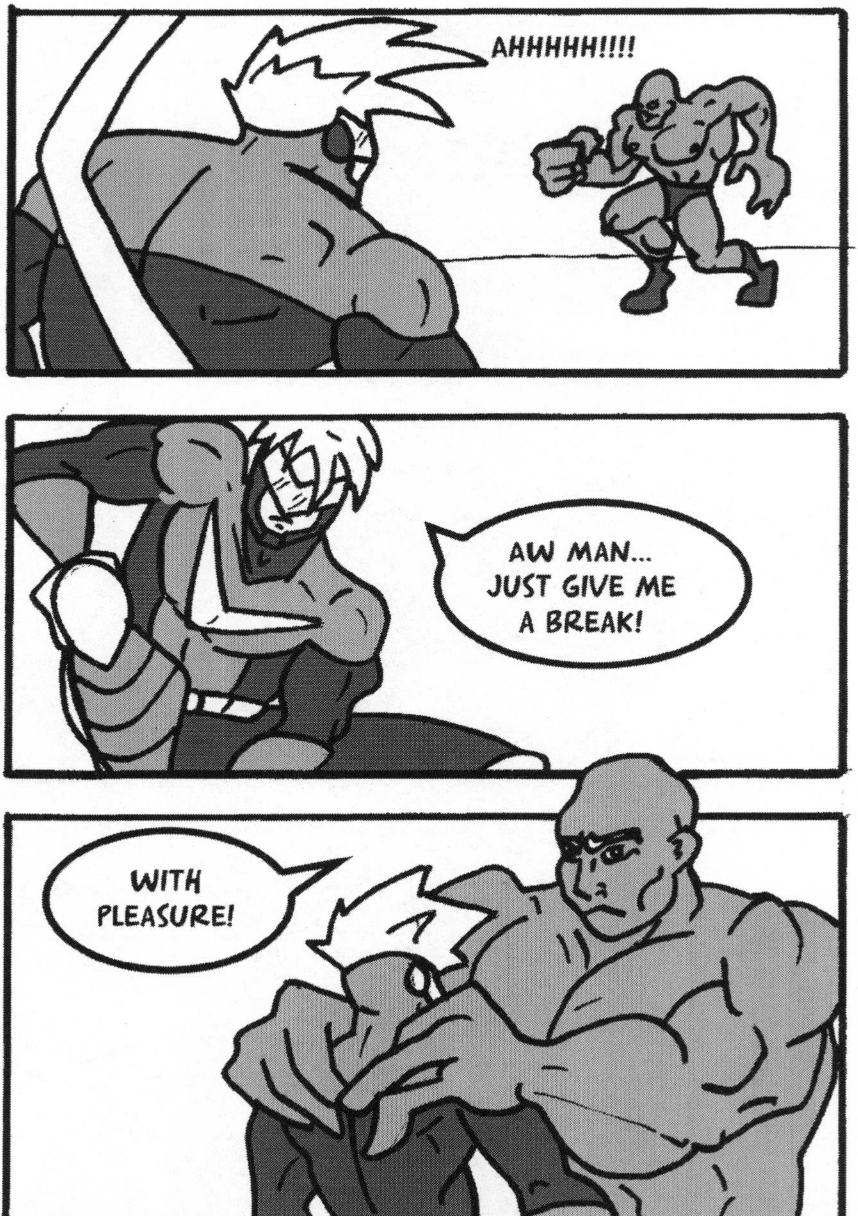
AHHHHH!!!!
AW MAN... JUST GIVE ME A BREAK!
WITH PLEASURE!

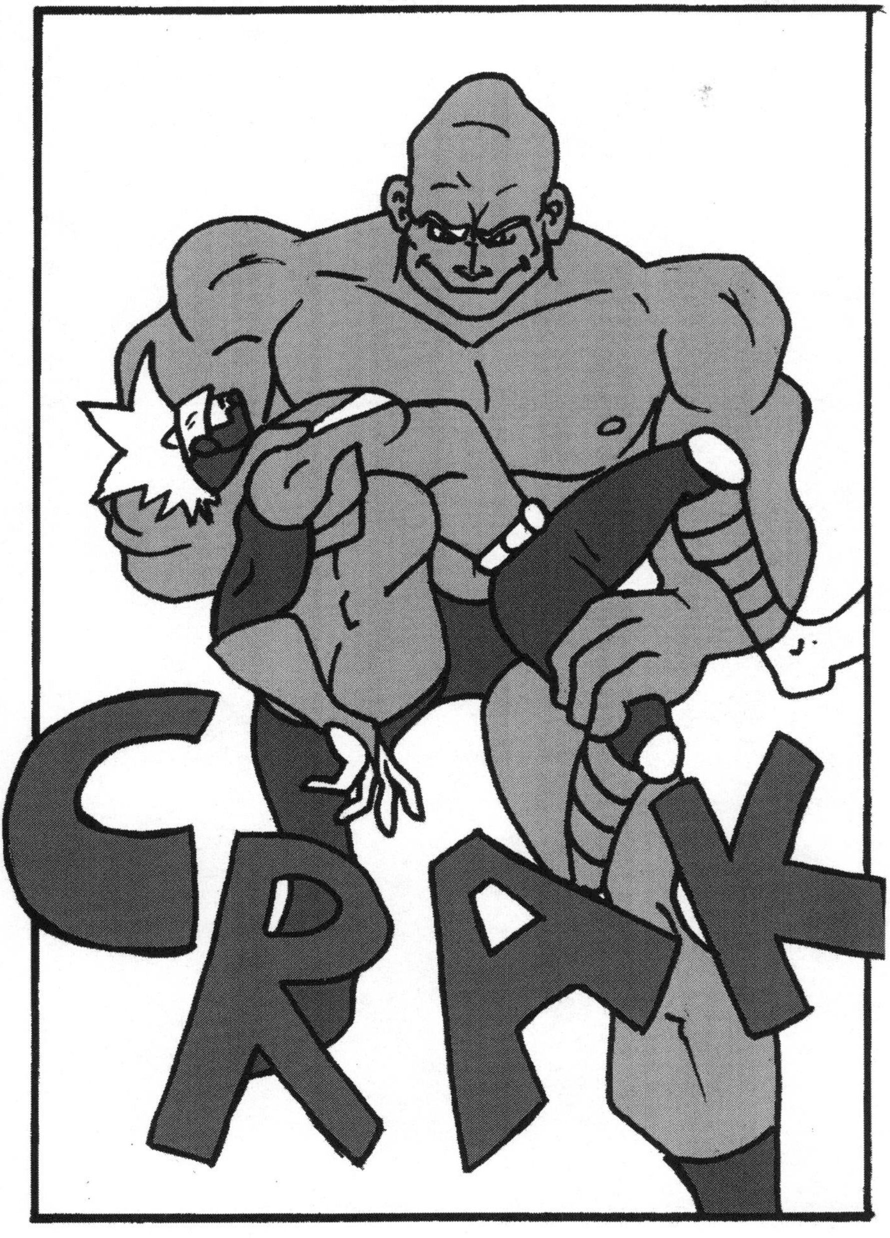
CRAK

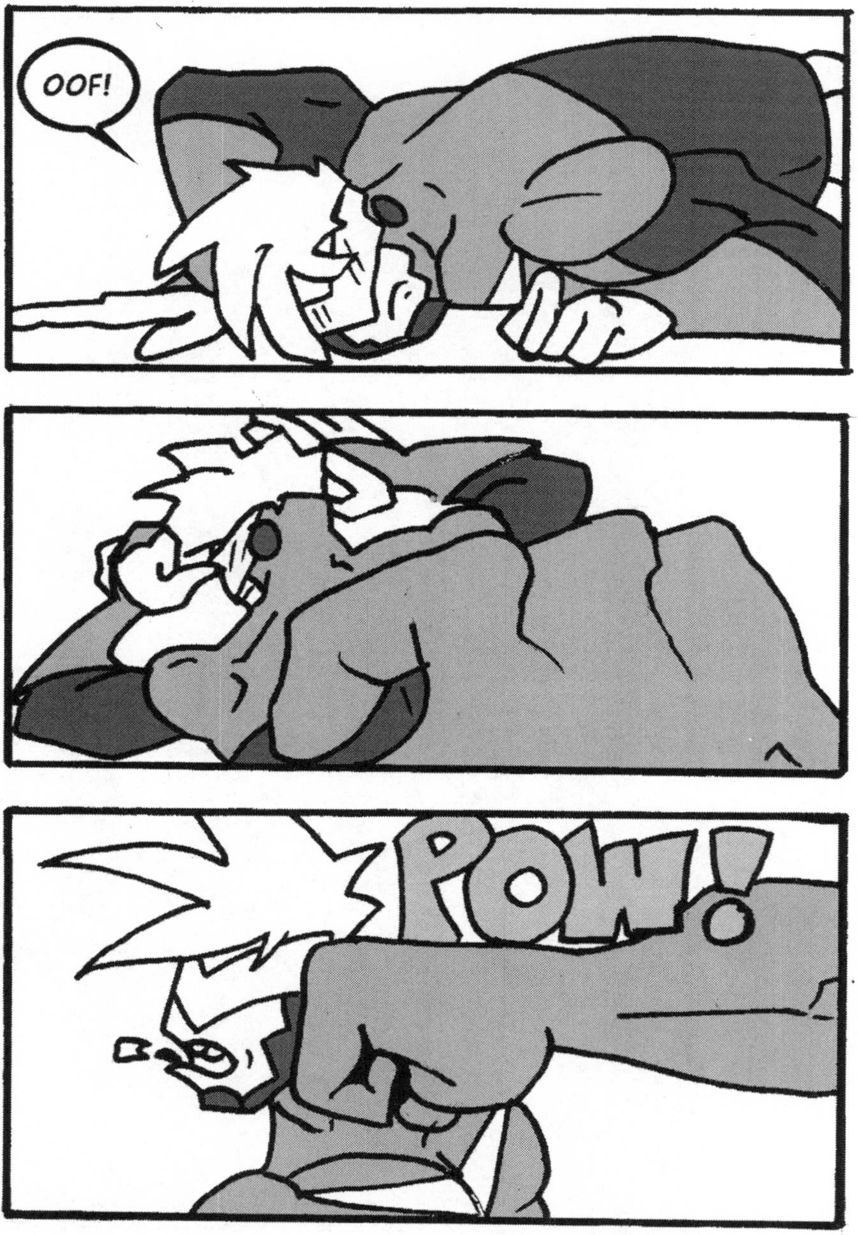
OOF!
POW!

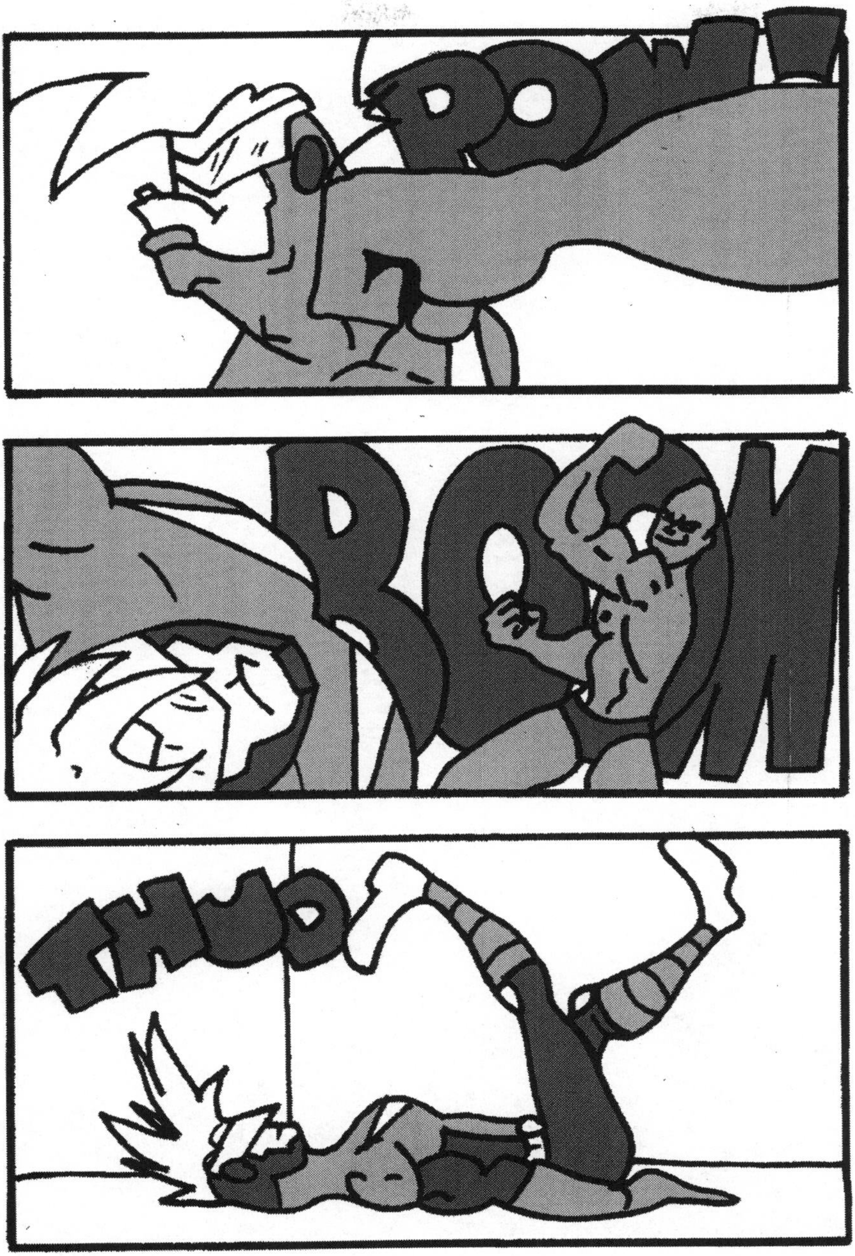
POW!!
BOOM
THUD

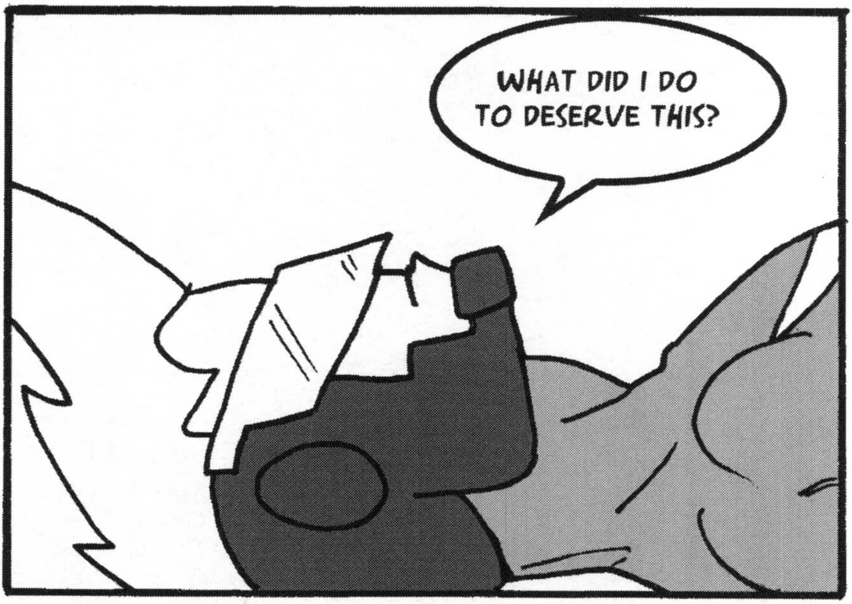
WHAT DID I DO
TO DESERVE THIS?

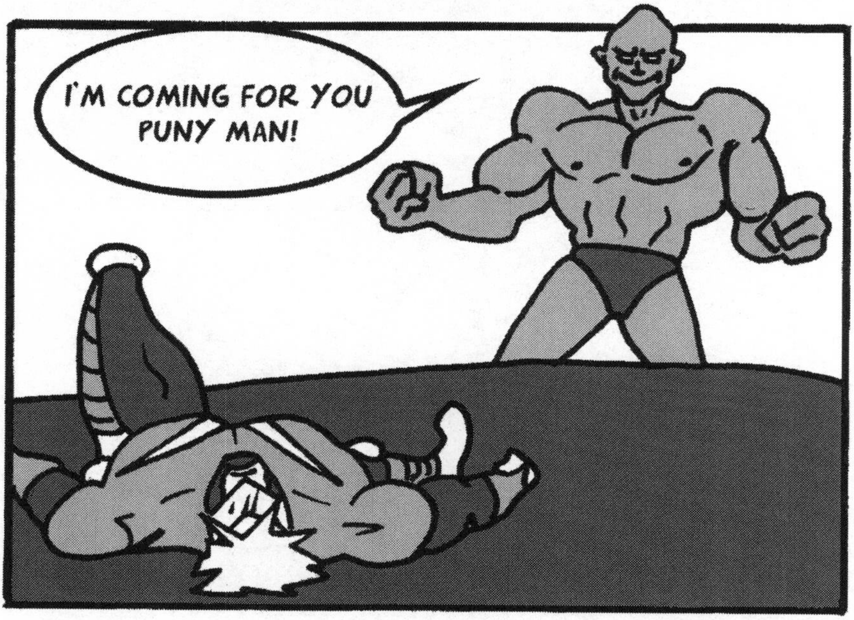
I'M COMING FOR YOU
PUNY MAN!

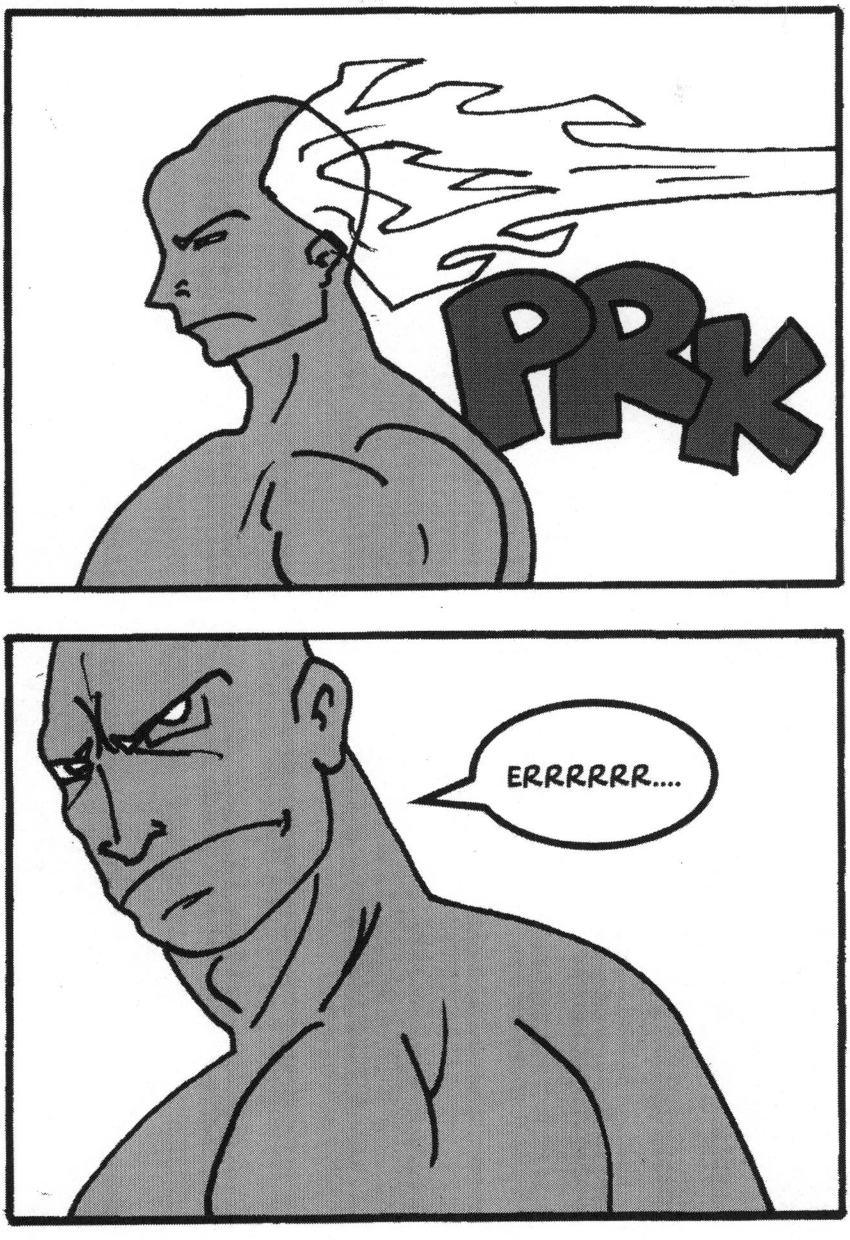
PRK
ERRRRRR....

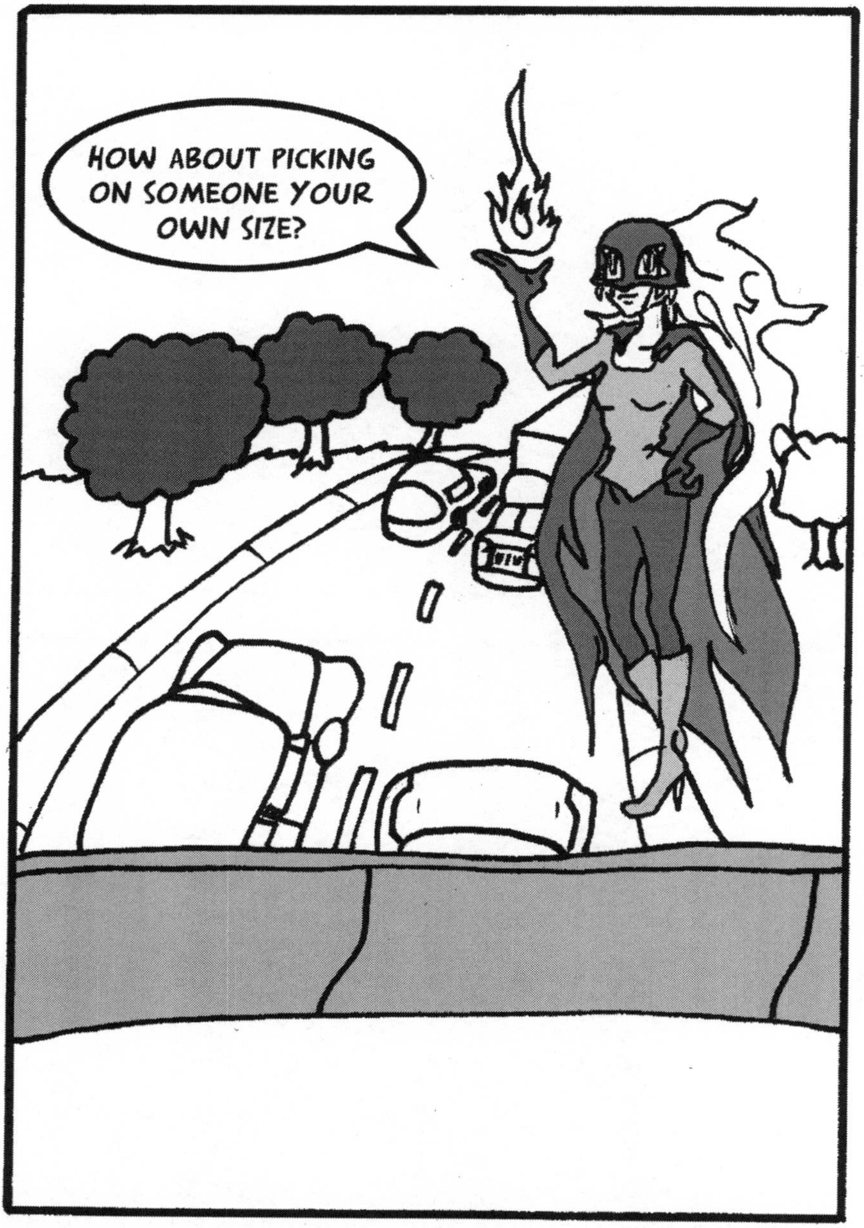
HOW ABOUT PICKING ON SOMEONE YOUR OWN SIZE?

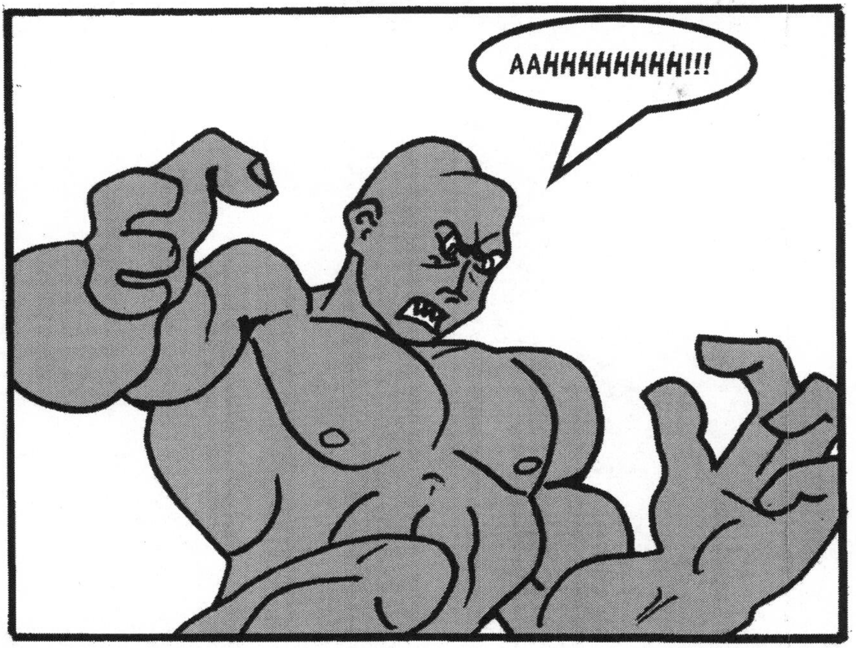
AAHHHHHHHH!!!

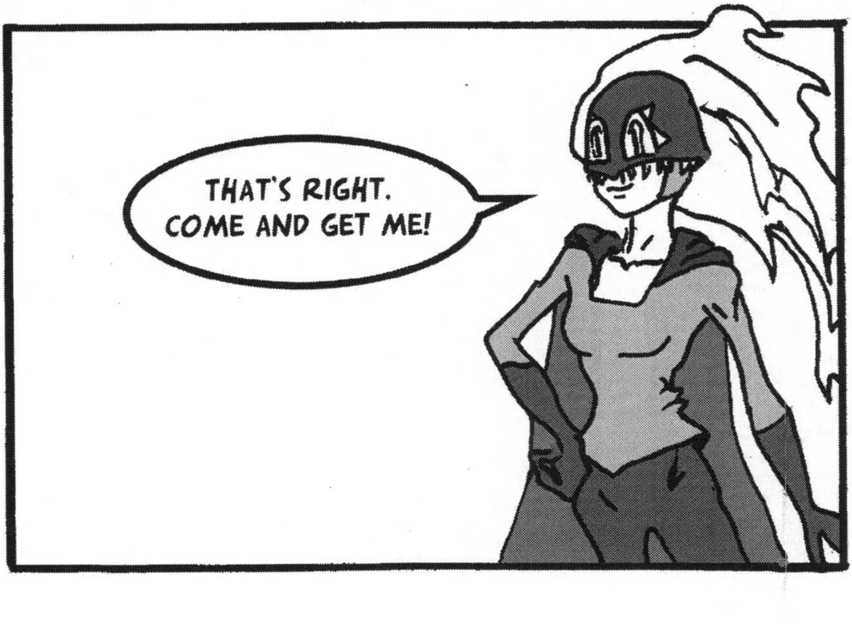
THAT'S RIGHT.
COME AND GET ME!

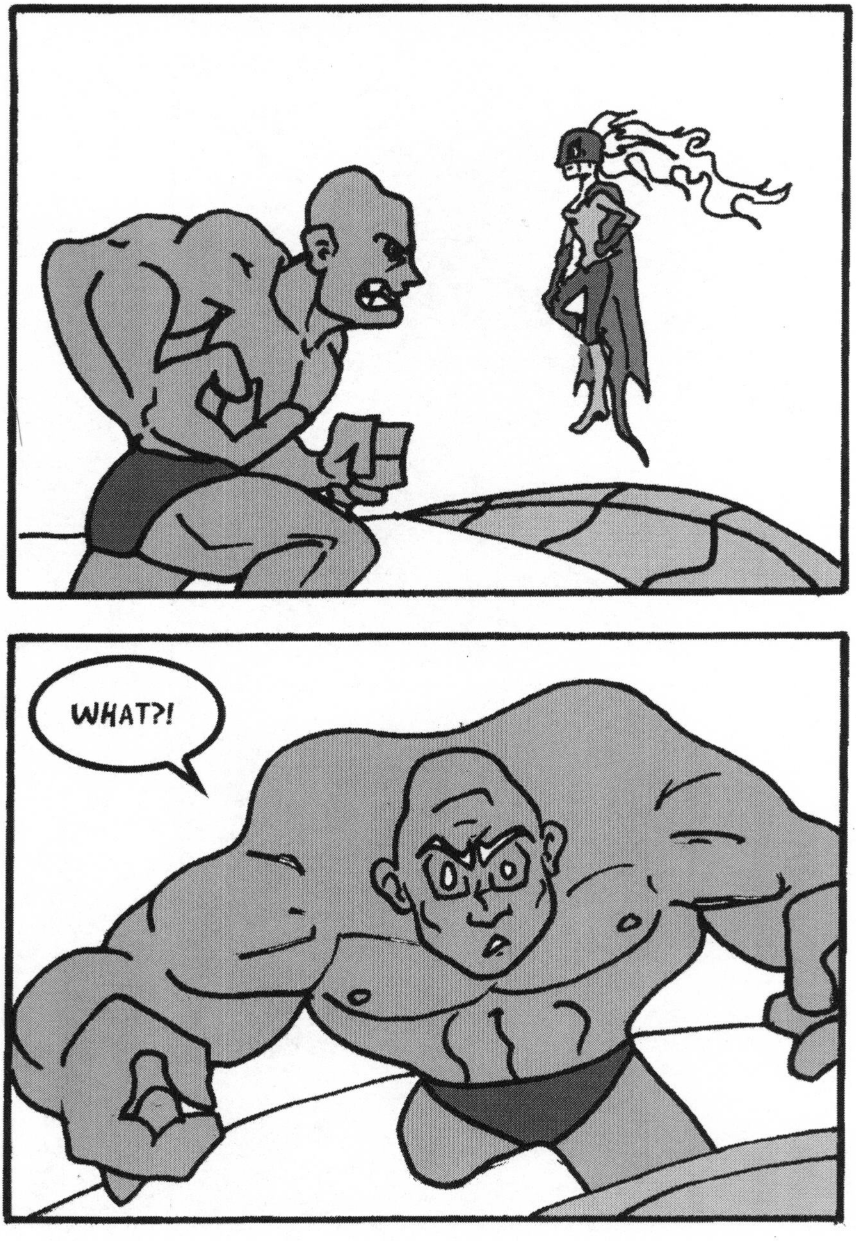
WHAT?!

BEEP
BEEP
BOOM
WHOOPS! DON'T MIND ME...

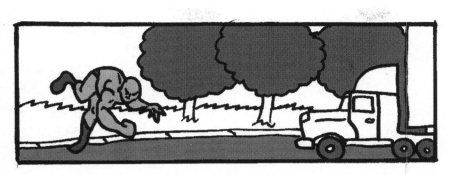

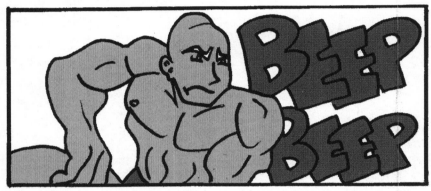

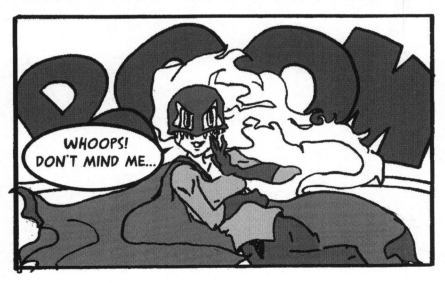

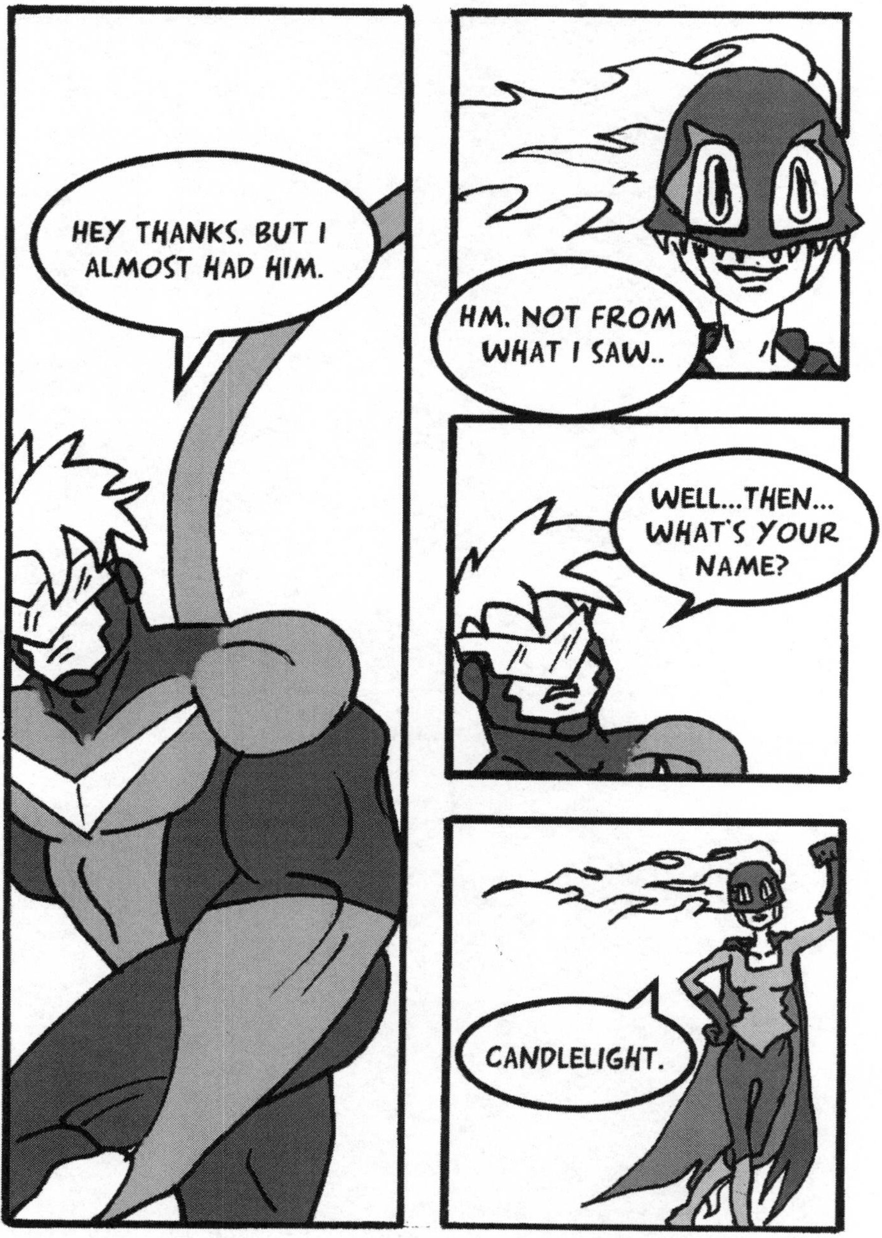
HEY THANKS. BUT I ALMOST HAD HIM.
HM. NOT FROM WHAT I SAW..
WELL...THEN... WHAT'S YOUR NAME?
CANDLELIGHT.

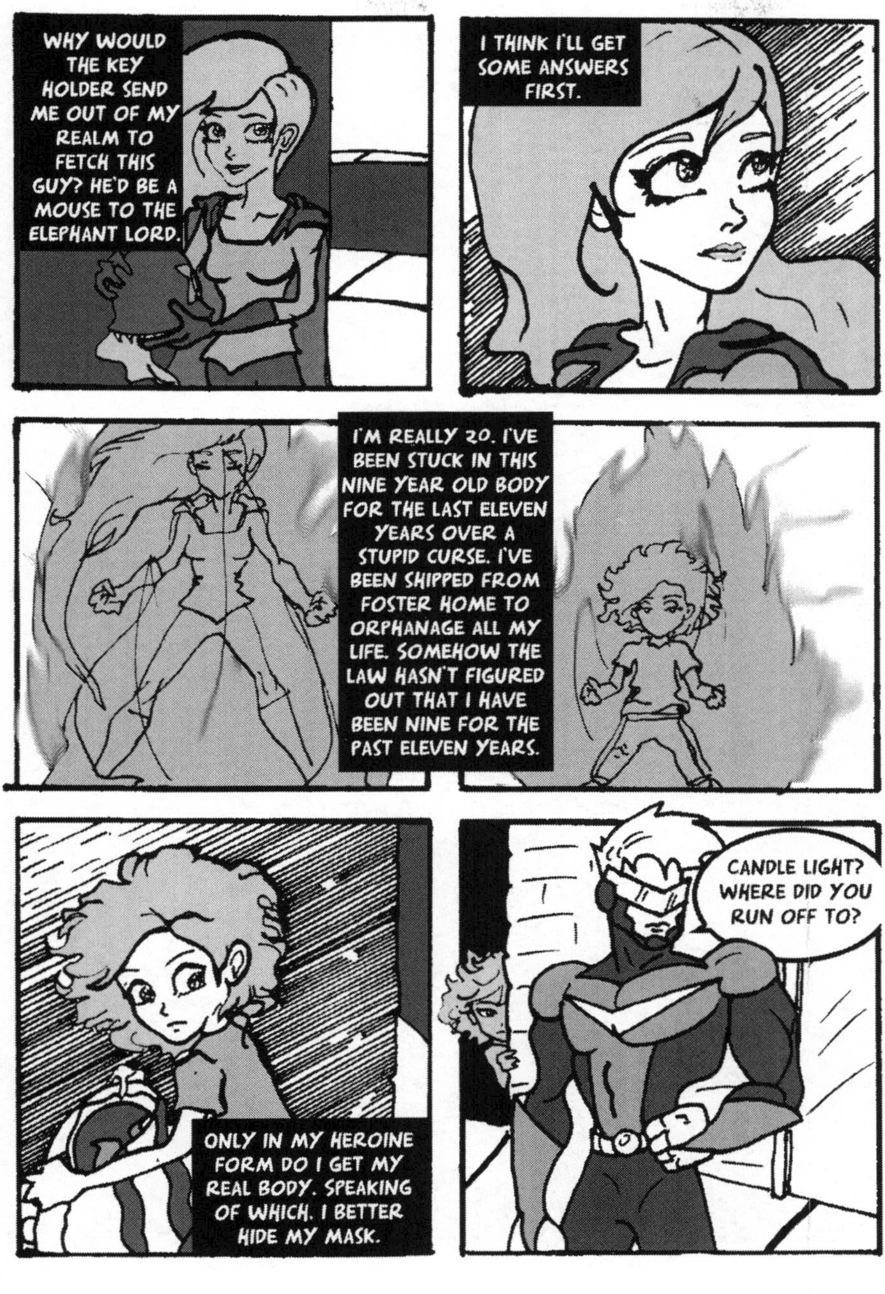
WHY WOULD THE KEY HOLDER SEND ME OUT OF MY REALM TO FETCH THIS GUY? HE'D BE A MOUSE TO THE ELEPHANT LORD.
I THINK I'LL GET SOME ANSWERS FIRST.
I'M REALLY 20. I'VE BEEN STUCK IN THIS NINE YEAR OLD BODY FOR THE LAST ELEVEN YEARS OVER A STUPID CURSE. I'VE BEEN SHIPPED FROM FOSTER HOME TO ORPHANAGE ALL MY LIFE. SOMEHOW THE LAW HASN'T FIGURED OUT THAT I HAVE BEEN NINE FOR THE PAST ELEVEN YEARS.
ONLY IN MY HEROINE FORM DO I GET MY REAL BODY. SPEAKING OF WHICH. I BETTER HIDE MY MASK.
CANDLE LIGHT? WHERE DID YOU RUN OFF TO?

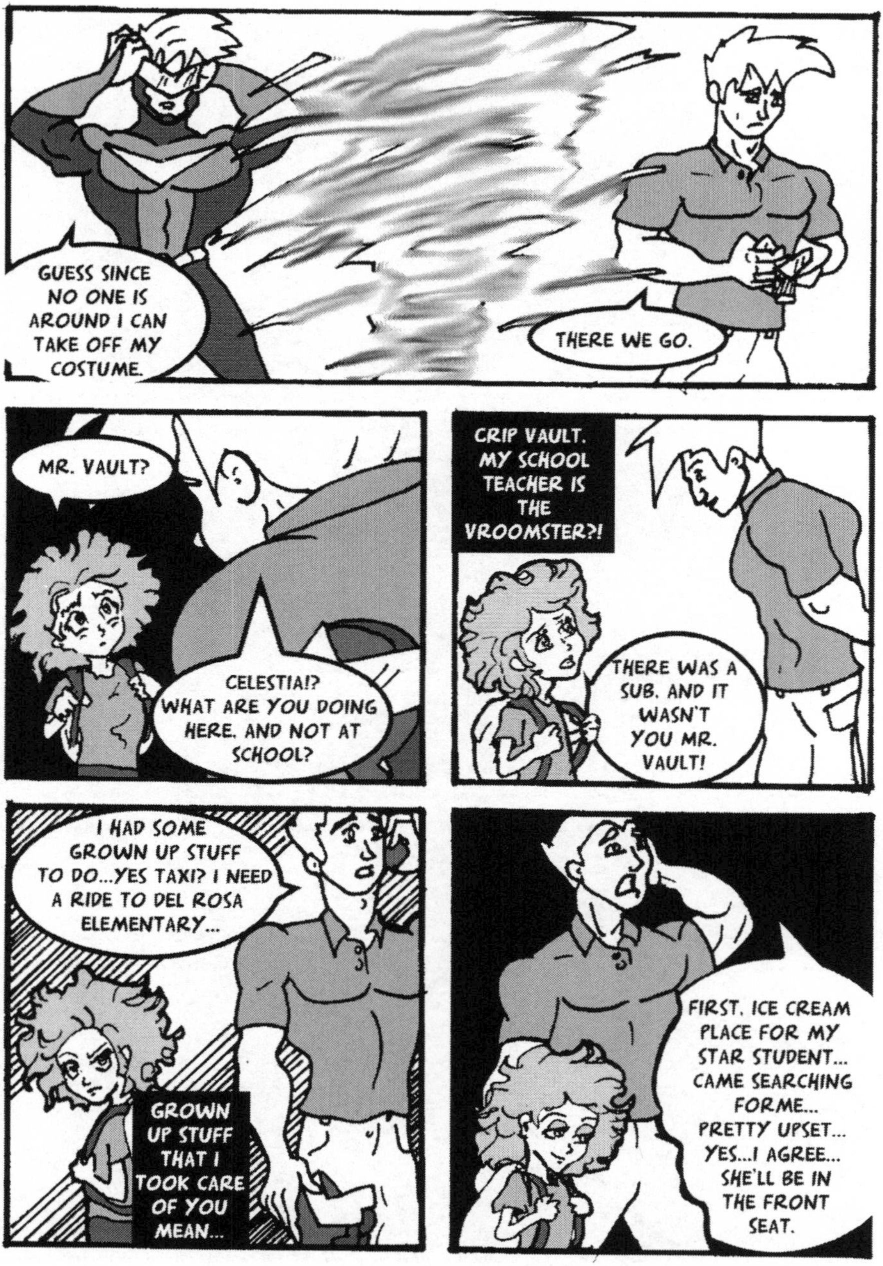
GUESS SINCE NO ONE IS AROUND I CAN TAKE OFF MY COSTUME.
THERE WE GO.
MR. VAULT?
CELESTIA!? WHAT ARE YOU DOING HERE. AND NOT AT SCHOOL?
CRIP VAULT. MY SCHOOL TEACHER IS THE VROOMSTER?!
THERE WAS A SUB. AND IT WASN'T YOU MR. VAULT!
I HAD SOME GROWN UP STUFF TO DO...YES TAXI? I NEED A RIDE TO DEL ROSA ELEMENTARY...
GROWN UP STUFF THAT I TOOK CARE OF YOU MEAN...
FIRST. ICE CREAM PLACE FOR MY STAR STUDENT... CAME SEARCHING FORME... PRETTY UPSET... YES...I AGREE... SHE'LL BE IN THE FRONT SEAT.

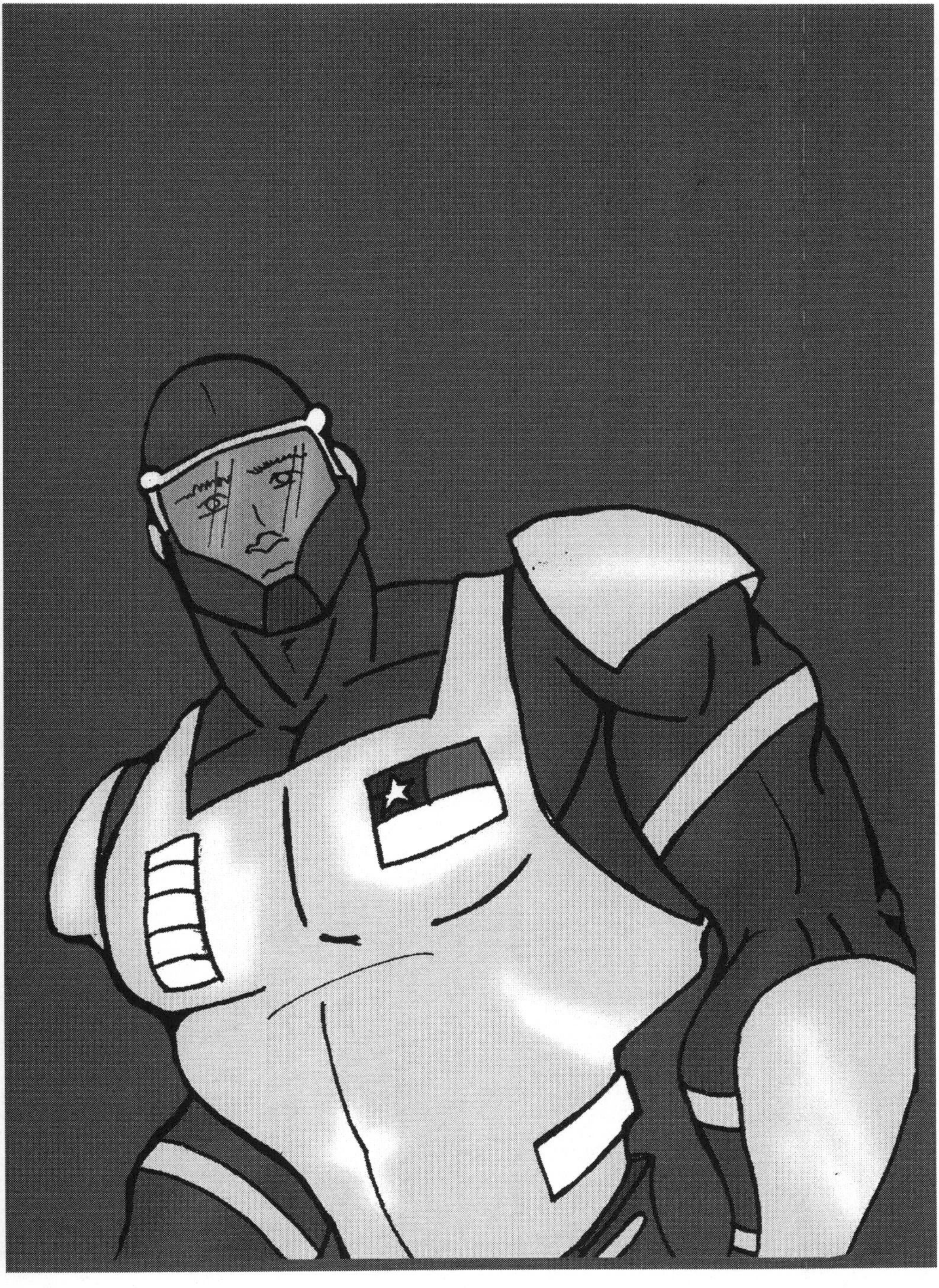

MATT'S NOTES:

This comic was my official first comic book. I think that it might have actually been drawn before The Salad Crew, but I put it here because it was the first official chapter of Zoom Man. I tried once to reboot the series, but decided against it.

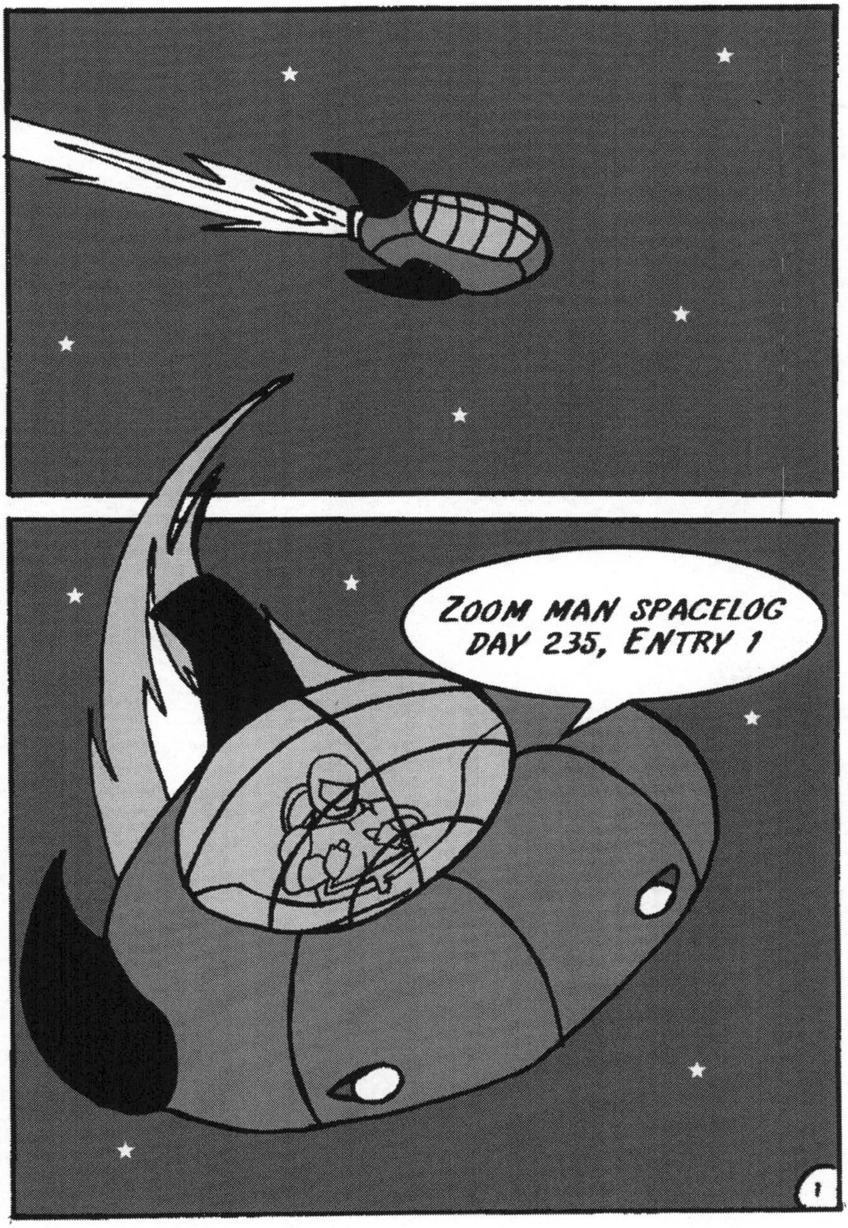
ZOOM MAN SPACELOG
DAY 235, ENTRY 1
1

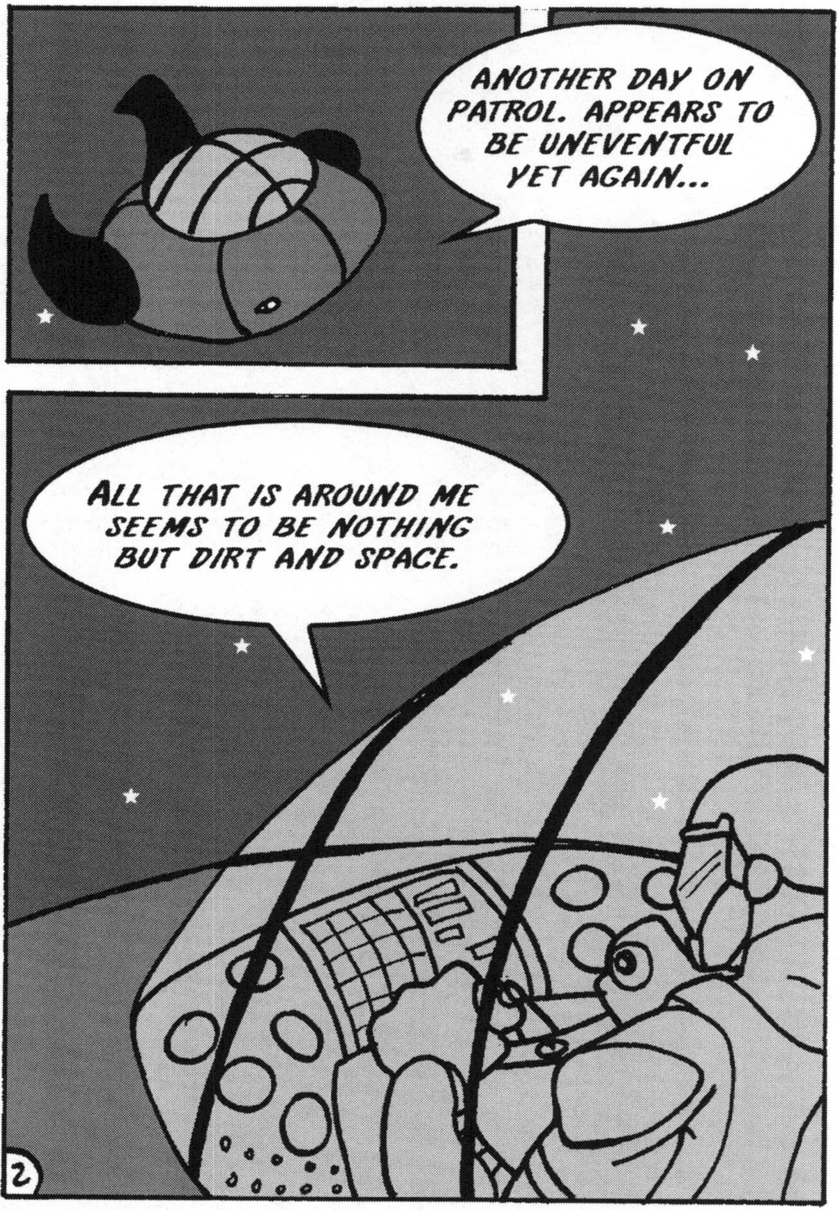
ANOTHER DAY ON PATROL. APPEARS TO BE UNEVENTFUL YET AGAIN...
ALL THAT IS AROUND ME SEEMS TO BE NOTHING BUT DIRT AND SPACE.
2

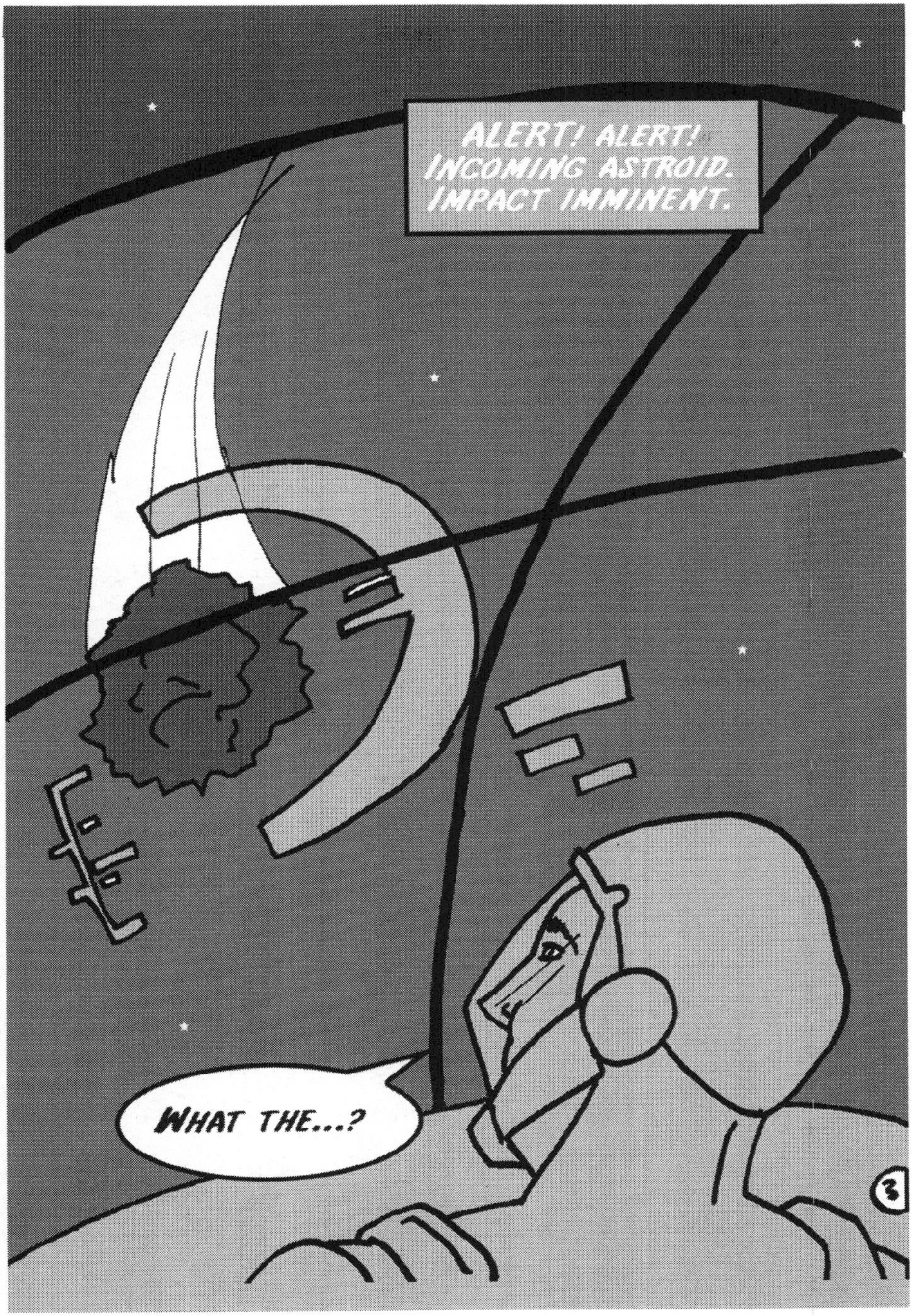
ALERT! ALERT!
INCOMING ASTROID.
IMPACT IMMINENT.
WHAT THE...?
3

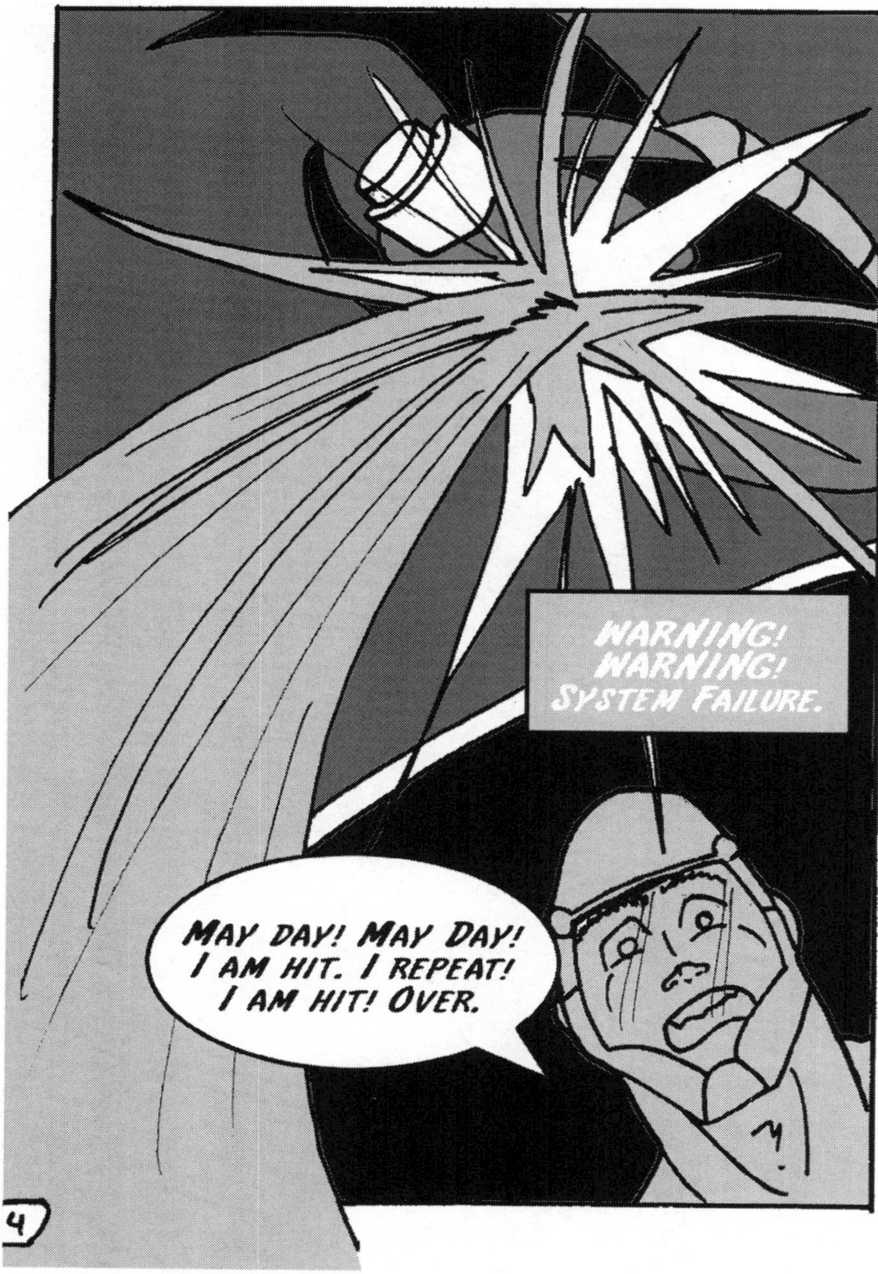
WARNING!
WARNING!
SYSTEM FAILURE.
MAY DAY! MAY DAY!
I AM HIT. I REPEAT!
I AM HIT! OVER.
4

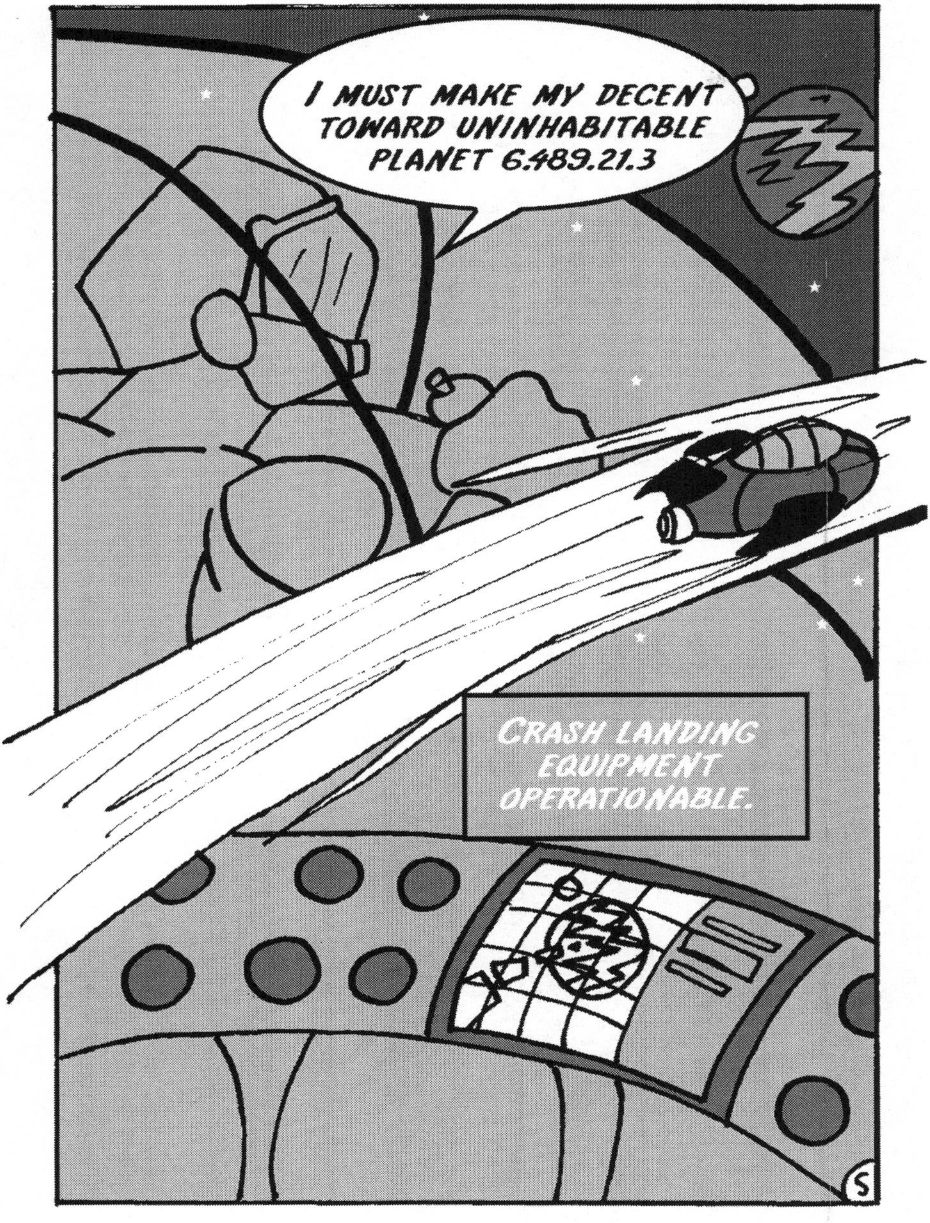
I MUST MAKE MY DECENT TOWARD UNINHABITABLE PLANET 6.489.21.3
CRASH LANDING EQUIPMENT OPERATIONABLE.

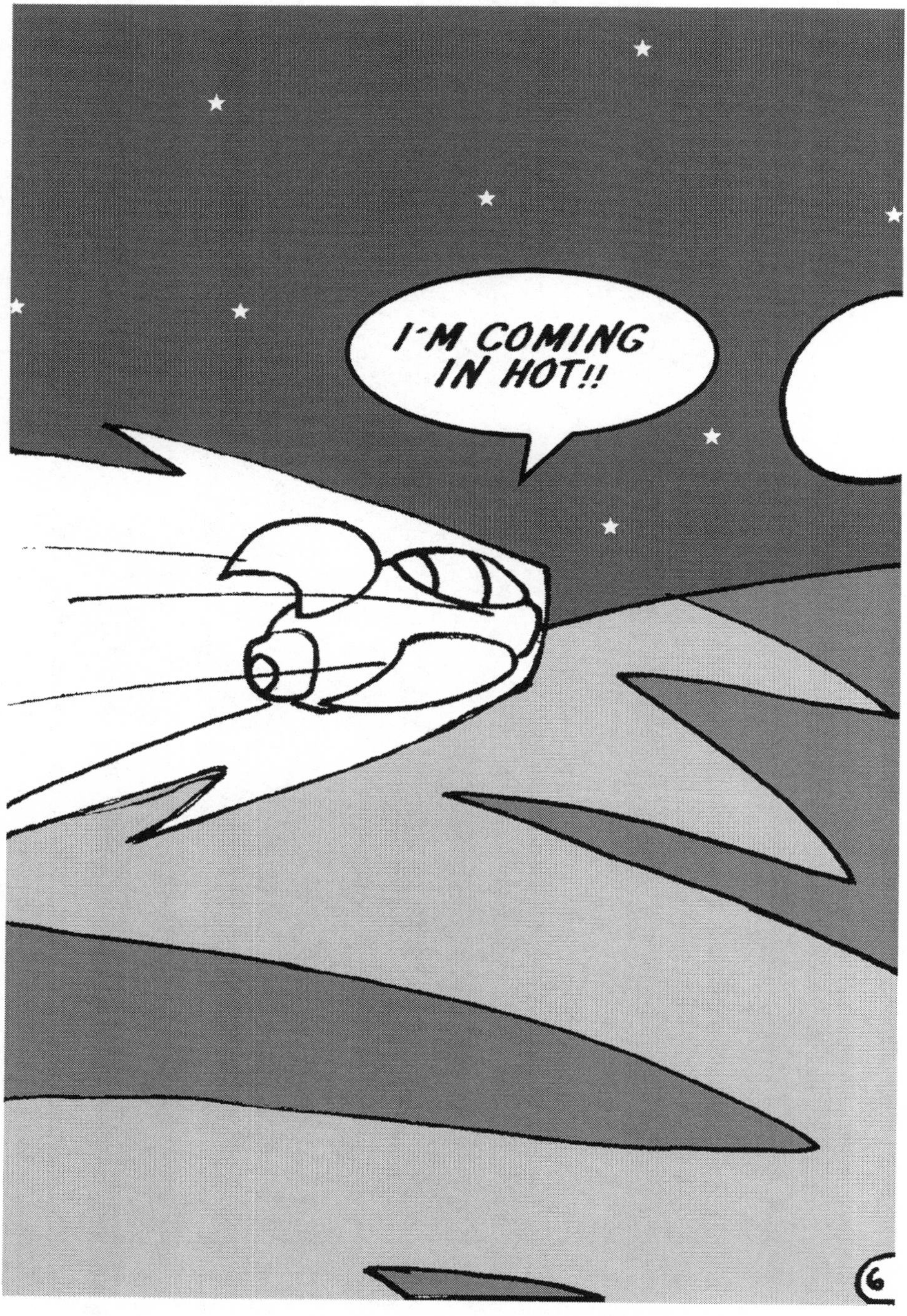
I'M COMING
IN HOT!!
6

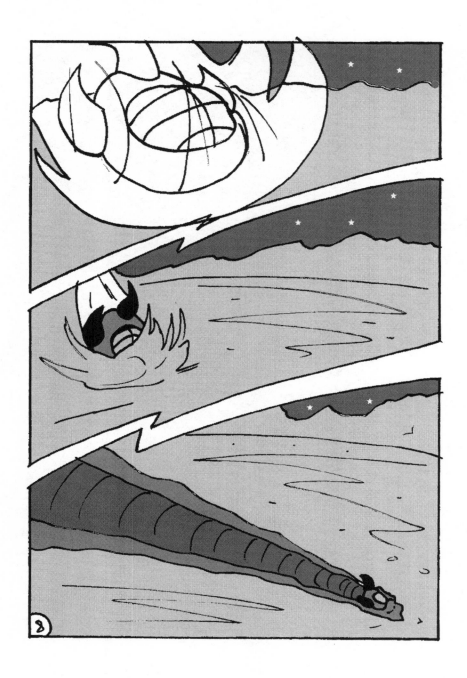

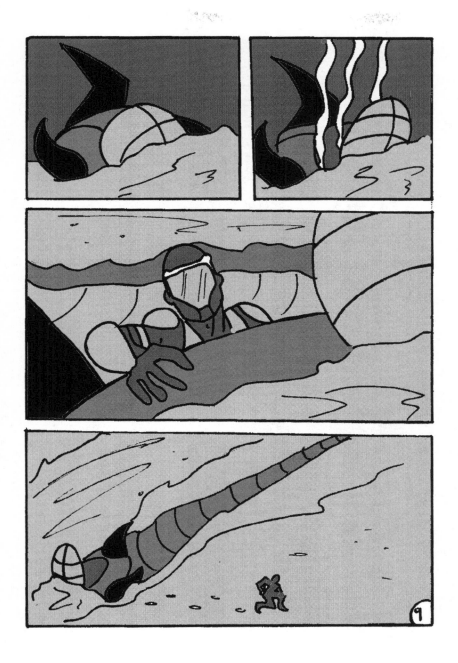

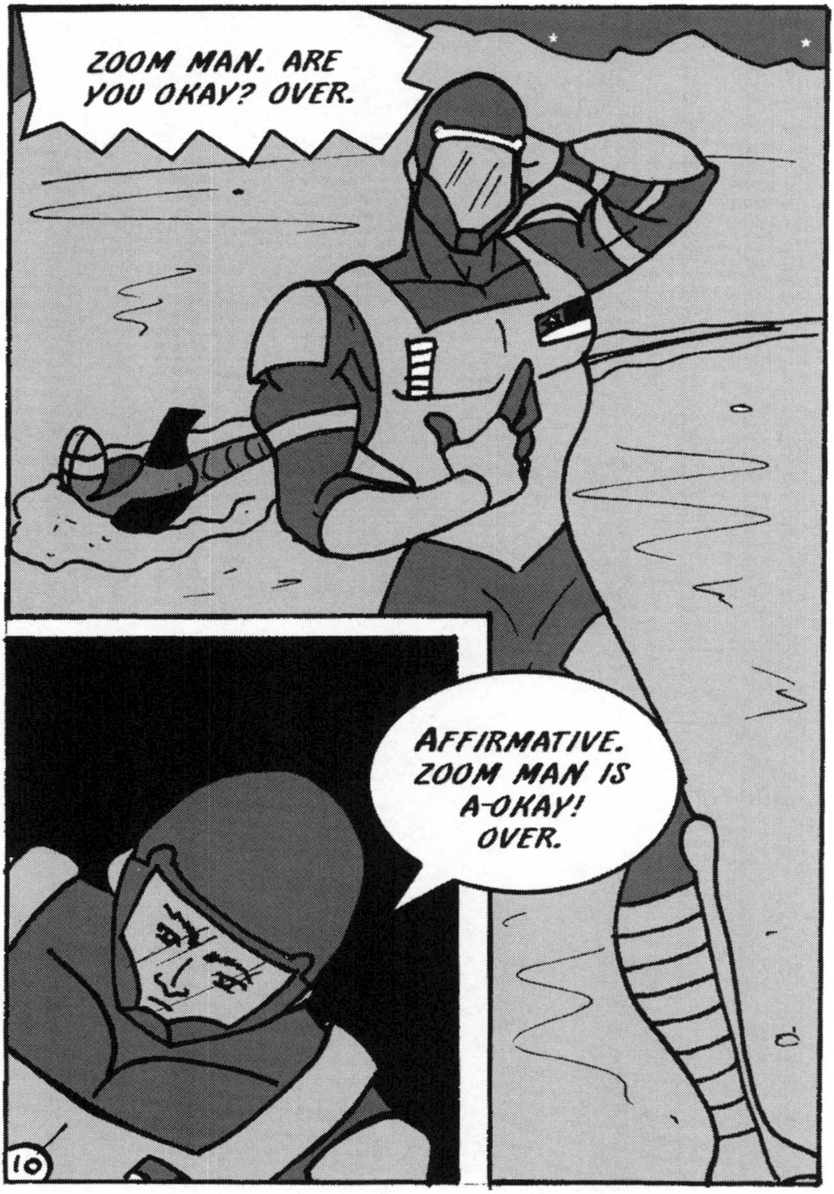
ZOOM MAN. ARE YOU OKAY? OVER.
AFFIRMATIVE. ZOOM MAN IS A-OKAY! OVER.
10

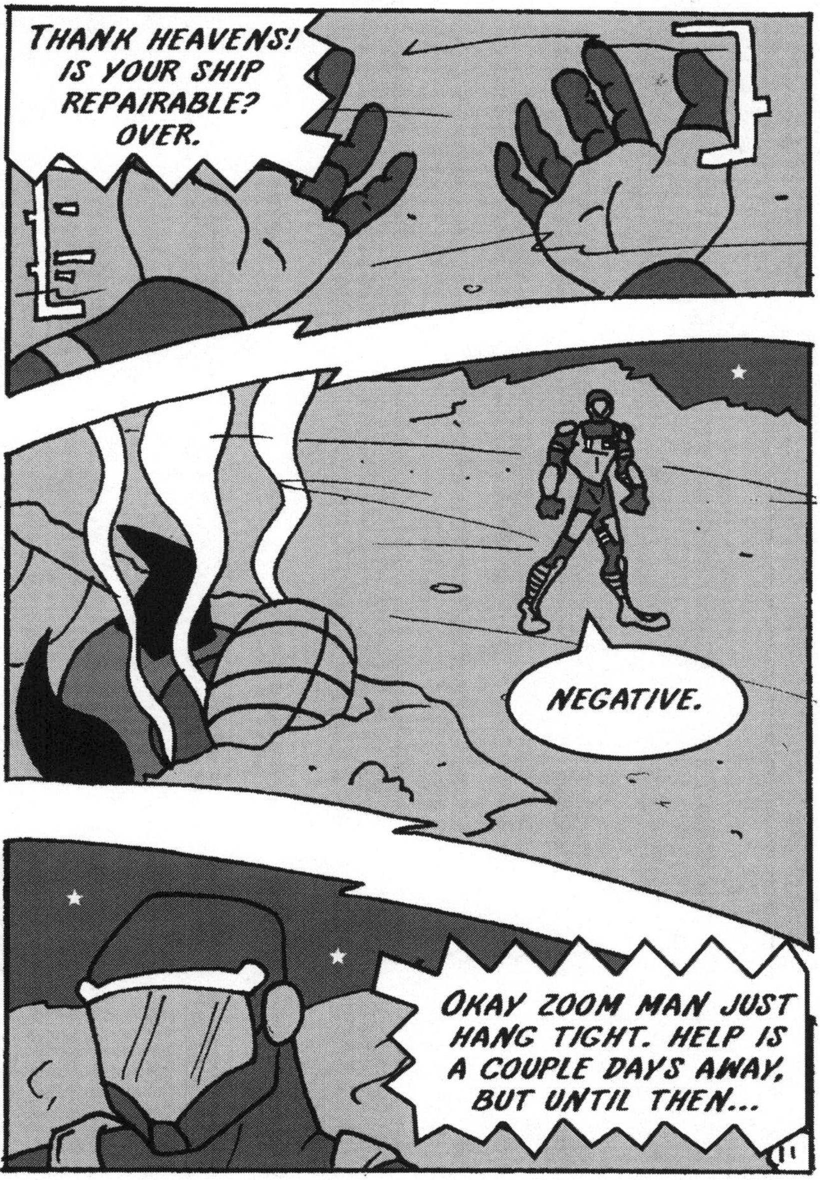
THANK HEAVENS! IS YOUR SHIP REPAIRABLE? OVER.
NEGATIVE.
OKAY ZOOM MAN JUST HANG TIGHT. HELP IS A COUPLE DAYS AWAY, BUT UNTIL THEN...
11

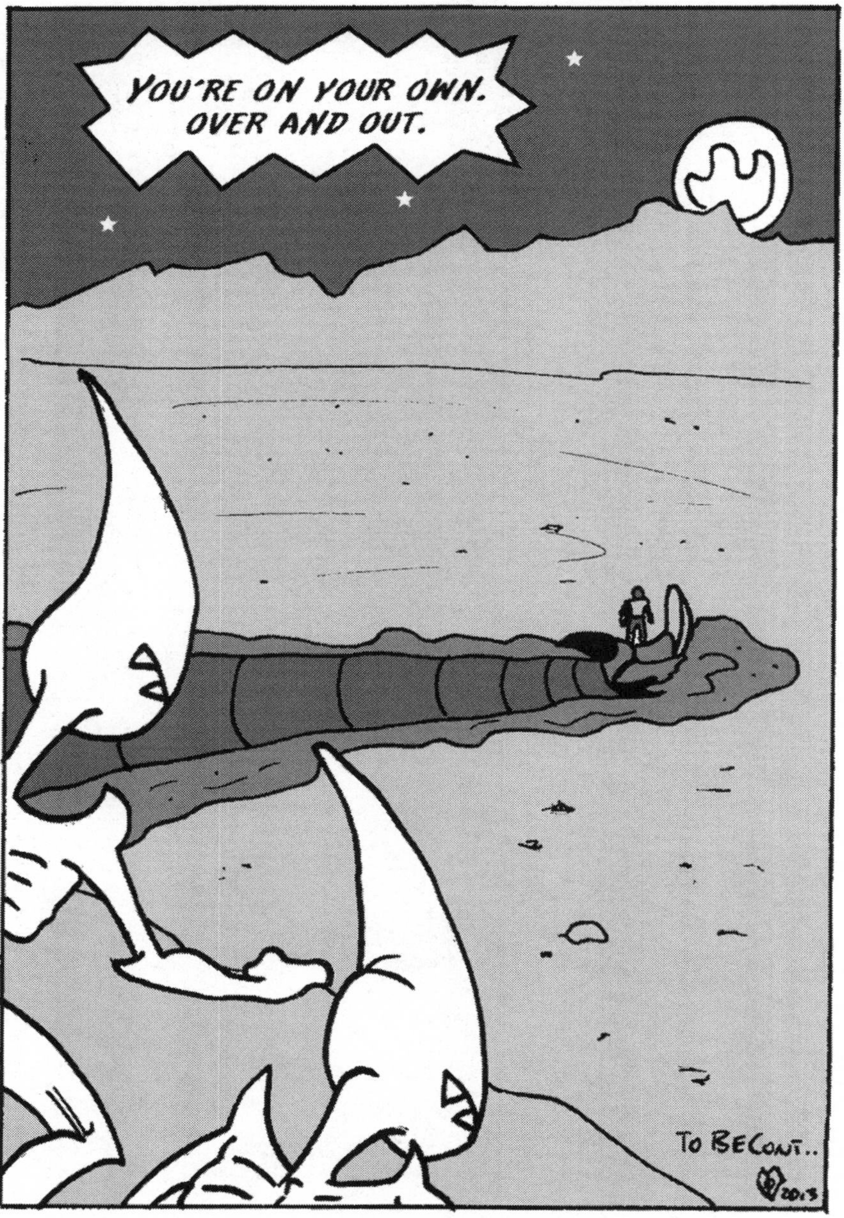
YOU'RE ON YOUR OWN.
OVER AND OUT.
TO BE CONT..
2013

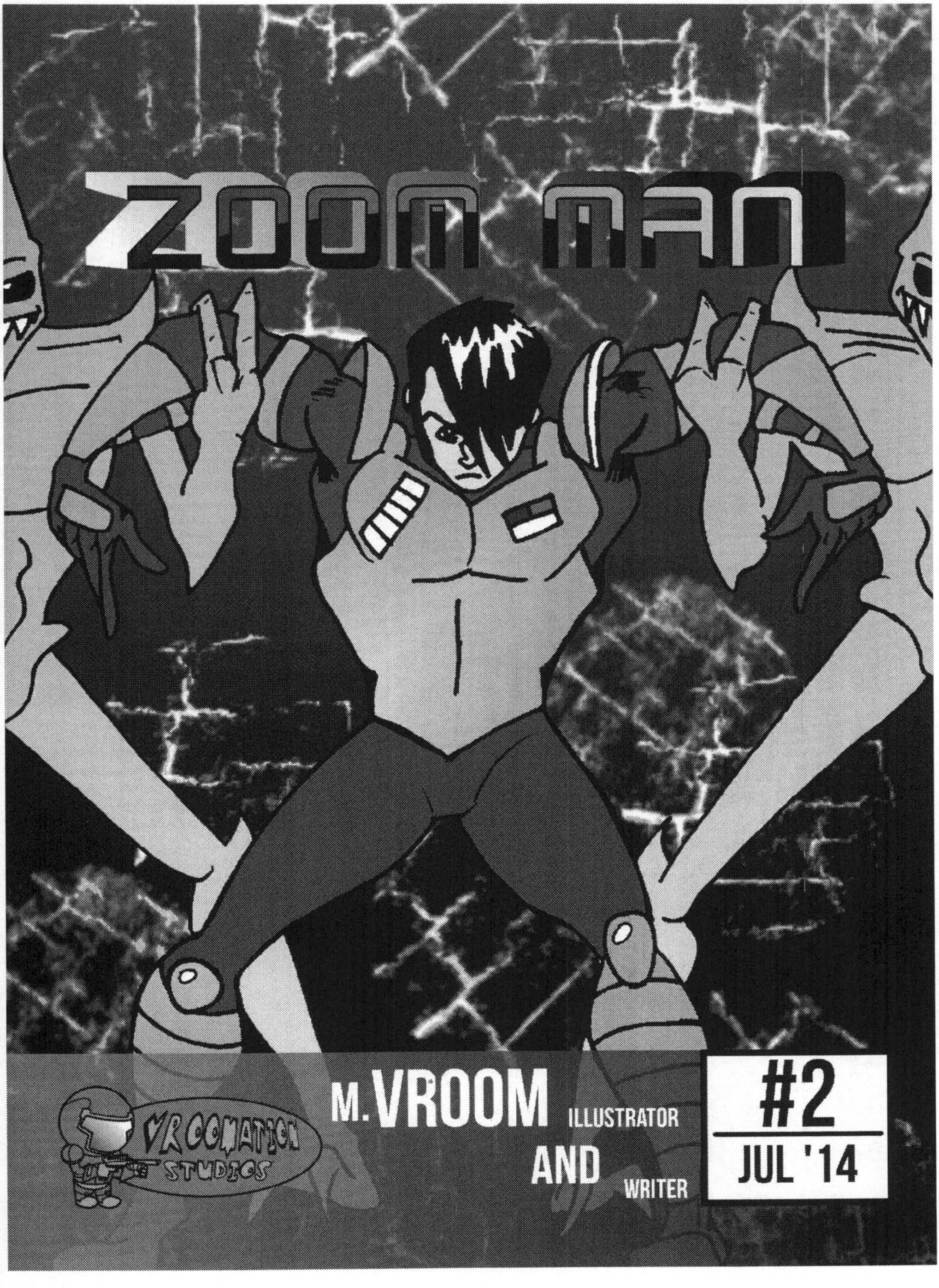
ZOOM MAN
M.VROOM ILLUSTRATOR
AND WRITER
#2
JUL '14
VROOMATION STUDIOS

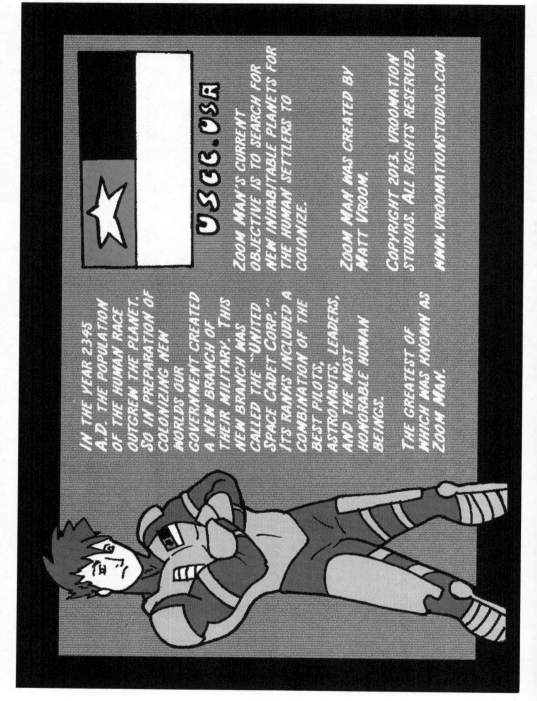

USCC.USA

IN THE YEAR 2345 A.D. THE POPULATION OF THE HUMAN RACE OUTGREW THE PLANET. SO IN PREPARATION OF COLONIZING NEW WORLDS OUR GOVERNMENT CREATED A NEW BRANCH OF THEIR MILITARY. THIS NEW BRANCH WAS CALLED THE "UNITED SPACE CADET CORP." ITS RANKS INCLUDED A COMBINATION OF THE BEST PILOTS, ASTRONAUTS, LEADERS, AND THE MOST HONORABLE HUMAN BEINGS.

THE GREATEST OF WHICH WAS KNOWN AS ZOOM MAN.

ZOOM MAN'S CURRENT OBJECTIVE IS TO SEARCH FOR NEW INHABITABLE PLANETS FOR THE HUMAN SETTLERS TO COLONIZE.

ZOOM MAN WAS CREATED BY MATT VROOM.

COPYRIGHT 2013, VROOMATION STUDIOS. ALL RIGHTS RESERVED.

WWW.VROOMATIONSTUDIOS.COM

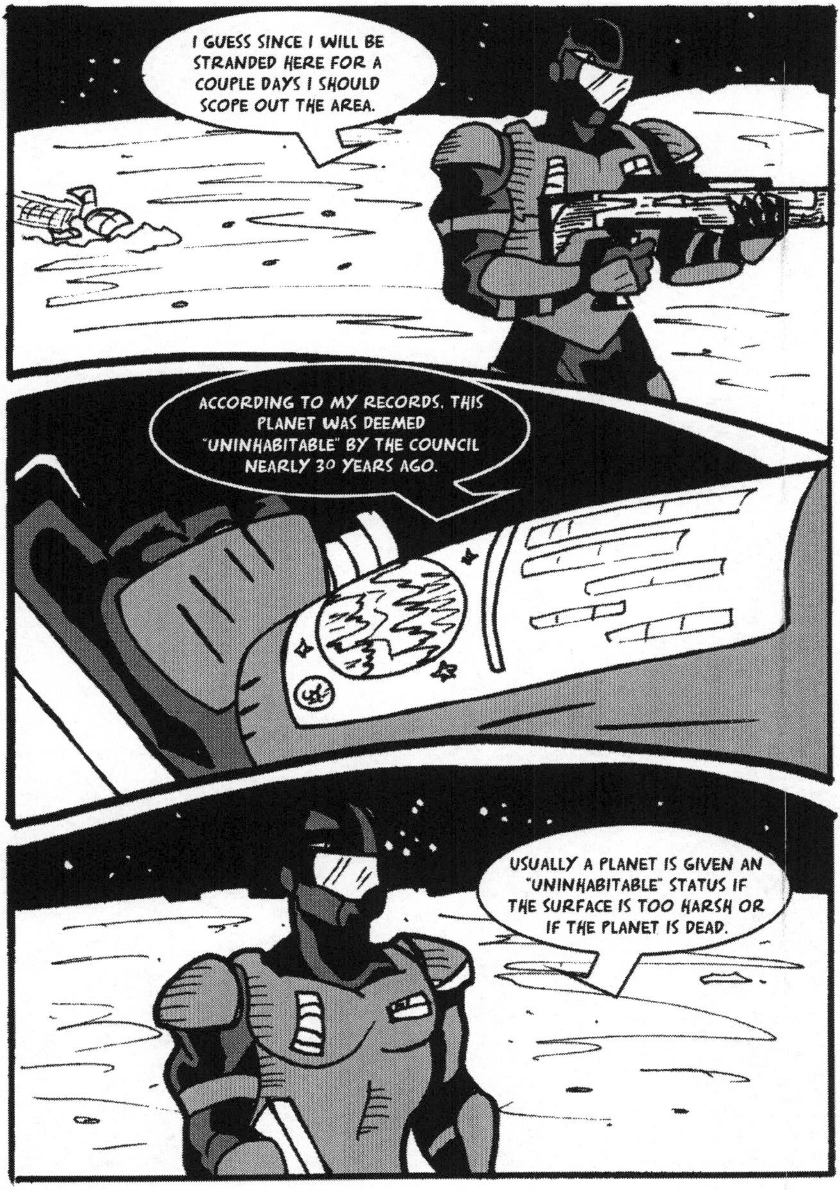
I GUESS SINCE I WILL BE STRANDED HERE FOR A COUPLE DAYS I SHOULD SCOPE OUT THE AREA.
ACCORDING TO MY RECORDS. THIS PLANET WAS DEEMED "UNINHABITABLE" BY THE COUNCIL NEARLY 30 YEARS AGO.
USUALLY A PLANET IS GIVEN AN "UNINHABITABLE" STATUS IF THE SURFACE IS TOO HARSH OR IF THE PLANET IS DEAD.

SCANNING... 30%
HOWEVER, IT APPEARS THAT THIS ISN'T THE CASE FOR EITHER ONE OF THOSE OPTIONS.
SCAN COMPLETE... ALIEN LIFE DETECTED.
THAT'S WHAT I THOUGHT...

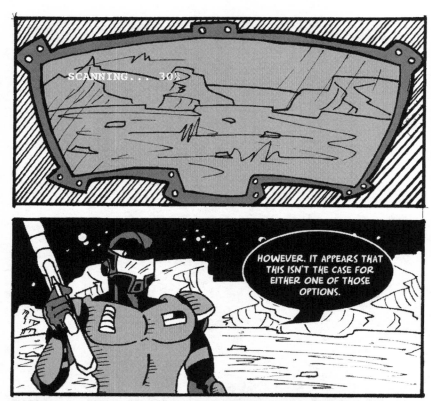

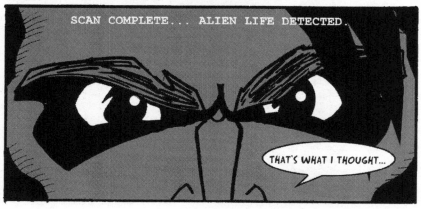

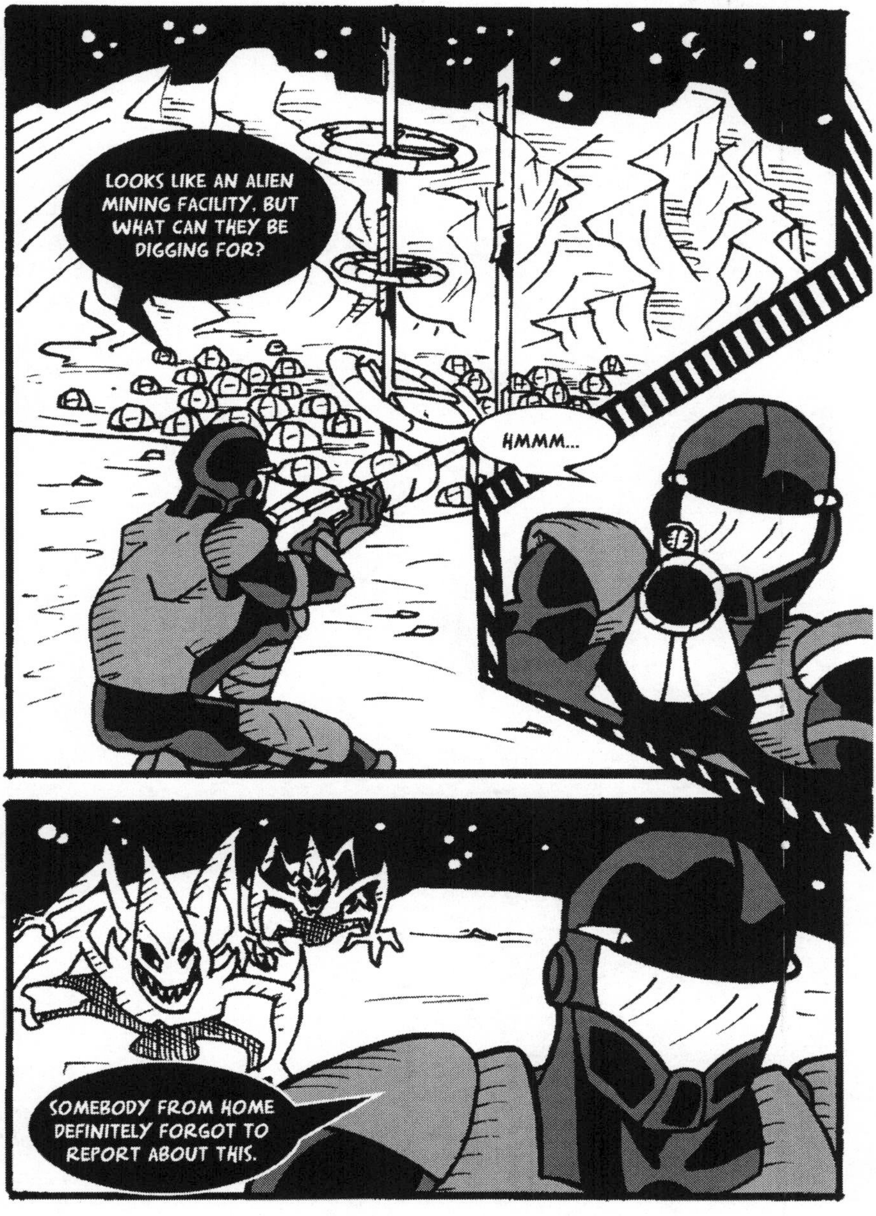
LOOKS LIKE AN ALIEN MINING FACILITY, BUT WHAT CAN THEY BE DIGGING FOR?
HMMM...
SOMEBODY FROM HOME DEFINITELY FORGOT TO REPORT ABOUT THIS.

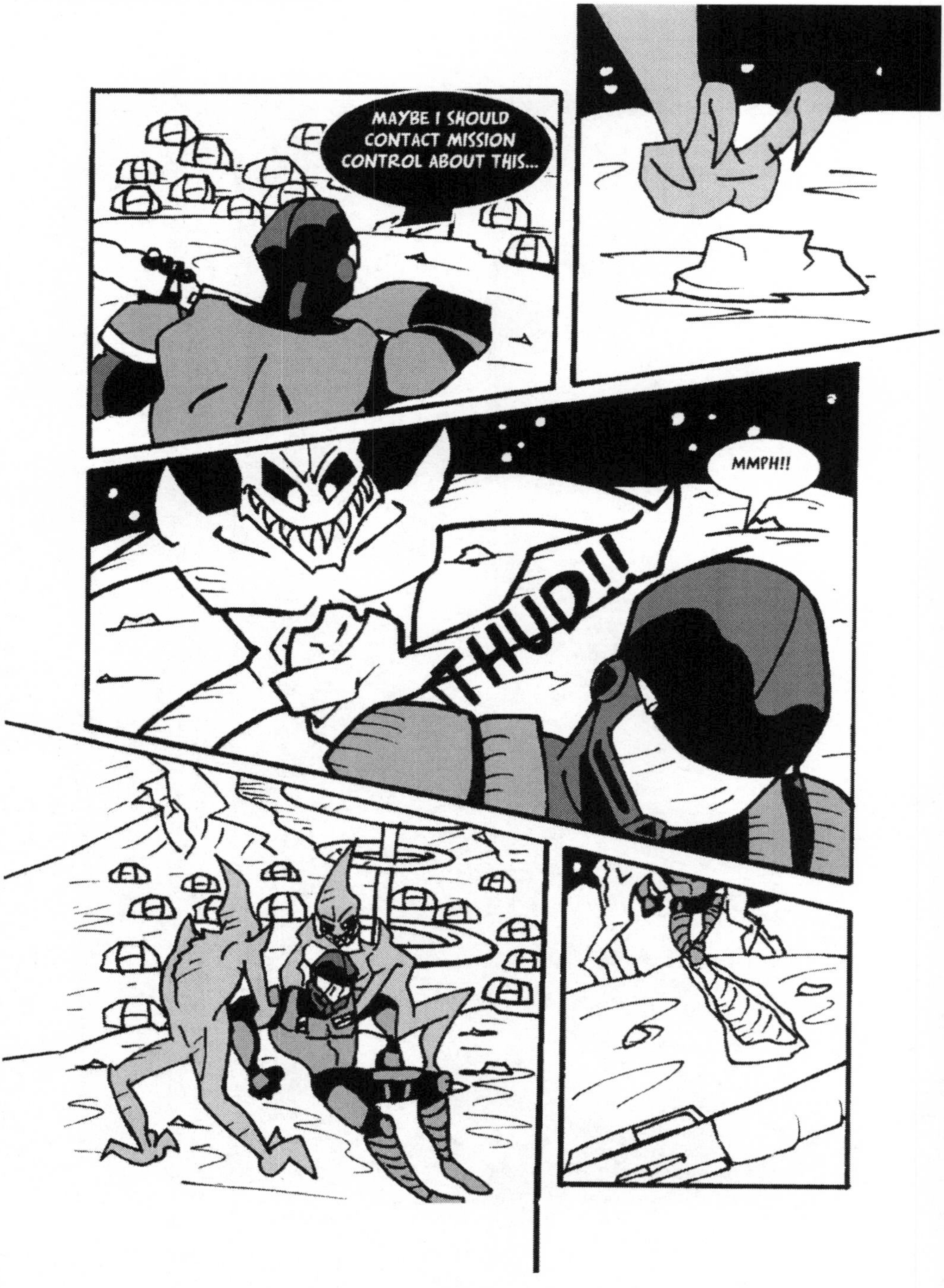
MAYBE I SHOULD CONTACT MISSION CONTROL ABOUT THIS...
MMPH!!
THUD!!

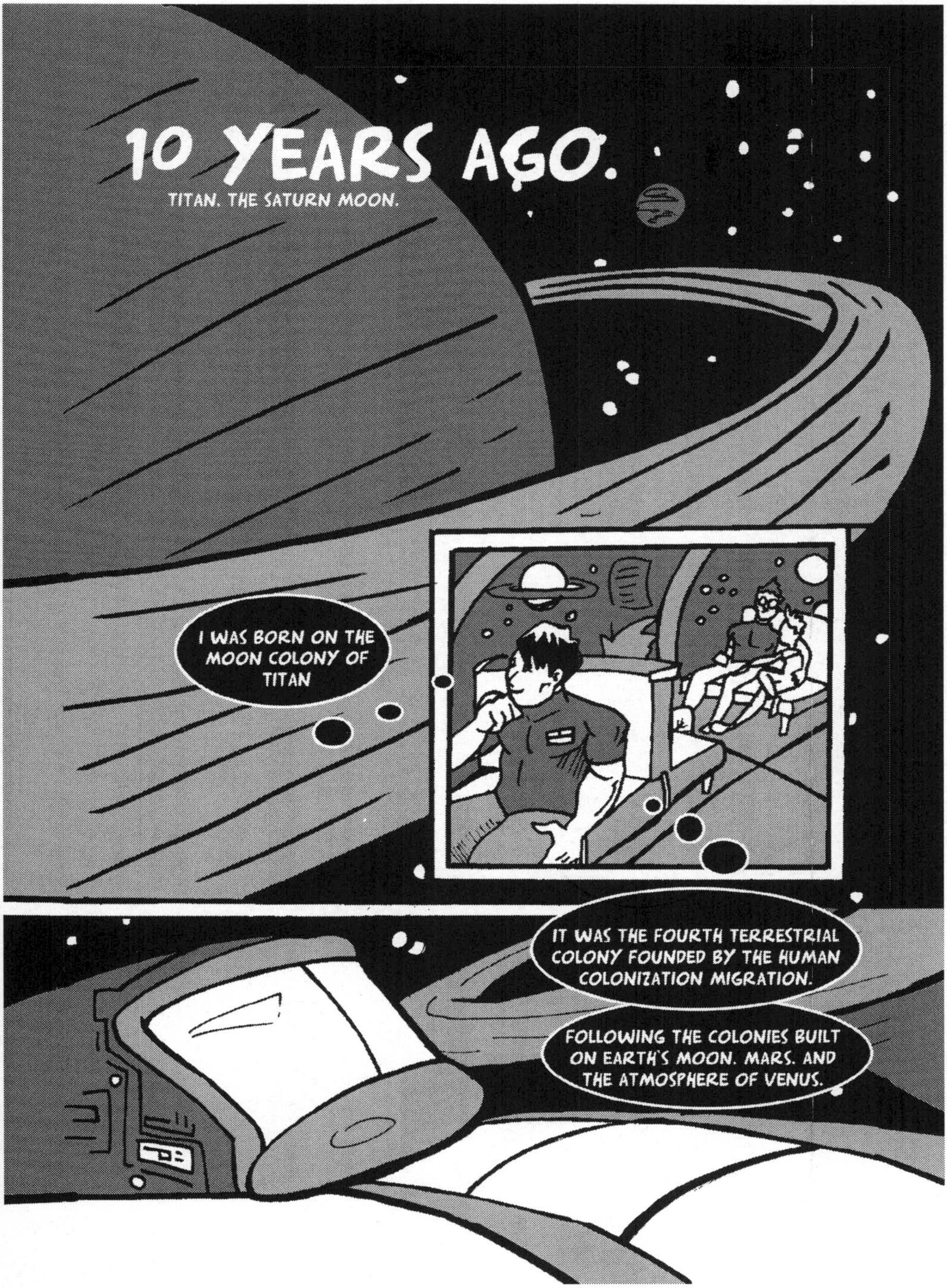
10 YEARS AGO.
TITAN. THE SATURN MOON.
I WAS BORN ON THE MOON COLONY OF TITAN
IT WAS THE FOURTH TERRESTRIAL COLONY FOUNDED BY THE HUMAN COLONIZATION MIGRATION.
FOLLOWING THE COLONIES BUILT ON EARTH'S MOON. MARS. AND THE ATMOSPHERE OF VENUS.

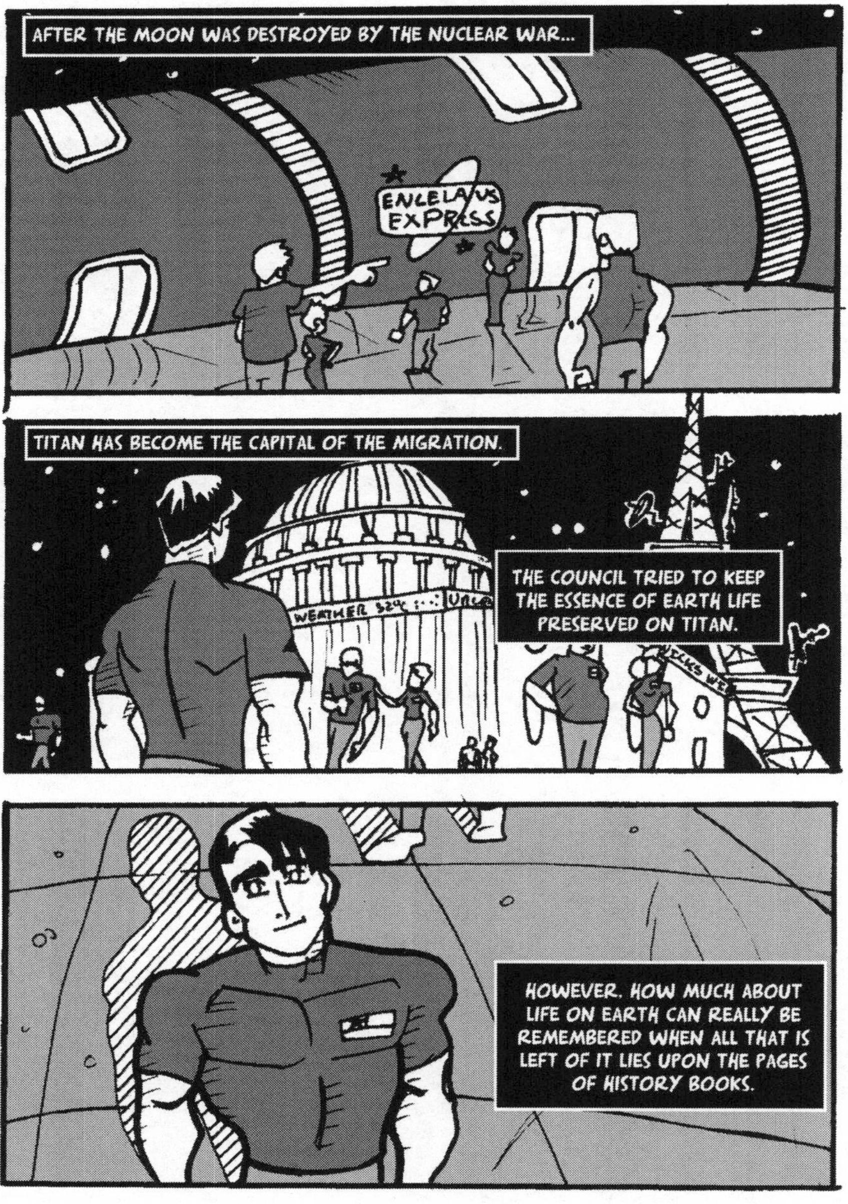
AFTER THE MOON WAS DESTROYED BY THE NUCLEAR WAR...
TITAN HAS BECOME THE CAPITAL OF THE MIGRATION.
THE COUNCIL TRIED TO KEEP THE ESSENCE OF EARTH LIFE PRESERVED ON TITAN.
HOWEVER. HOW MUCH ABOUT LIFE ON EARTH CAN REALLY BE REMEMBERED WHEN ALL THAT IS LEFT OF IT LIES UPON THE PAGES OF HISTORY BOOKS.

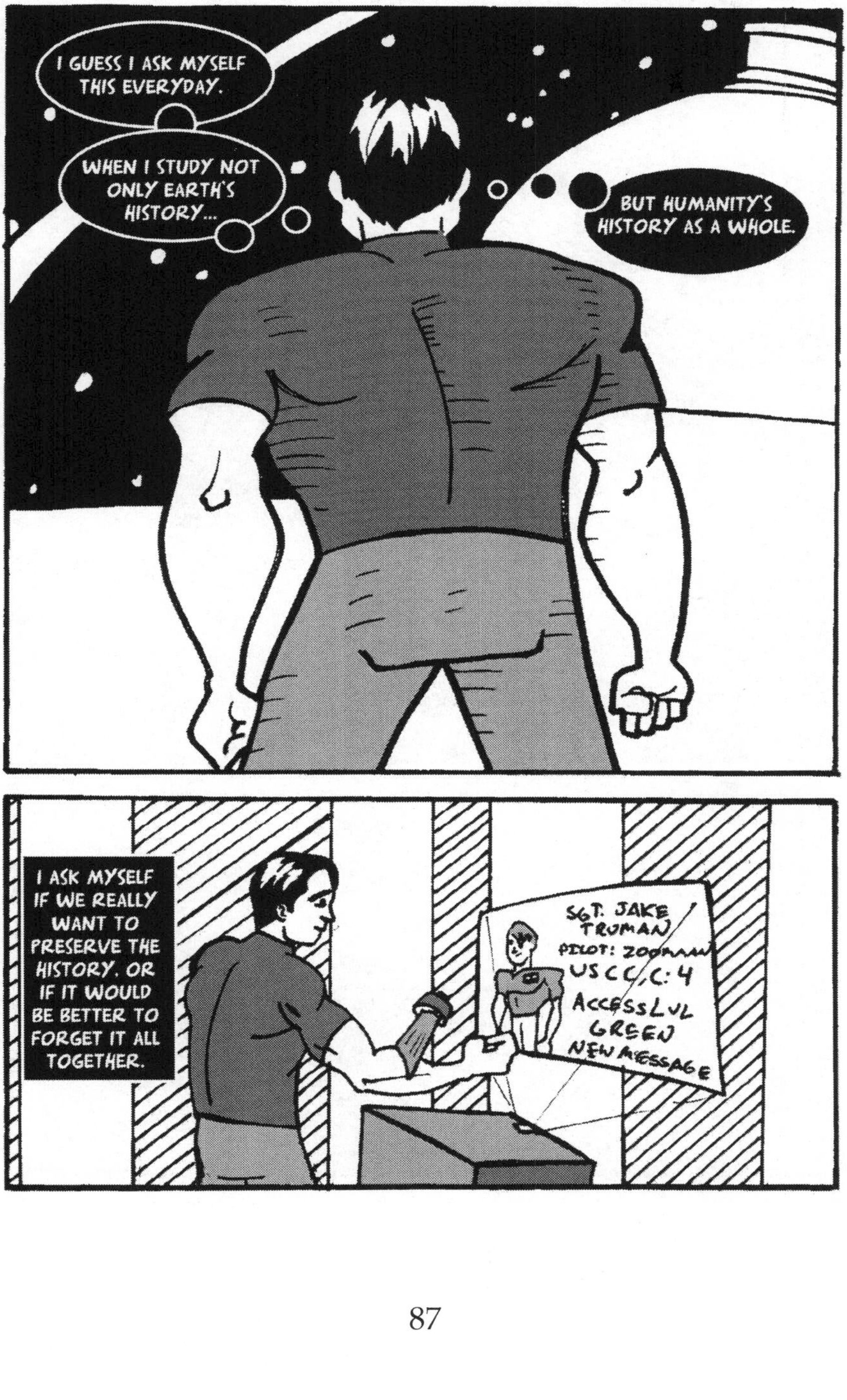
I GUESS I ASK MYSELF THIS EVERYDAY.
WHEN I STUDY NOT ONLY EARTH'S HISTORY...
BUT HUMANITY'S HISTORY AS A WHOLE.
I ASK MYSELF IF WE REALLY WANT TO PRESERVE THE HISTORY, OR IF IT WOULD BE BETTER TO FORGET IT ALL TOGETHER.
SGT. JAKE TRUMAN
PILOT: ZOOMAN
USCC,C:4
ACCESS LVL GREEN
NEW MESSAGE

NEW ASSIGNME
SYSTEM 6.489.21
SPYDER.23
LONG DISTANCE CRUSSER
USCC
AT 23 YEARS OLD I AM THE YOUNGEST SPACE CADET IN THE UNITED SPACE CADET CORP.
TODAY I RECEIVE MY FIRST INTERGALACTIC MISSION TO EXPLORE A WORLD LIGHT YEARS AWAY.
A LOT CAN HAPPEN IN SPACE AND I MIGHT BE GONE FOR A LONG TIME.
I GUESS I SHOULD PROBABLY KISS MY MOTHER GOODBYE.

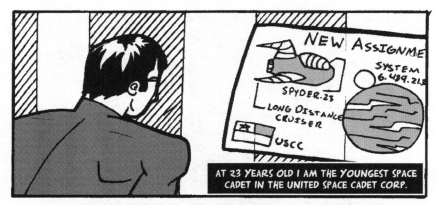

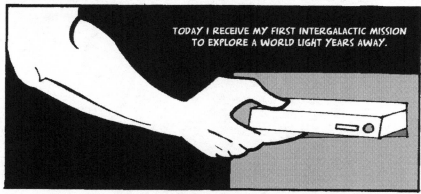

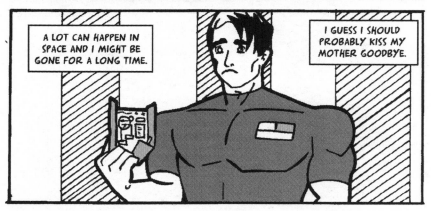

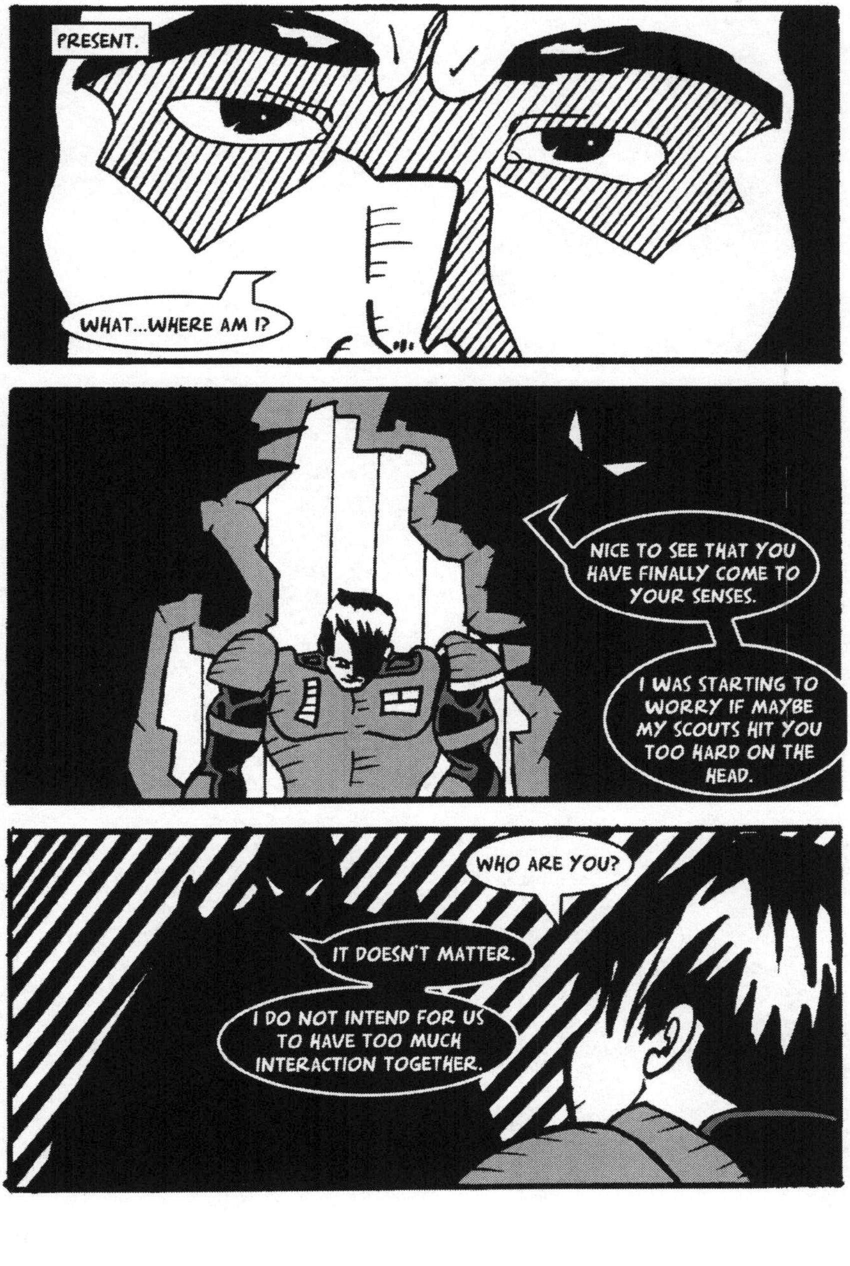
PRESENT.
WHAT...WHERE AM I?
NICE TO SEE THAT YOU HAVE FINALLY COME TO YOUR SENSES.
I WAS STARTING TO WORRY IF MAYBE MY SCOUTS HIT YOU TOO HARD ON THE HEAD.
WHO ARE YOU?
IT DOESN'T MATTER.
I DO NOT INTEND FOR US TO HAVE TOO MUCH INTERACTION TOGETHER.

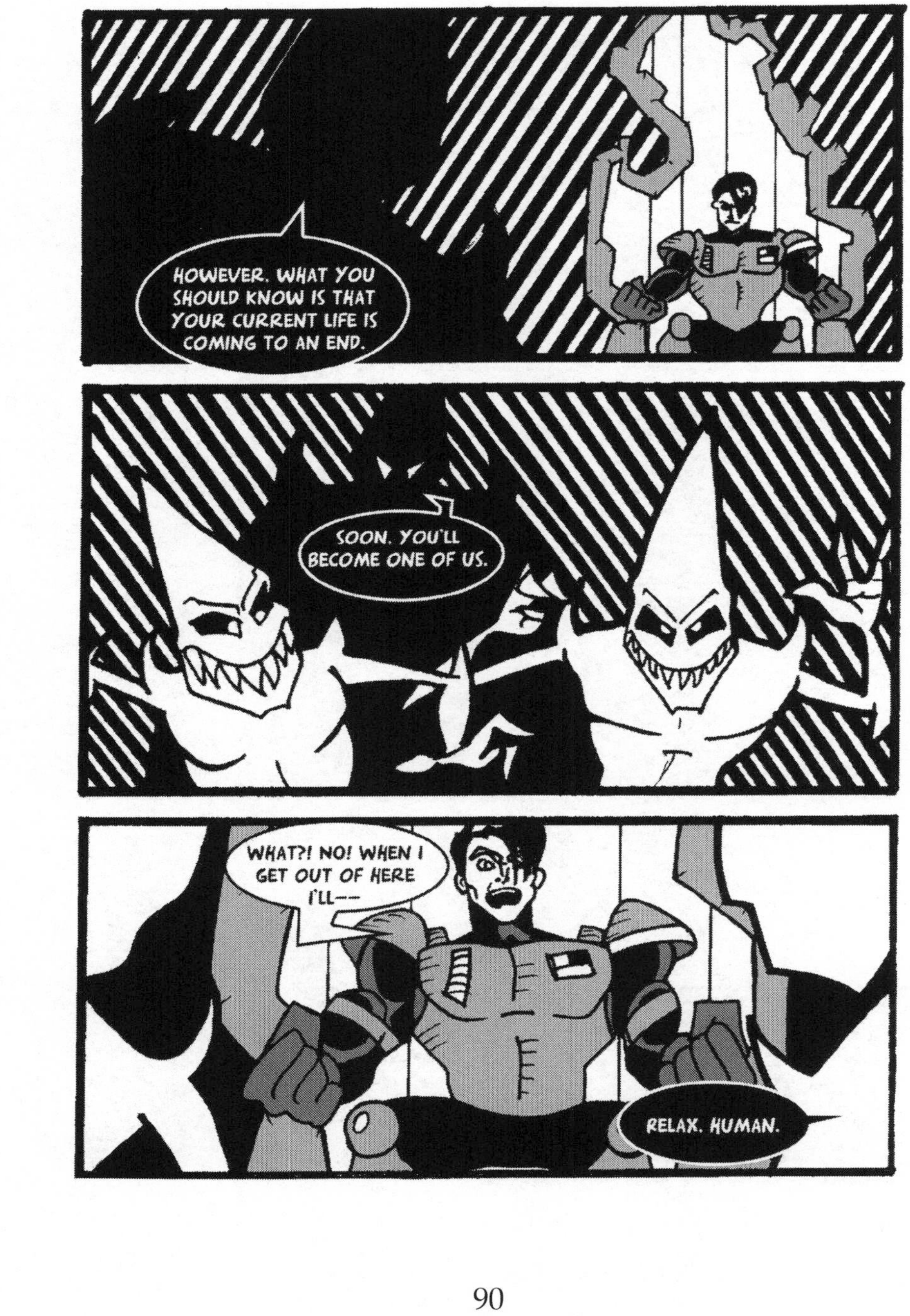
HOWEVER, WHAT YOU SHOULD KNOW IS THAT YOUR CURRENT LIFE IS COMING TO AN END.
SOON, YOU'LL BECOME ONE OF US.
WHAT?! NO! WHEN I GET OUT OF HERE I'LL--
RELAX, HUMAN.

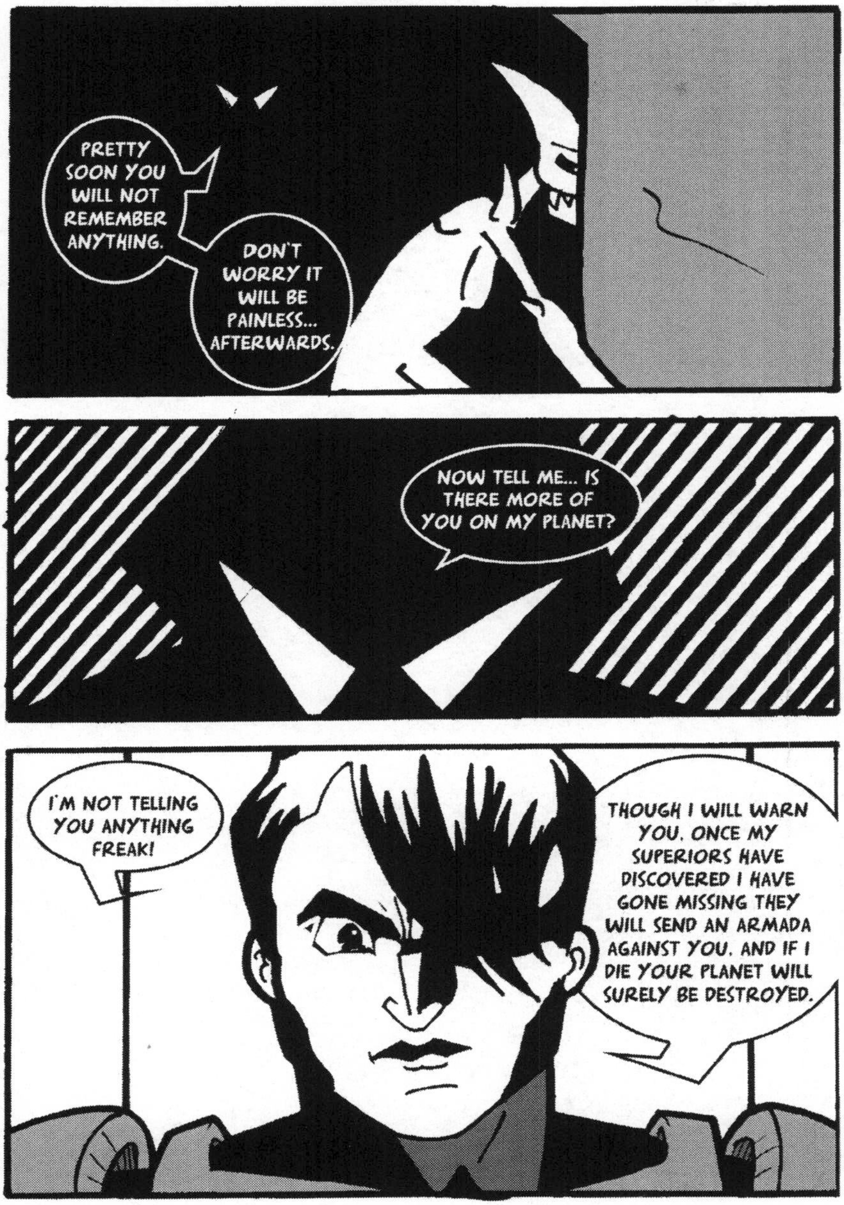
PRETTY SOON YOU WILL NOT REMEMBER ANYTHING.
DON'T WORRY IT WILL BE PAINLESS... AFTERWARDS.
NOW TELL ME... IS THERE MORE OF YOU ON MY PLANET?
I'M NOT TELLING YOU ANYTHING FREAK!
THOUGH I WILL WARN YOU. ONCE MY SUPERIORS HAVE DISCOVERED I HAVE GONE MISSING THEY WILL SEND AN ARMADA AGAINST YOU. AND IF I DIE YOUR PLANET WILL SURELY BE DESTROYED.

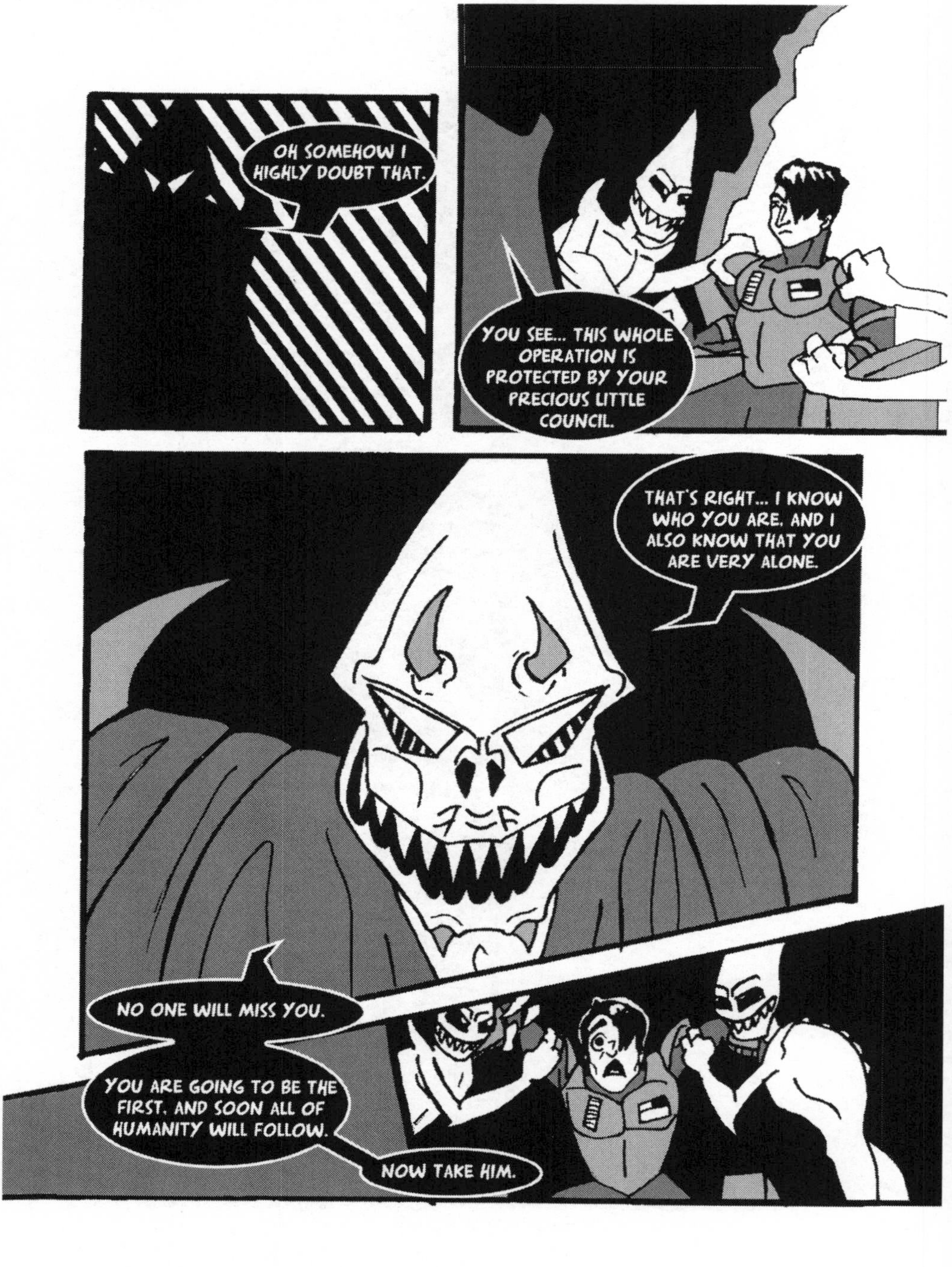
OH SOMEHOW I HIGHLY DOUBT THAT.
YOU SEE... THIS WHOLE OPERATION IS PROTECTED BY YOUR PRECIOUS LITTLE COUNCIL.
THAT'S RIGHT... I KNOW WHO YOU ARE. AND I ALSO KNOW THAT YOU ARE VERY ALONE.
NO ONE WILL MISS YOU.
YOU ARE GOING TO BE THE FIRST. AND SOON ALL OF HUMANITY WILL FOLLOW.
NOW TAKE HIM.

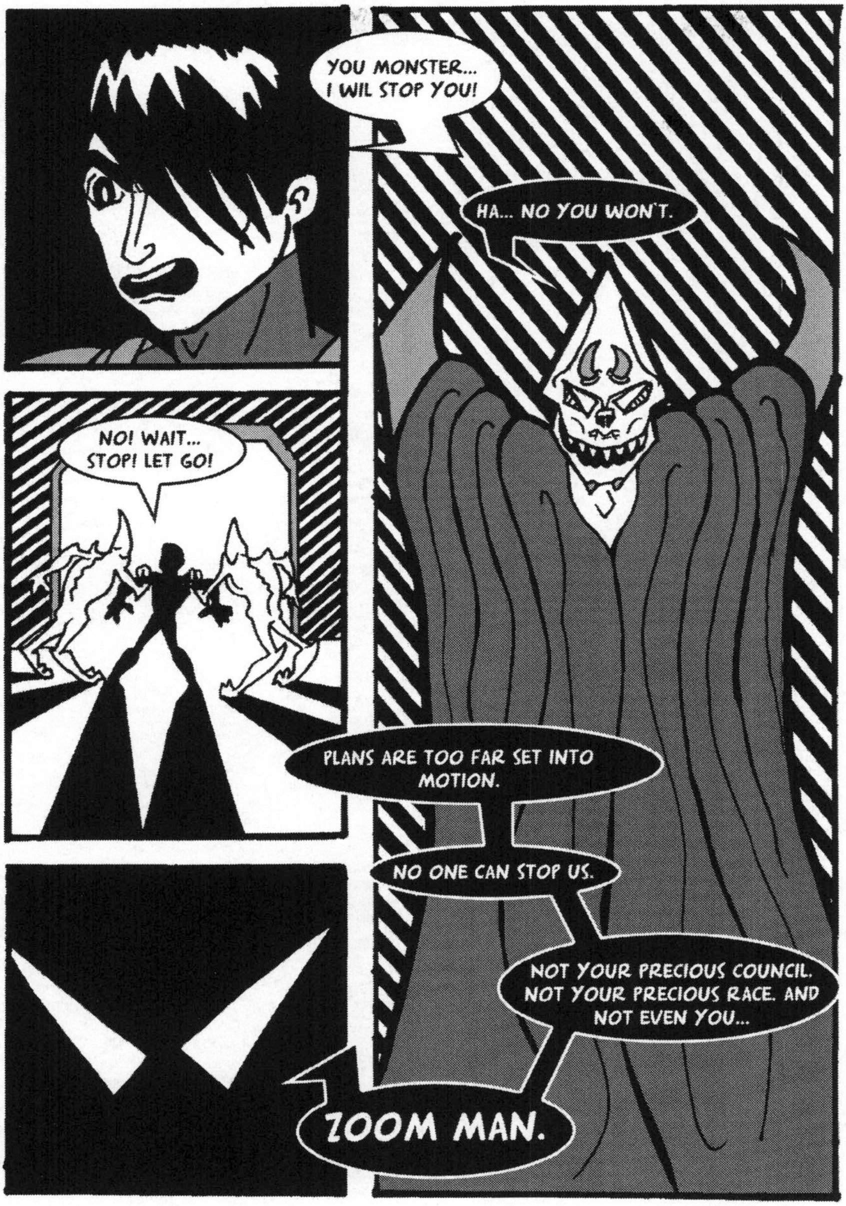
YOU MONSTER...
I WIL STOP YOU!
HA... NO YOU WON'T.
NO! WAIT...
STOP! LET GO!
PLANS ARE TOO FAR SET INTO MOTION.
NO ONE CAN STOP US.
NOT YOUR PRECIOUS COUNCIL. NOT YOUR PRECIOUS RACE. AND NOT EVEN YOU...
ZOOM MAN.

MATT'S NOTES:

This comic was co-written by one of
my close friends, Samuel Clemens.
It was meant to be the turning point
for the Zoom Man story. We will
probably explore the rest of this saga
sometime in the future.

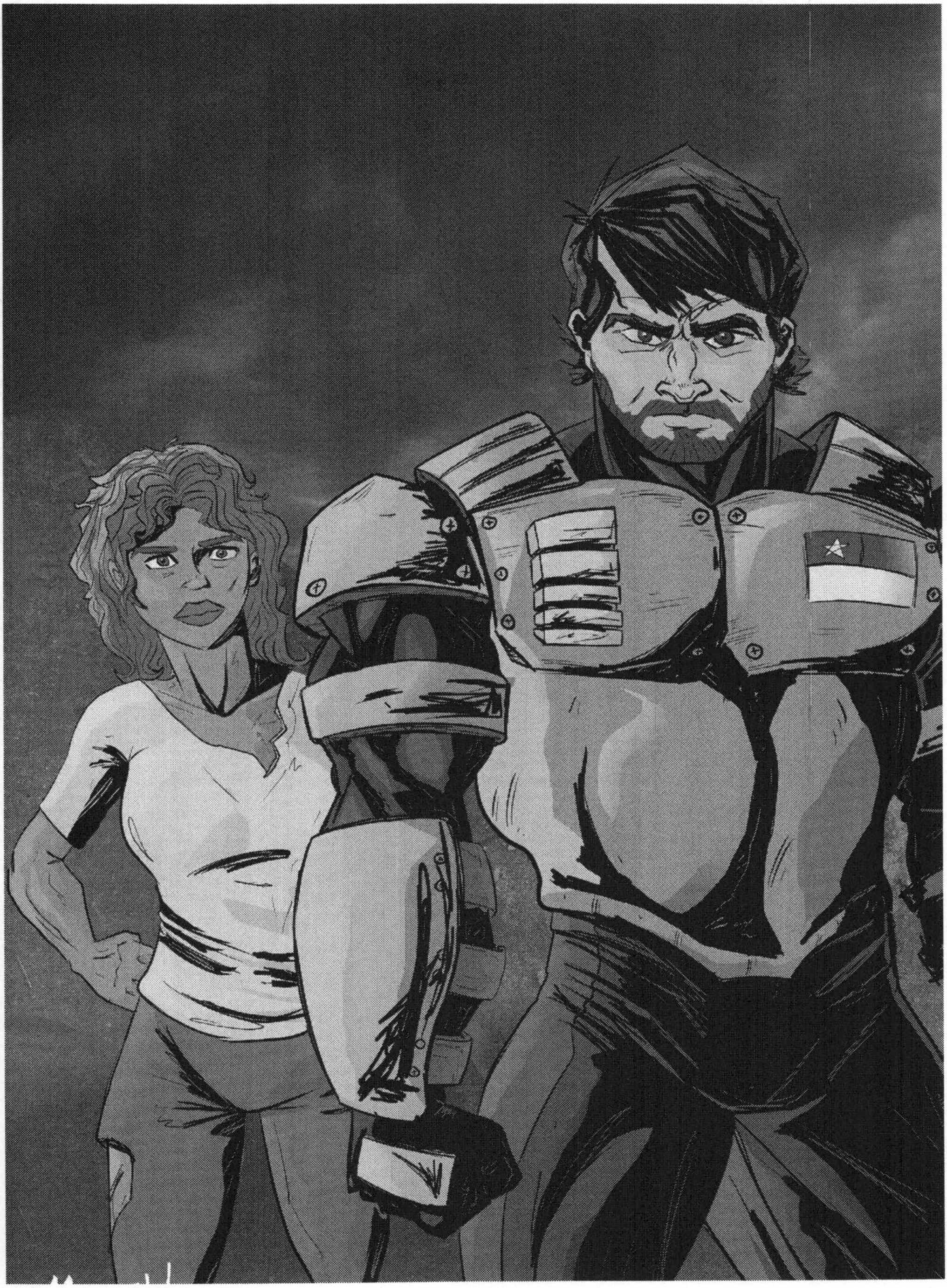

Vroom Toons - Volume One

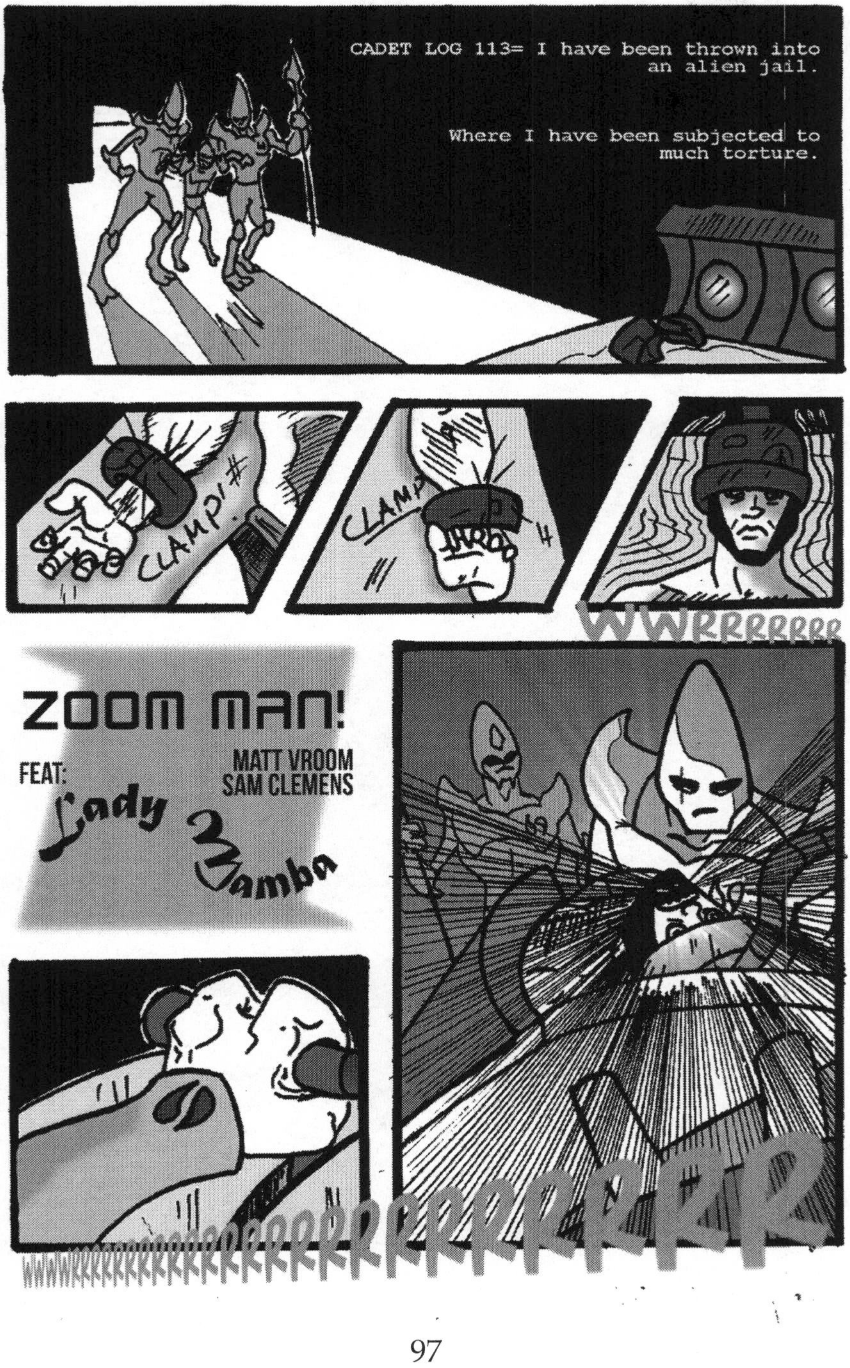
CADET LOG 113= I have been thrown into an alien jail.
Where I have been subjected to much torture.
CLAMP!#
CLAMP
WWRRRRRRR
ZOOM MAN!
FEAT:
MATT VROOM
SAM CLEMENS
Lady Mamba
wwwwRRRRRRRRRRRRRRRRRRRRRRRRRRRRR

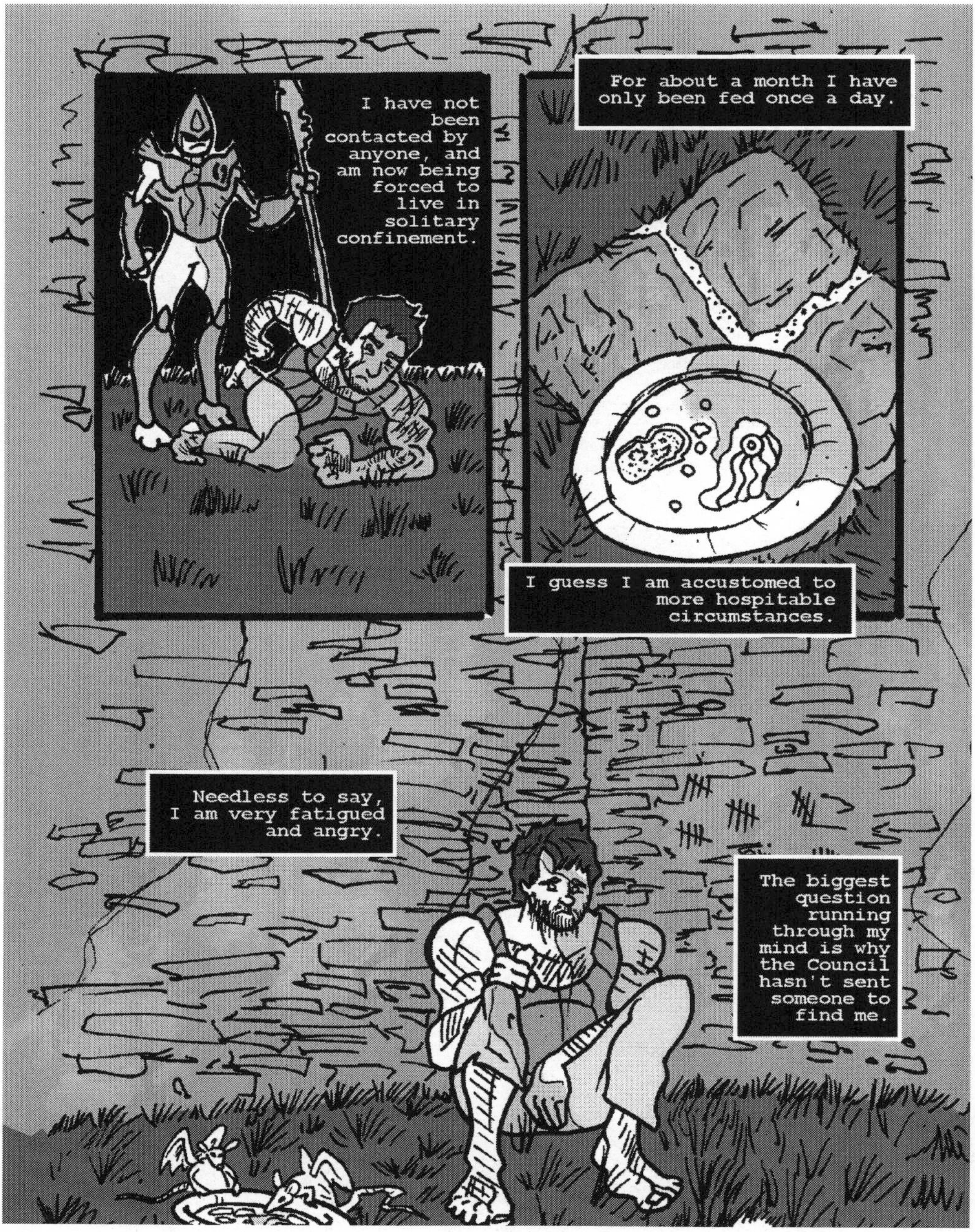
I have not been contacted by anyone, and am now being forced to live in solitary confinement.
For about a month I have only been fed once a day.
I guess I am accustomed to more hospitable circumstances.
Needless to say, I am very fatigued and angry.
The biggest question running through my mind is why the Council hasn't sent someone to find me.

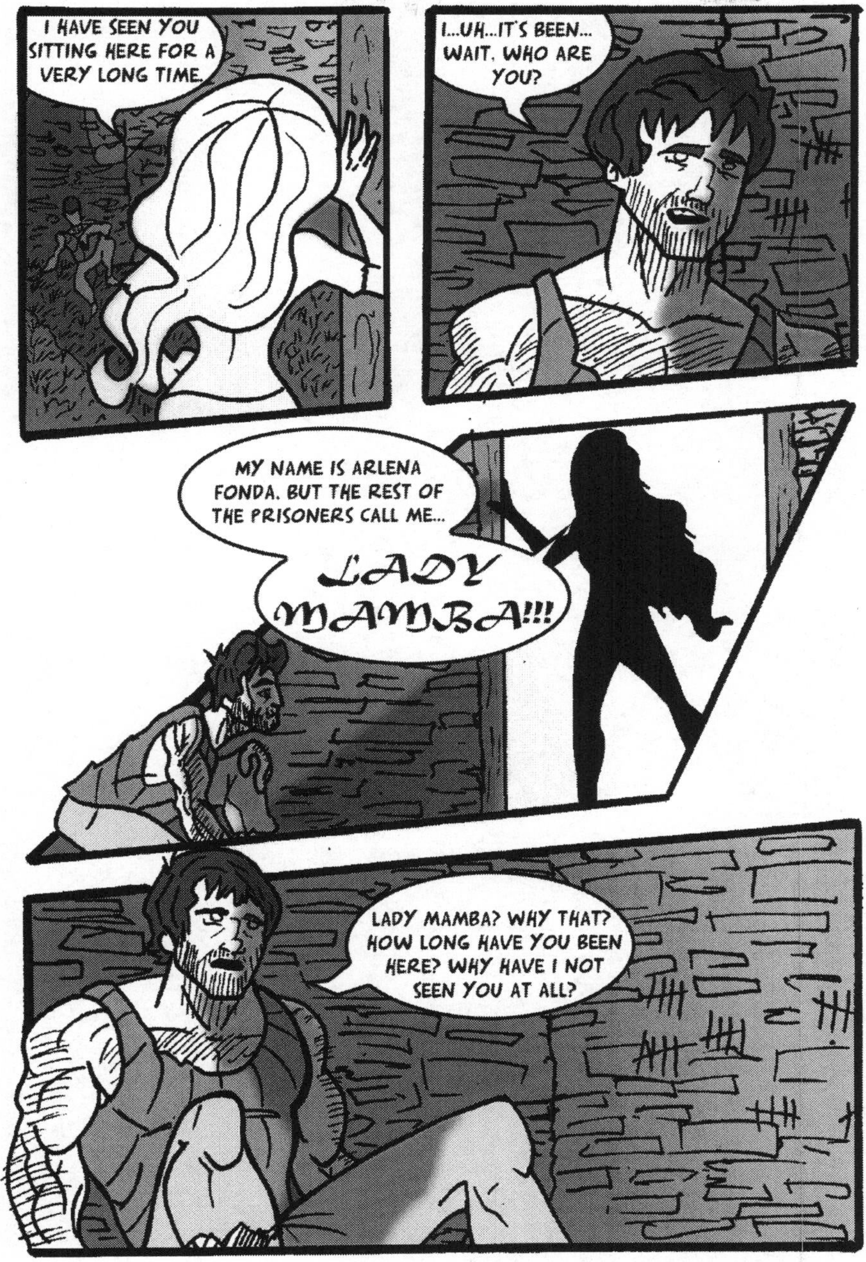
I HAVE SEEN YOU SITTING HERE FOR A VERY LONG TIME.
I...UH...IT'S BEEN... WAIT, WHO ARE YOU?
MY NAME IS ARLENA FONDA. BUT THE REST OF THE PRISONERS CALL ME...
LADY MAMBA!!!
LADY MAMBA? WHY THAT? HOW LONG HAVE YOU BEEN HERE? WHY HAVE I NOT SEEN YOU AT ALL?

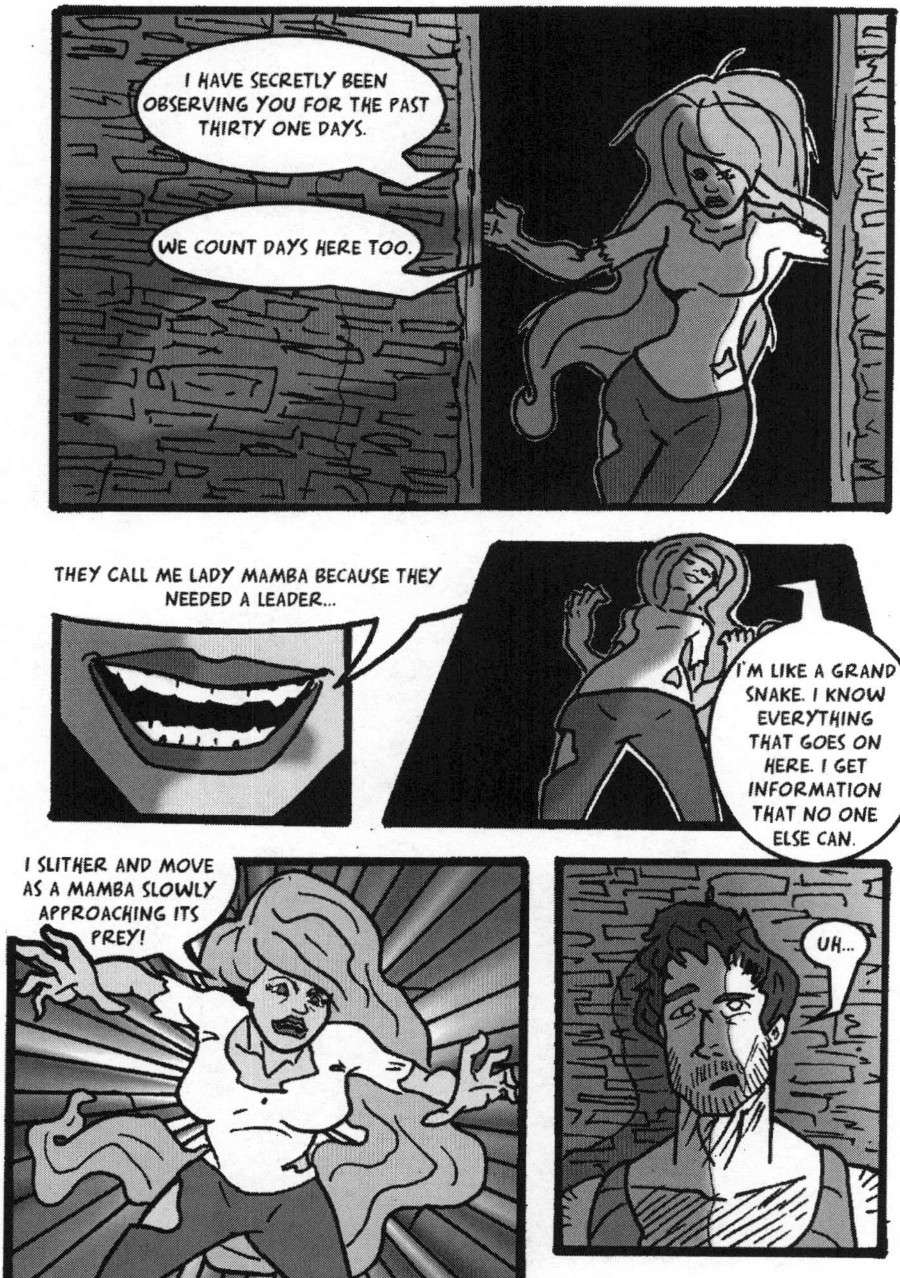
I HAVE SECRETLY BEEN OBSERVING YOU FOR THE PAST THIRTY ONE DAYS.
WE COUNT DAYS HERE TOO.
THEY CALL ME LADY MAMBA BECAUSE THEY NEEDED A LEADER...
I'M LIKE A GRAND SNAKE. I KNOW EVERYTHING THAT GOES ON HERE. I GET INFORMATION THAT NO ONE ELSE CAN.
I SLITHER AND MOVE AS A MAMBA SLOWLY APPROACHING ITS PREY!
UH...

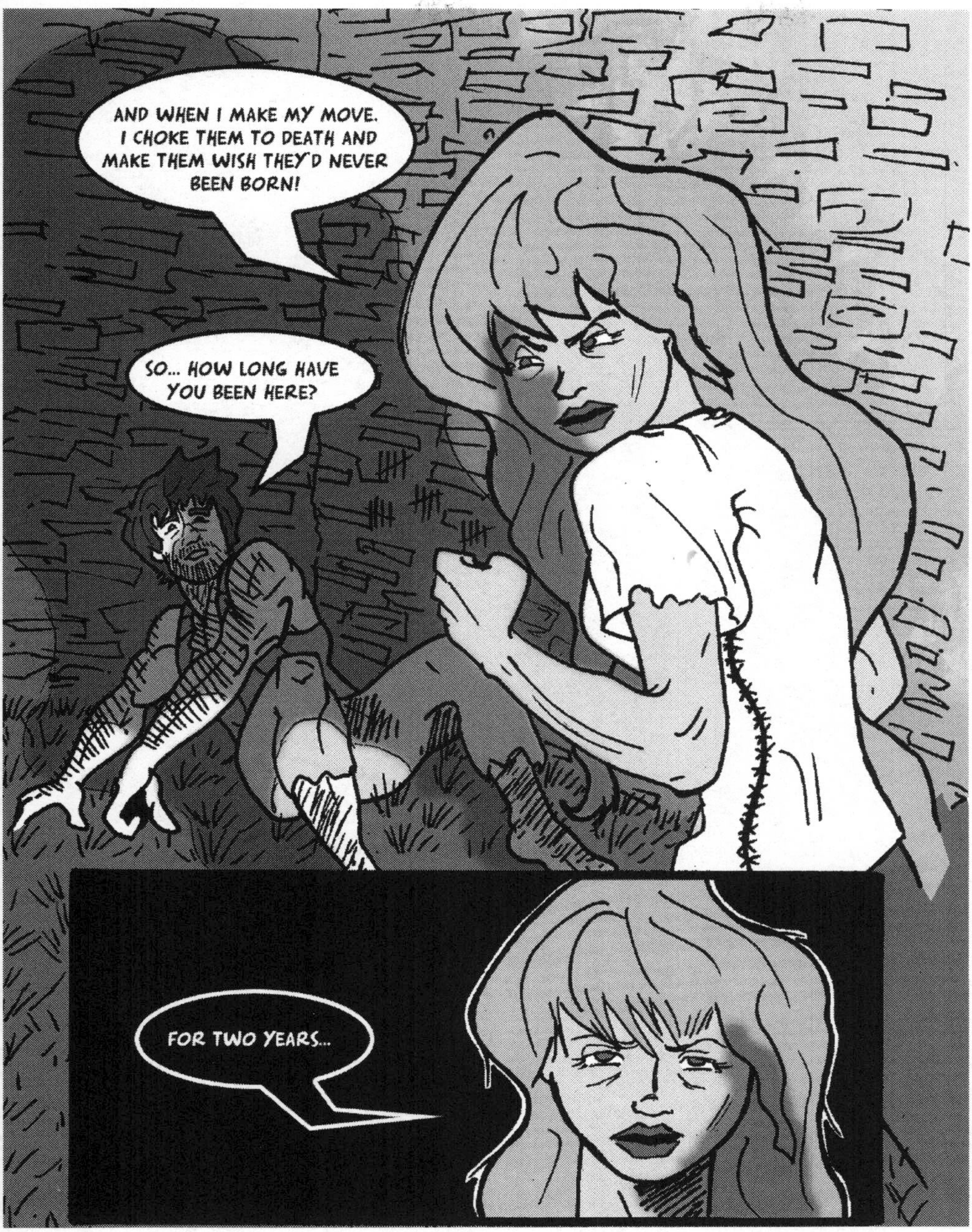
AND WHEN I MAKE MY MOVE. I CHOKE THEM TO DEATH AND MAKE THEM WISH THEY'D NEVER BEEN BORN!
SO... HOW LONG HAVE YOU BEEN HERE?
FOR TWO YEARS...

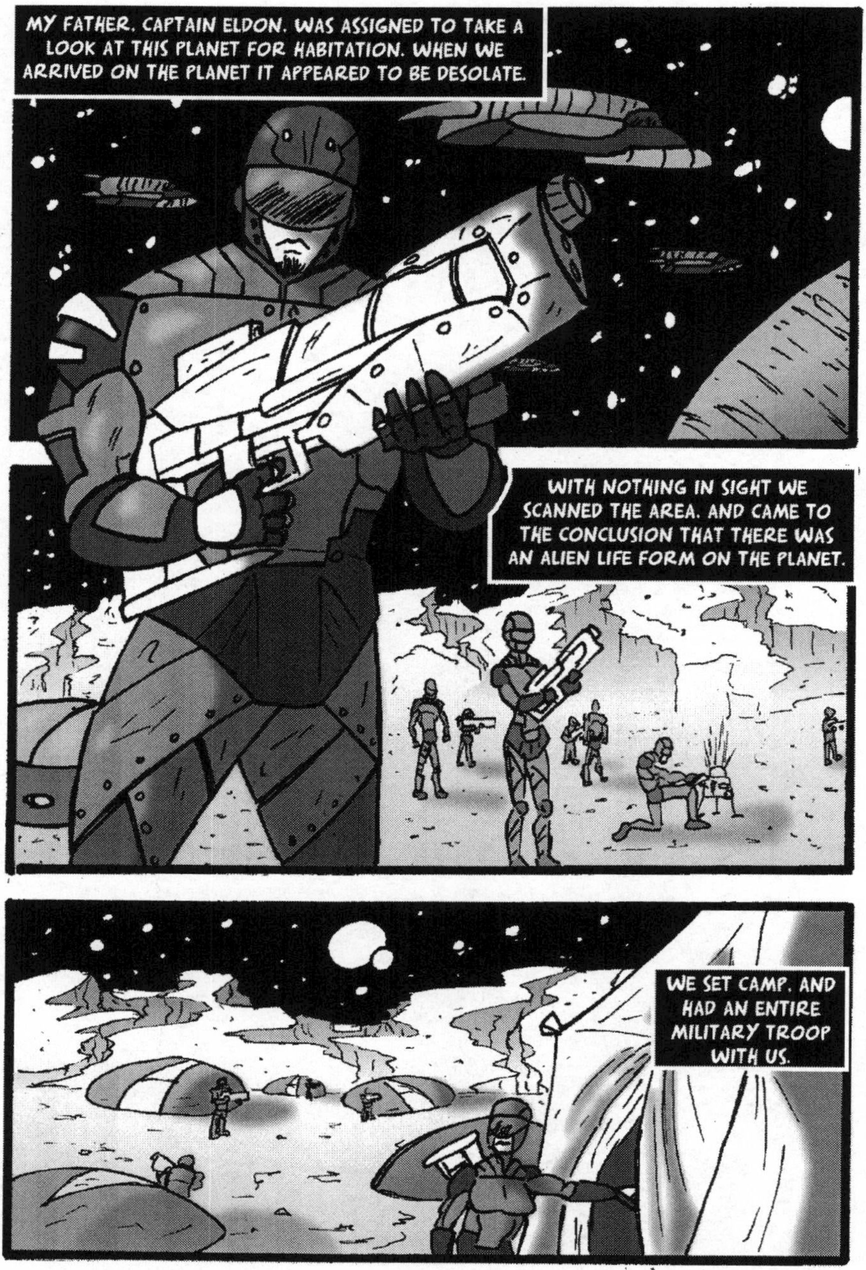
MY FATHER. CAPTAIN ELDON. WAS ASSIGNED TO TAKE A LOOK AT THIS PLANET FOR HABITATION. WHEN WE ARRIVED ON THE PLANET IT APPEARED TO BE DESOLATE.
WITH NOTHING IN SIGHT WE SCANNED THE AREA. AND CAME TO THE CONCLUSION THAT THERE WAS AN ALIEN LIFE FORM ON THE PLANET.
WE SET CAMP. AND HAD AN ENTIRE MILITARY TROOP WITH US.

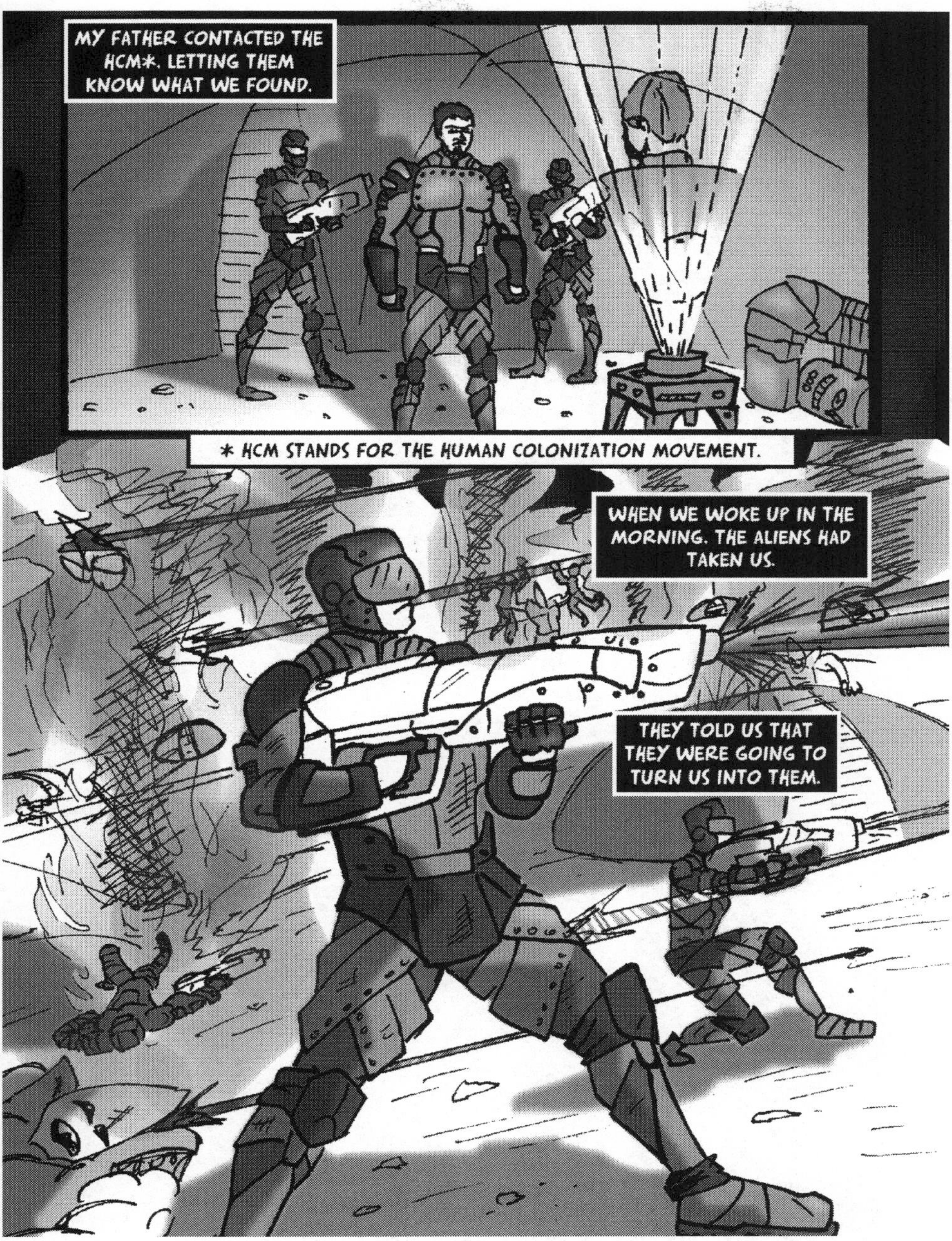
MY FATHER CONTACTED THE HCM*. LETTING THEM KNOW WHAT WE FOUND.
* HCM STANDS FOR THE HUMAN COLONIZATION MOVEMENT.
WHEN WE WOKE UP IN THE MORNING. THE ALIENS HAD TAKEN US.
THEY TOLD US THAT THEY WERE GOING TO TURN US INTO THEM.

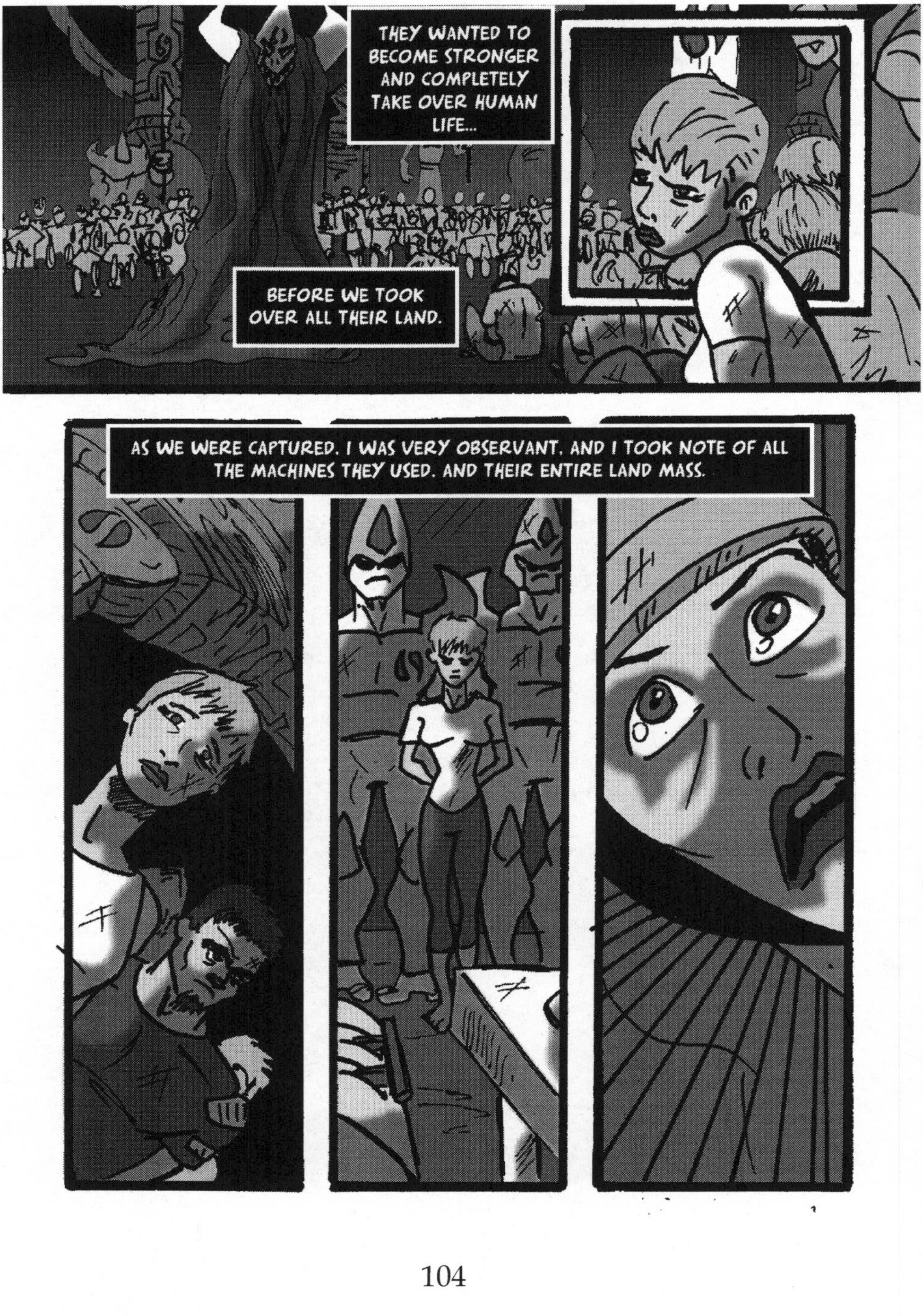
THEY WANTED TO BECOME STRONGER AND COMPLETELY TAKE OVER HUMAN LIFE...
BEFORE WE TOOK OVER ALL THEIR LAND.
AS WE WERE CAPTURED. I WAS VERY OBSERVANT. AND I TOOK NOTE OF ALL THE MACHINES THEY USED. AND THEIR ENTIRE LAND MASS.

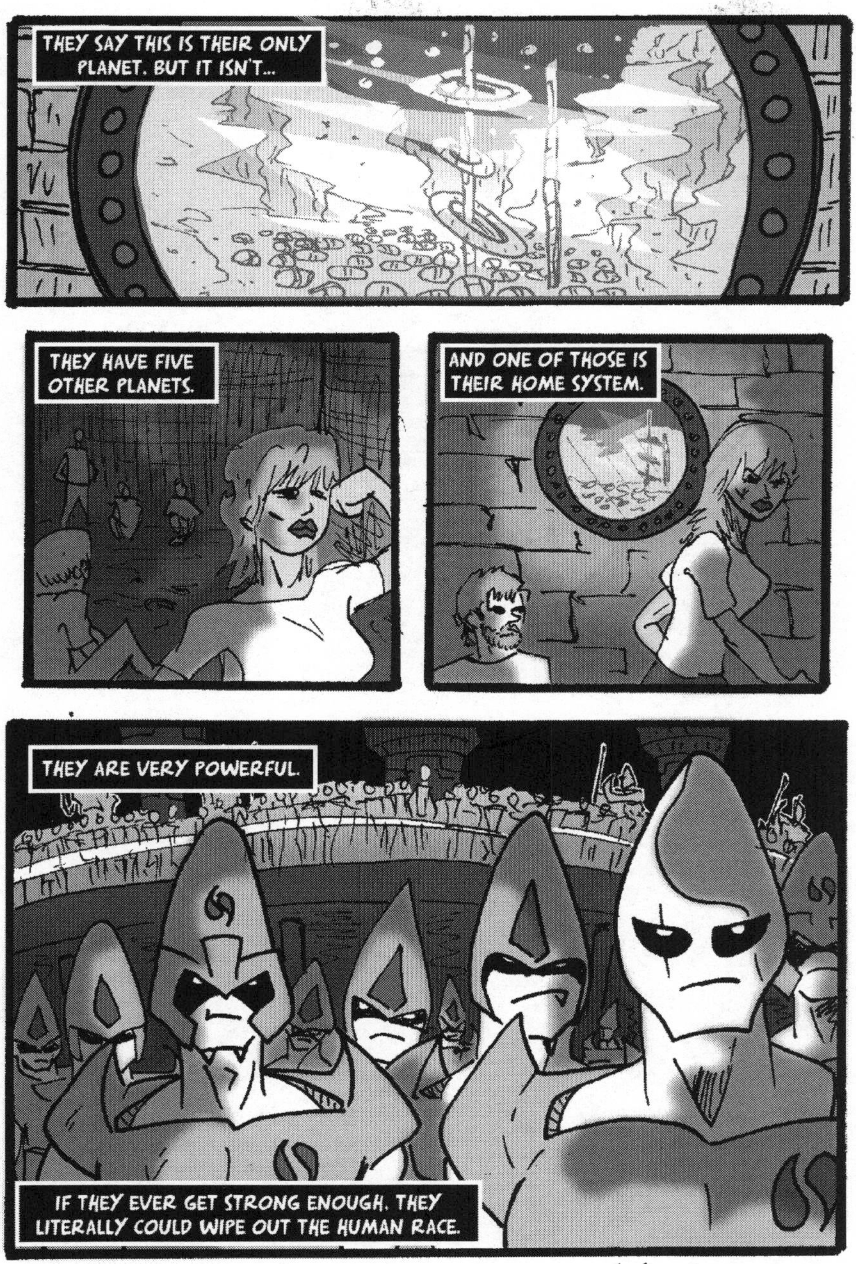
THEY SAY THIS IS THEIR ONLY PLANET. BUT IT ISN'T...
THEY HAVE FIVE OTHER PLANETS.
AND ONE OF THOSE IS THEIR HOME SYSTEM.
THEY ARE VERY POWERFUL.
IF THEY EVER GET STRONG ENOUGH, THEY LITERALLY COULD WIPE OUT THE HUMAN RACE.

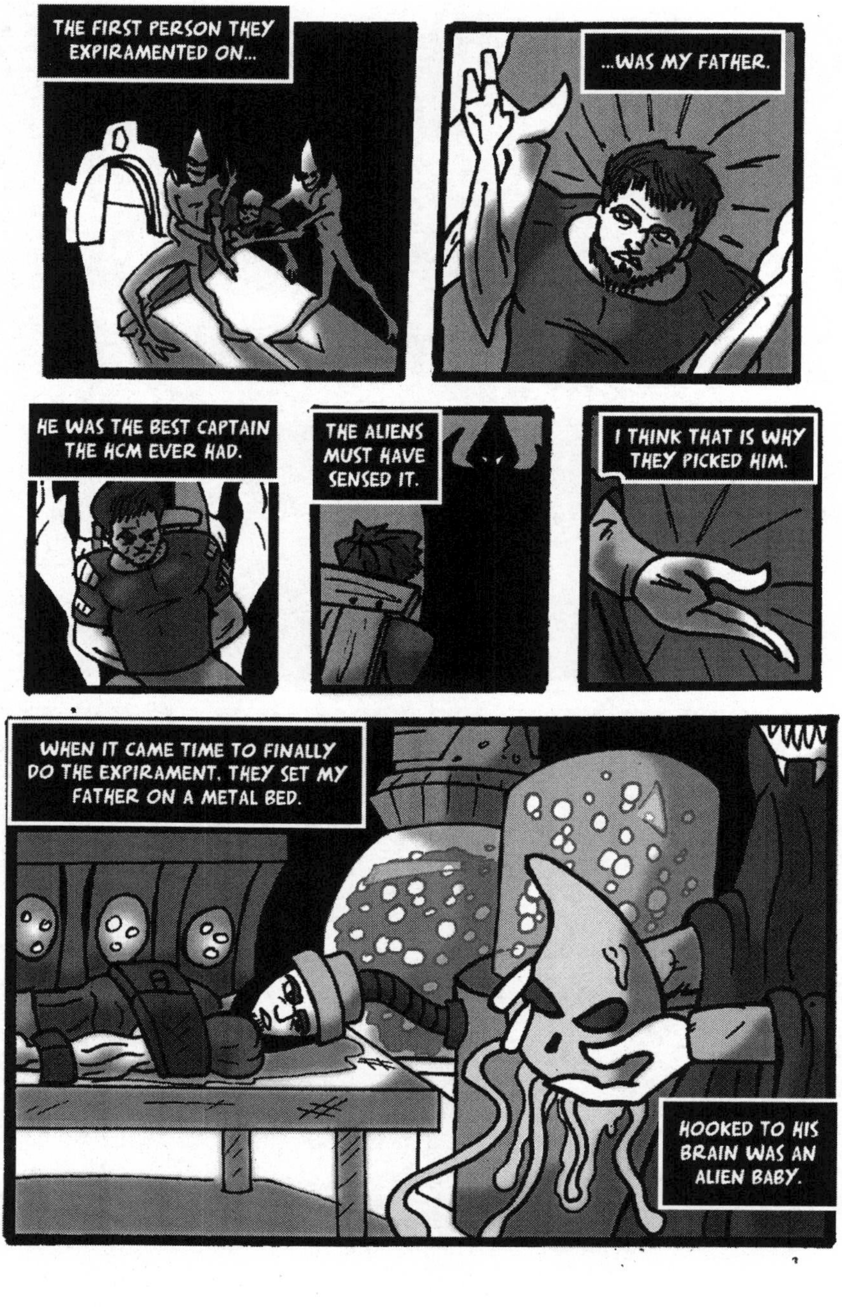
THE FIRST PERSON THEY EXPIRAMENTED ON...
...WAS MY FATHER.
HE WAS THE BEST CAPTAIN THE HCM EVER HAD.
THE ALIENS MUST HAVE SENSED IT.
I THINK THAT IS WHY THEY PICKED HIM.
WHEN IT CAME TIME TO FINALLY DO THE EXPIRAMENT, THEY SET MY FATHER ON A METAL BED.
HOOKED TO HIS BRAIN WAS AN ALIEN BABY.

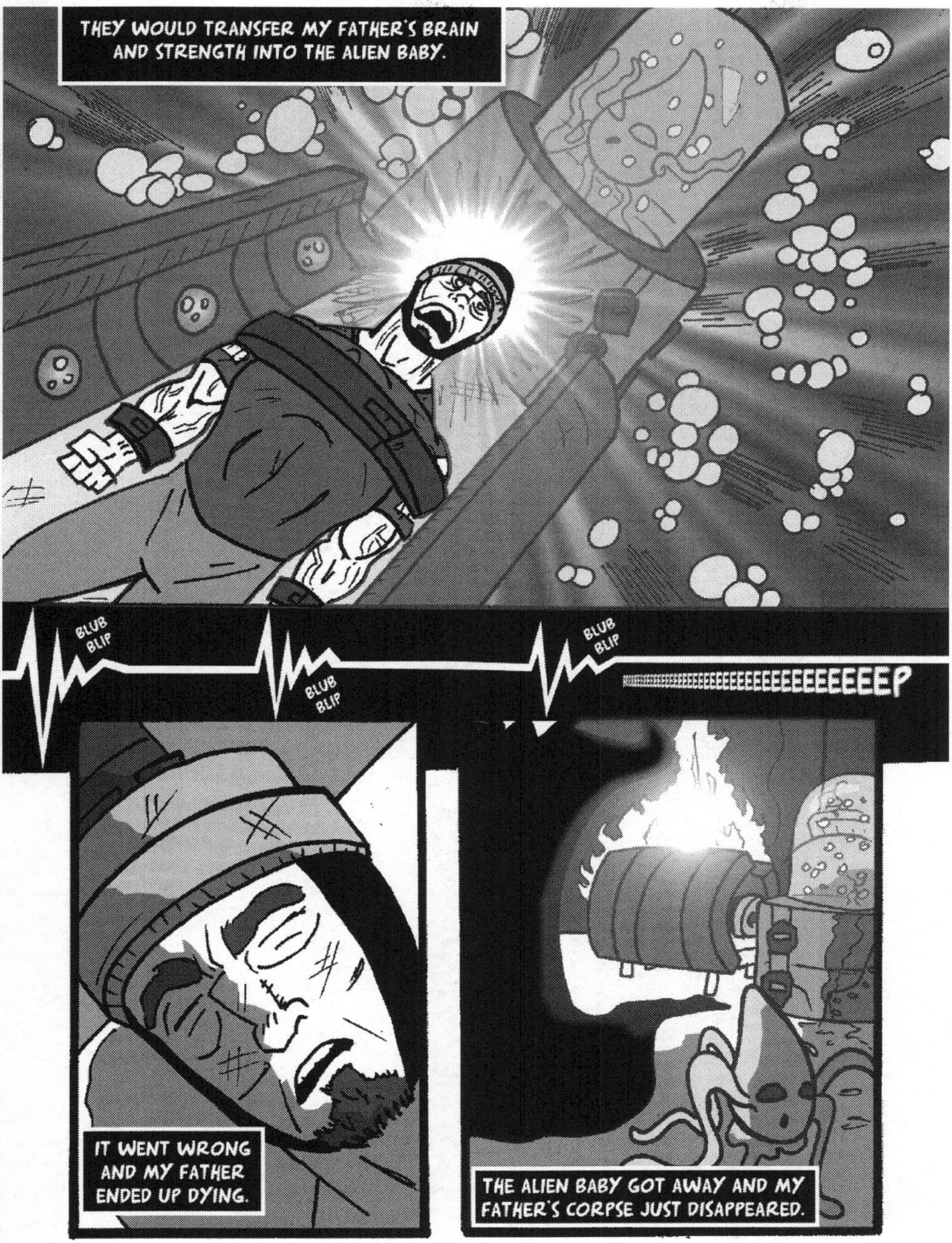
THEY WOULD TRANSFER MY FATHER'S BRAIN AND STRENGTH INTO THE ALIEN BABY.
BLUB BLIP
BLUB BLIP
BLUB BLIP
EEEEEEEEEEEEEEEEEEEEEEEEEEEEEEEEEEEEP
IT WENT WRONG AND MY FATHER ENDED UP DYING.
THE ALIEN BABY GOT AWAY AND MY FATHER'S CORPSE JUST DISAPPEARED.

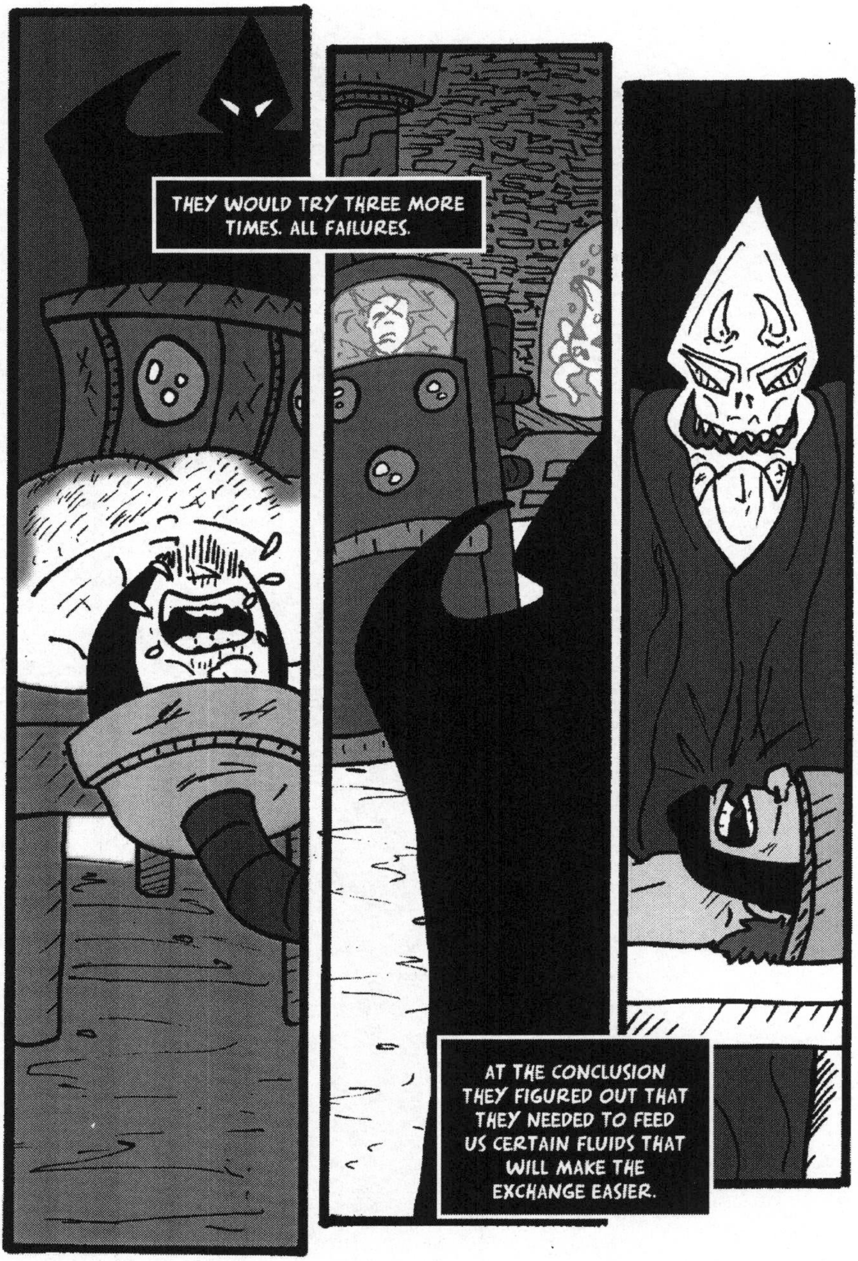
THEY WOULD TRY THREE MORE TIMES. ALL FAILURES.
AT THE CONCLUSION THEY FIGURED OUT THAT THEY NEEDED TO FEED US CERTAIN FLUIDS THAT WILL MAKE THE EXCHANGE EASIER.

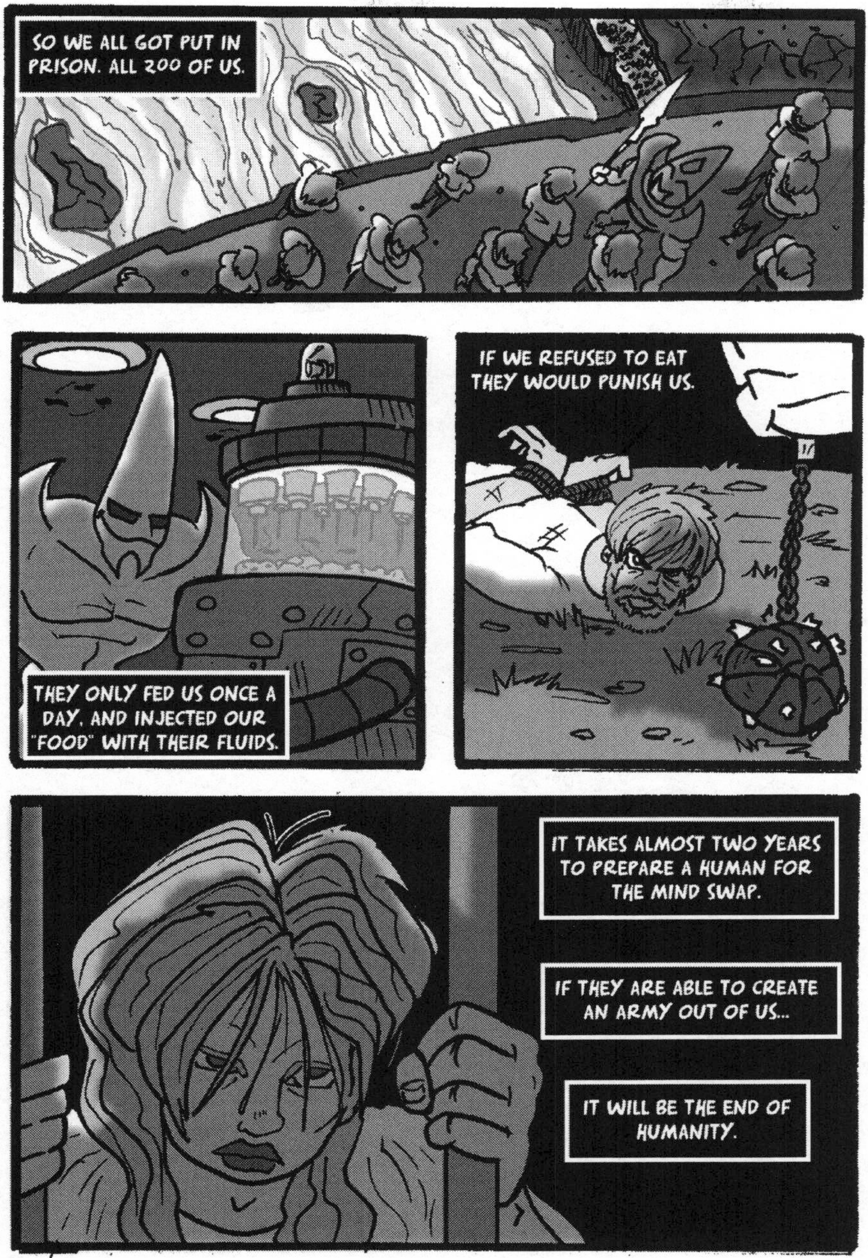
SO WE ALL GOT PUT IN PRISON. ALL 200 OF US.
THEY ONLY FED US ONCE A DAY, AND INJECTED OUR "FOOD" WITH THEIR FLUIDS.
IF WE REFUSED TO EAT THEY WOULD PUNISH US.
IT TAKES ALMOST TWO YEARS TO PREPARE A HUMAN FOR THE MIND SWAP.
IF THEY ARE ABLE TO CREATE AN ARMY OUT OF US...
IT WILL BE THE END OF HUMANITY.

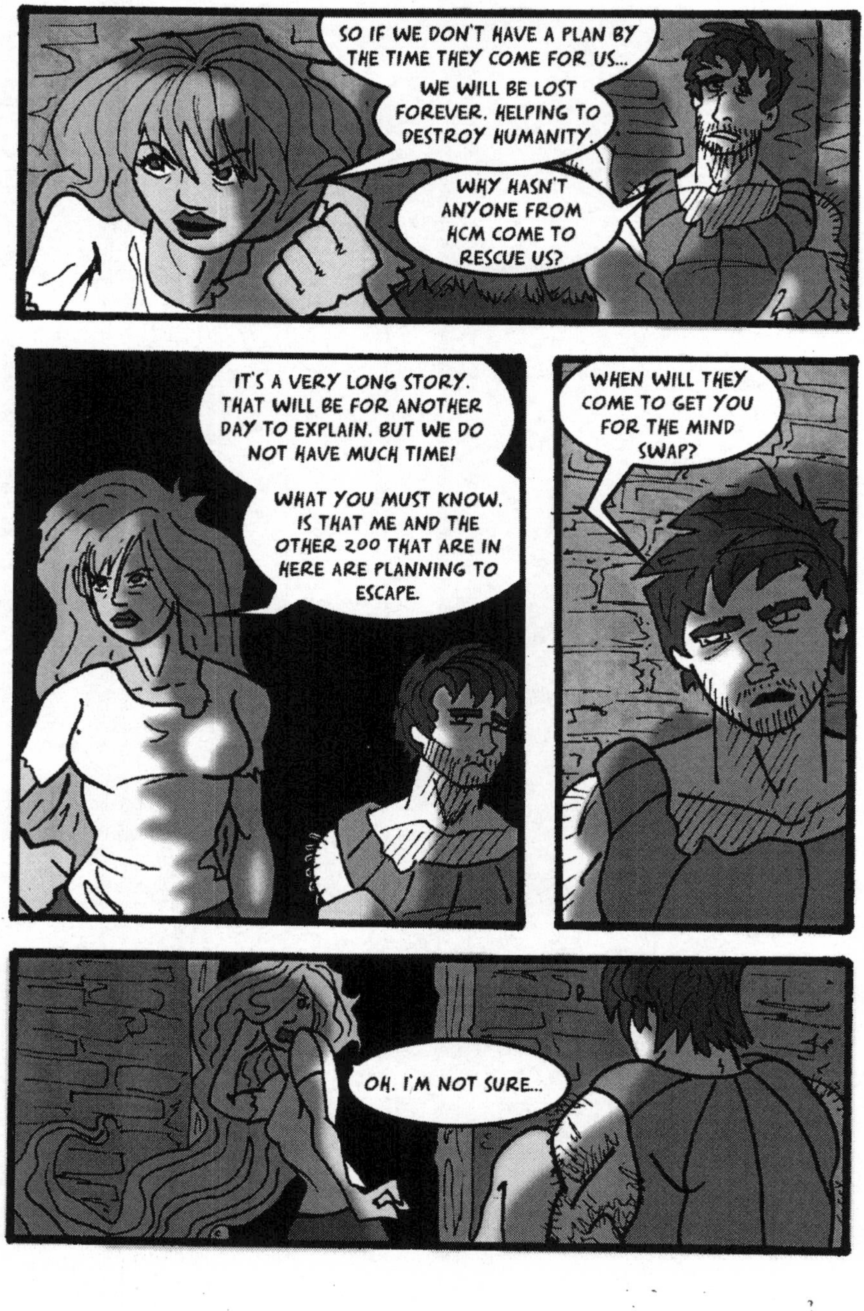
SO IF WE DON'T HAVE A PLAN BY THE TIME THEY COME FOR US...
WE WILL BE LOST FOREVER. HELPING TO DESTROY HUMANITY.
WHY HASN'T ANYONE FROM HCM COME TO RESCUE US?
IT'S A VERY LONG STORY. THAT WILL BE FOR ANOTHER DAY TO EXPLAIN. BUT WE DO NOT HAVE MUCH TIME!
WHAT YOU MUST KNOW. IS THAT ME AND THE OTHER 200 THAT ARE IN HERE ARE PLANNING TO ESCAPE.
WHEN WILL THEY COME TO GET YOU FOR THE MIND SWAP?
OH. I'M NOT SURE...

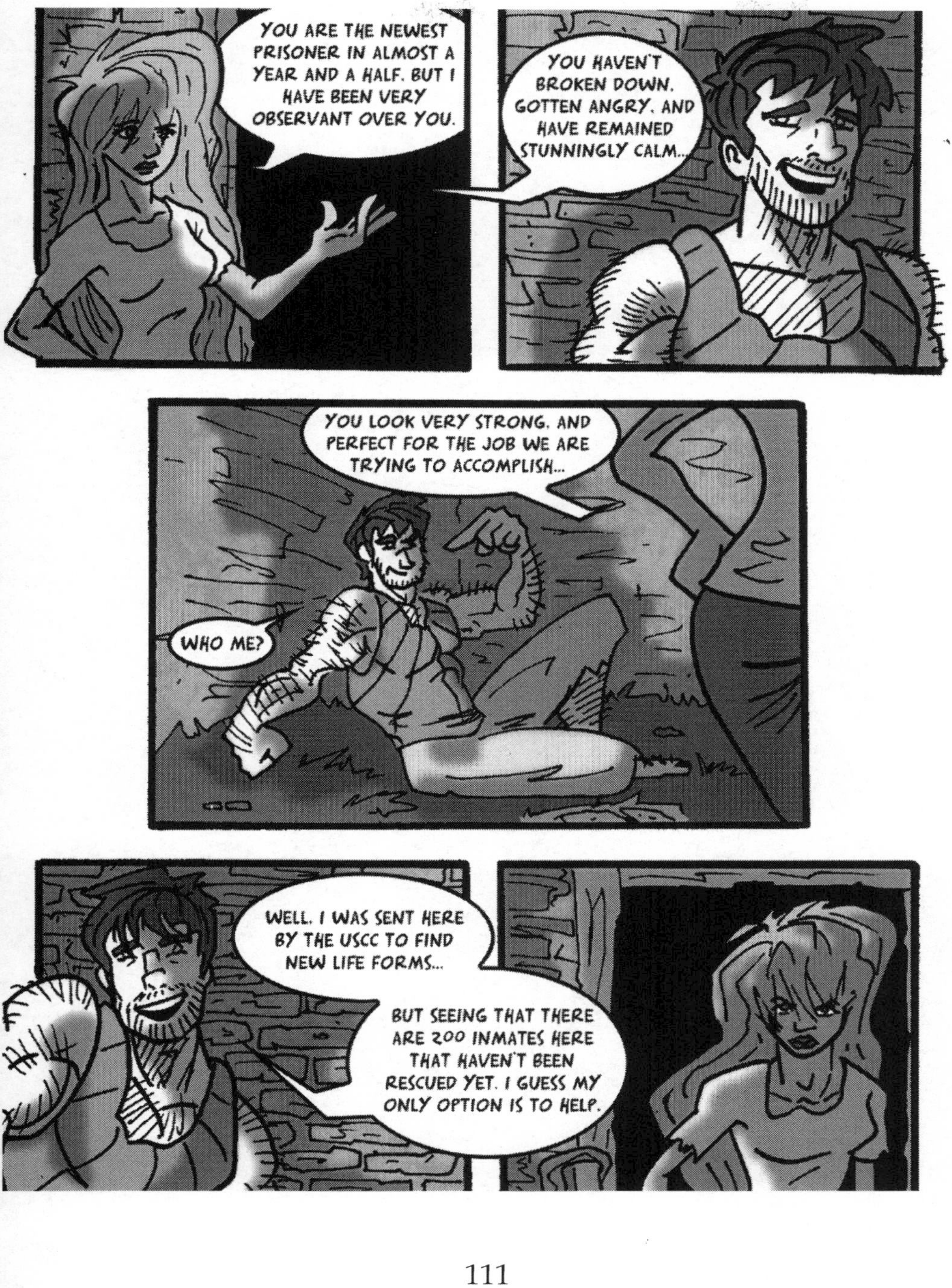
YOU ARE THE NEWEST PRISONER IN ALMOST A YEAR AND A HALF. BUT I HAVE BEEN VERY OBSERVANT OVER YOU.
YOU HAVEN'T BROKEN DOWN. GOTTEN ANGRY. AND HAVE REMAINED STUNNINGLY CALM...
YOU LOOK VERY STRONG. AND PERFECT FOR THE JOB WE ARE TRYING TO ACCOMPLISH...
WHO ME?
WELL. I WAS SENT HERE BY THE USCC TO FIND NEW LIFE FORMS...
BUT SEEING THAT THERE ARE 200 INMATES HERE THAT HAVEN'T BEEN RESCUED YET. I GUESS MY ONLY OPTION IS TO HELP.

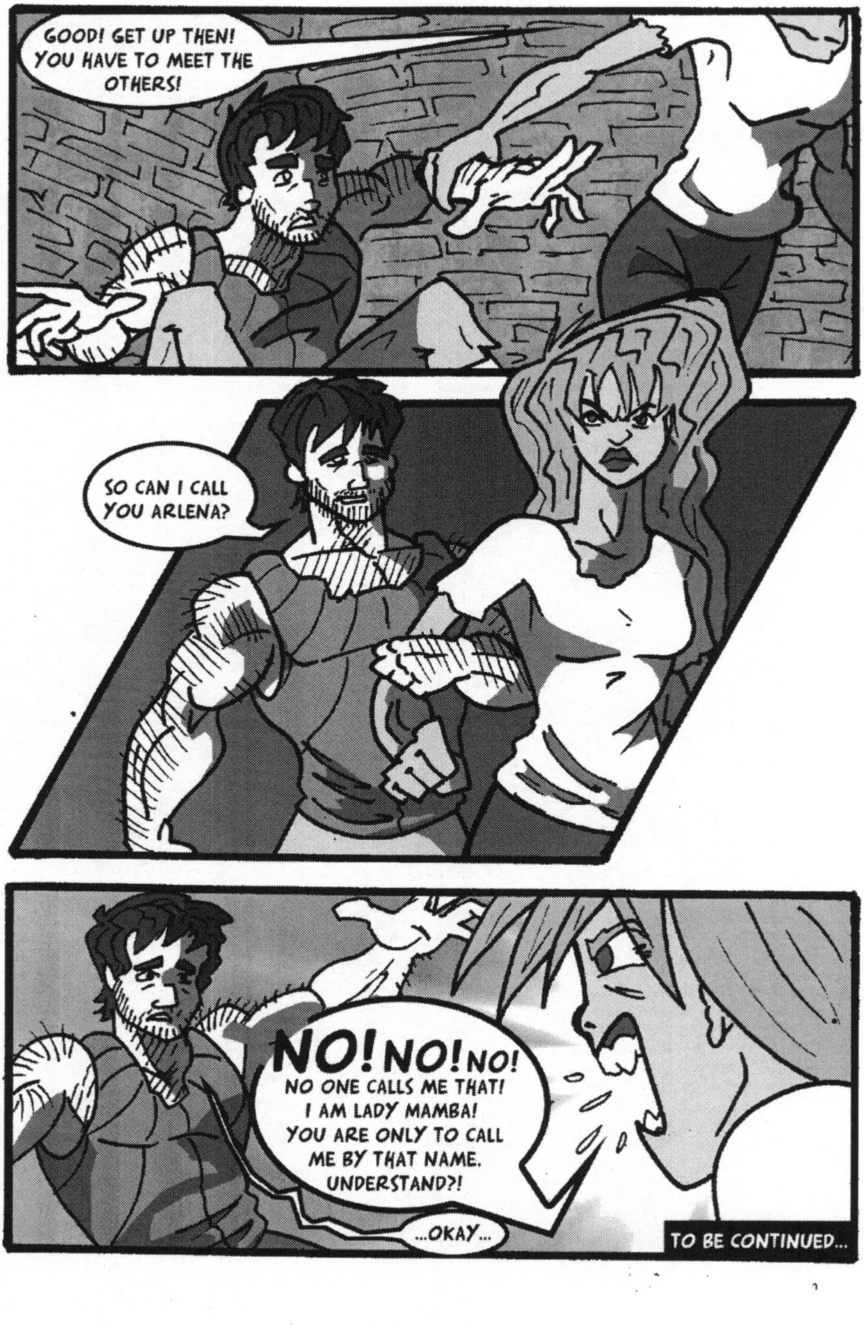
GOOD! GET UP THEN! YOU HAVE TO MEET THE OTHERS!
SO CAN I CALL YOU ARLENA?
NO! NO! NO! NO ONE CALLS ME THAT! I AM LADY MAMBA! YOU ARE ONLY TO CALL ME BY THAT NAME. UNDERSTAND?!
...OKAY...
TO BE CONTINUED...

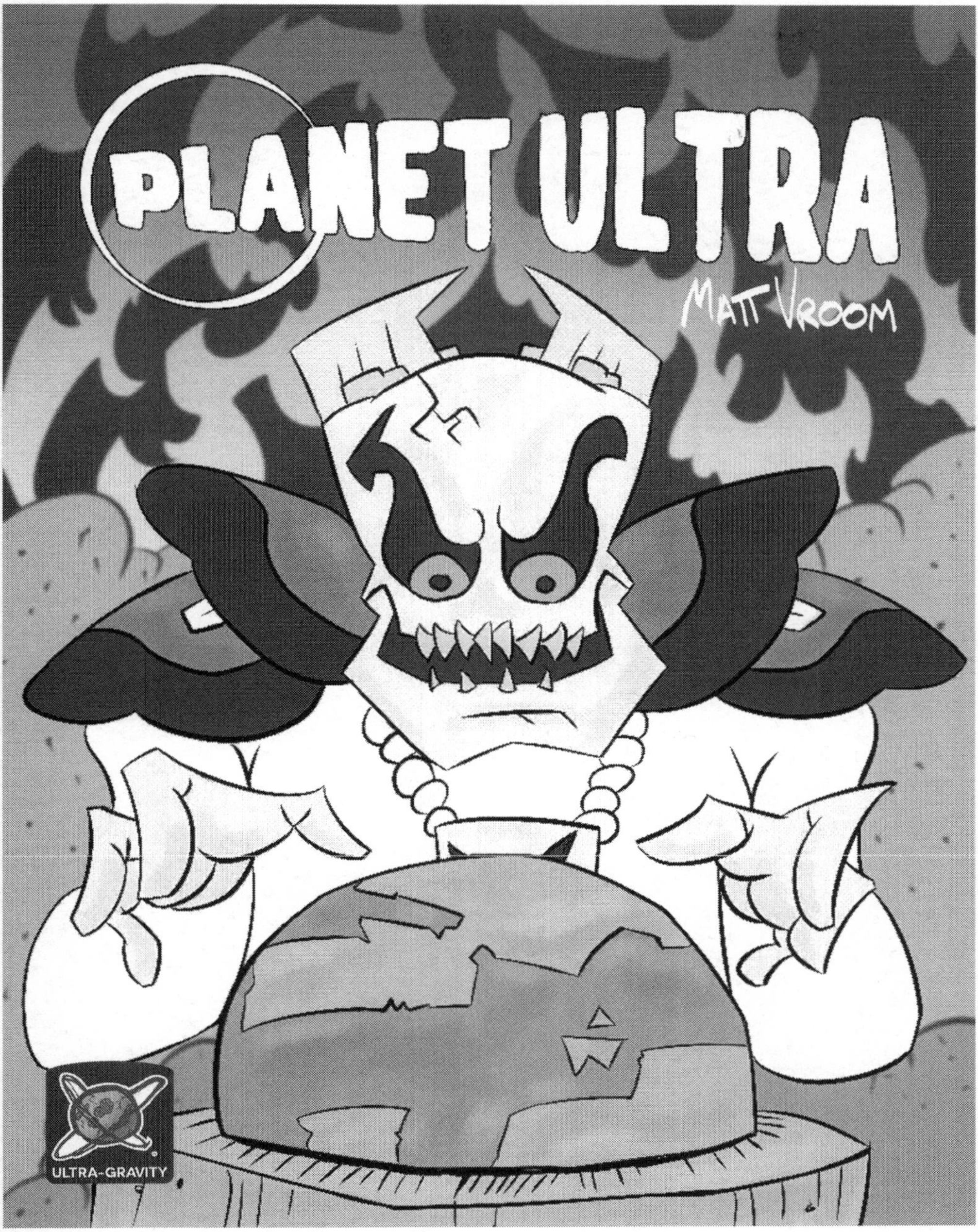
PLANET ULTRA
MATT VROOM
ULTRA-GRAVITY

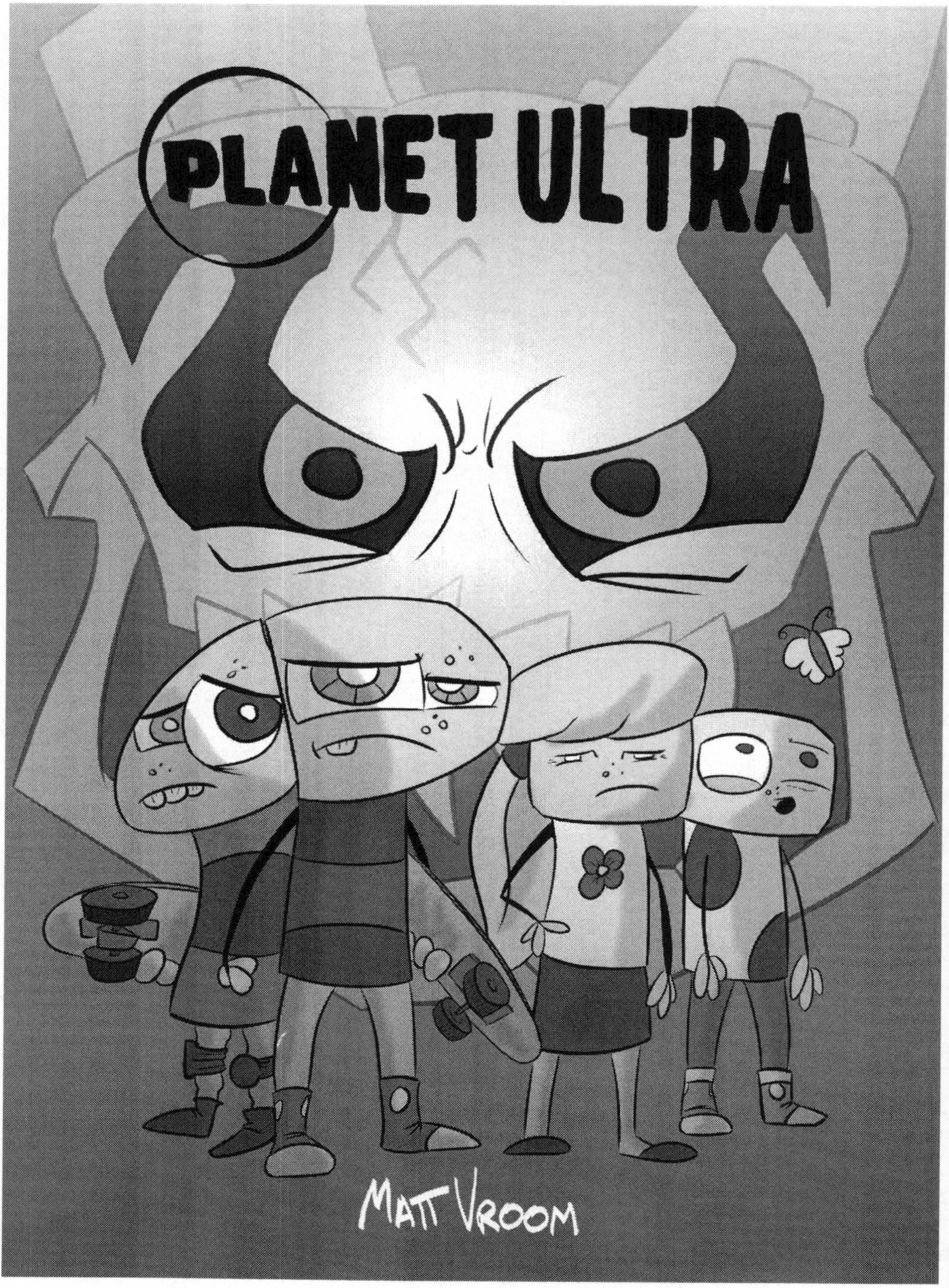
PLANET ULTRA
MATT VROOM

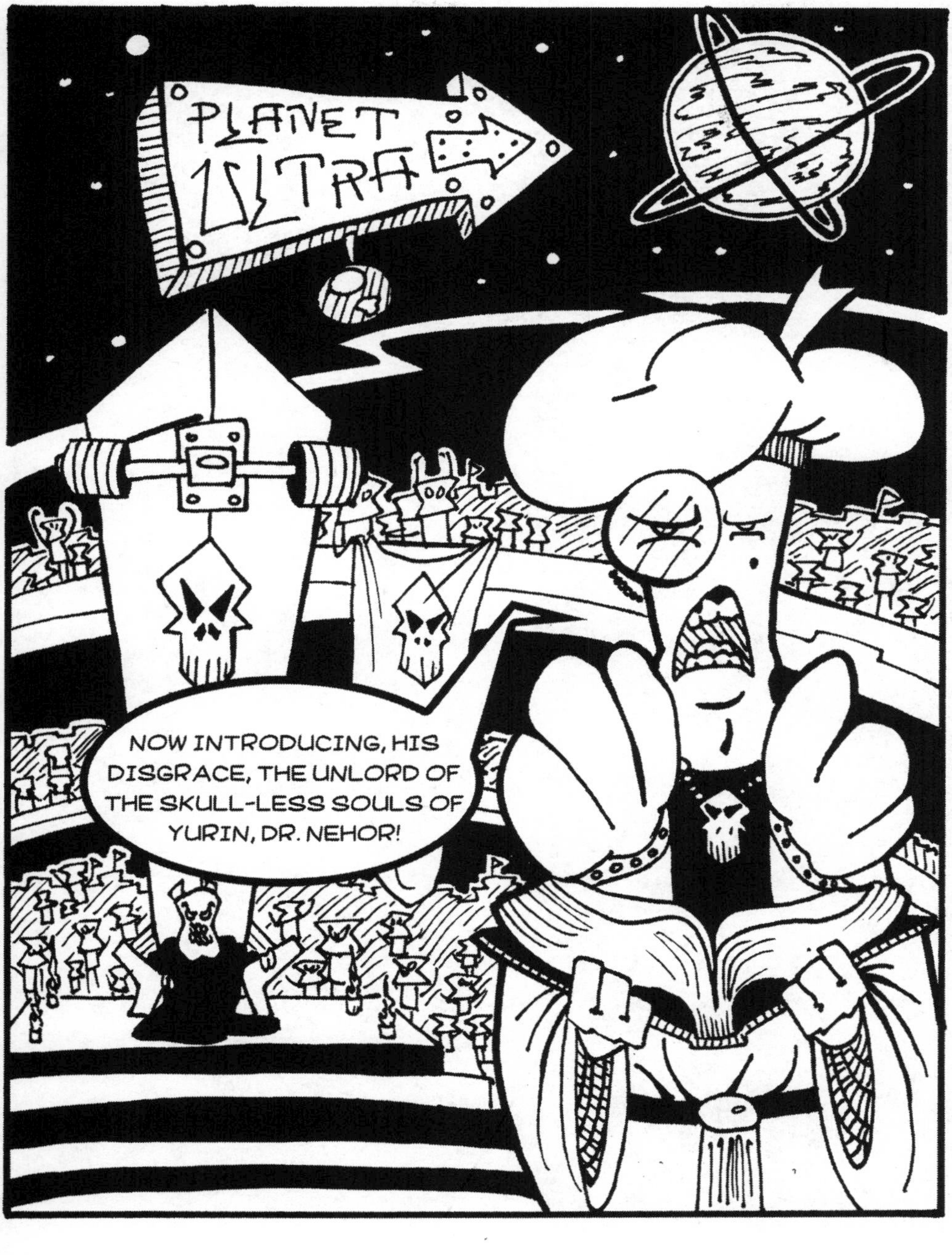
PLANET ULTRA
NOW INTRODUCING, HIS DISGRACE, THE UNLORD OF THE SKULL-LESS SOULS OF YURIN, DR. NEHOR!

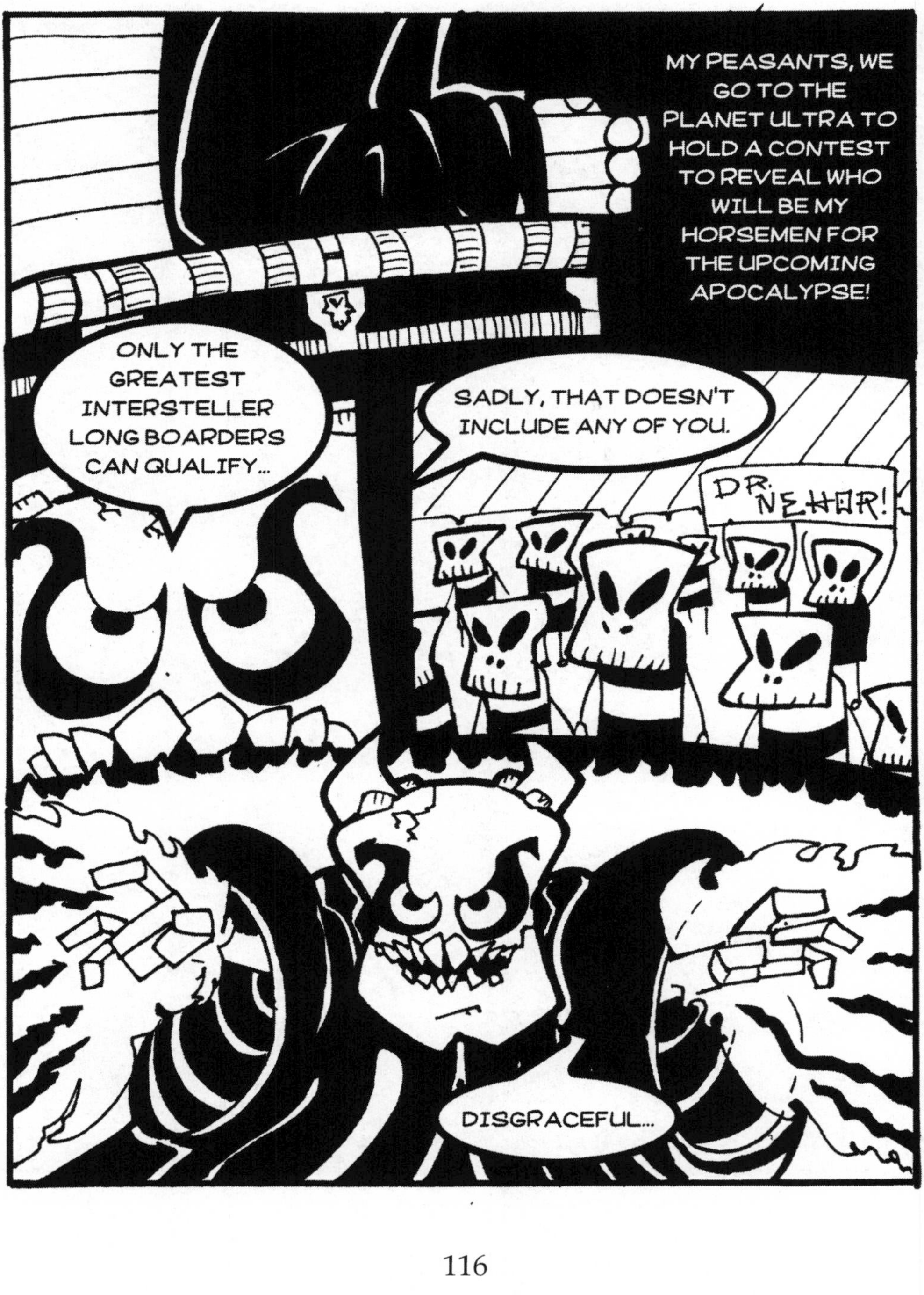
MY PEASANTS, WE GO TO THE PLANET ULTRA TO HOLD A CONTEST TO REVEAL WHO WILL BE MY HORSEMEN FOR THE UPCOMING APOCALYPSE!
ONLY THE GREATEST INTERSTELLER LONG BOARDERS CAN QUALIFY...
SADLY, THAT DOESN'T INCLUDE ANY OF YOU.
DR. NEHOR!
DISGRACEFUL...

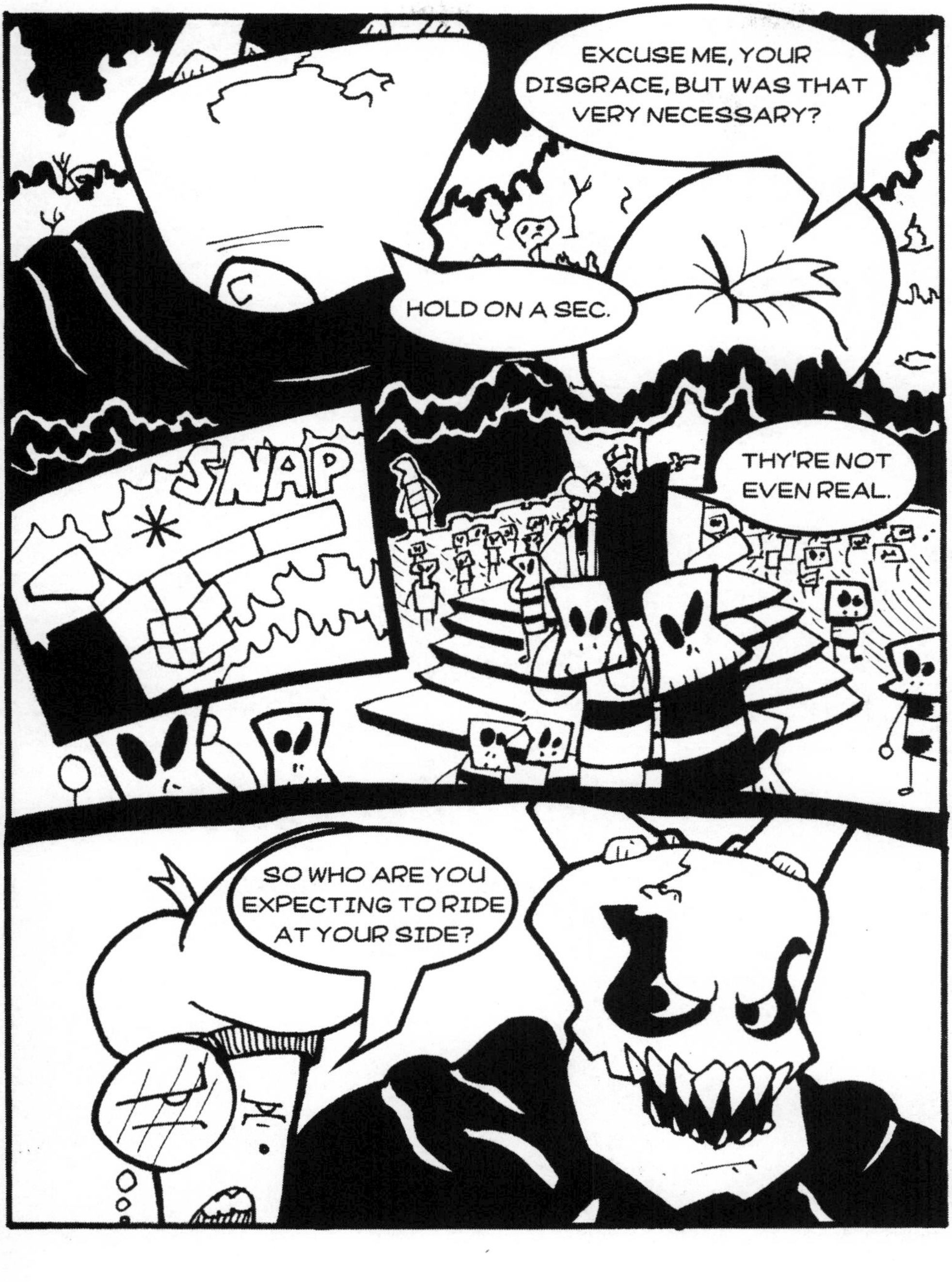
EXCUSE ME, YOUR DISGRACE, BUT WAS THAT VERY NECESSARY?
HOLD ON A SEC.
SNAP
THY'RE NOT EVEN REAL.
SO WHO ARE YOU EXPECTING TO RIDE AT YOUR SIDE?

WE SHALL SEE...
INTER GALATIC DOWNHILL RACE! - TODAY -
YOU GUYS IN?
OH, YEAH!

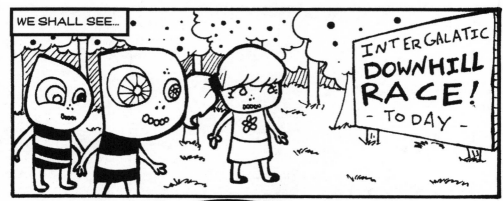

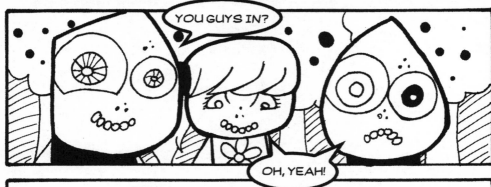

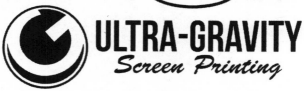

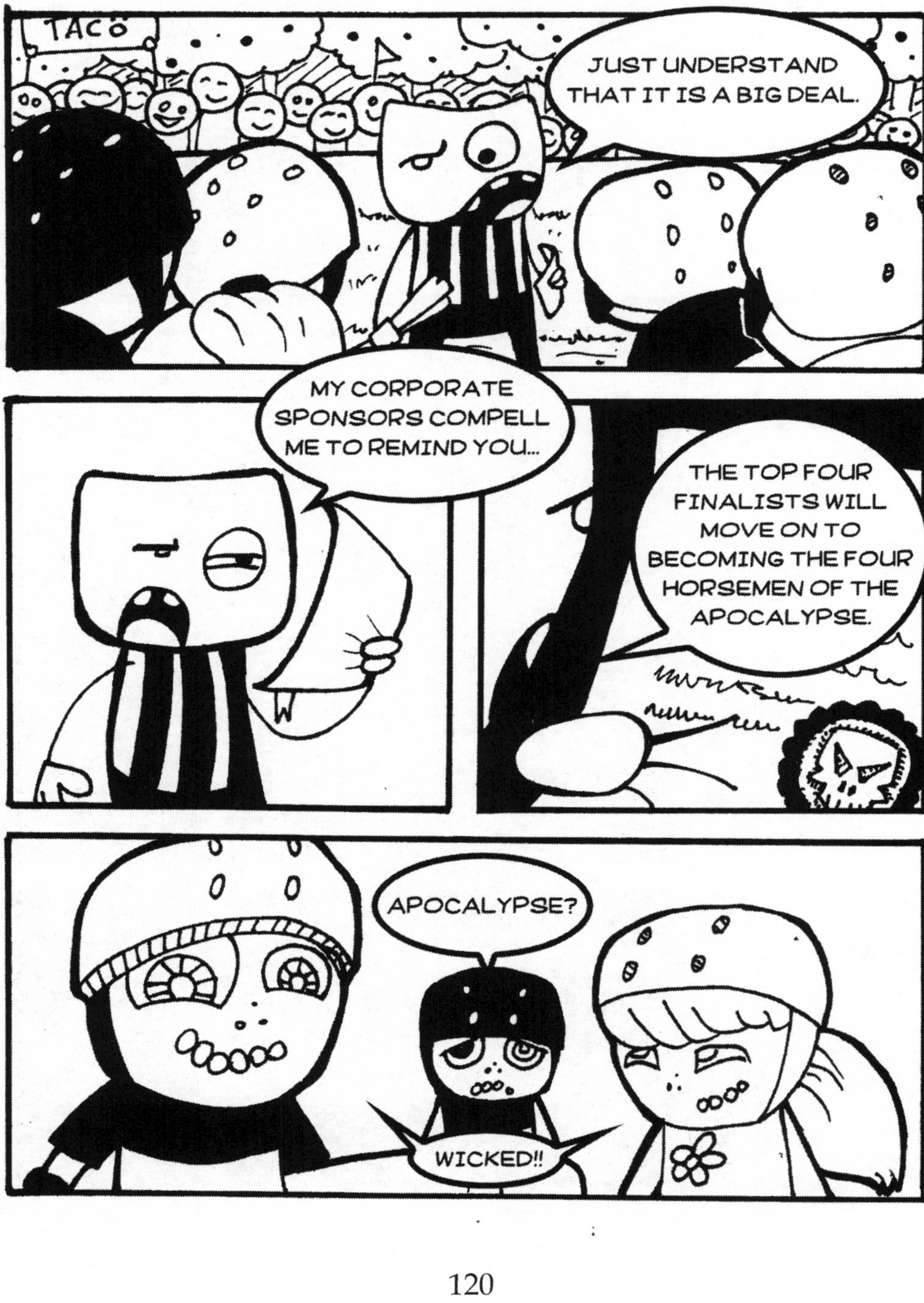
TACO
JUST UNDERSTAND THAT IT IS A BIG DEAL.
MY CORPORATE SPONSORS COMPELL ME TO REMIND YOU...
THE TOP FOUR FINALISTS WILL MOVE ON TO BECOMING THE FOUR HORSEMEN OF THE APOCALYPSE.
APOCALYPSE?
WICKED!!

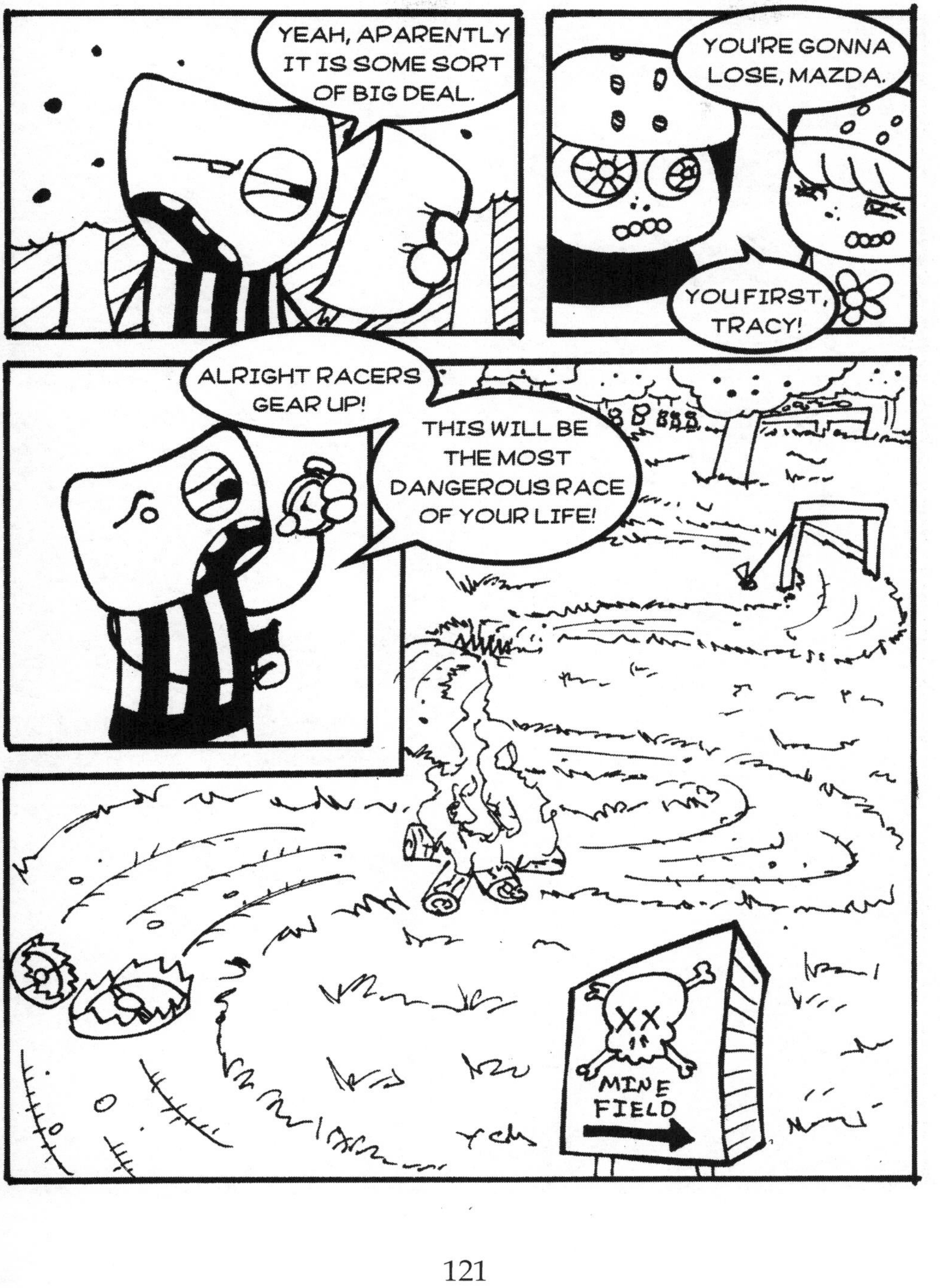
YEAH, APARENTLY IT IS SOME SORT OF BIG DEAL.
YOU'RE GONNA LOSE, MAZDA.
YOU FIRST, TRACY!
ALRIGHT RACERS GEAR UP!
THIS WILL BE THE MOST DANGEROUS RACE OF YOUR LIFE!
MINE FIELD

RACERS ON THE READY!
MAZDA
STEADY.
TRACY
GET SET!
TACO
BANG
GO!

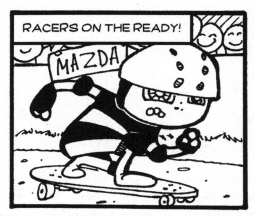

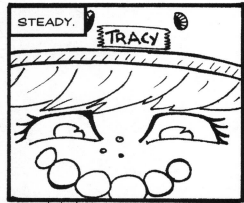

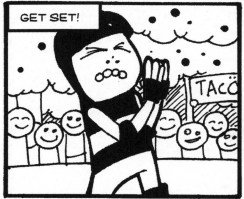

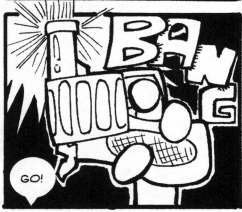

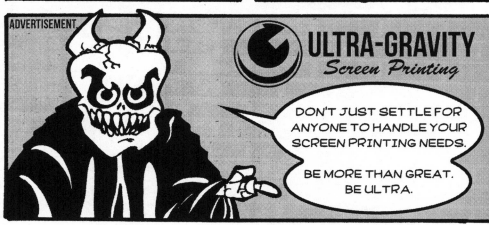

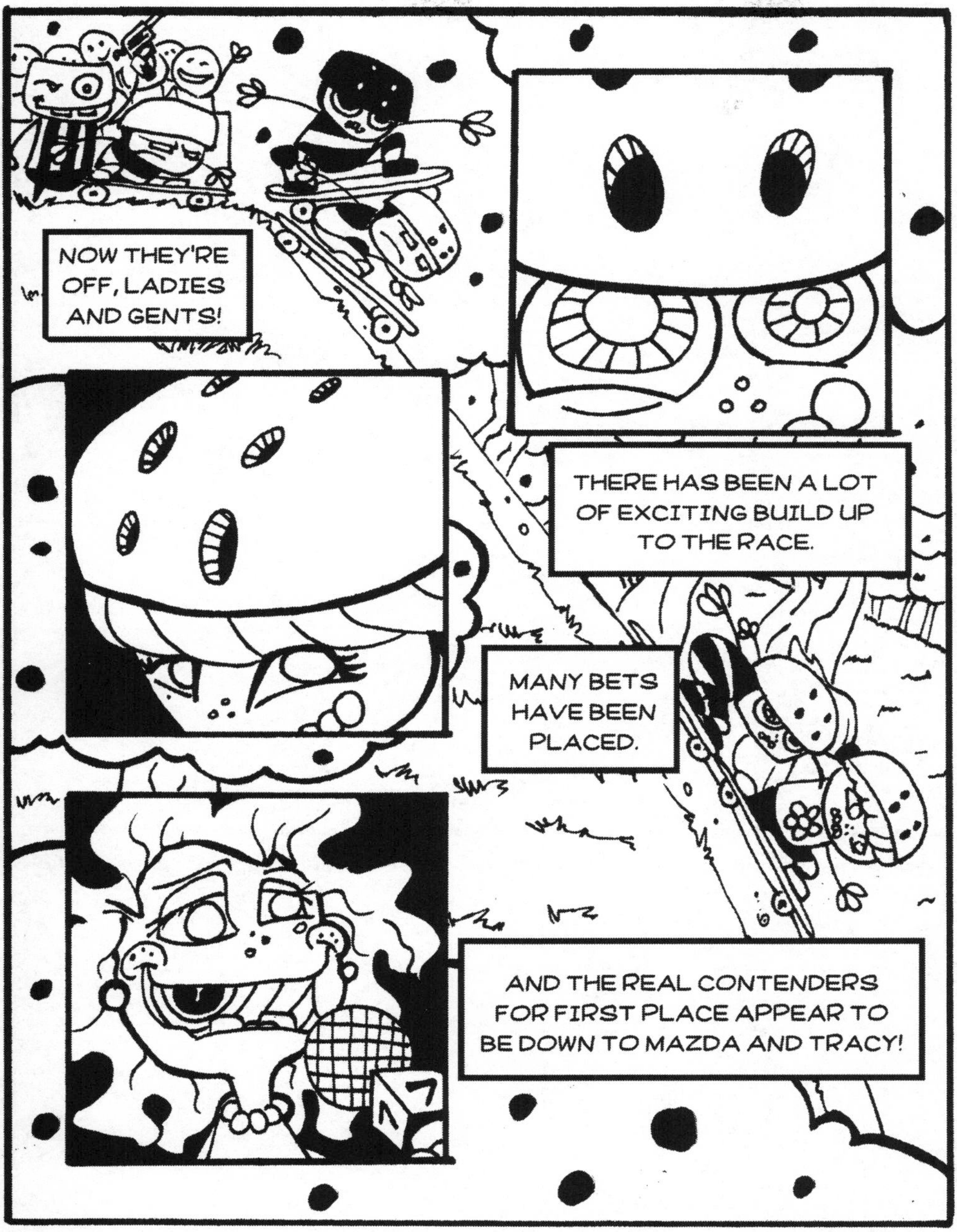
NOW THEY'RE OFF, LADIES AND GENTS!
THERE HAS BEEN A LOT OF EXCITING BUILD UP TO THE RACE.
MANY BETS HAVE BEEN PLACED.
AND THE REAL CONTENDERS FOR FIRST PLACE APPEAR TO BE DOWN TO MAZDA AND TRACY!

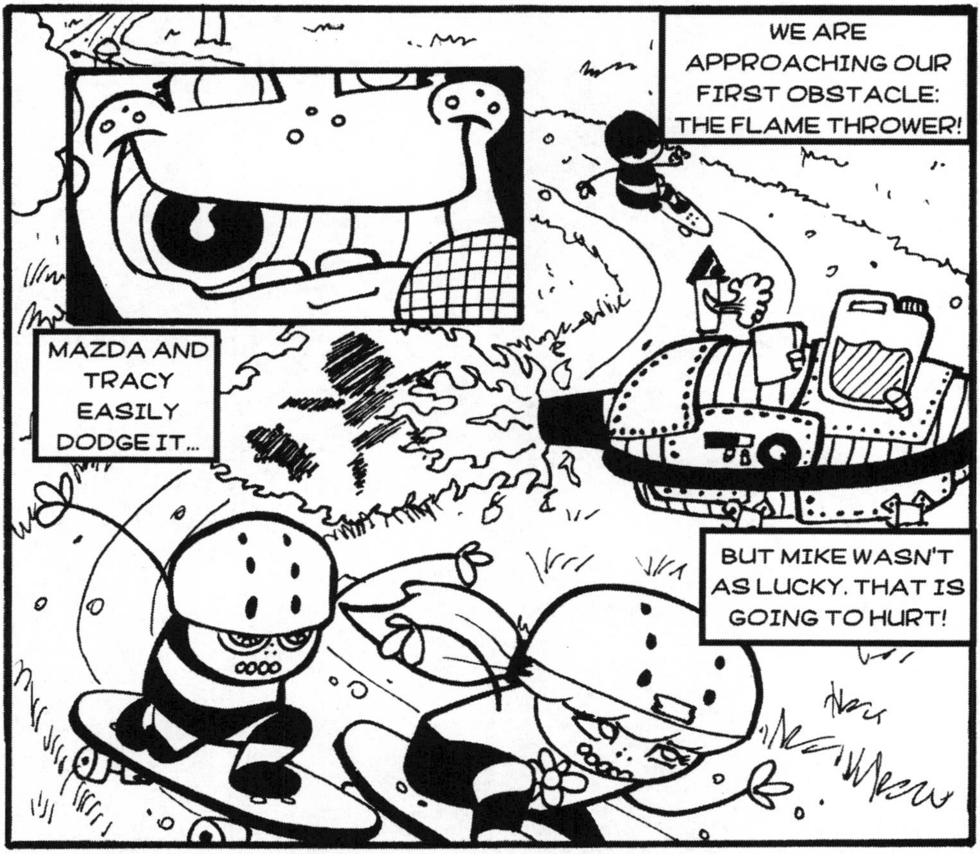
WE ARE APPROACHING OUR FIRST OBSTACLE: THE FLAME THROWER!
MAZDA AND TRACY EASILY DODGE IT...
BUT MIKE WASN'T AS LUCKY. THAT IS GOING TO HURT!

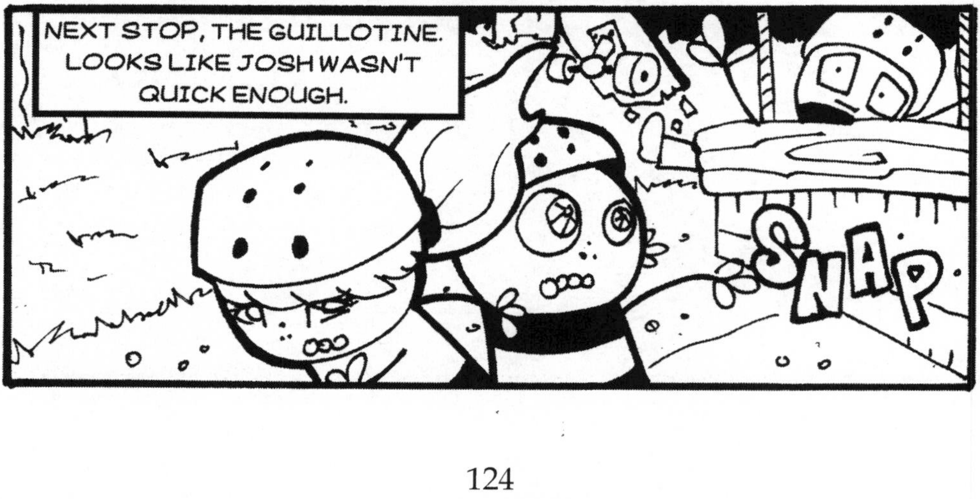
NEXT STOP, THE GUILLOTINE. LOOKS LIKE JOSH WASN'T QUICK ENOUGH.
SNAP

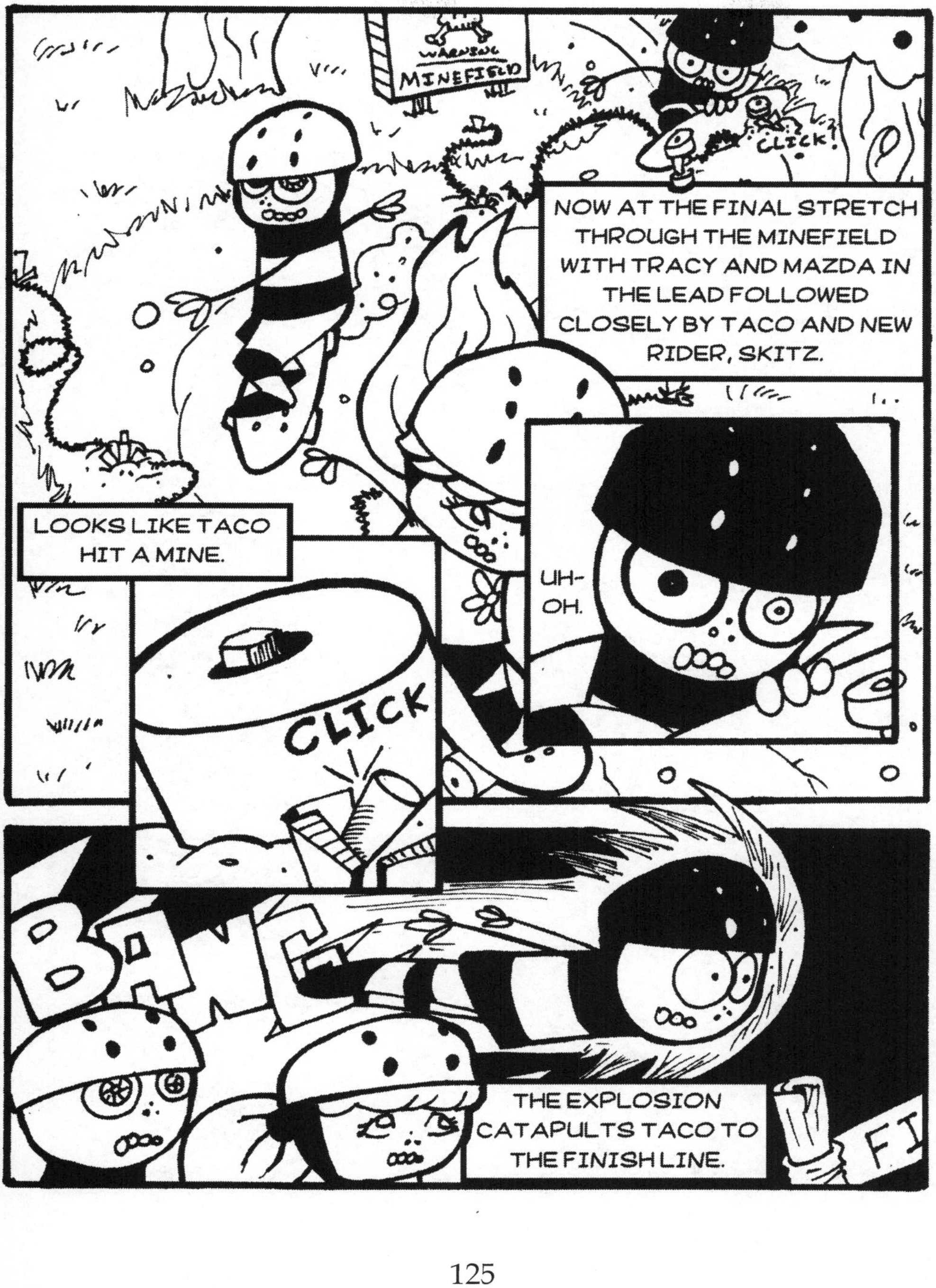
WARNING
MINEFIELD
CLICK!
NOW AT THE FINAL STRETCH THROUGH THE MINEFIELD WITH TRACY AND MAZDA IN THE LEAD FOLLOWED CLOSELY BY TACO AND NEW RIDER, SKITZ.
LOOKS LIKE TACO HIT A MINE.
CLICK
UH-OH.
BANG
THE EXPLOSION CATAPULTS TACO TO THE FINISH LINE.
FI

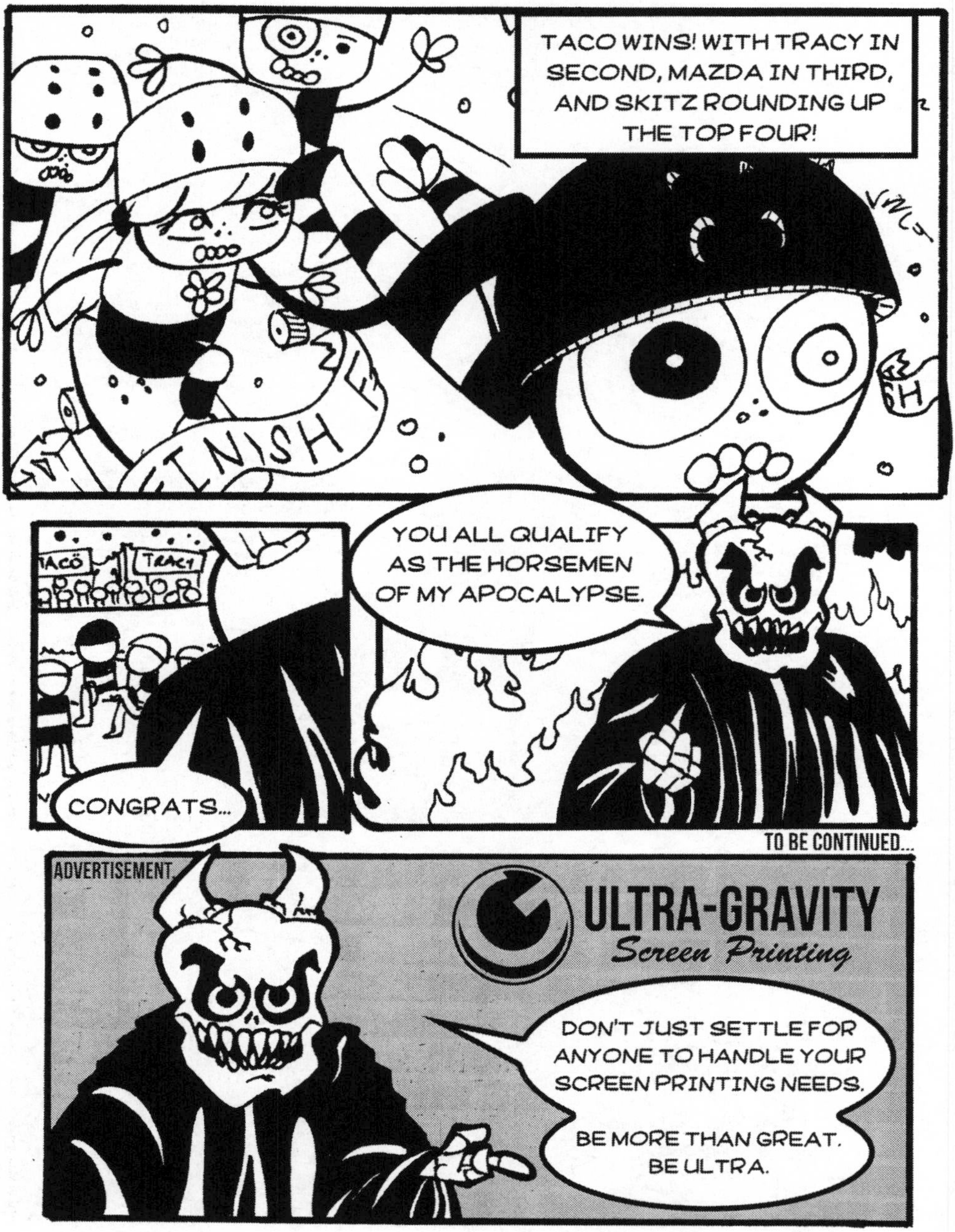
TACO WINS! WITH TRACY IN SECOND, MAZDA IN THIRD, AND SKITZ ROUNDING UP THE TOP FOUR!
FINISH
TACO
TRACY
CONGRATS...
YOU ALL QUALIFY AS THE HORSEMEN OF MY APOCALYPSE.
TO BE CONTINUED...
ADVERTISEMENT
ULTRA-GRAVITY
Screen Printing
DON'T JUST SETTLE FOR ANYONE TO HANDLE YOUR SCREEN PRINTING NEEDS.
BE MORE THAN GREAT. BE ULTRA.

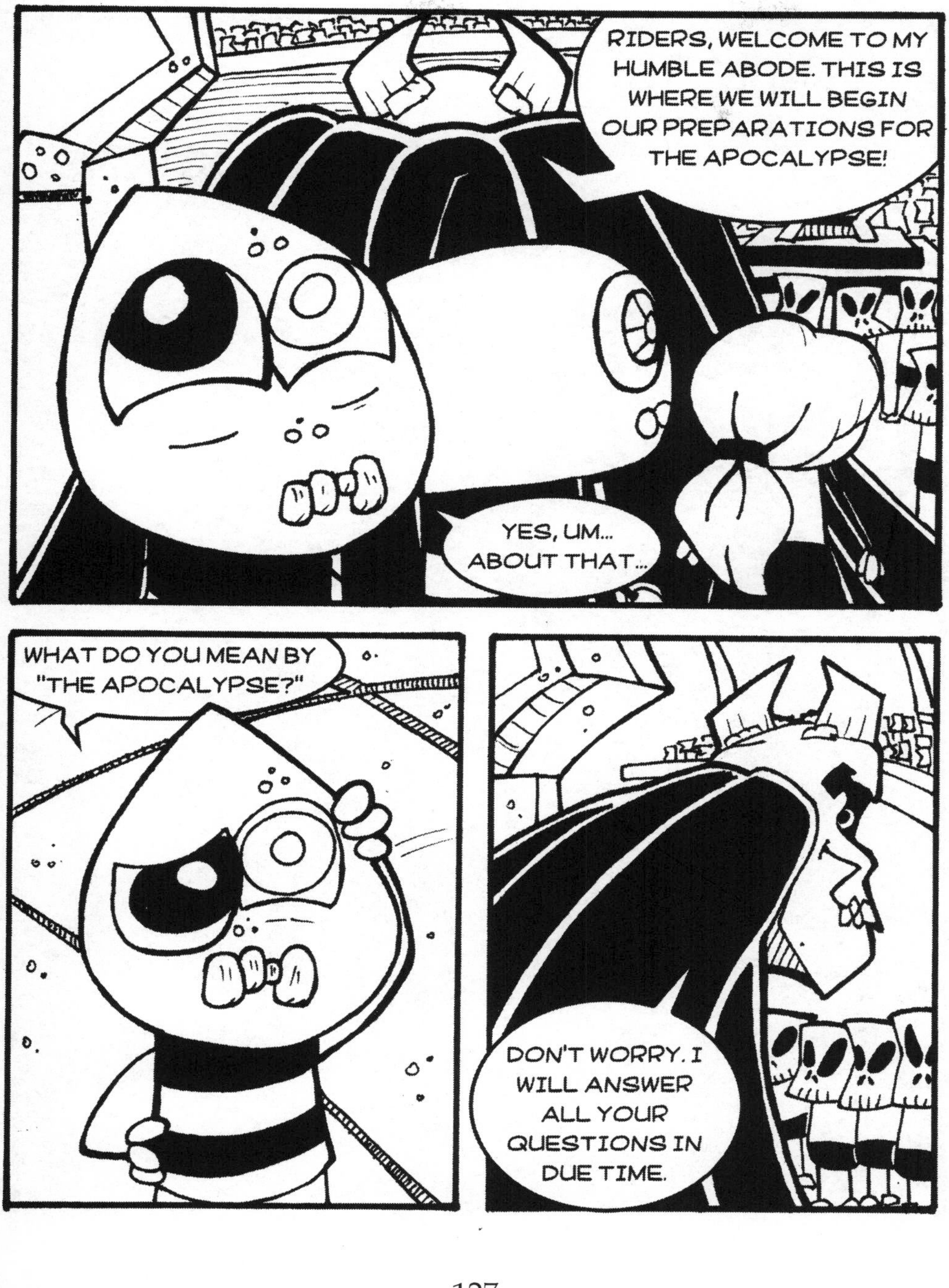
RIDERS, WELCOME TO MY HUMBLE ABODE. THIS IS WHERE WE WILL BEGIN OUR PREPARATIONS FOR THE APOCALYPSE!
YES, UM... ABOUT THAT...
WHAT DO YOU MEAN BY "THE APOCALYPSE?"
DON'T WORRY. I WILL ANSWER ALL YOUR QUESTIONS IN DUE TIME.

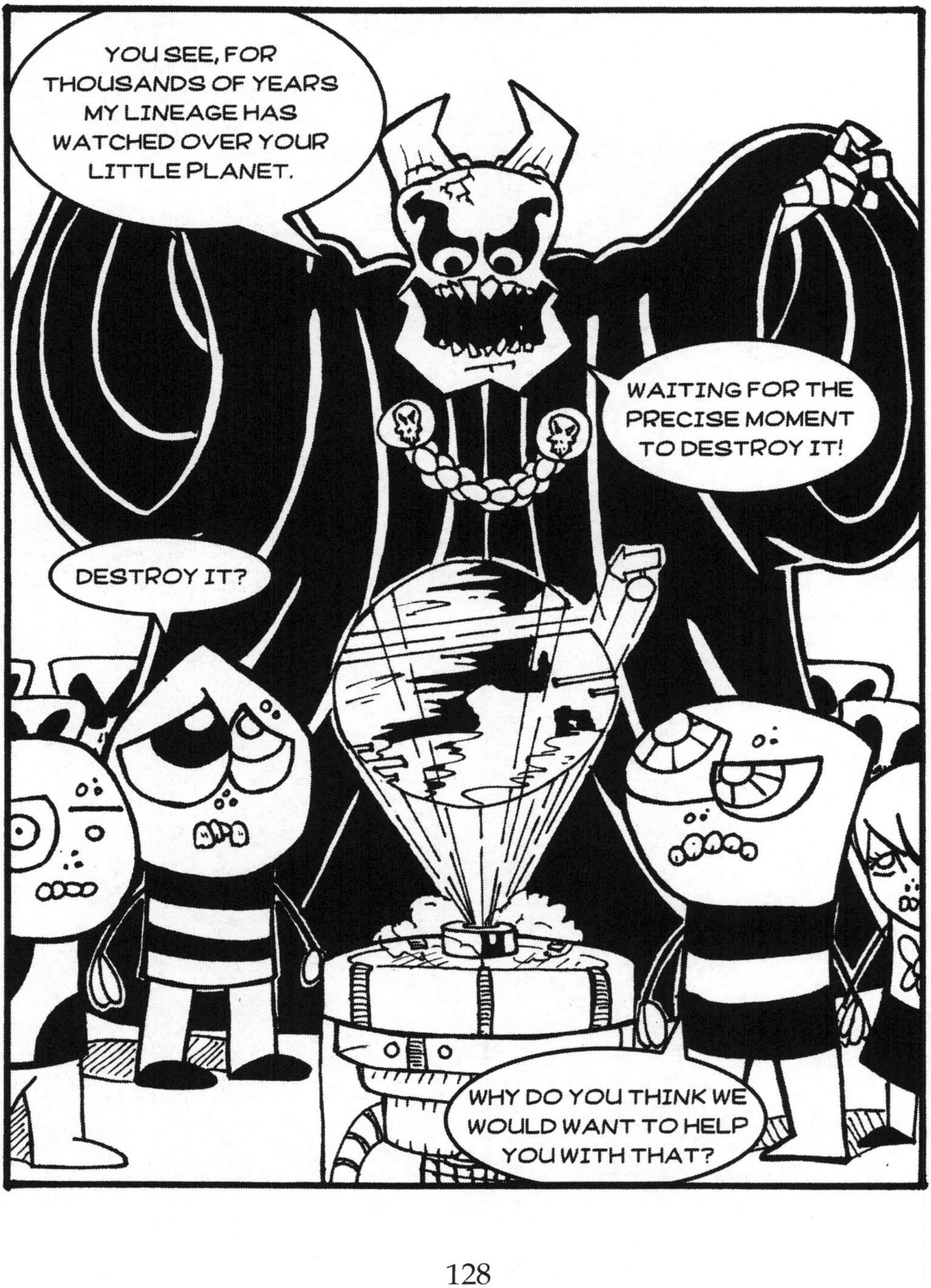
YOU SEE, FOR THOUSANDS OF YEARS MY LINEAGE HAS WATCHED OVER YOUR LITTLE PLANET.
WAITING FOR THE PRECISE MOMENT TO DESTROY IT!
DESTROY IT?
WHY DO YOU THINK WE WOULD WANT TO HELP YOU WITH THAT?

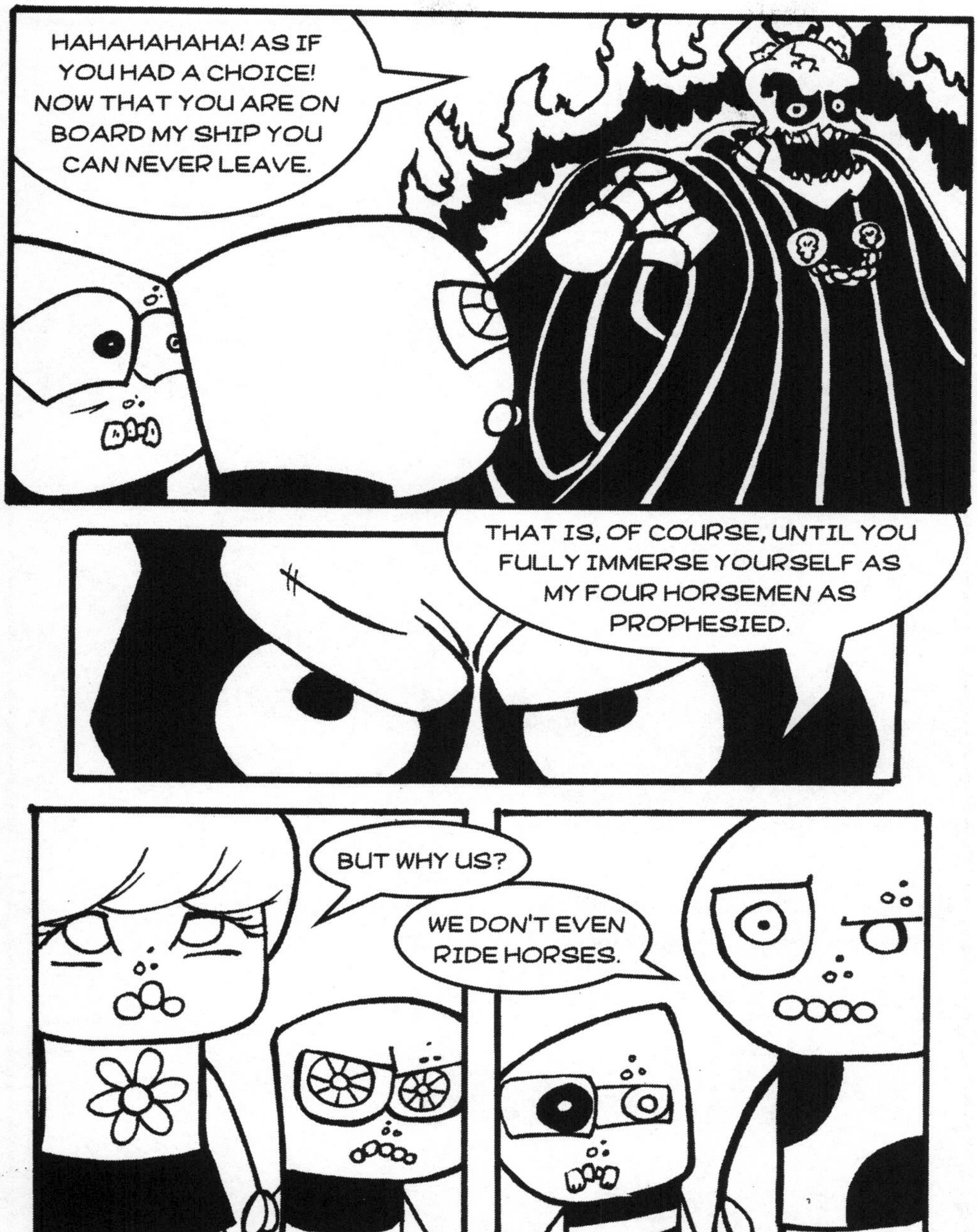
HAHAHAHAHA! AS IF YOU HAD A CHOICE! NOW THAT YOU ARE ON BOARD MY SHIP YOU CAN NEVER LEAVE.
THAT IS, OF COURSE, UNTIL YOU FULLY IMMERSE YOURSELF AS MY FOUR HORSEMEN AS PROPHESIED.
BUT WHY US?
WE DON'T EVEN RIDE HORSES.

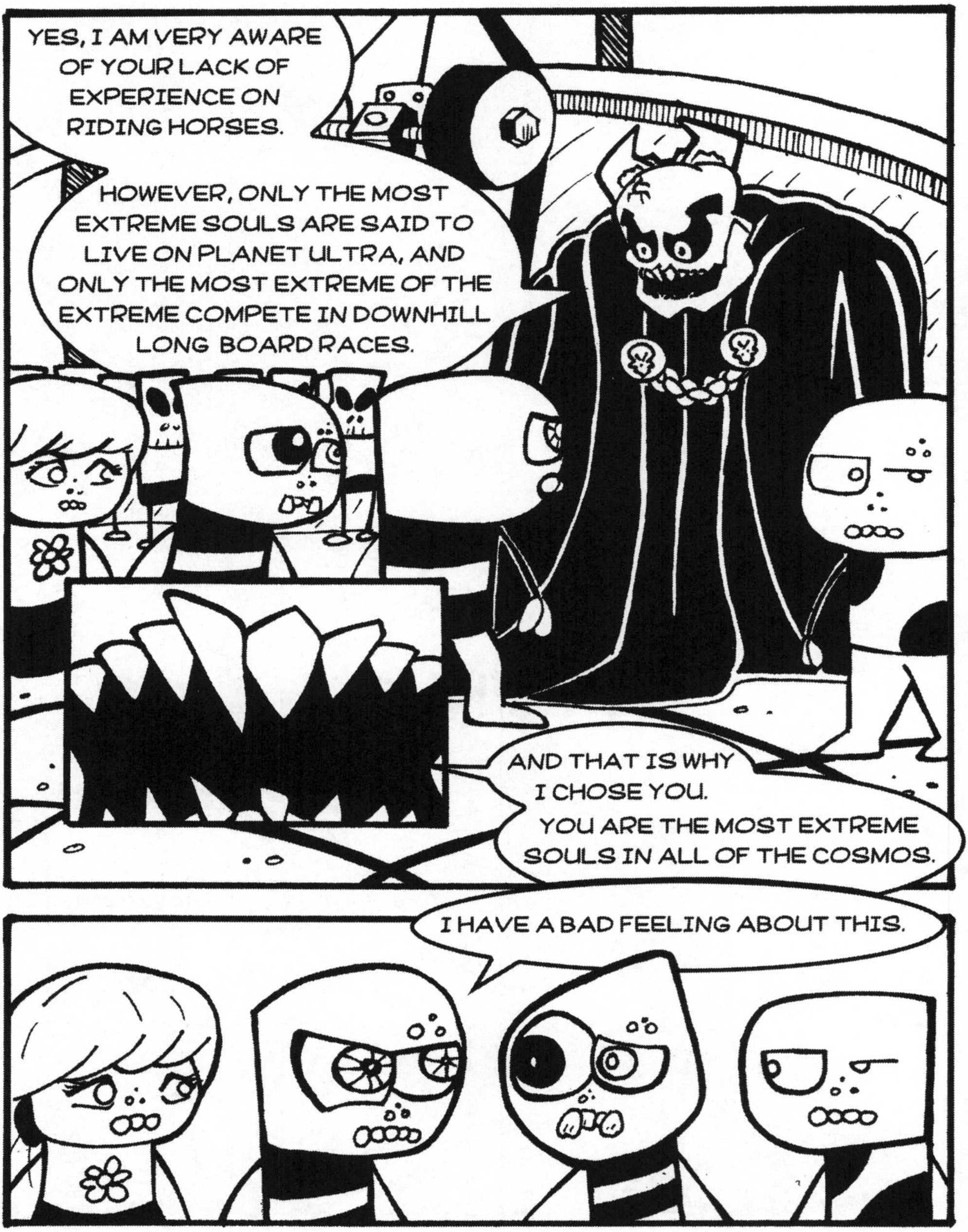
YES, I AM VERY AWARE OF YOUR LACK OF EXPERIENCE ON RIDING HORSES.
HOWEVER, ONLY THE MOST EXTREME SOULS ARE SAID TO LIVE ON PLANET ULTRA, AND ONLY THE MOST EXTREME OF THE EXTREME COMPETE IN DOWNHILL LONG BOARD RACES.
AND THAT IS WHY I CHOSE YOU.
YOU ARE THE MOST EXTREME SOULS IN ALL OF THE COSMOS.
I HAVE A BAD FEELING ABOUT THIS.

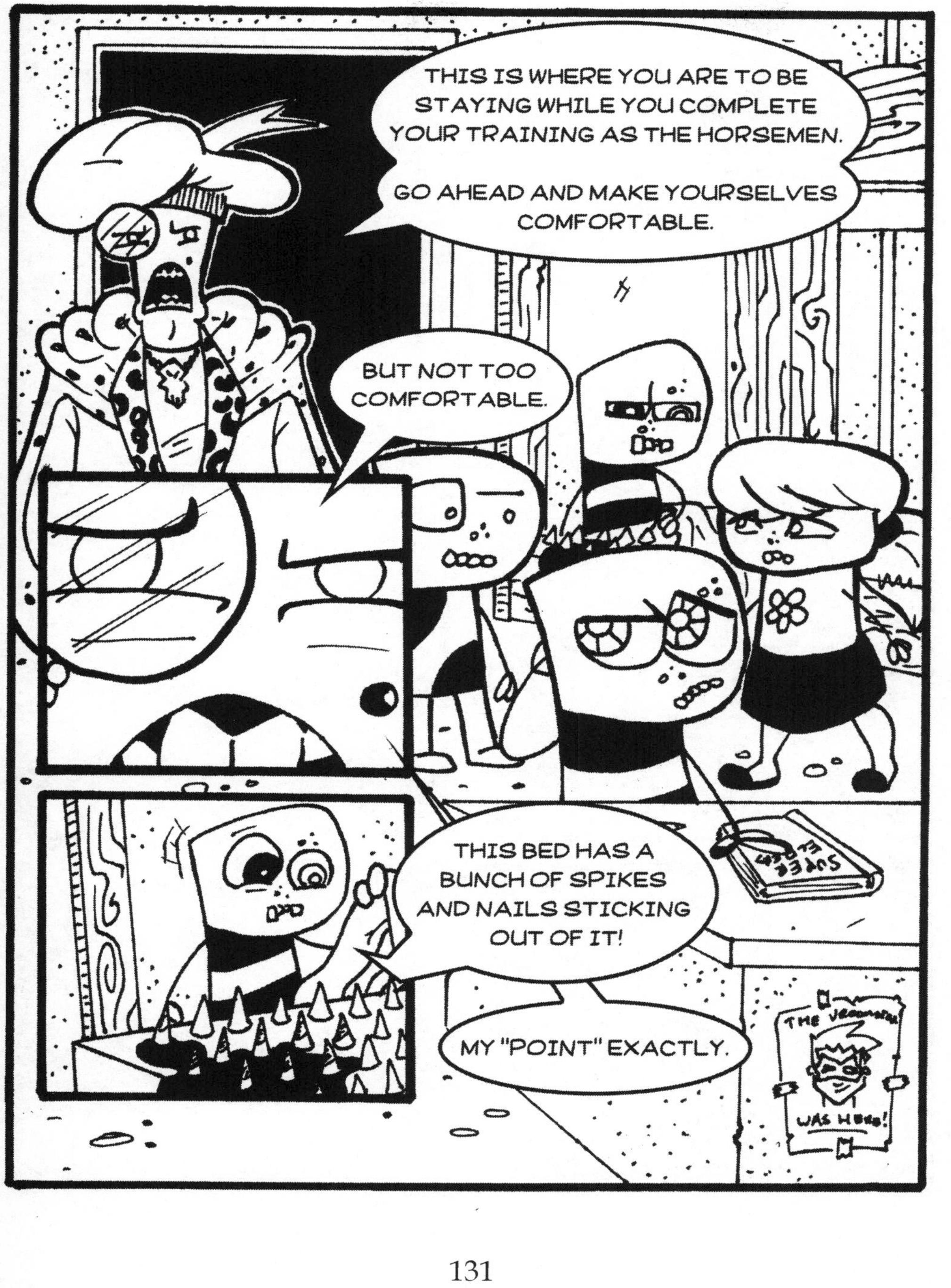
THIS IS WHERE YOU ARE TO BE STAYING WHILE YOU COMPLETE YOUR TRAINING AS THE HORSEMEN.
GO AHEAD AND MAKE YOURSELVES COMFORTABLE.
BUT NOT TOO COMFORTABLE.
THIS BED HAS A BUNCH OF SPIKES AND NAILS STICKING OUT OF IT!
MY "POINT" EXACTLY.
WAS HERE!

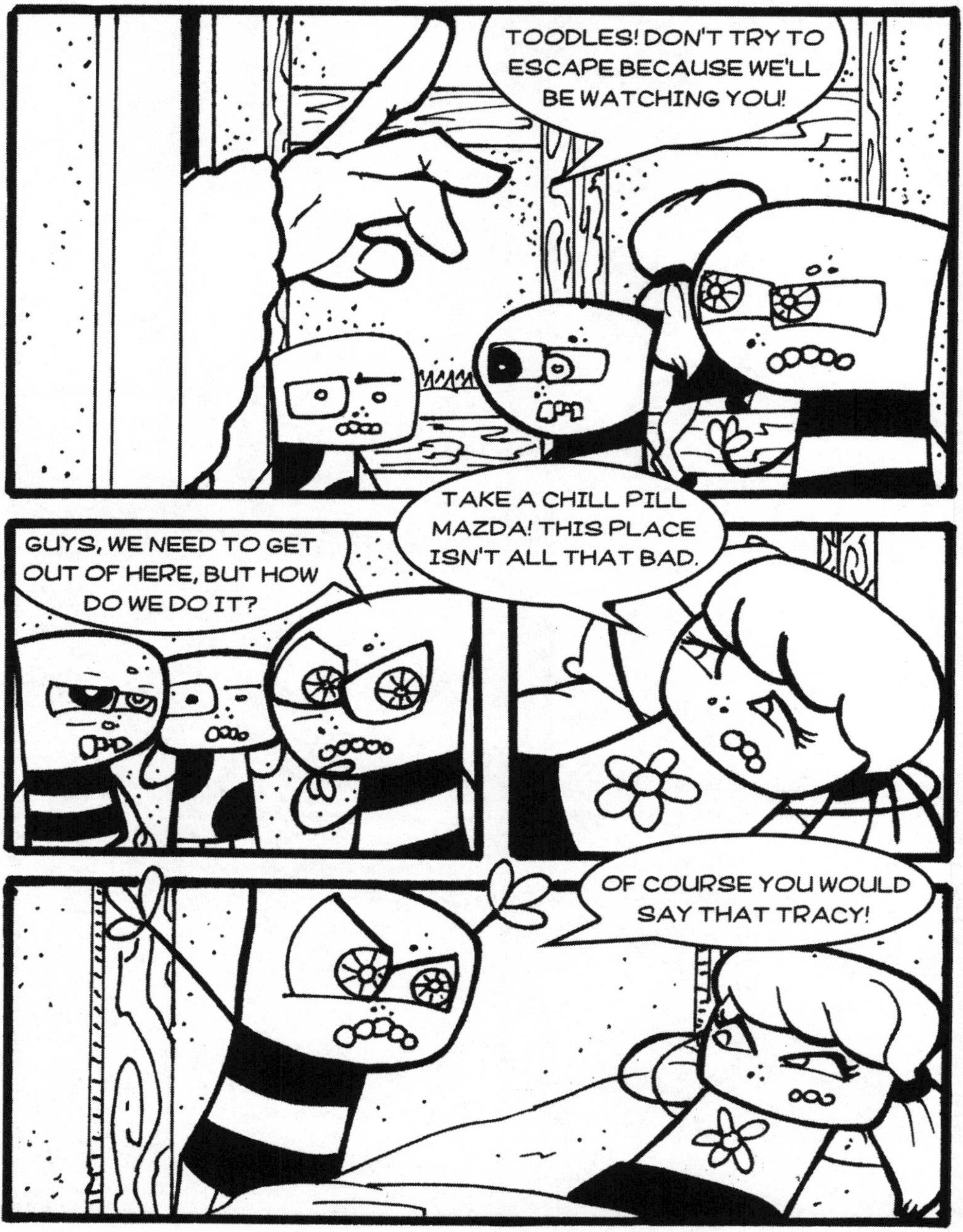
TOODLES! DON'T TRY TO ESCAPE BECAUSE WE'LL BE WATCHING YOU!
GUYS, WE NEED TO GET OUT OF HERE, BUT HOW DO WE DO IT?
TAKE A CHILL PILL MAZDA! THIS PLACE ISN'T ALL THAT BAD.
OF COURSE YOU WOULD SAY THAT TRACY!

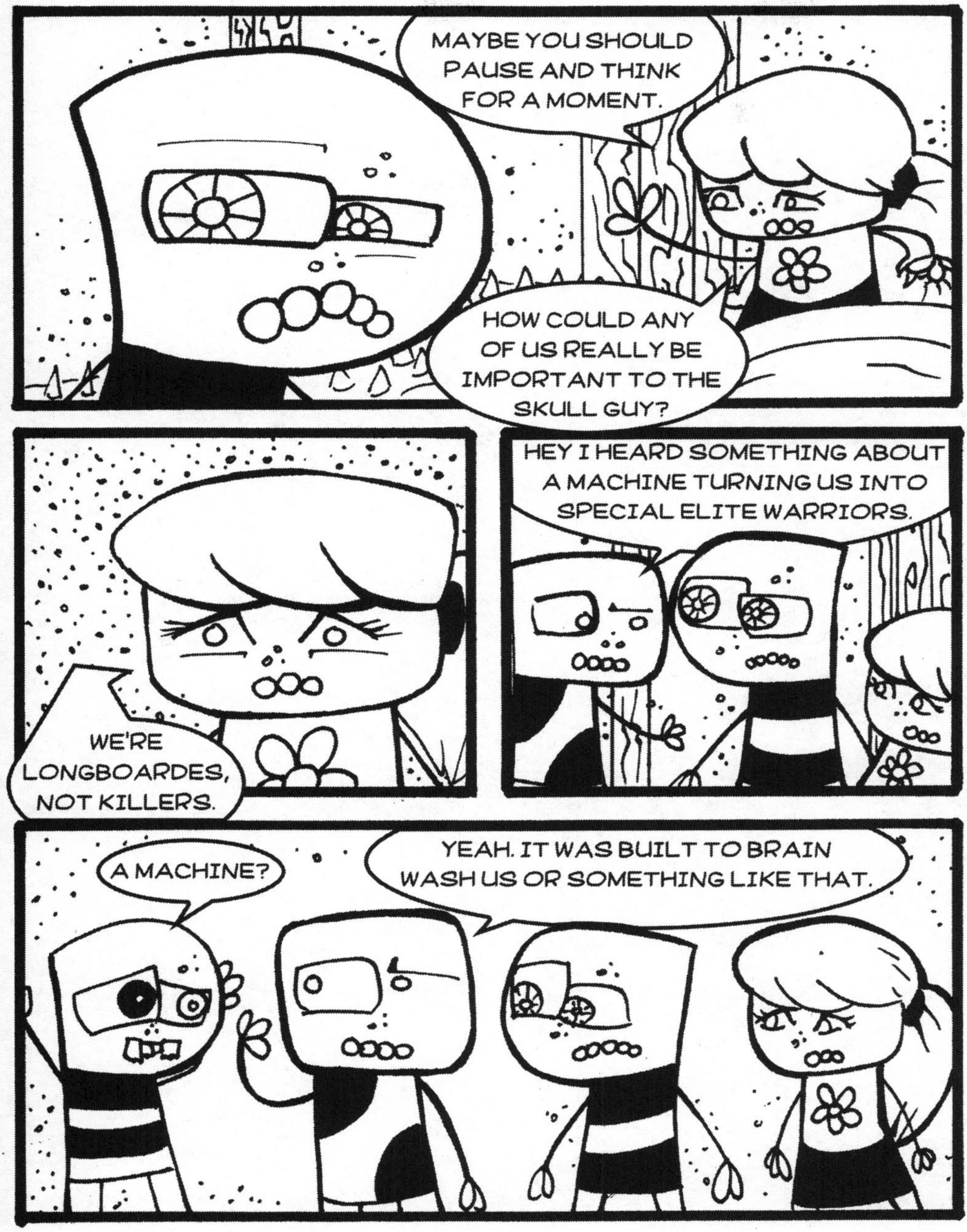
MAYBE YOU SHOULD PAUSE AND THINK FOR A MOMENT.
HOW COULD ANY OF US REALLY BE IMPORTANT TO THE SKULL GUY?
WE'RE LONGBOARDES, NOT KILLERS.
HEY I HEARD SOMETHING ABOUT A MACHINE TURNING US INTO SPECIAL ELITE WARRIORS.
A MACHINE?
YEAH. IT WAS BUILT TO BRAIN WASH US OR SOMETHING LIKE THAT.

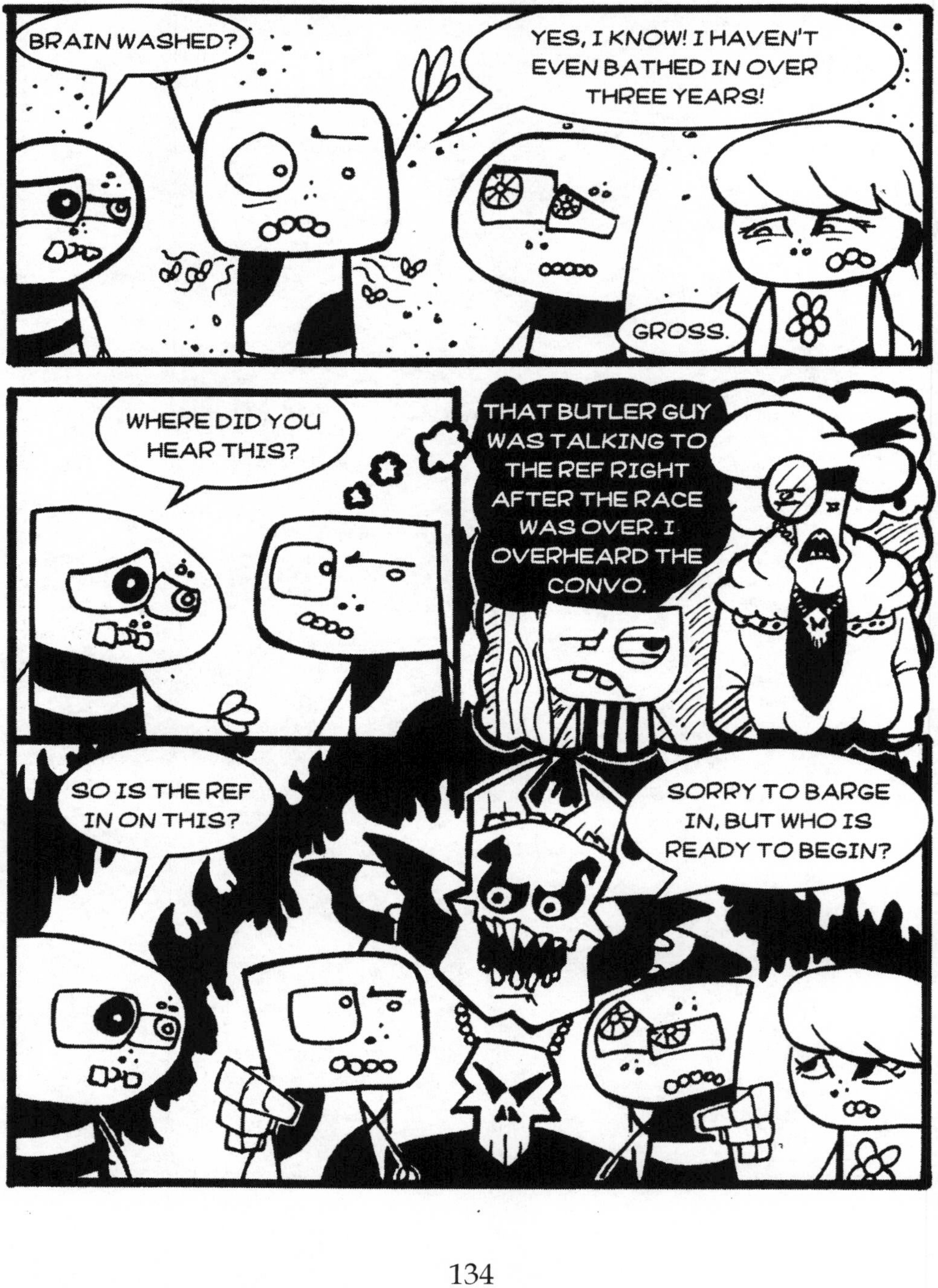

BRAIN WASHED?
YES, I KNOW! I HAVEN'T EVEN BATHED IN OVER THREE YEARS!
GROSS.
WHERE DID YOU HEAR THIS?
THAT BUTLER GUY WAS TALKING TO THE REF RIGHT AFTER THE RACE WAS OVER. I OVERHEARD THE CONVO.
SO IS THE REF IN ON THIS?
SORRY TO BARGE IN, BUT WHO IS READY TO BEGIN?

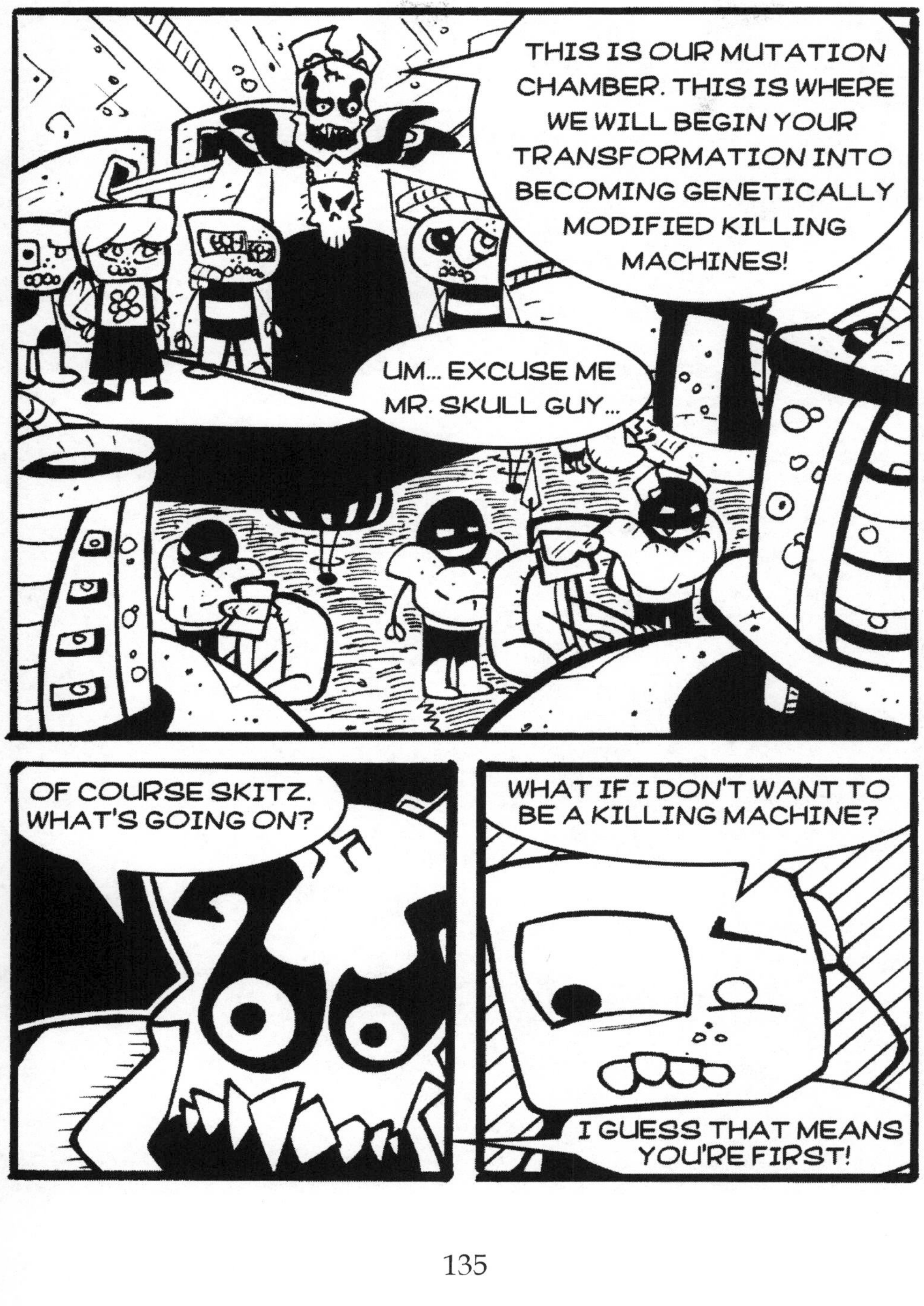
THIS IS OUR MUTATION CHAMBER. THIS IS WHERE WE WILL BEGIN YOUR TRANSFORMATION INTO BECOMING GENETICALLY MODIFIED KILLING MACHINES!
UM... EXCUSE ME MR. SKULL GUY...
OF COURSE SKITZ. WHAT'S GOING ON?
WHAT IF I DON'T WANT TO BE A KILLING MACHINE?
I GUESS THAT MEANS YOU'RE FIRST!

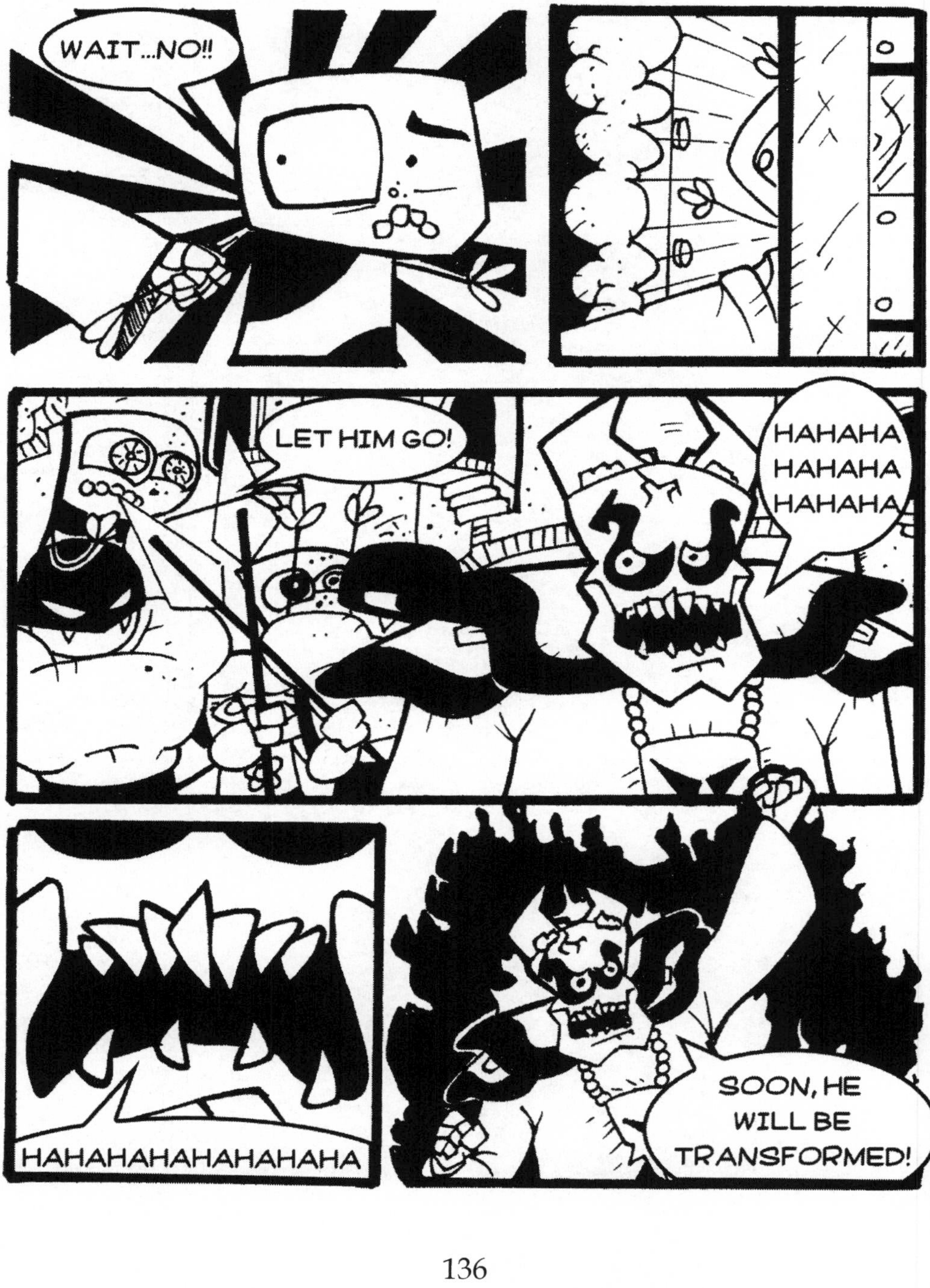
WAIT...NO!!
LET HIM GO!
HAHAHA HAHAHA HAHAHA
HAHAHAHAHAHAHAHA
SOON, HE WILL BE TRANSFORMED!

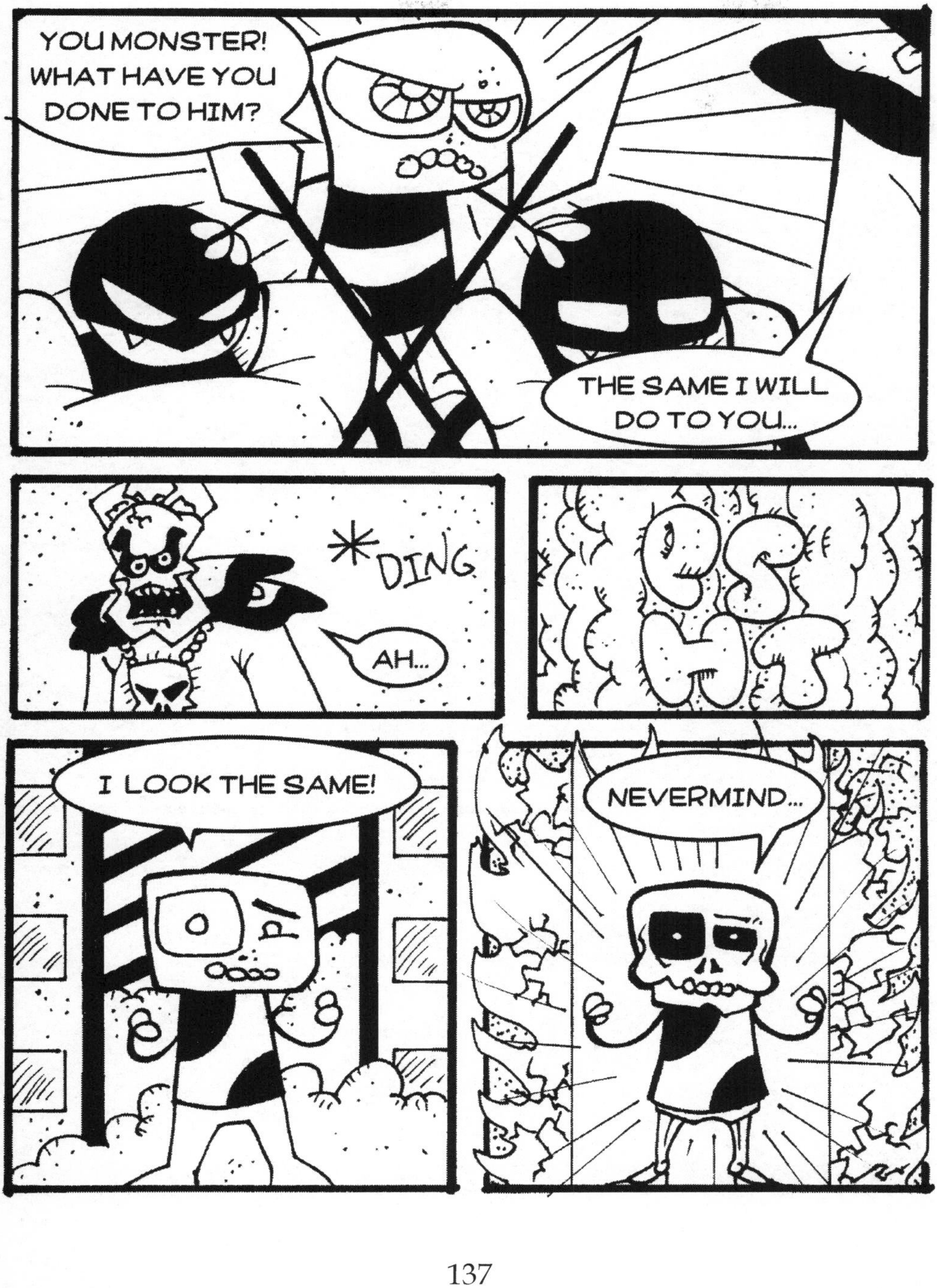
YOU MONSTER! WHAT HAVE YOU DONE TO HIM?
THE SAME I WILL DO TO YOU...
*DING
AH...
PSHT
I LOOK THE SAME!
NEVERMIND...

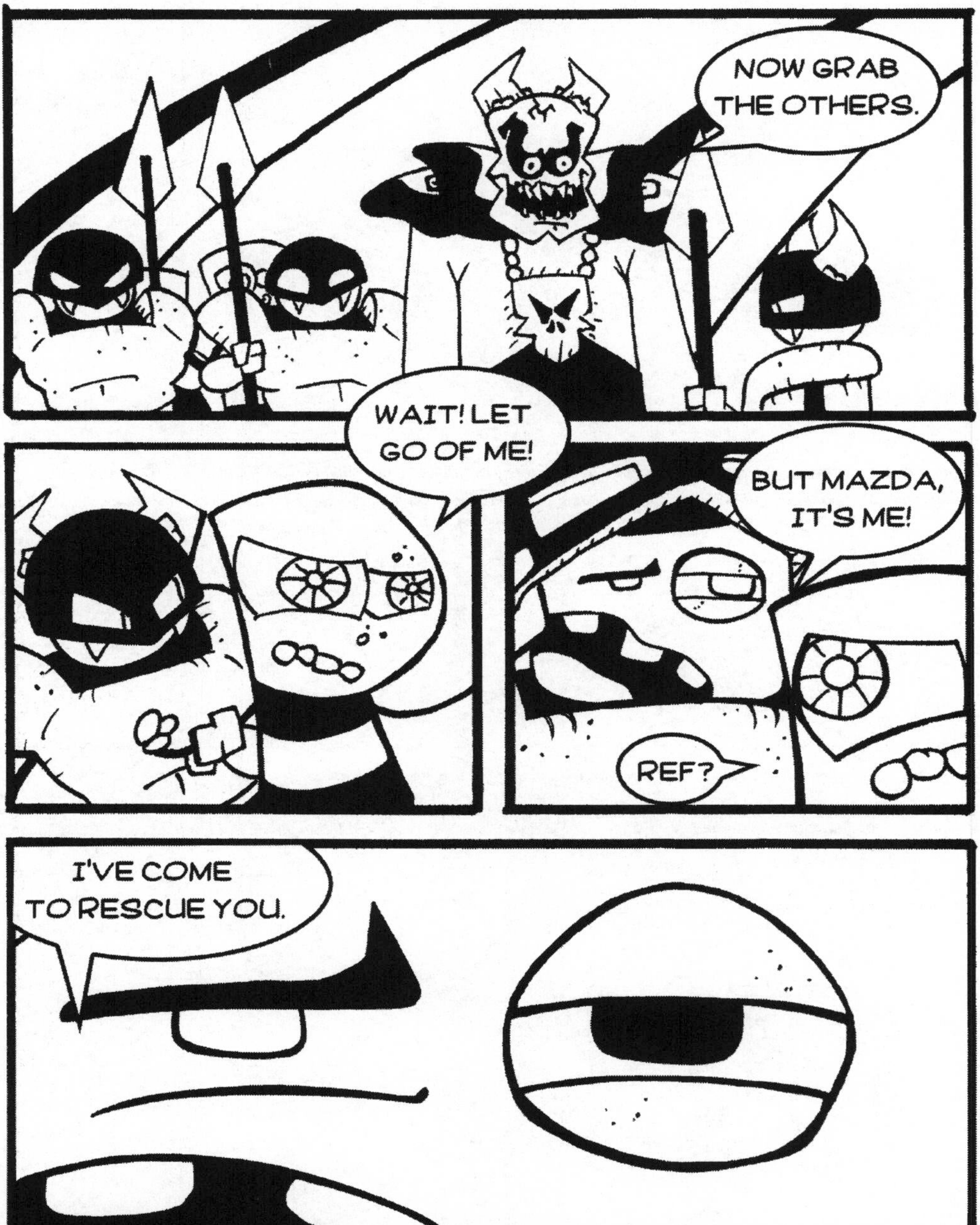
NOW GRAB THE OTHERS.
WAIT! LET GO OF ME!
BUT MAZDA, IT'S ME!
REF?
I'VE COME TO RESCUE YOU.

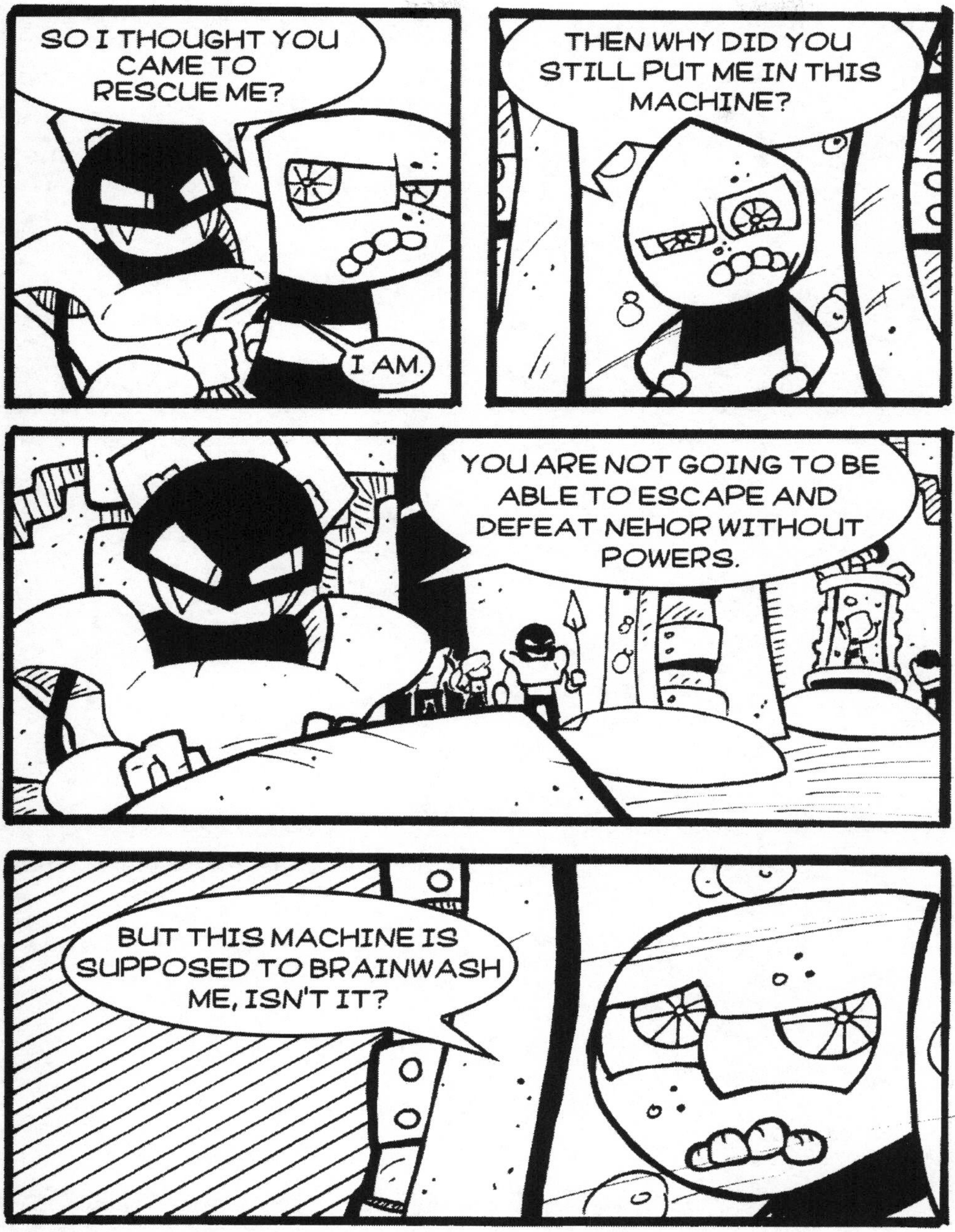
SO I THOUGHT YOU CAME TO RESCUE ME?
I AM.
THEN WHY DID YOU STILL PUT ME IN THIS MACHINE?
YOU ARE NOT GOING TO BE ABLE TO ESCAPE AND DEFEAT NEHOR WITHOUT POWERS.
BUT THIS MACHINE IS SUPPOSED TO BRAINWASH ME, ISN'T IT?

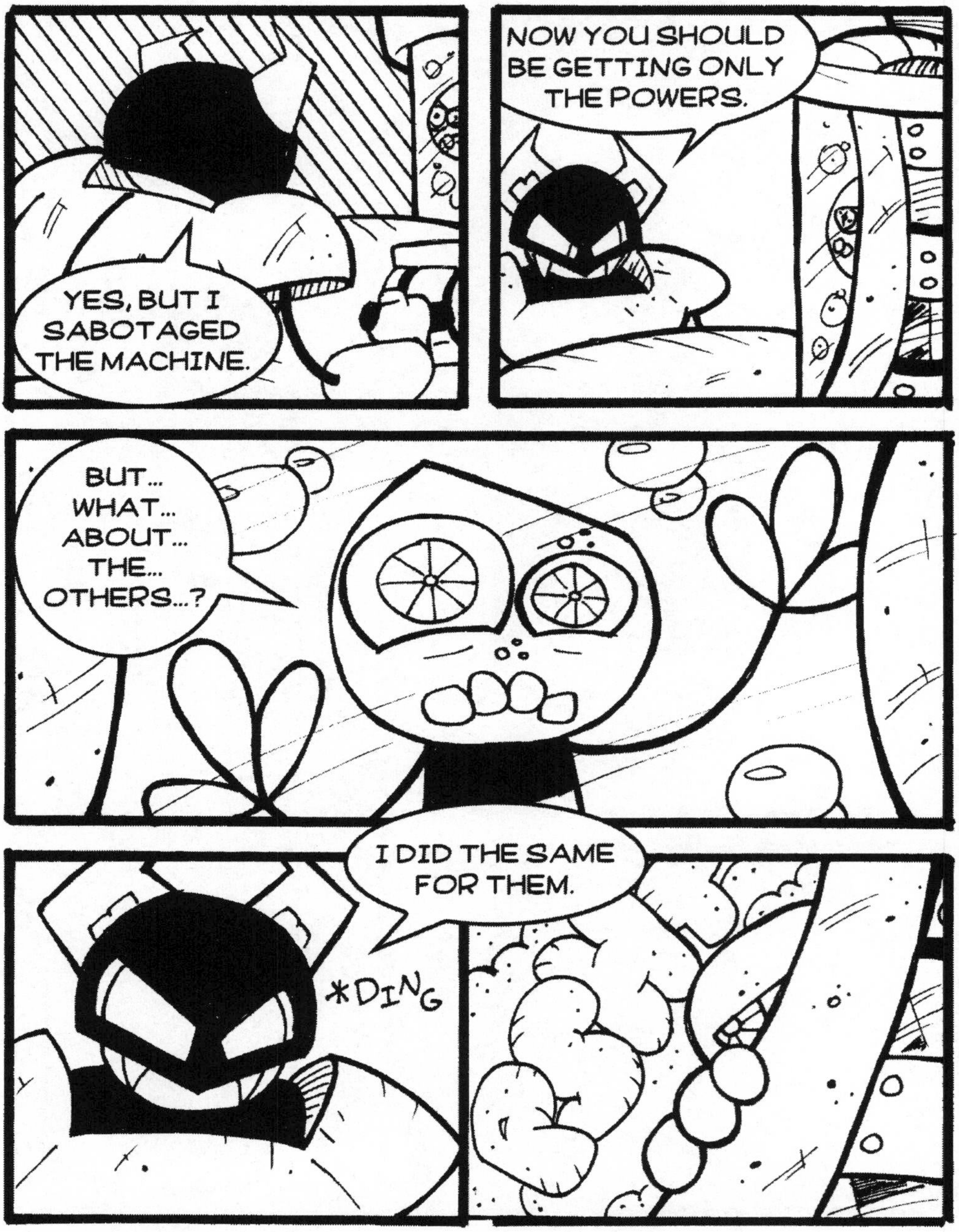
YES, BUT I SABOTAGED THE MACHINE.
NOW YOU SHOULD BE GETTING ONLY THE POWERS.
BUT... WHAT... ABOUT... THE... OTHERS...?
I DID THE SAME FOR THEM.
*DING

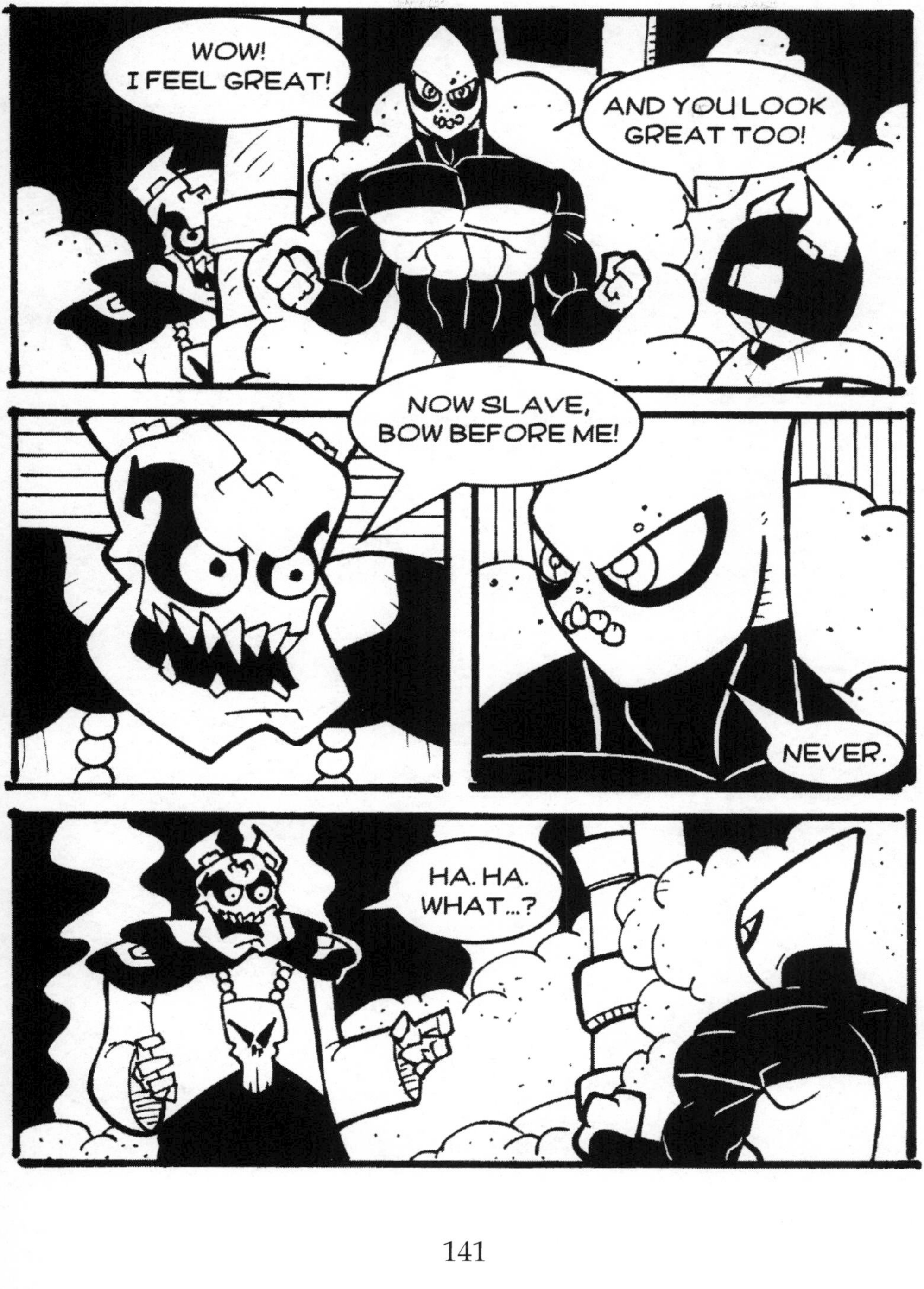
WOW!
I FEEL GREAT!
AND YOU LOOK GREAT TOO!
NOW SLAVE, BOW BEFORE ME!
NEVER.
HA. HA. WHAT...?

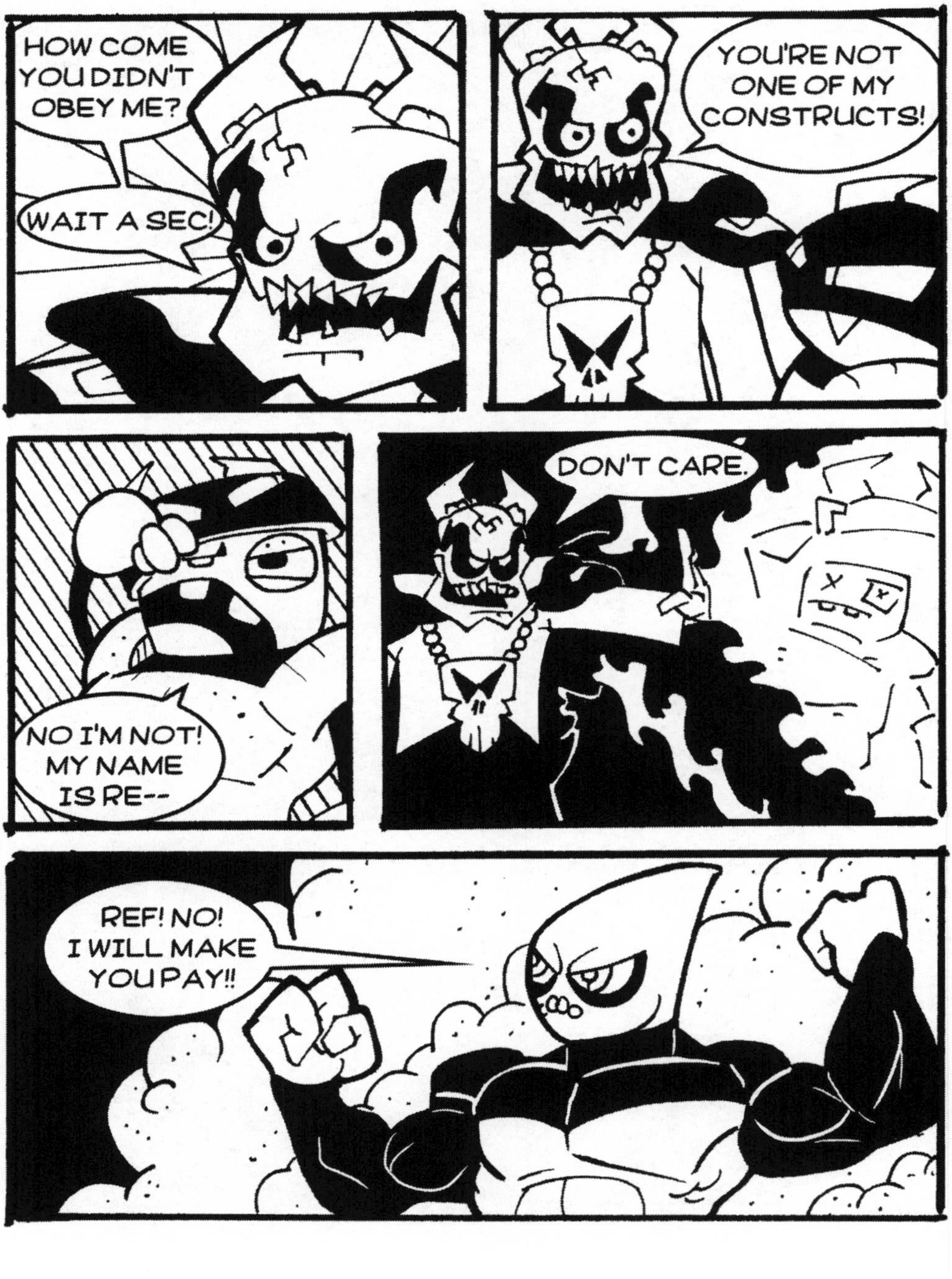
HOW COME YOU DIDN'T OBEY ME?
WAIT A SEC!
YOU'RE NOT ONE OF MY CONSTRUCTS!
NO I'M NOT! MY NAME IS RE--
DON'T CARE.
REF! NO! I WILL MAKE YOU PAY!!

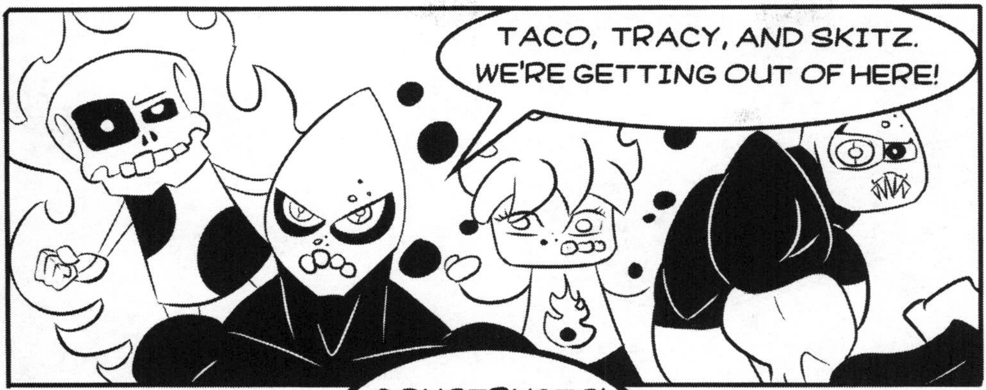
TACO, TRACY, AND SKITZ. WE'RE GETTING OUT OF HERE!

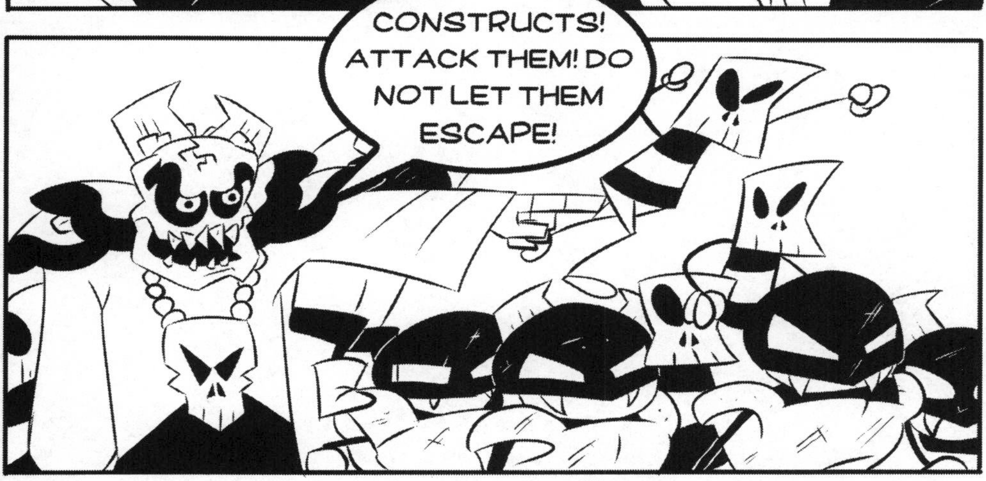
CONSTRUCTS! ATTACK THEM! DO NOT LET THEM ESCAPE!

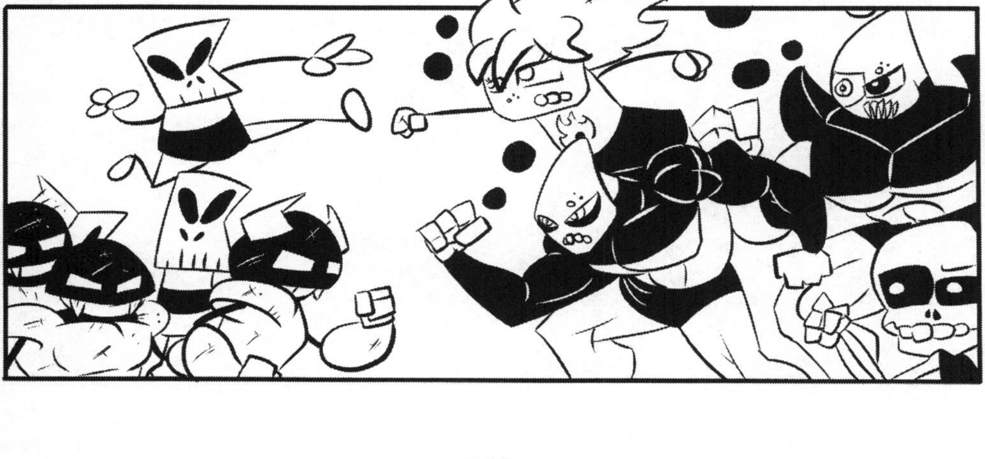

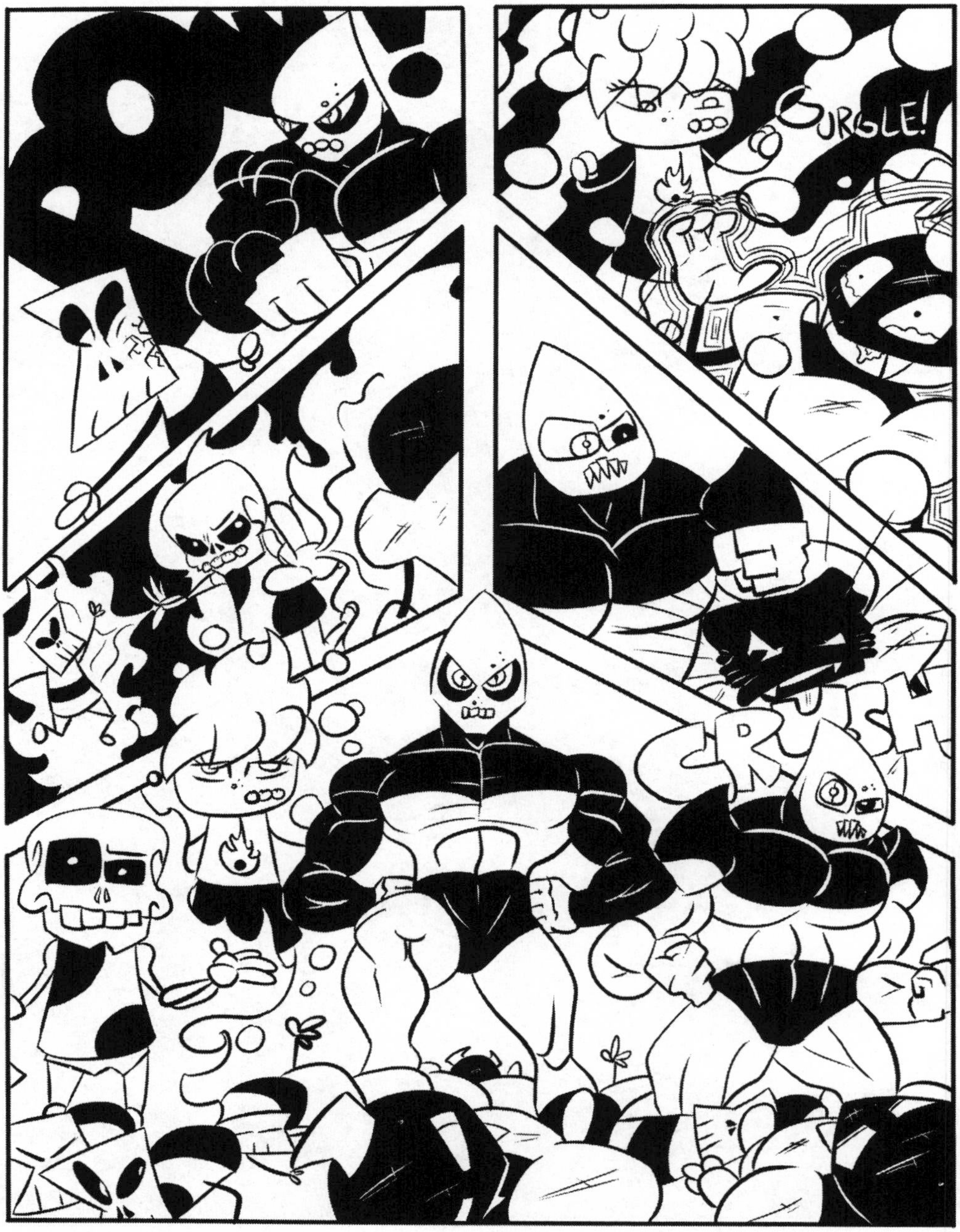
GURGLE!
CRUSH

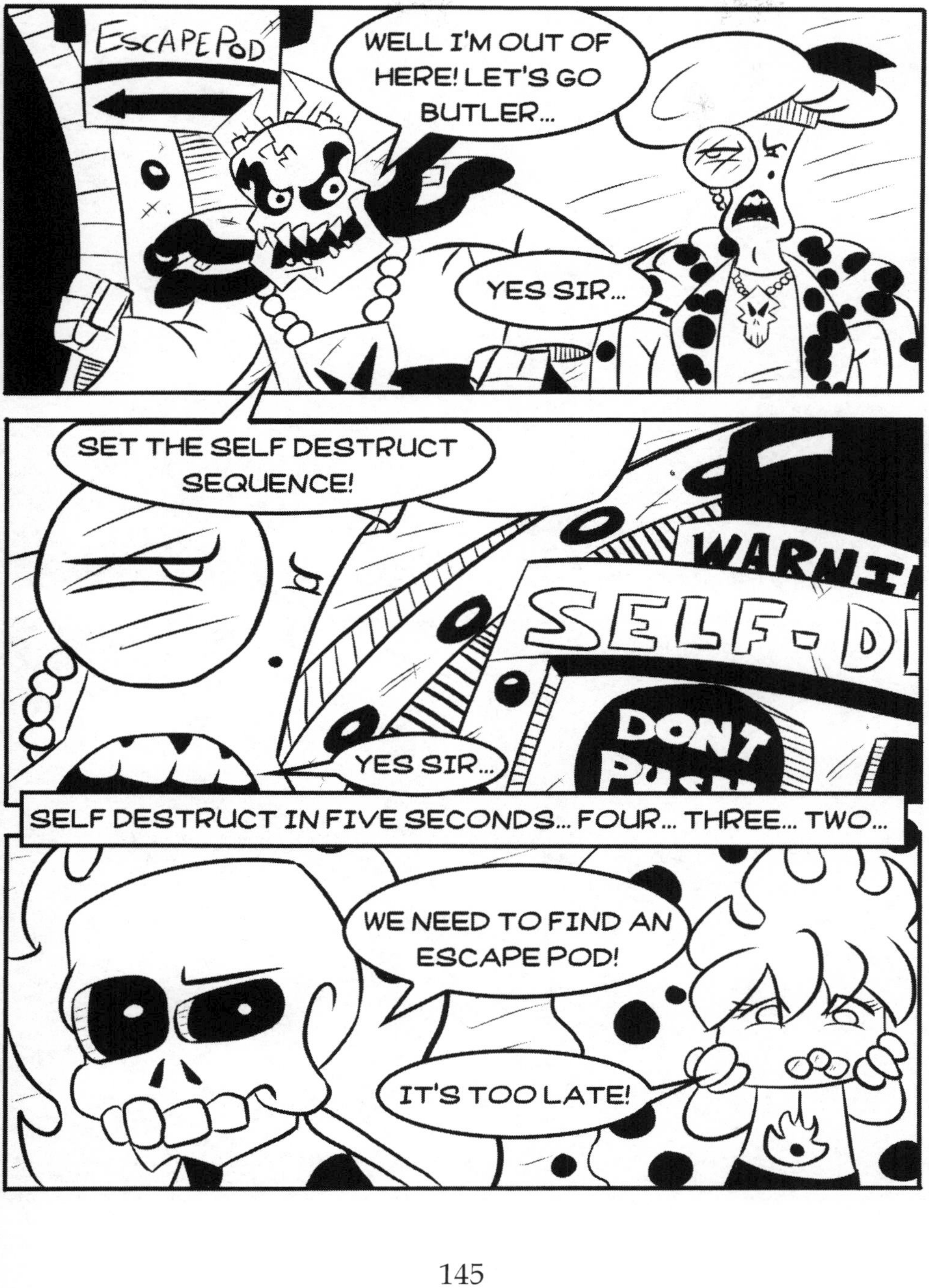
ESCAPE POD
WELL I'M OUT OF HERE! LET'S GO BUTLER...
YES SIR...
SET THE SELF DESTRUCT SEQUENCE!
DONT
YES SIR...
SELF DESTRUCT IN FIVE SECONDS... FOUR... THREE... TWO...
WE NEED TO FIND AN ESCAPE POD!
IT'S TOO LATE!

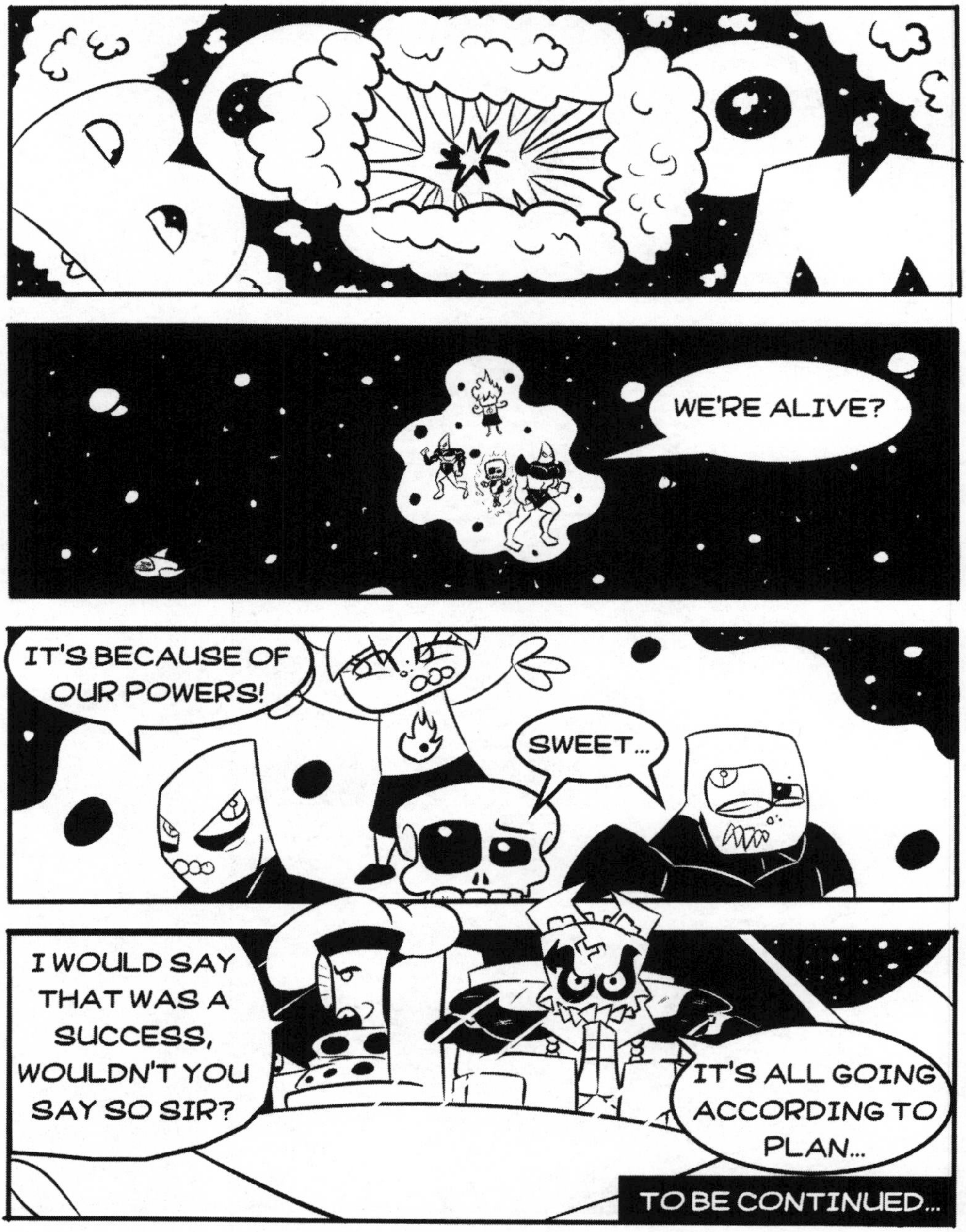
WE'RE ALIVE?
IT'S BECAUSE OF OUR POWERS!
SWEET...
I WOULD SAY THAT WAS A SUCCESS, WOULDN'T YOU SAY SO SIR?
IT'S ALL GOING ACCORDING TO PLAN...
TO BE CONTINUED...

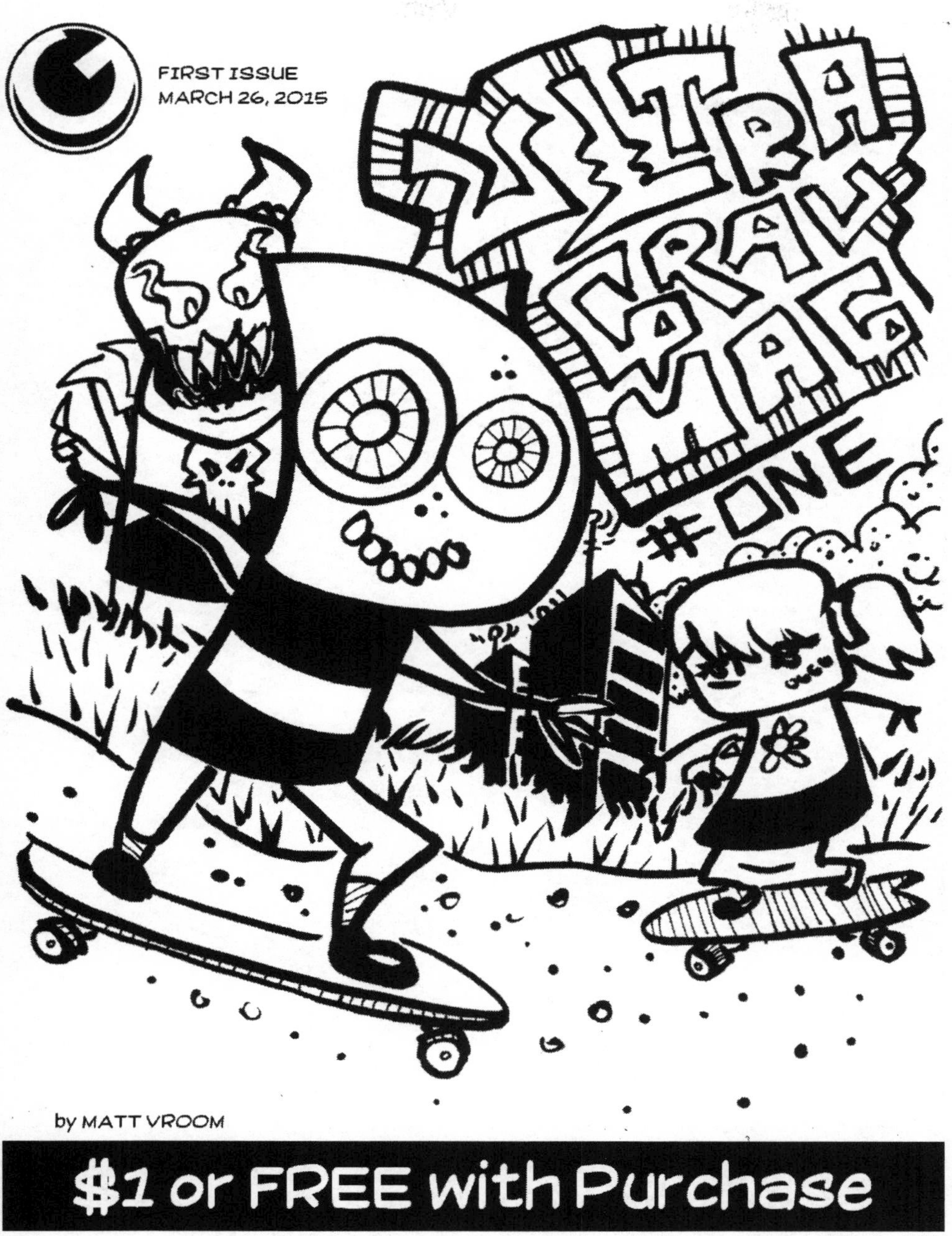
FIRST ISSUE
MARCH 26, 2015
ULTRA CRAY MAG
#ONE
by MATT VROOM
$1 or FREE with Purchase

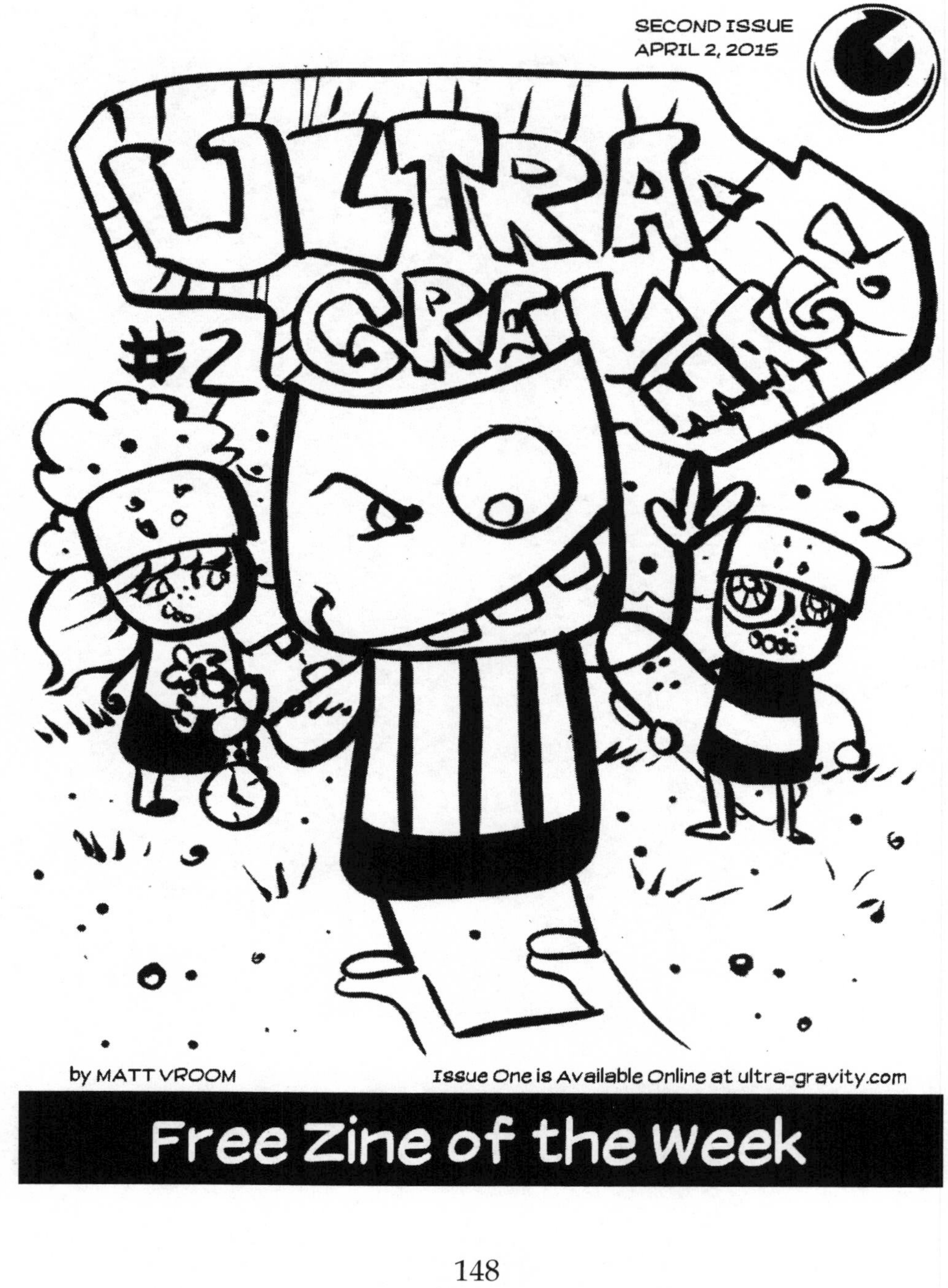
SECOND ISSUE
APRIL 2, 2015
ULTRA
#2
by MATT VROOM
Issue One is Available Online at ultra-gravity.com
Free Zine of the Week

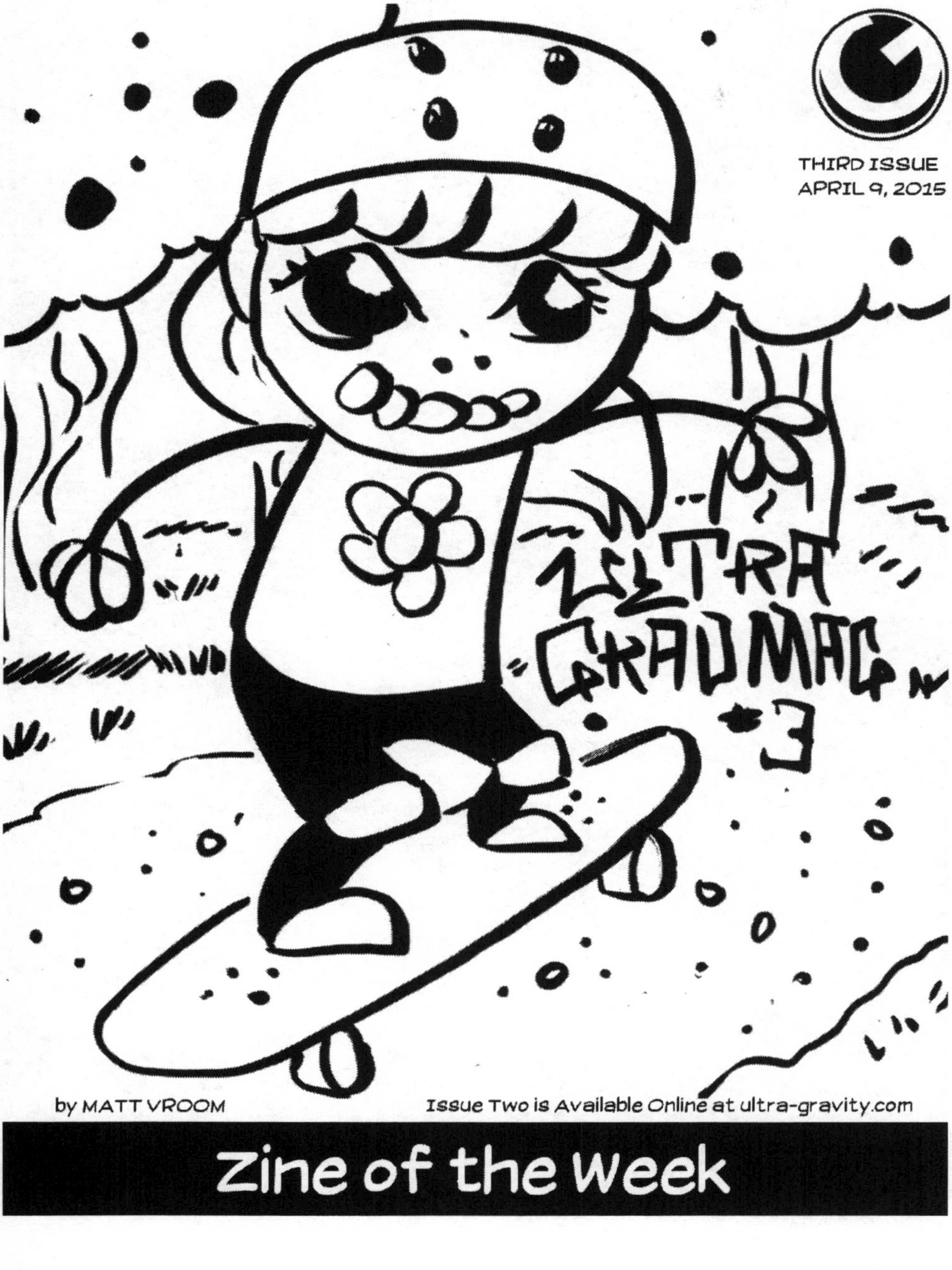
THIRD ISSUE
APRIL 9, 2015
ULTRA GRAVMAG
#3
by MATT VROOM
Issue Two is Available Online at ultra-gravity.com
Zine of the Week

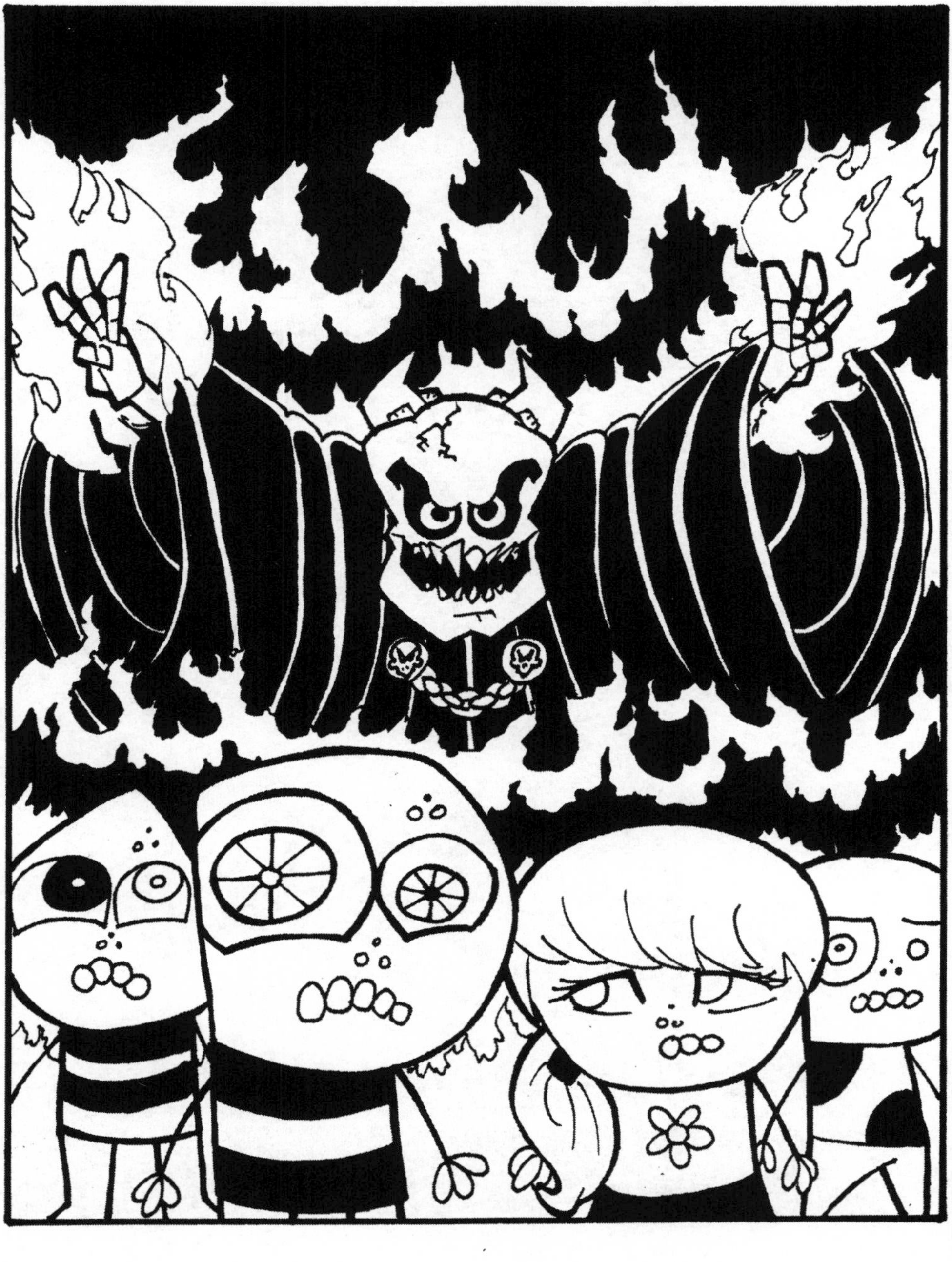

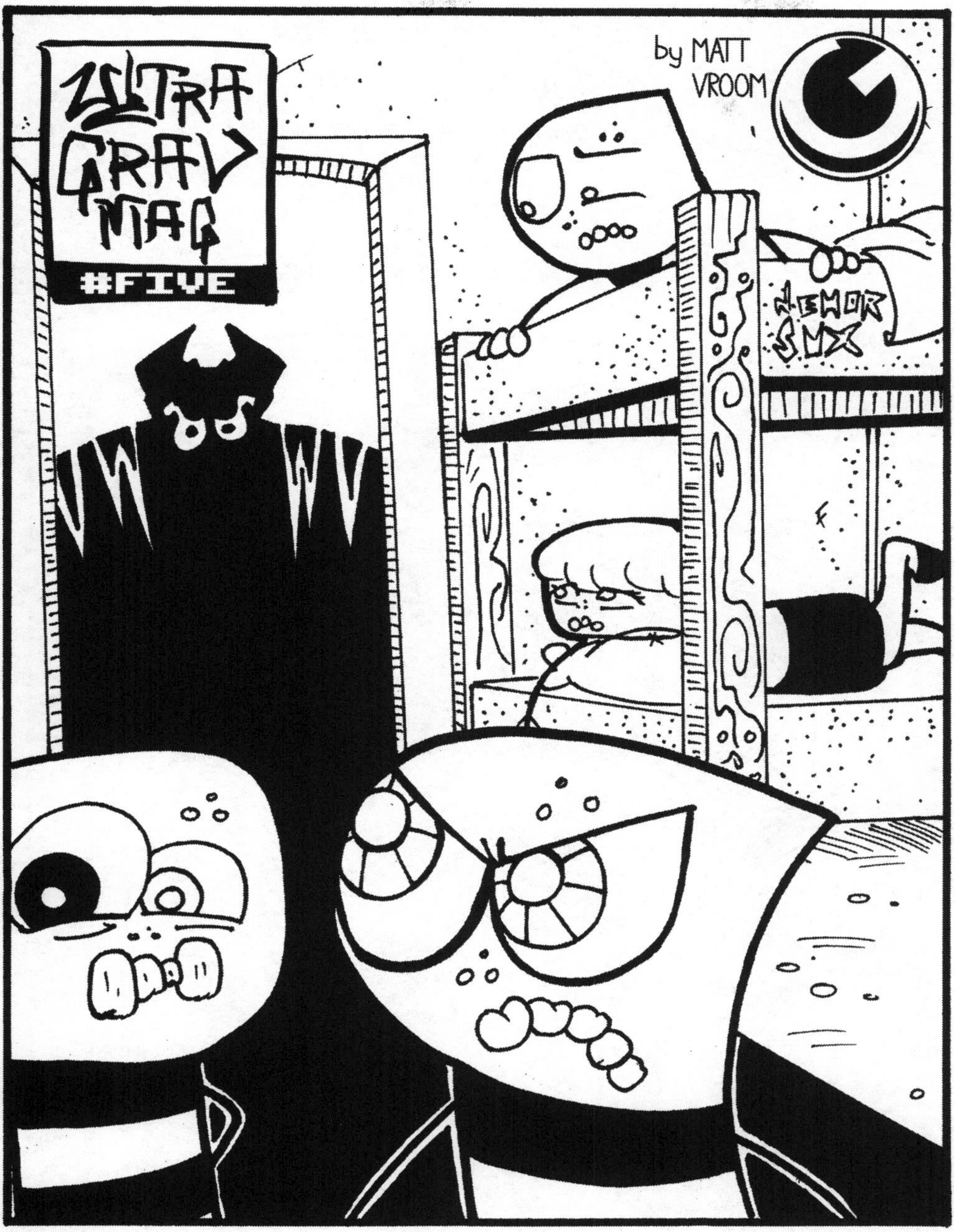
ULTRA GRAV MAG
#FIVE
by MATT VROOM
DEMOR SUX

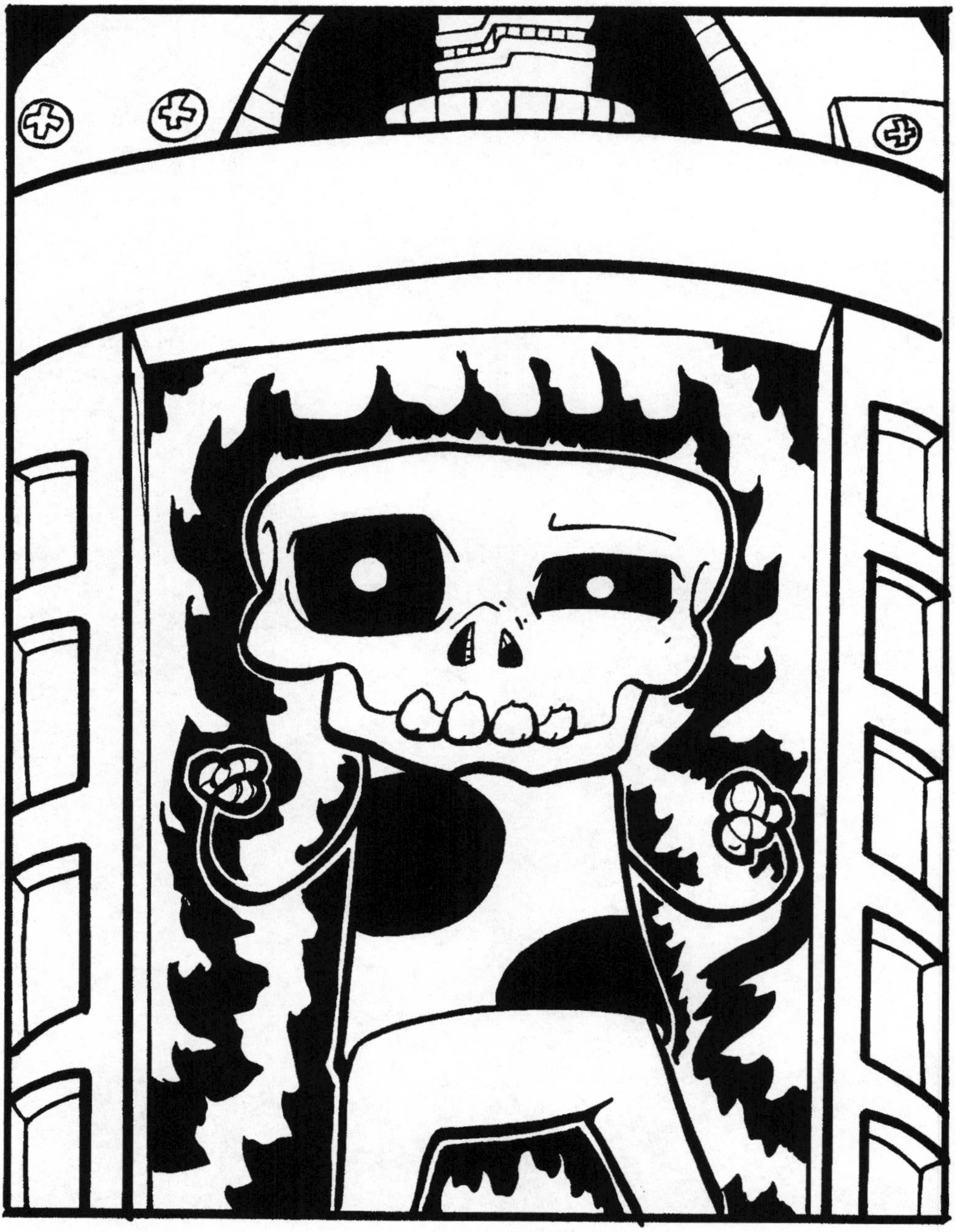

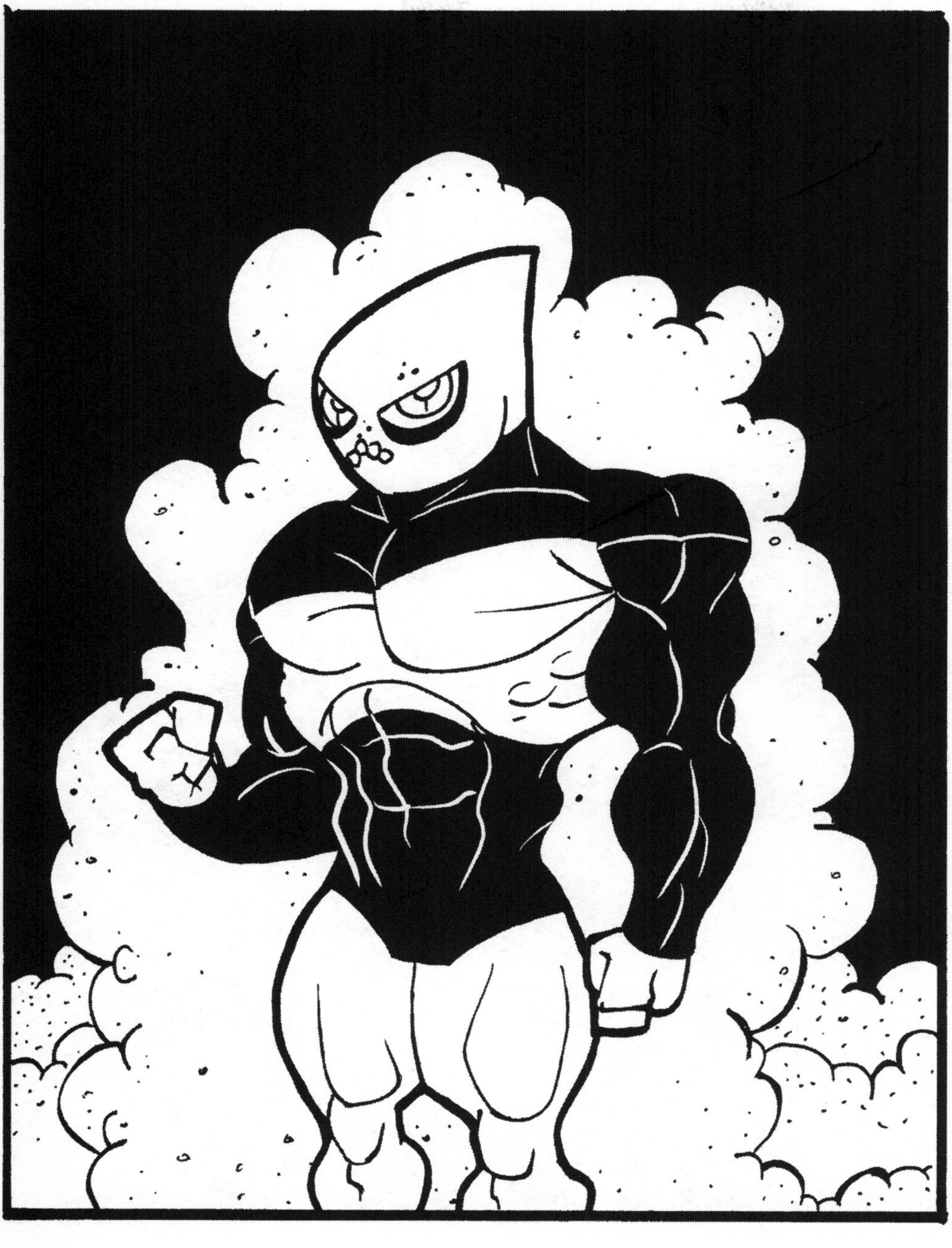

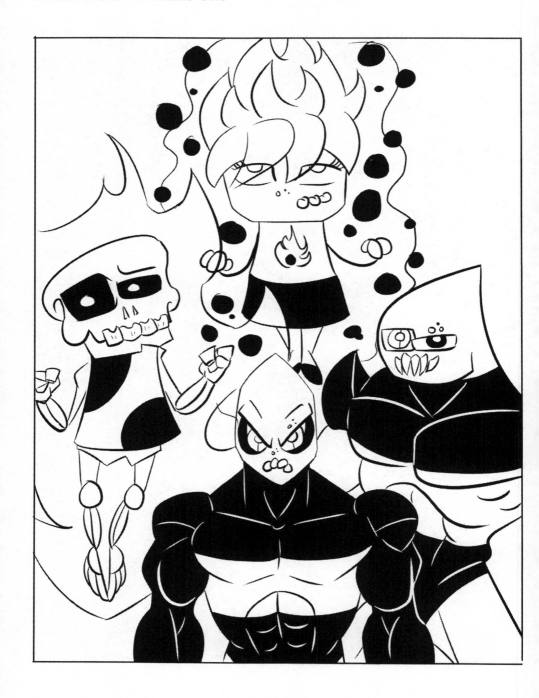

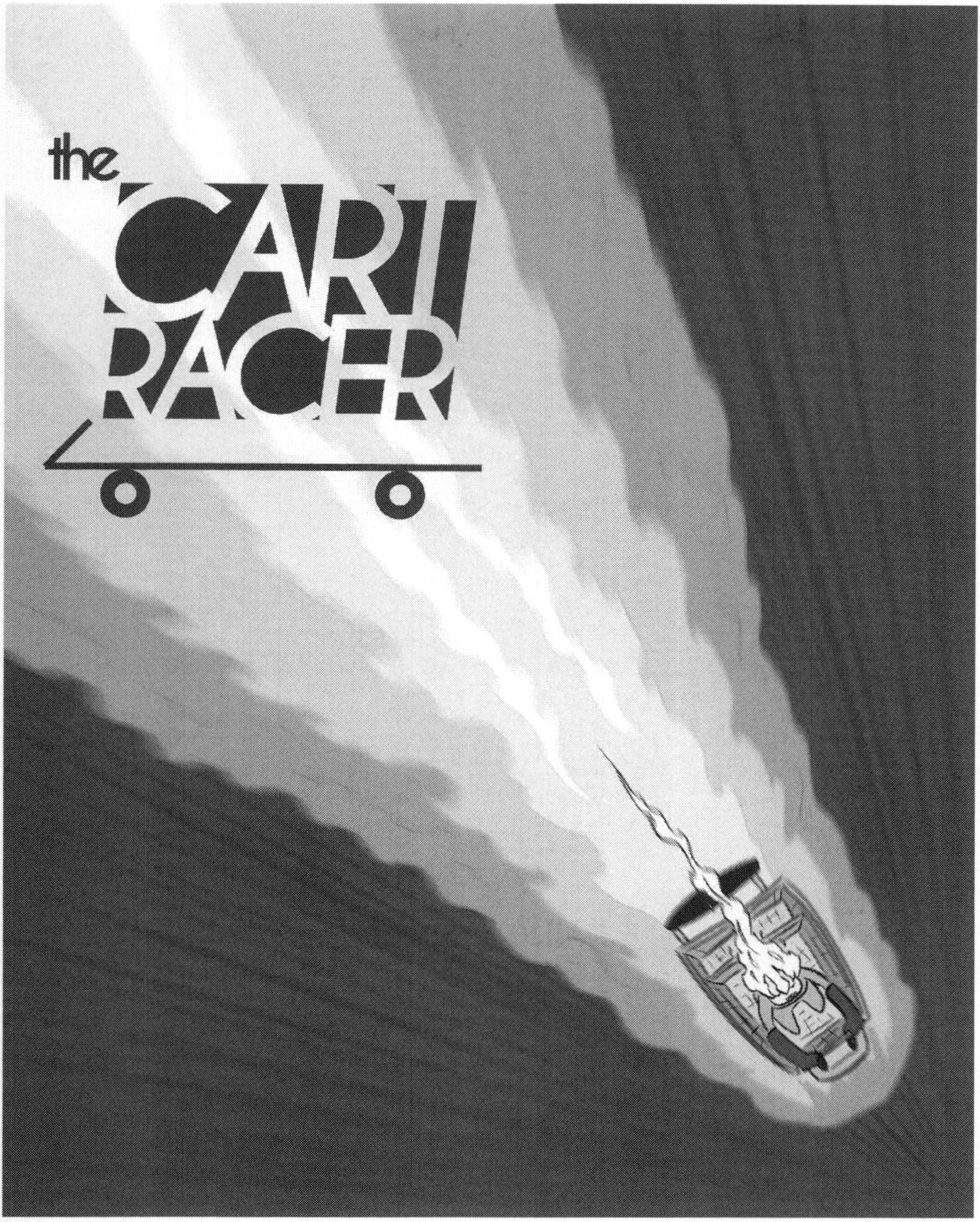
the
CART
RACER

MATT'S NOTES:

This comic was originally created to be a filler episode to introduce a character that we wanted to use in a sequel. After creating the character I decided that she will ultimately be served as the main antagonist in Planet Ultra II: The Cart Racer.

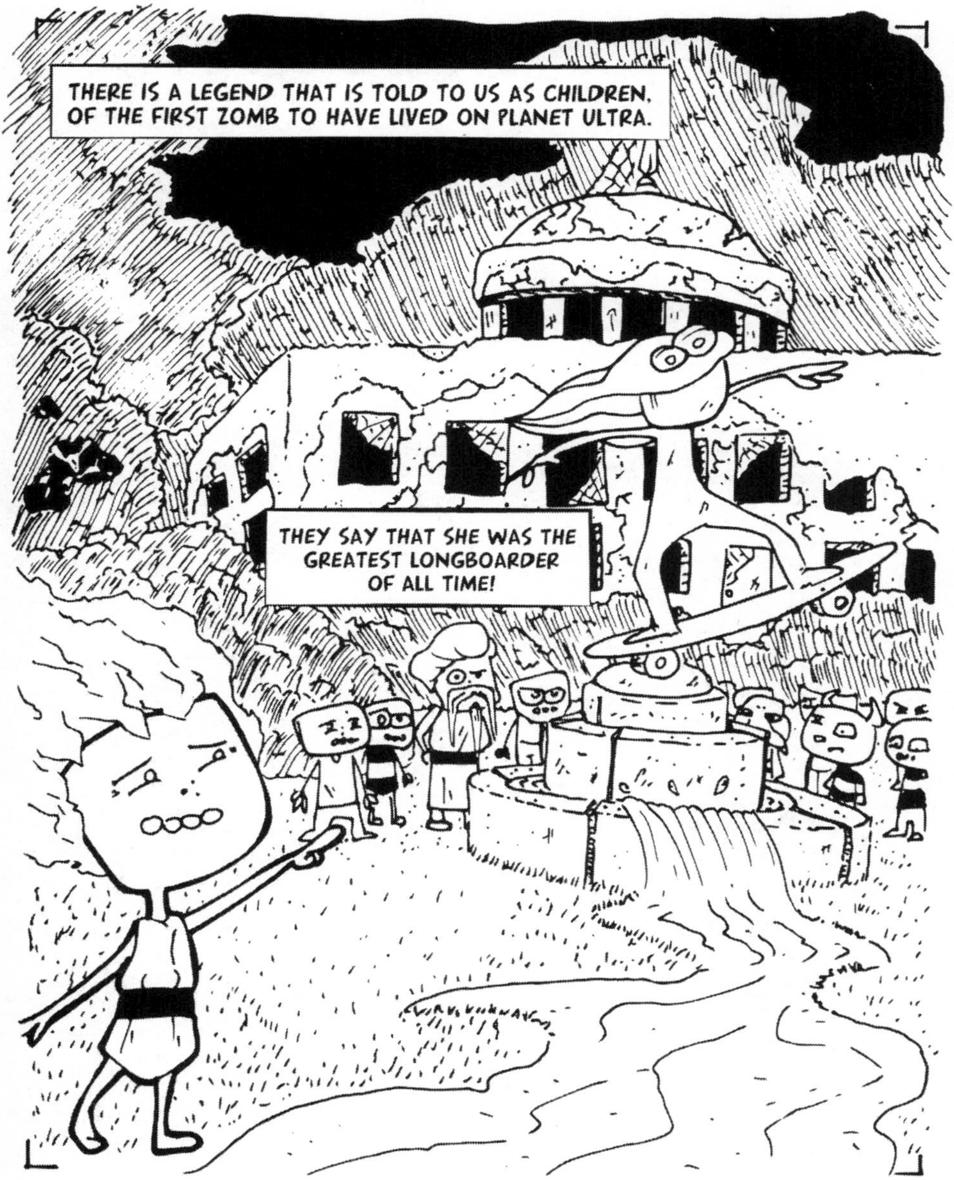
THERE IS A LEGEND THAT IS TOLD TO US AS CHILDREN, OF THE FIRST ZOMB TO HAVE LIVED ON PLANET ULTRA.
THEY SAY THAT SHE WAS THE GREATEST LONGBOARDER OF ALL TIME!

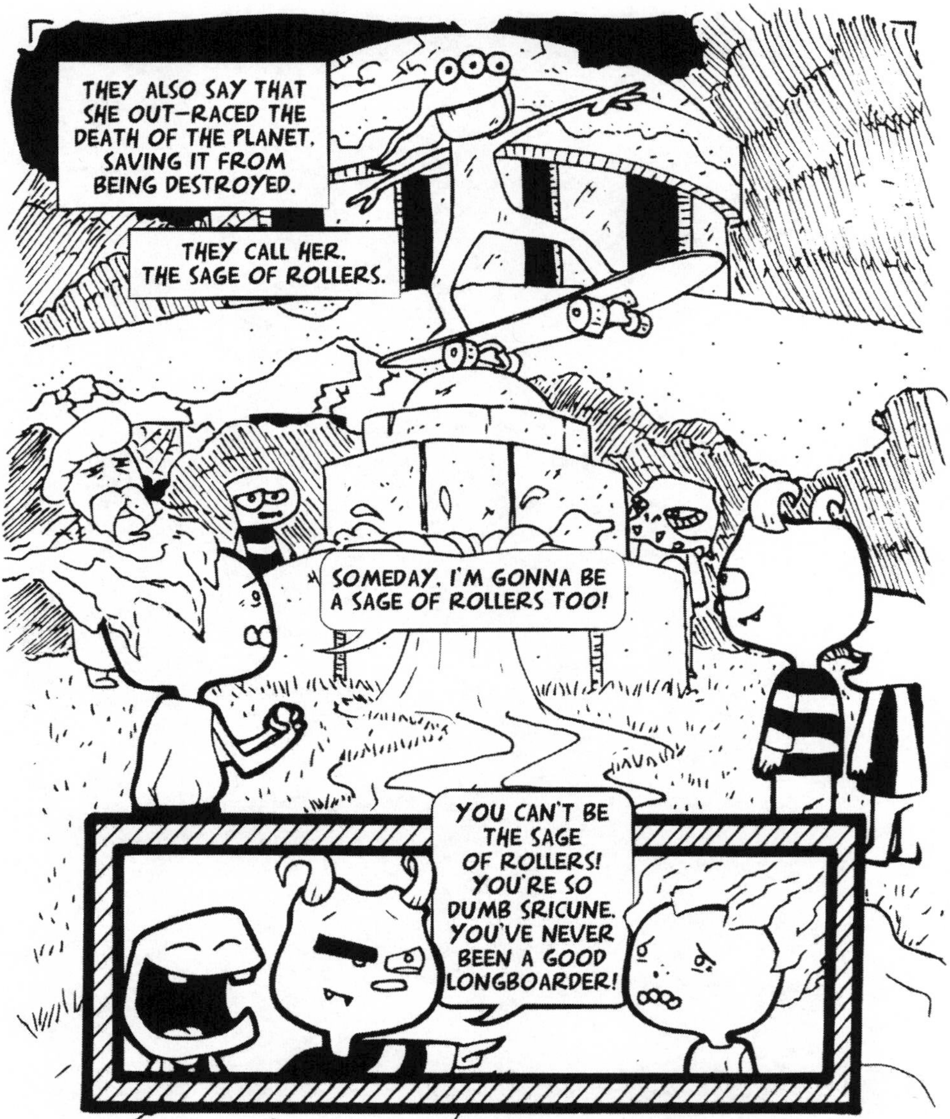
THEY ALSO SAY THAT SHE OUT-RACED THE DEATH OF THE PLANET. SAVING IT FROM BEING DESTROYED.
THEY CALL HER. THE SAGE OF ROLLERS.
SOMEDAY. I'M GONNA BE A SAGE OF ROLLERS TOO!
YOU CAN'T BE THE SAGE OF ROLLERS! YOU'RE SO DUMB SRICUNE. YOU'VE NEVER BEEN A GOOD LONGBOARDER!

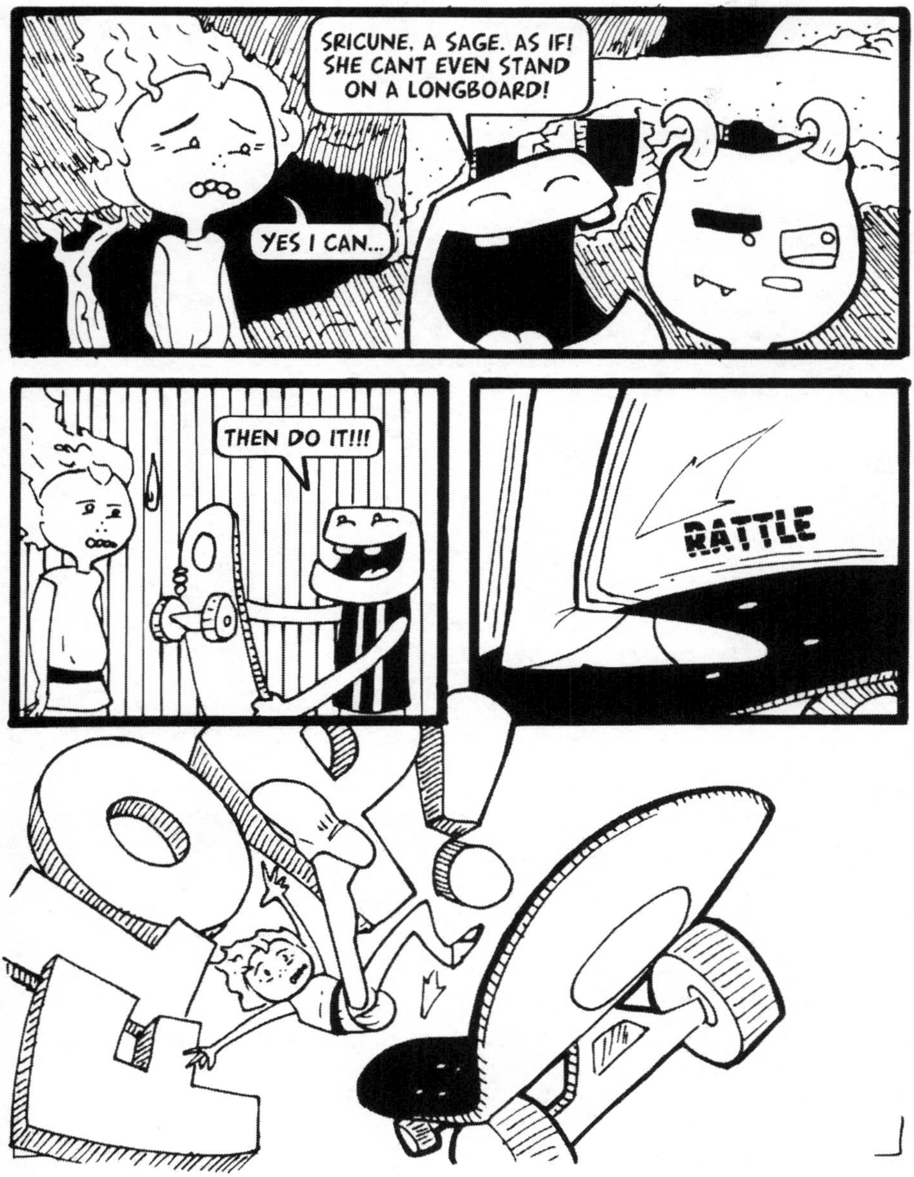
SRICUNE, A SAGE. AS IF! SHE CANT EVEN STAND ON A LONGBOARD!
YES I CAN...
THEN DO IT!!!
RATTLE

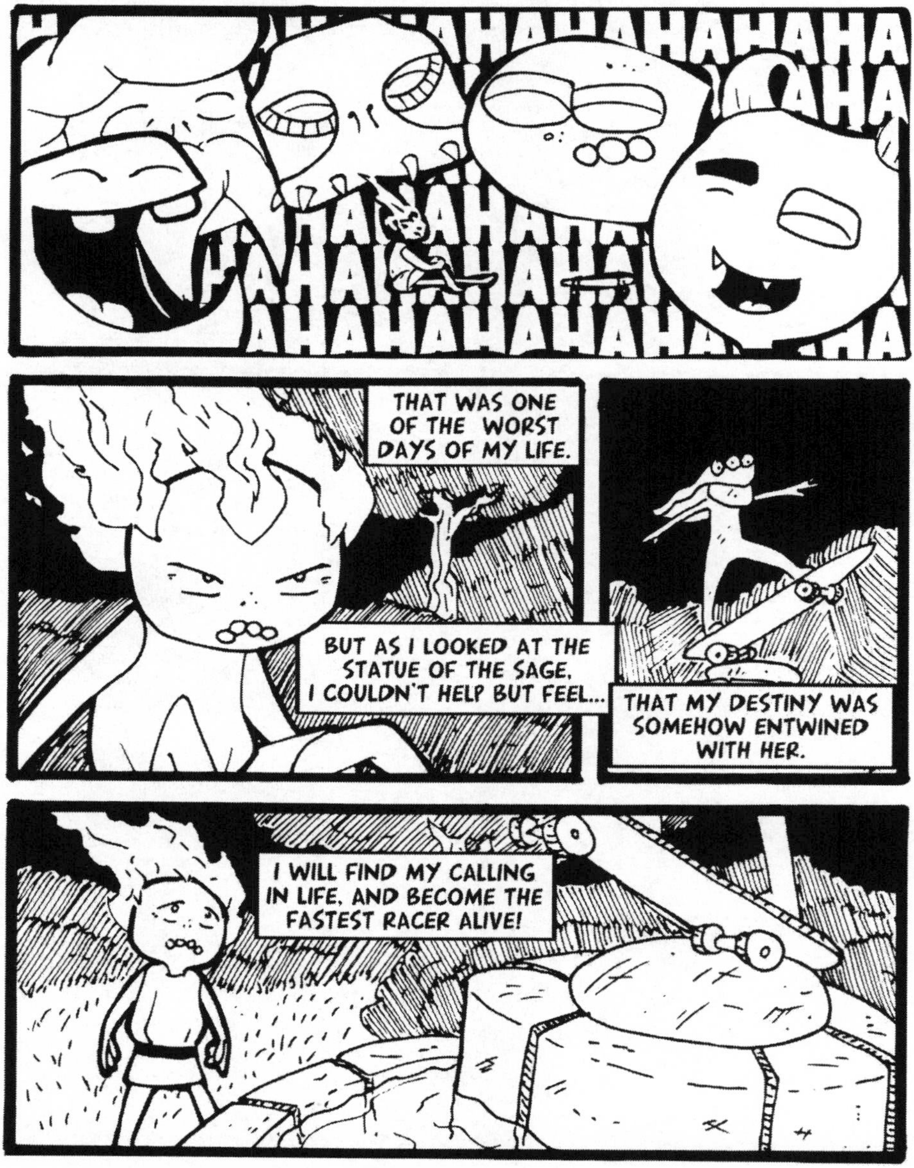
HAHAHAHAHAHA
THAT WAS ONE OF THE WORST DAYS OF MY LIFE.
BUT AS I LOOKED AT THE STATUE OF THE SAGE, I COULDN'T HELP BUT FEEL...
THAT MY DESTINY WAS SOMEHOW ENTWINED WITH HER.
I WILL FIND MY CALLING IN LIFE, AND BECOME THE FASTEST RACER ALIVE!

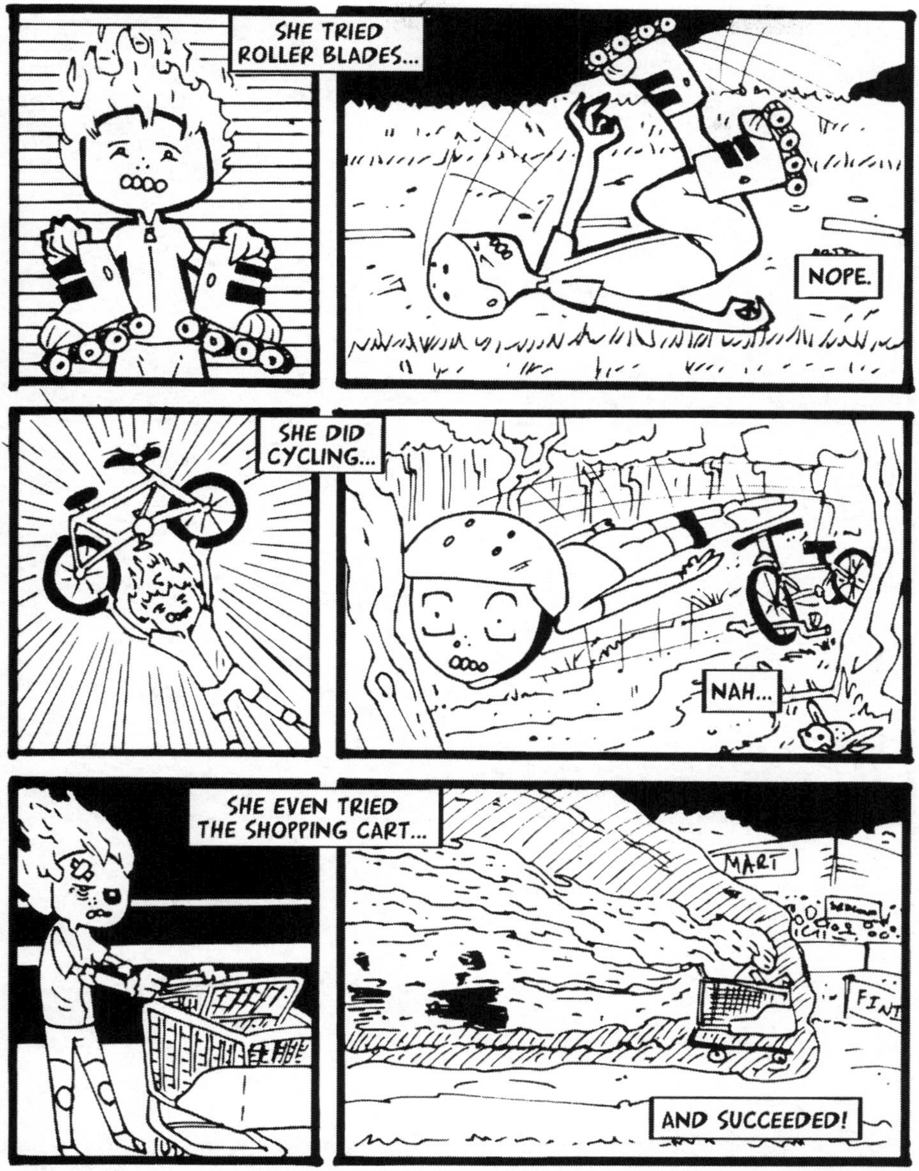
SHE TRIED ROLLER BLADES...
NOPE.
SHE DID CYCLING...
NAH...
SHE EVEN TRIED THE SHOPPING CART...
MART
AND SUCCEEDED!

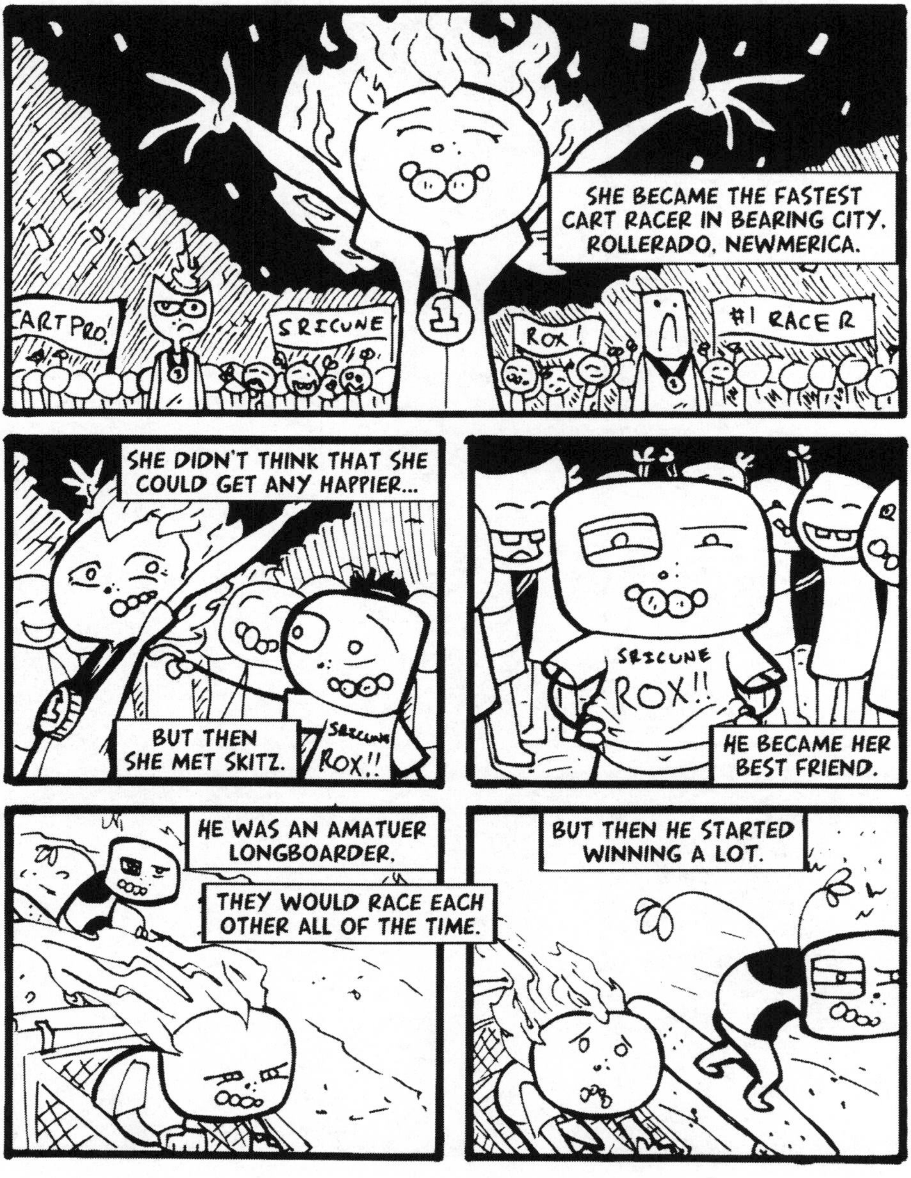
SHE BECAME THE FASTEST CART RACER IN BEARING CITY, ROLLERADO, NEWMERICA.
CART PRO!
SRICUNE
ROX!
#1 RACER
SHE DIDN'T THINK THAT SHE COULD GET ANY HAPPIER...
BUT THEN SHE MET SKITZ.
SRICUNE ROX!!
SRICUNE ROX!!
HE BECAME HER BEST FRIEND.
HE WAS AN AMATUER LONGBOARDER.
THEY WOULD RACE EACH OTHER ALL OF THE TIME.
BUT THEN HE STARTED WINNING A LOT.

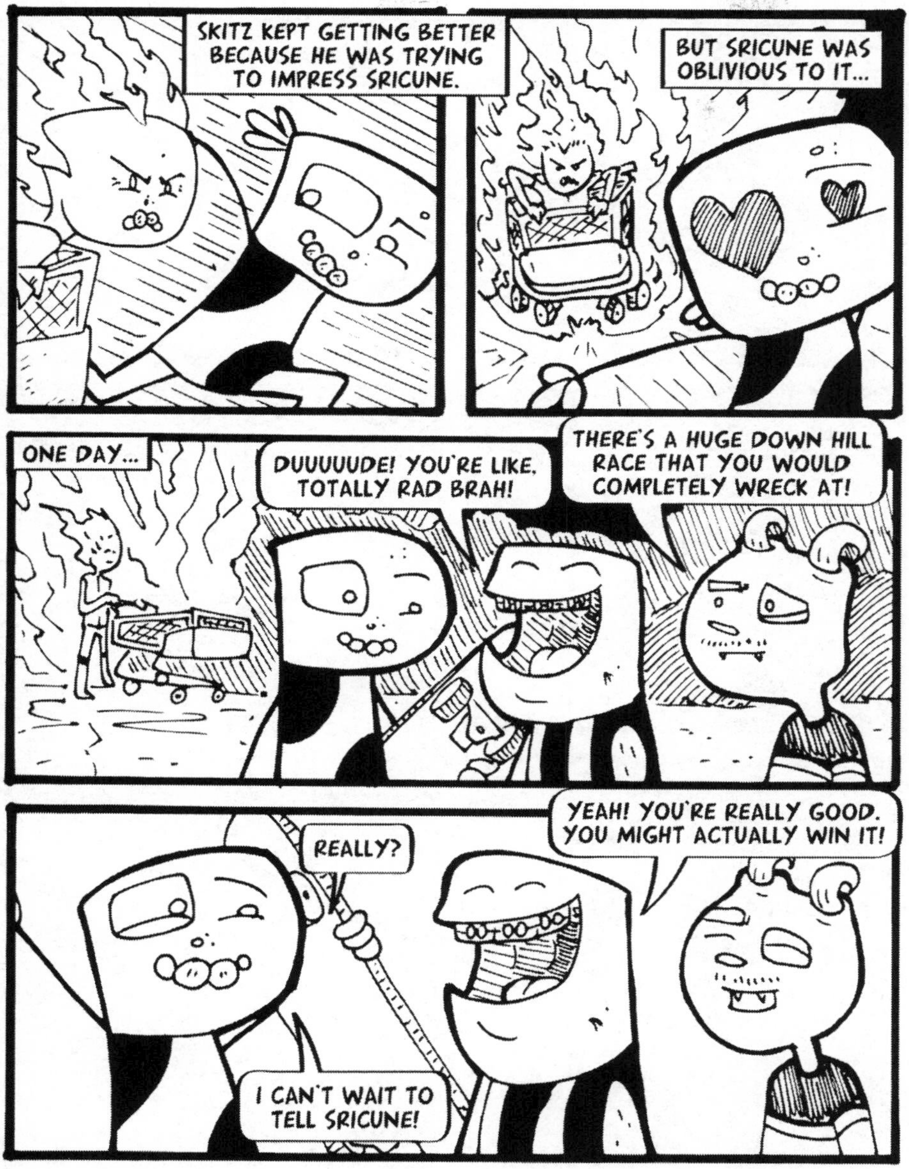
SKITZ KEPT GETTING BETTER BECAUSE HE WAS TRYING TO IMPRESS SRICUNE.
BUT SRICUNE WAS OBLIVIOUS TO IT...
ONE DAY...
DUUUUUDE! YOU'RE LIKE. TOTALLY RAD BRAH!
THERE'S A HUGE DOWN HILL RACE THAT YOU WOULD COMPLETELY WRECK AT!
REALLY?
YEAH! YOU'RE REALLY GOOD. YOU MIGHT ACTUALLY WIN IT!
I CAN'T WAIT TO TELL SRICUNE!

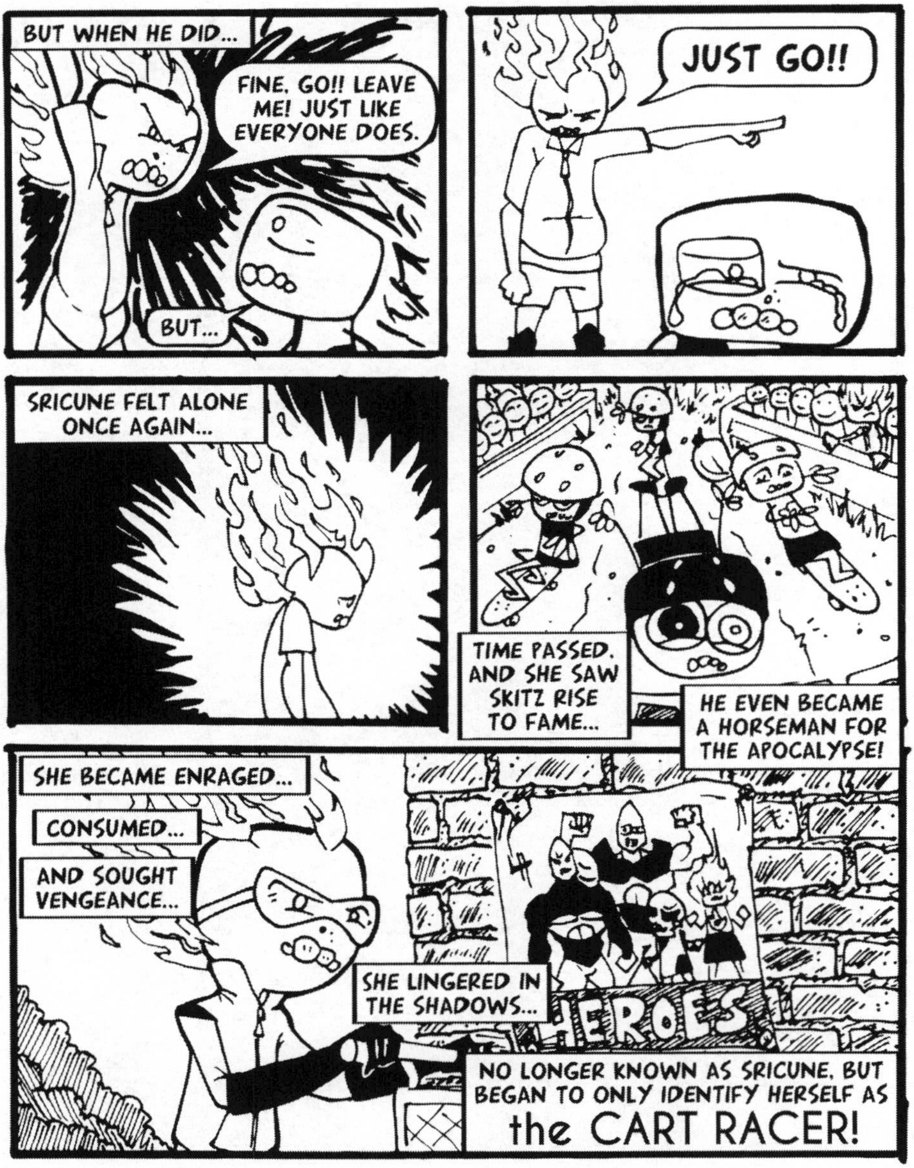
BUT WHEN HE DID...
FINE, GO!! LEAVE ME! JUST LIKE EVERYONE DOES.
BUT...
JUST GO!!
SRICUNE FELT ALONE ONCE AGAIN...
TIME PASSED, AND SHE SAW SKITZ RISE TO FAME...
HE EVEN BECAME A HORSEMAN FOR THE APOCALYPSE!
SHE BECAME ENRAGED...
CONSUMED...
AND SOUGHT VENGEANCE...
SHE LINGERED IN THE SHADOWS...
HEROES
NO LONGER KNOWN AS SRICUNE, BUT BEGAN TO ONLY IDENTIFY HERSELF AS
the CART RACER!

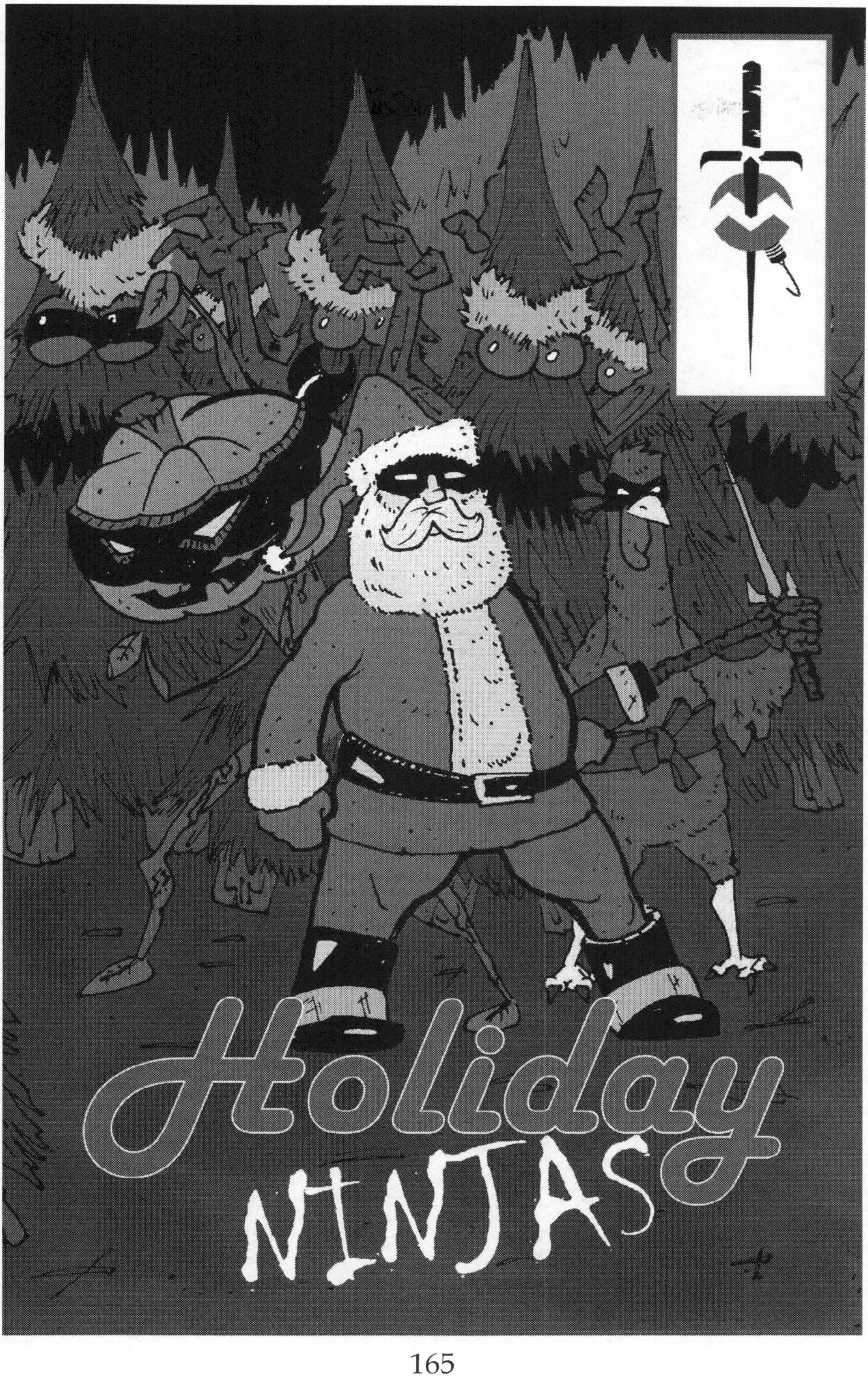
Holiday
NINJAS

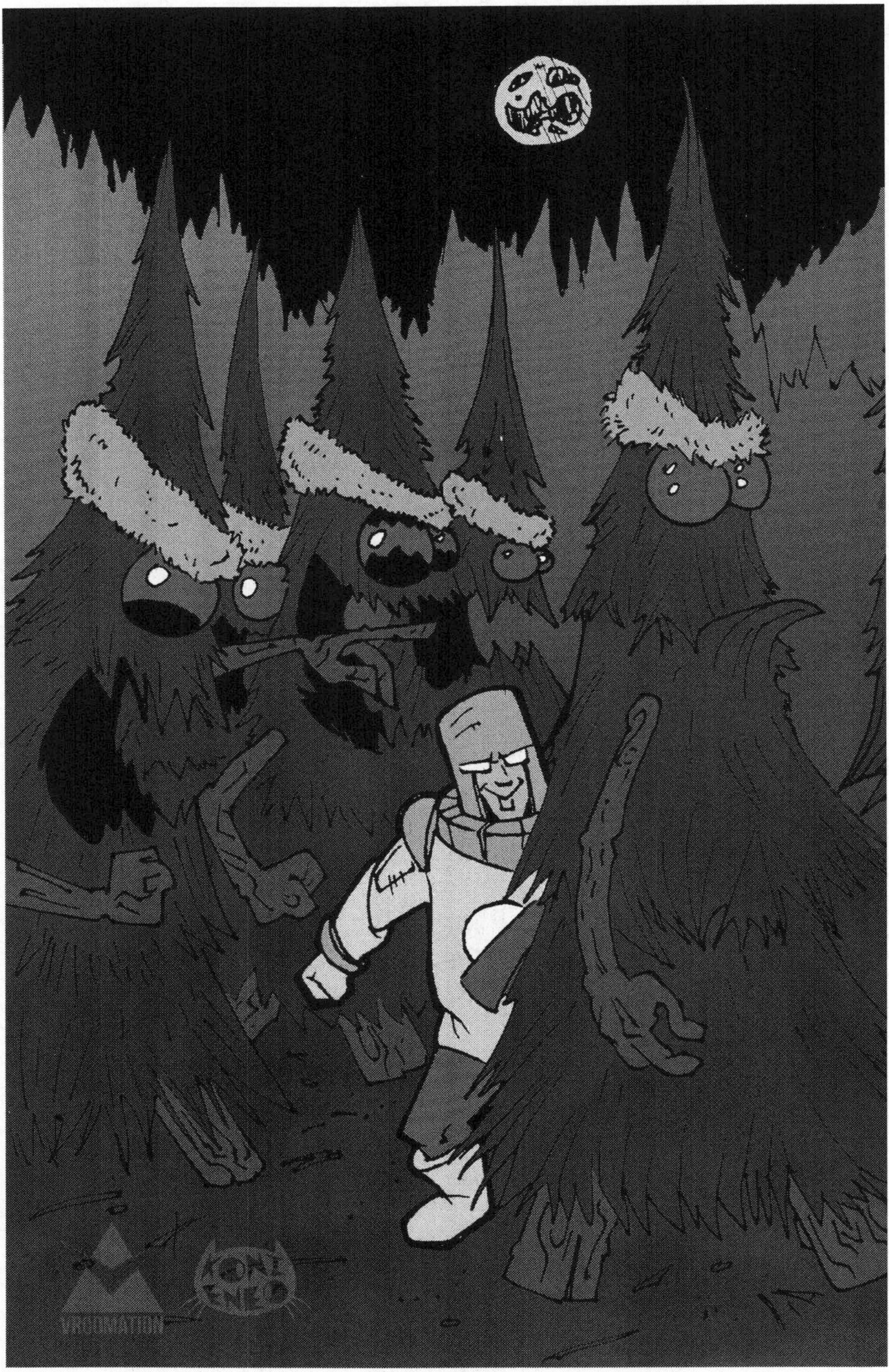

Holiday
NINJAS
BY MATT VROOM
PINE CITY, CALIF.
HE-HE-HE...

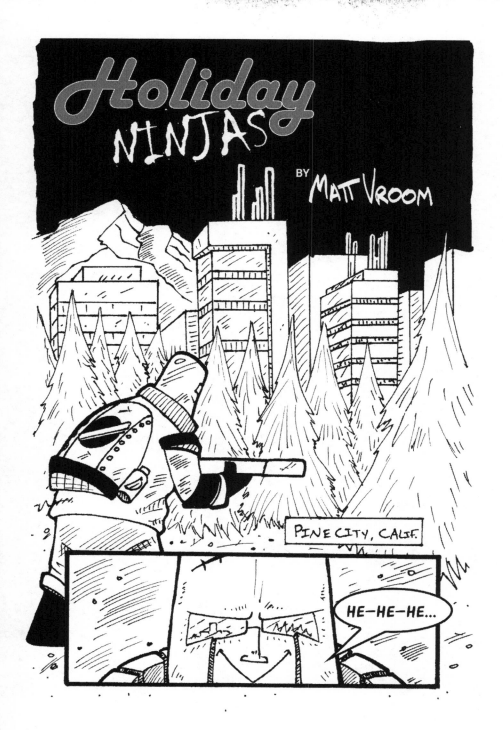

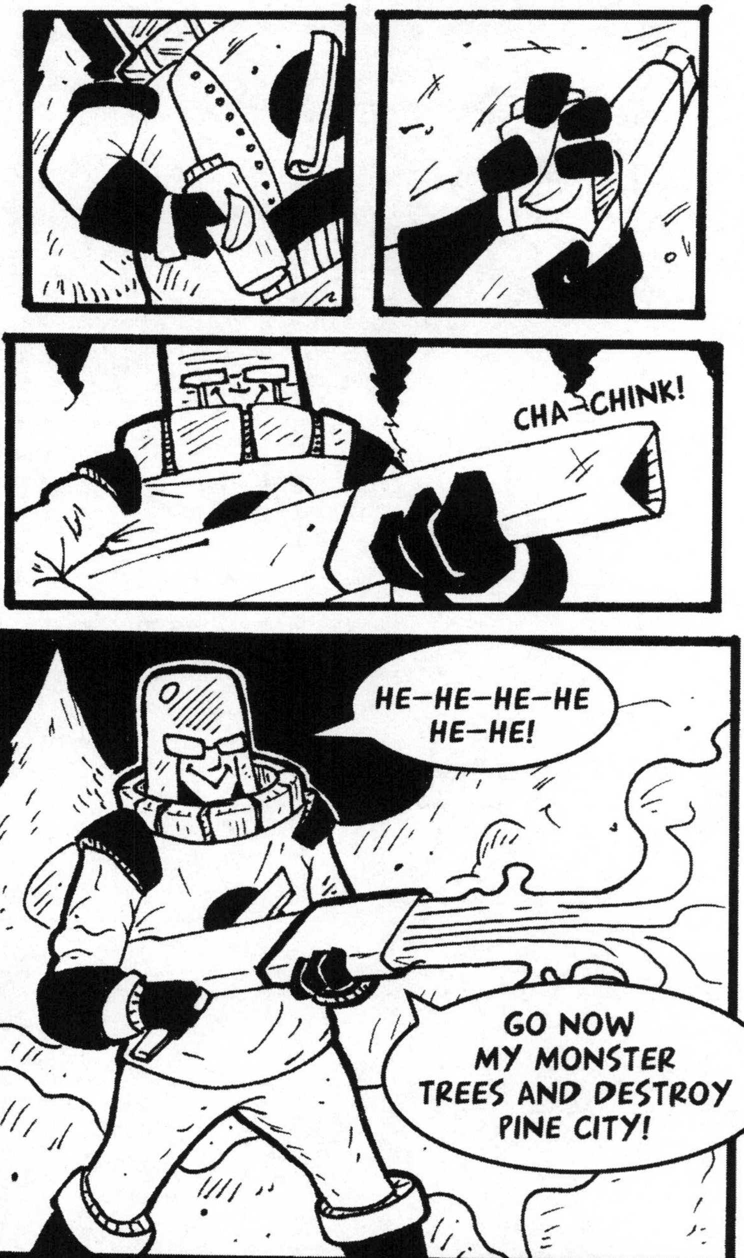
CHA-CHINK!
HE-HE-HE-HE HE-HE!
GO NOW MY MONSTER TREES AND DESTROY PINE CITY!

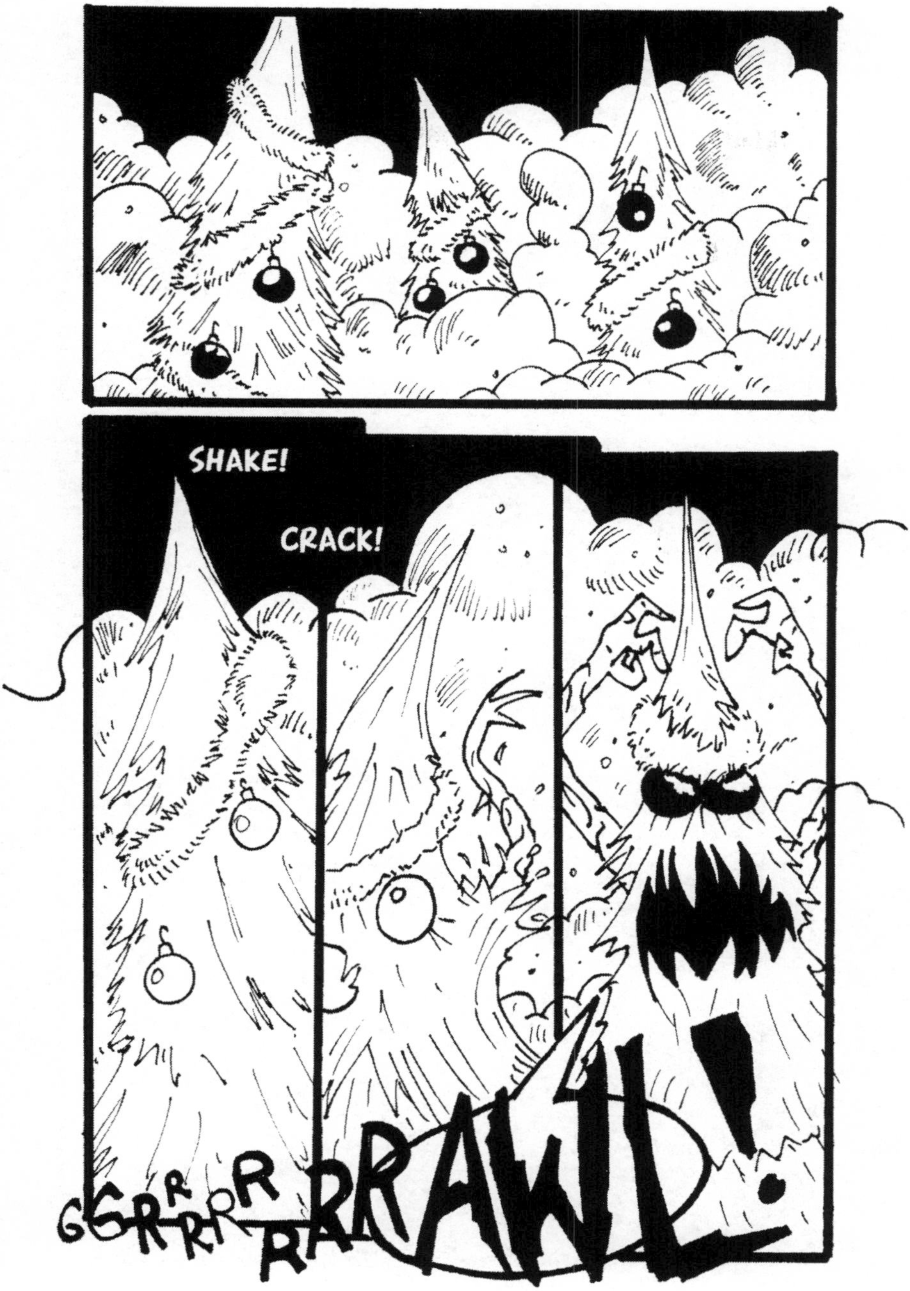
SHAKE!
CRACK!
GGRRRRRRRRAWL!

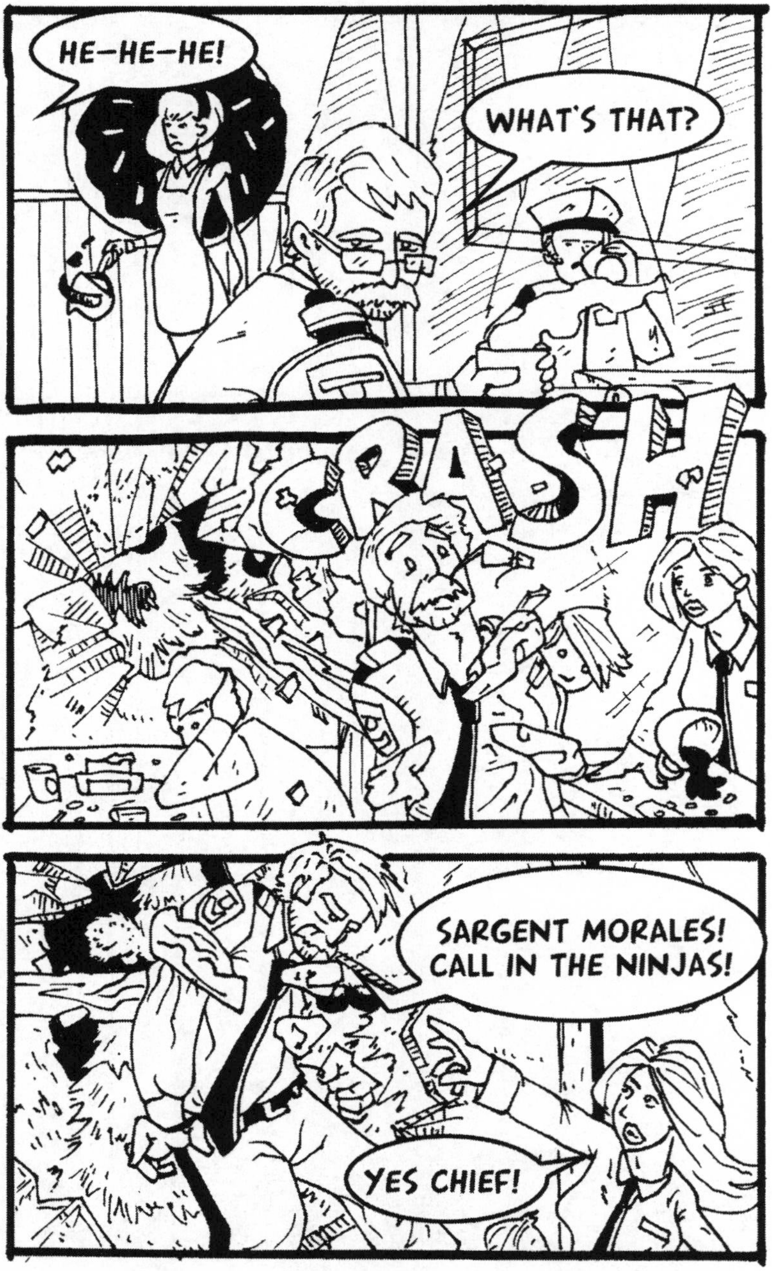
HE-HE-HE!
WHAT'S THAT?
CRASH
SARGENT MORALES! CALL IN THE NINJAS!
YES CHIEF!

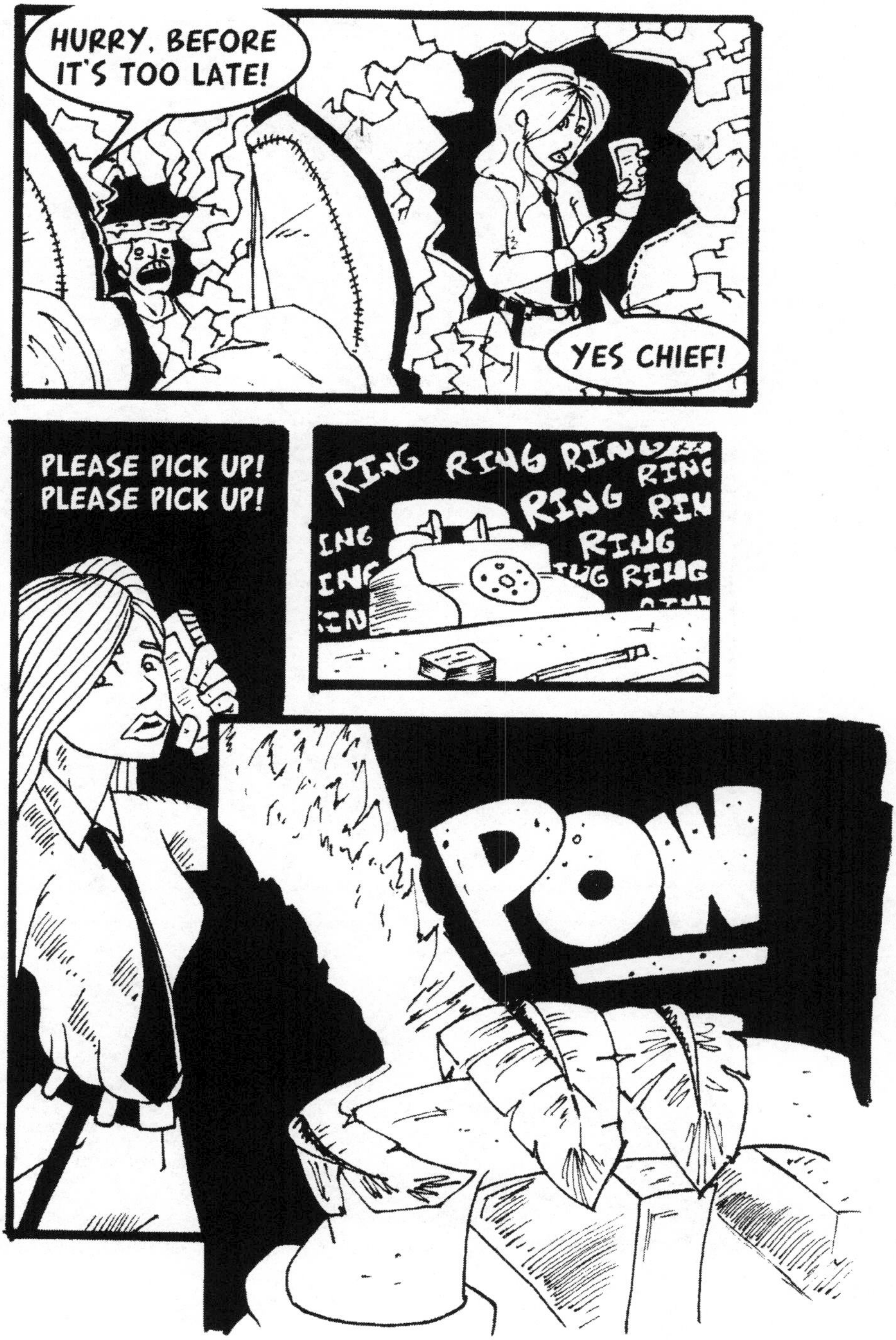
HURRY, BEFORE IT'S TOO LATE!
YES CHIEF!
PLEASE PICK UP! PLEASE PICK UP!
RING RING RING
RING
RING
RING
RING RING
POW

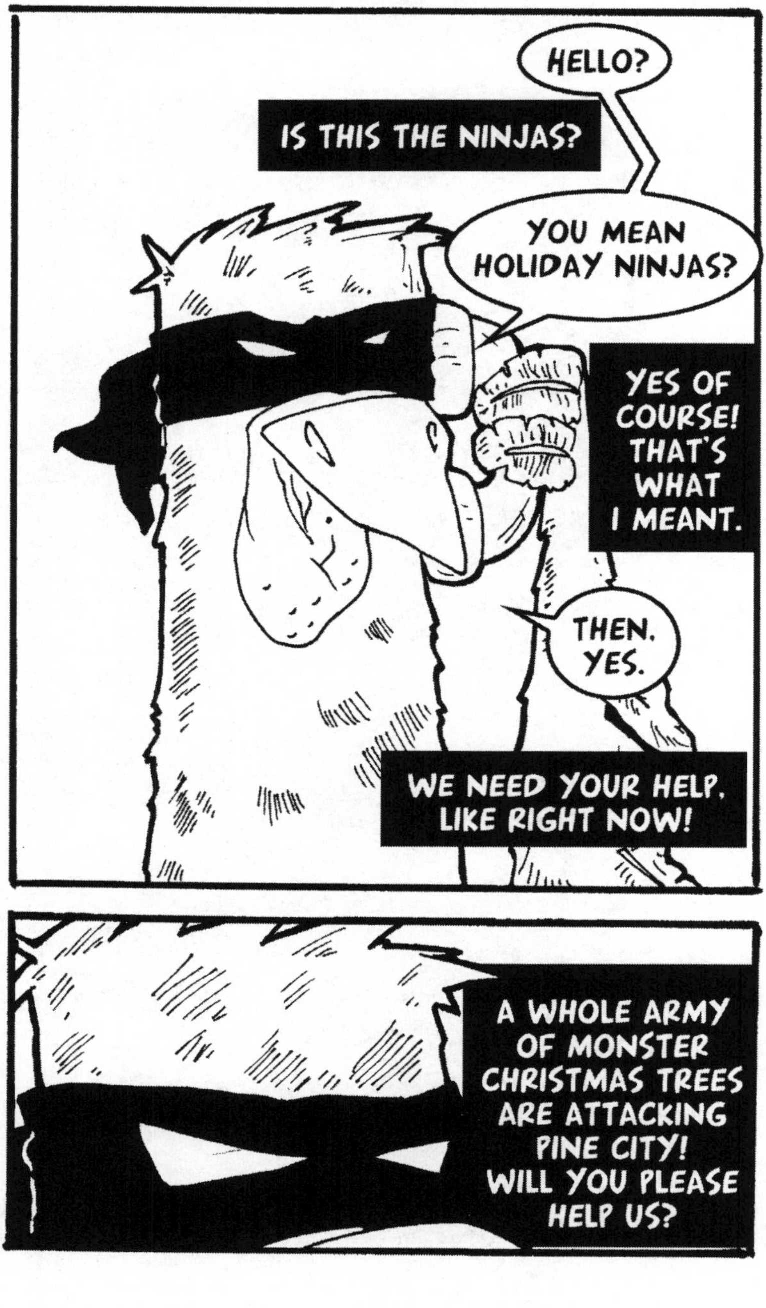
HELLO?
IS THIS THE NINJAS?
YOU MEAN HOLIDAY NINJAS?
YES OF COURSE! THAT'S WHAT I MEANT.
THEN. YES.
WE NEED YOUR HELP. LIKE RIGHT NOW!
A WHOLE ARMY OF MONSTER CHRISTMAS TREES ARE ATTACKING PINE CITY! WILL YOU PLEASE HELP US?

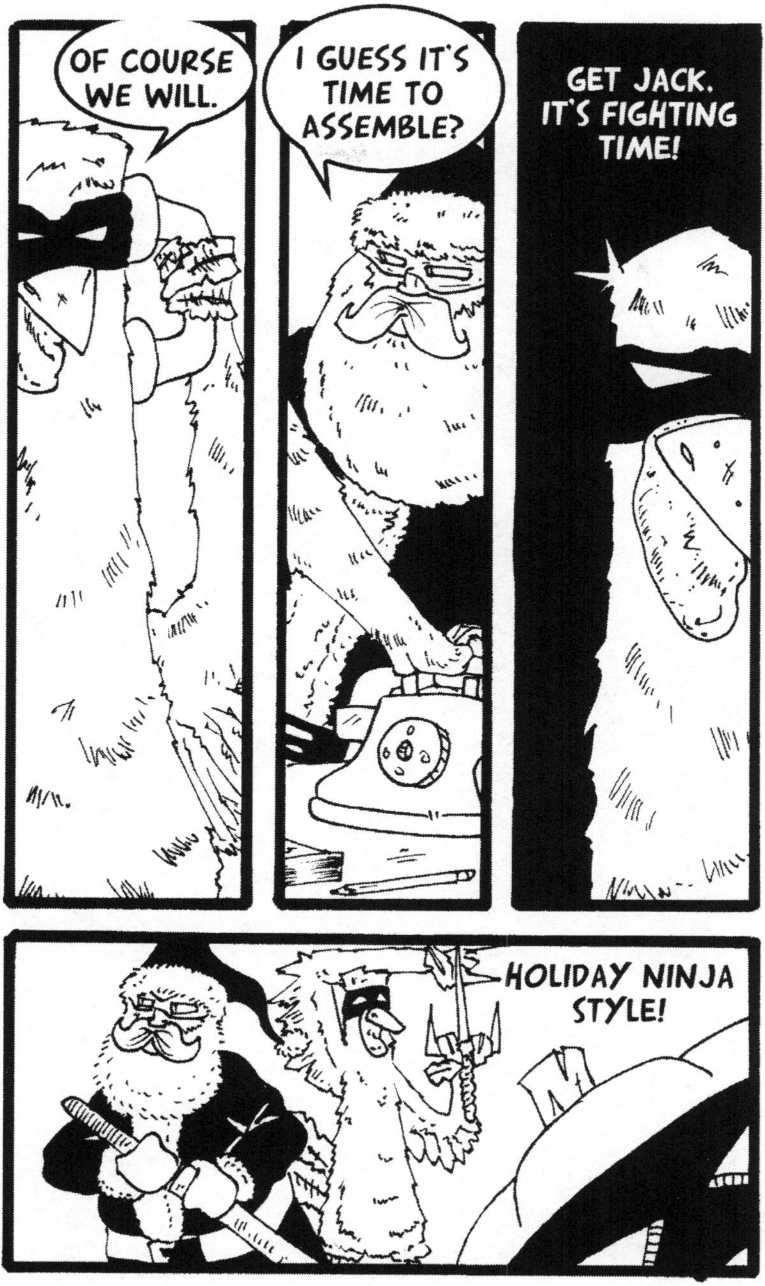
OF COURSE WE WILL.
I GUESS IT'S TIME TO ASSEMBLE?
GET JACK. IT'S FIGHTING TIME!
HOLIDAY NINJA STYLE!

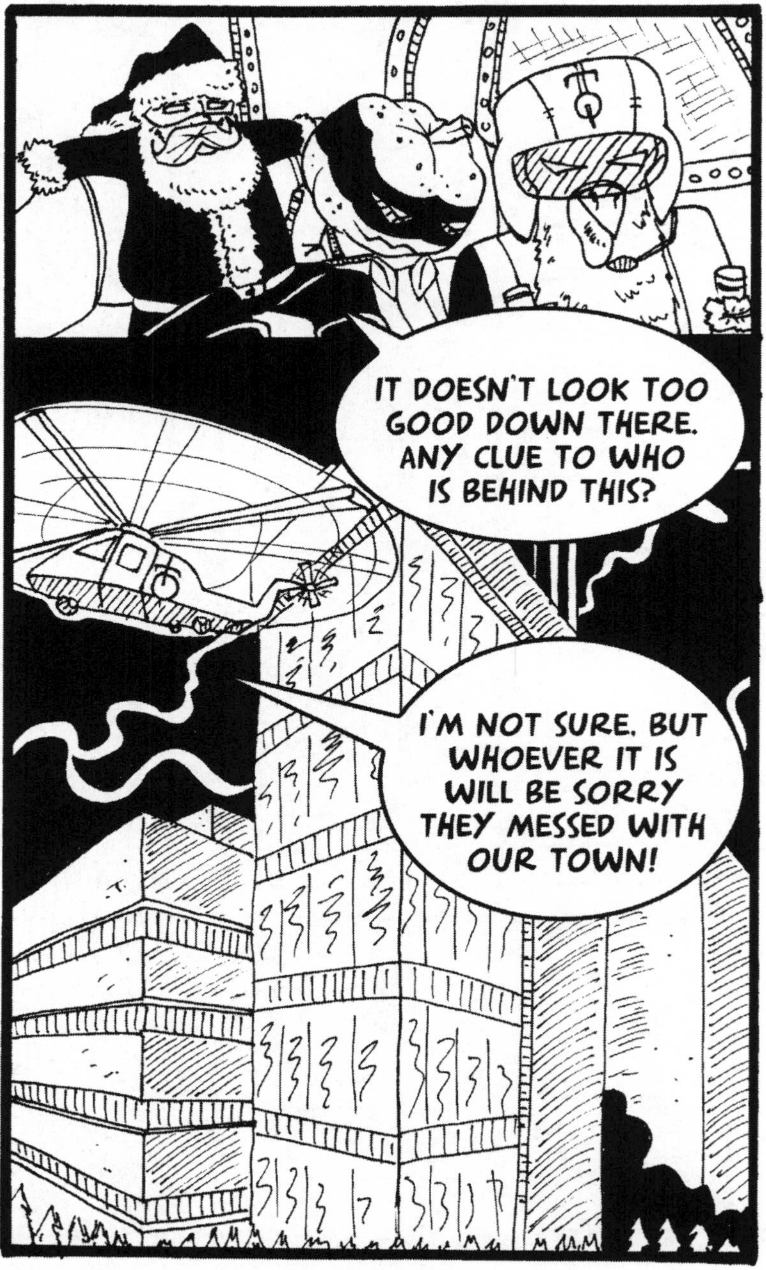
IT DOESN'T LOOK TOO GOOD DOWN THERE. ANY CLUE TO WHO IS BEHIND THIS?
I'M NOT SURE. BUT WHOEVER IT IS WILL BE SORRY THEY MESSED WITH OUR TOWN!

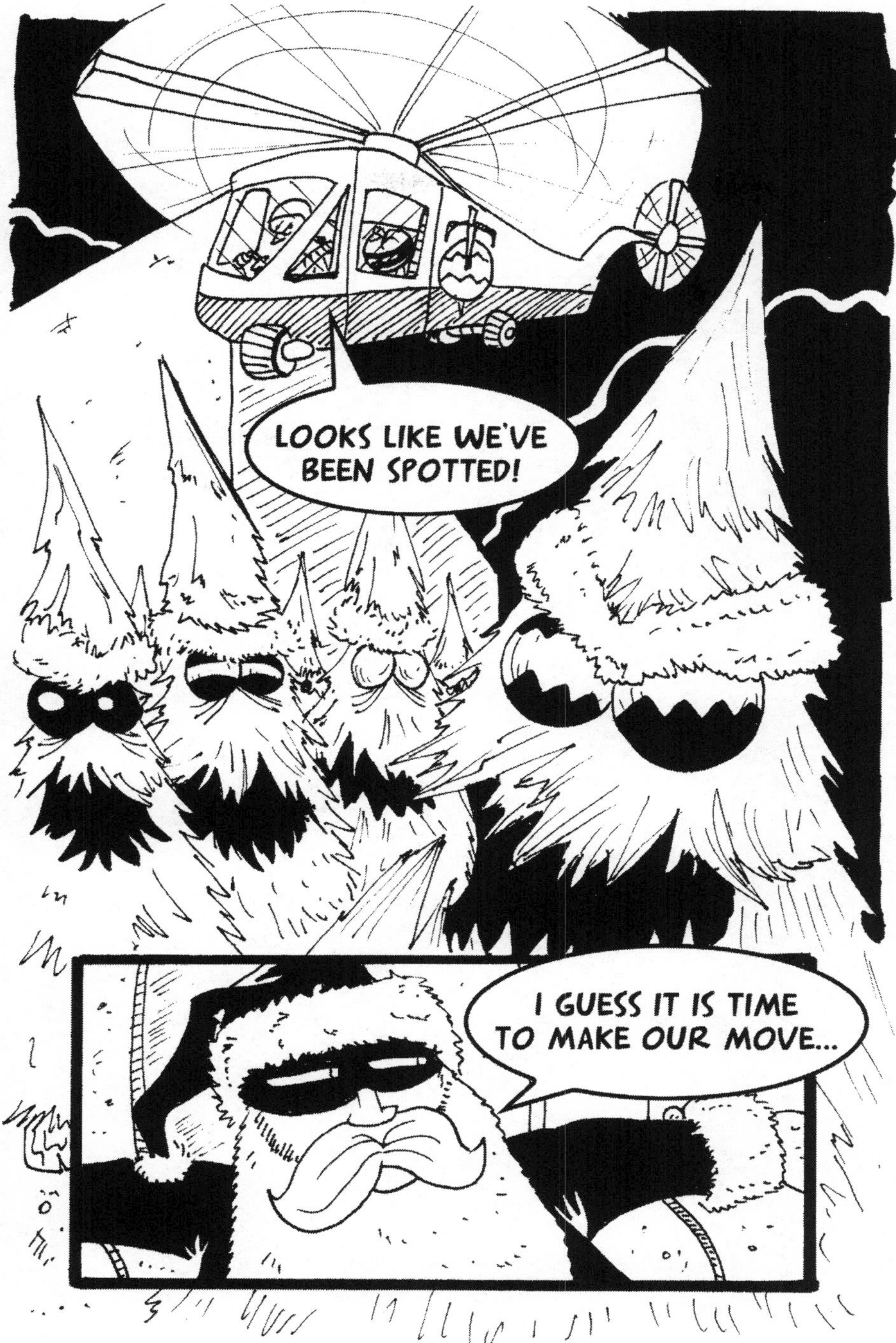
LOOKS LIKE WE'VE BEEN SPOTTED!
I GUESS IT IS TIME TO MAKE OUR MOVE...

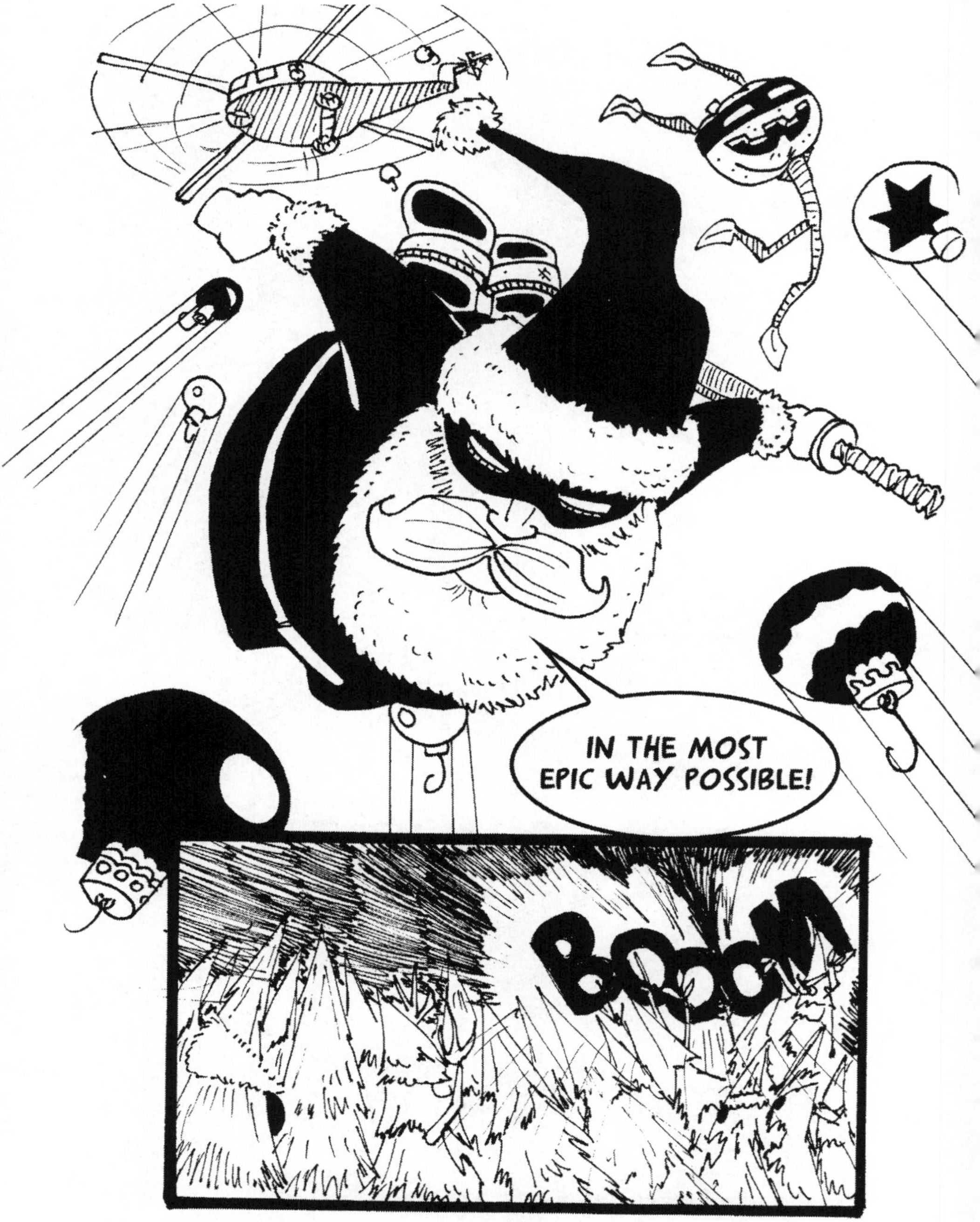
IN THE MOST EPIC WAY POSSIBLE!
BOOM

CLINK!
SANTA SAMURAI

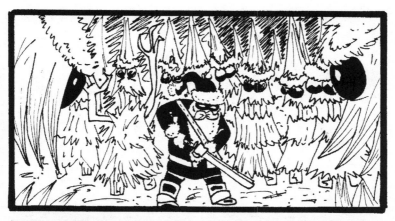

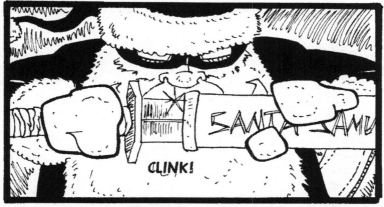

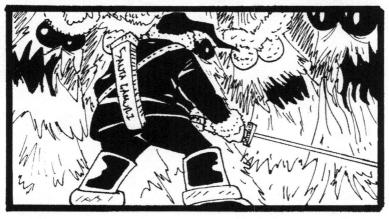

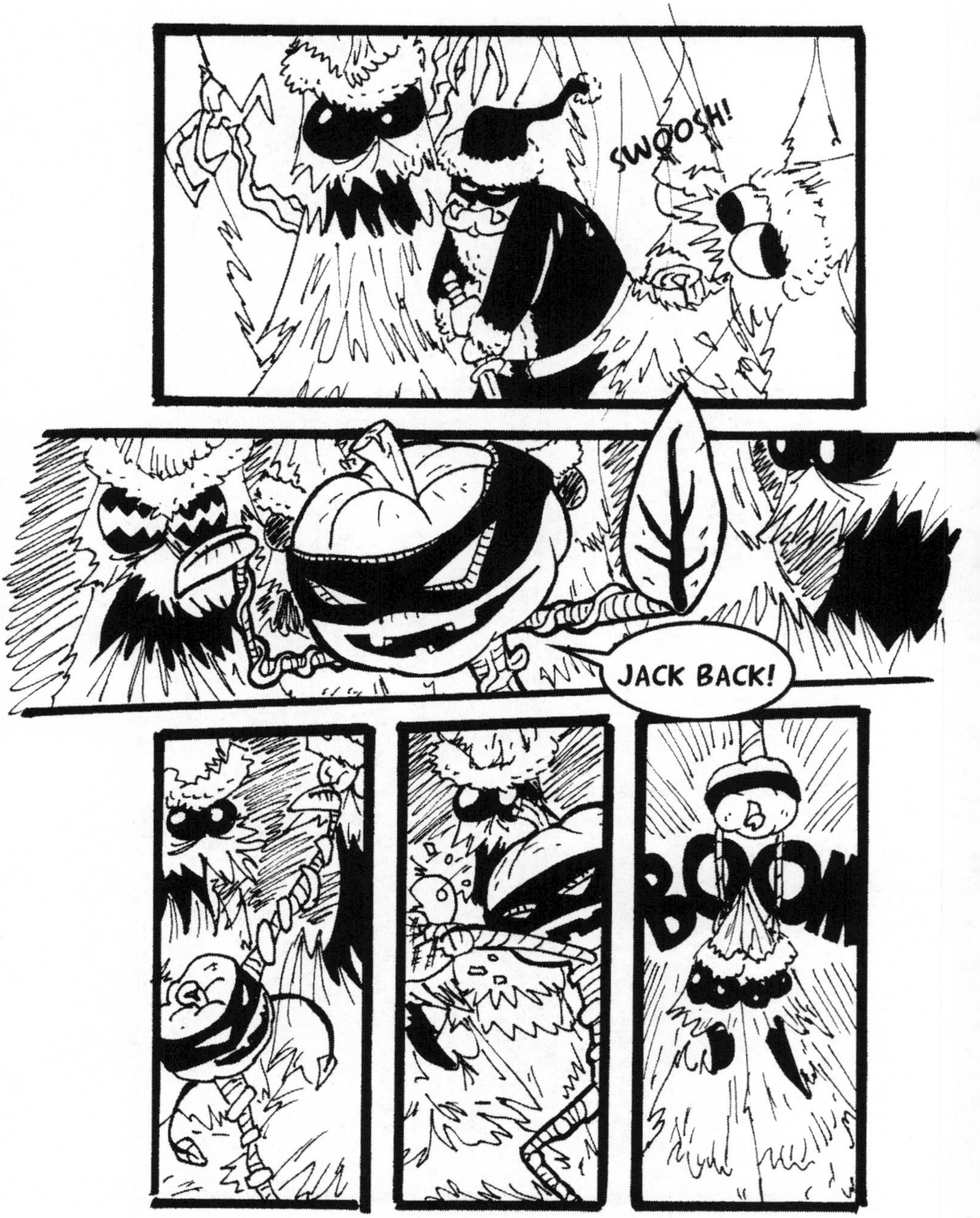
SWOOSH!
JACK BACK!
BOOM

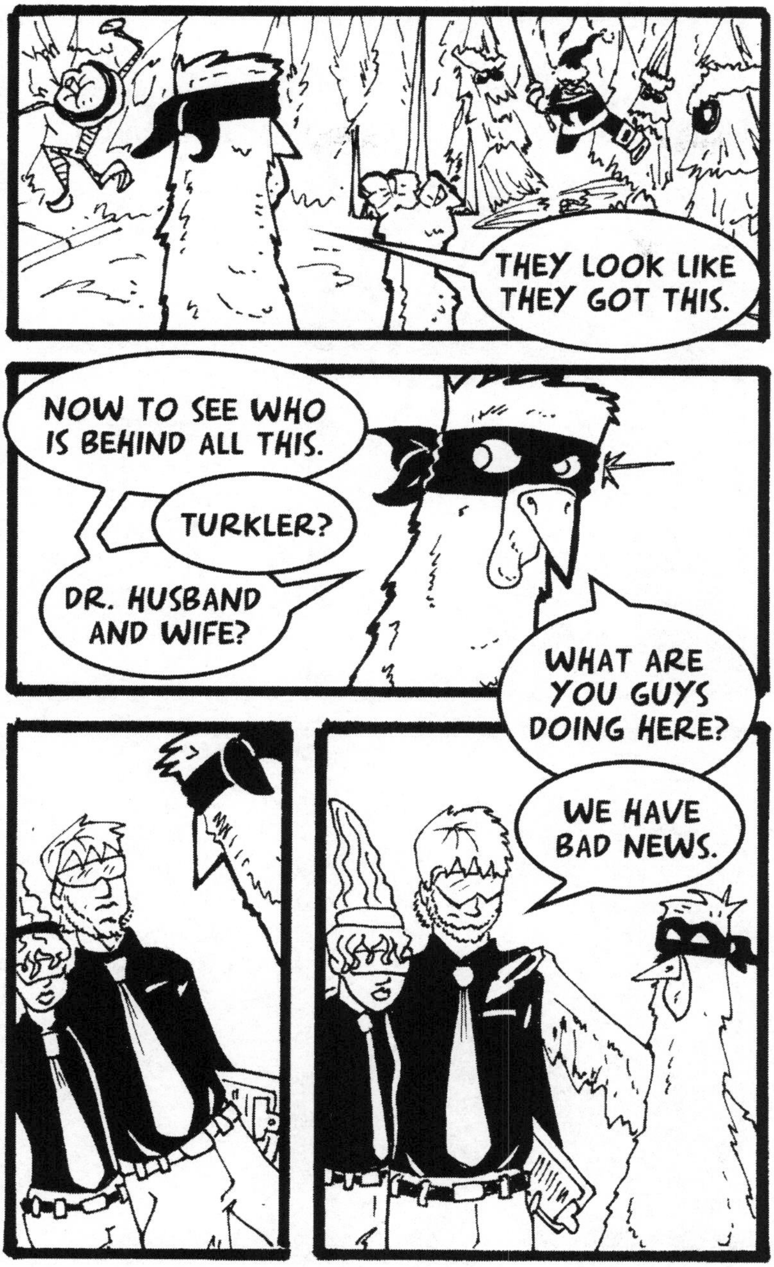
THEY LOOK LIKE THEY GOT THIS.
NOW TO SEE WHO IS BEHIND ALL THIS.
TURKLER?
DR. HUSBAND AND WIFE?
WHAT ARE YOU GUYS DOING HERE?
WE HAVE BAD NEWS.

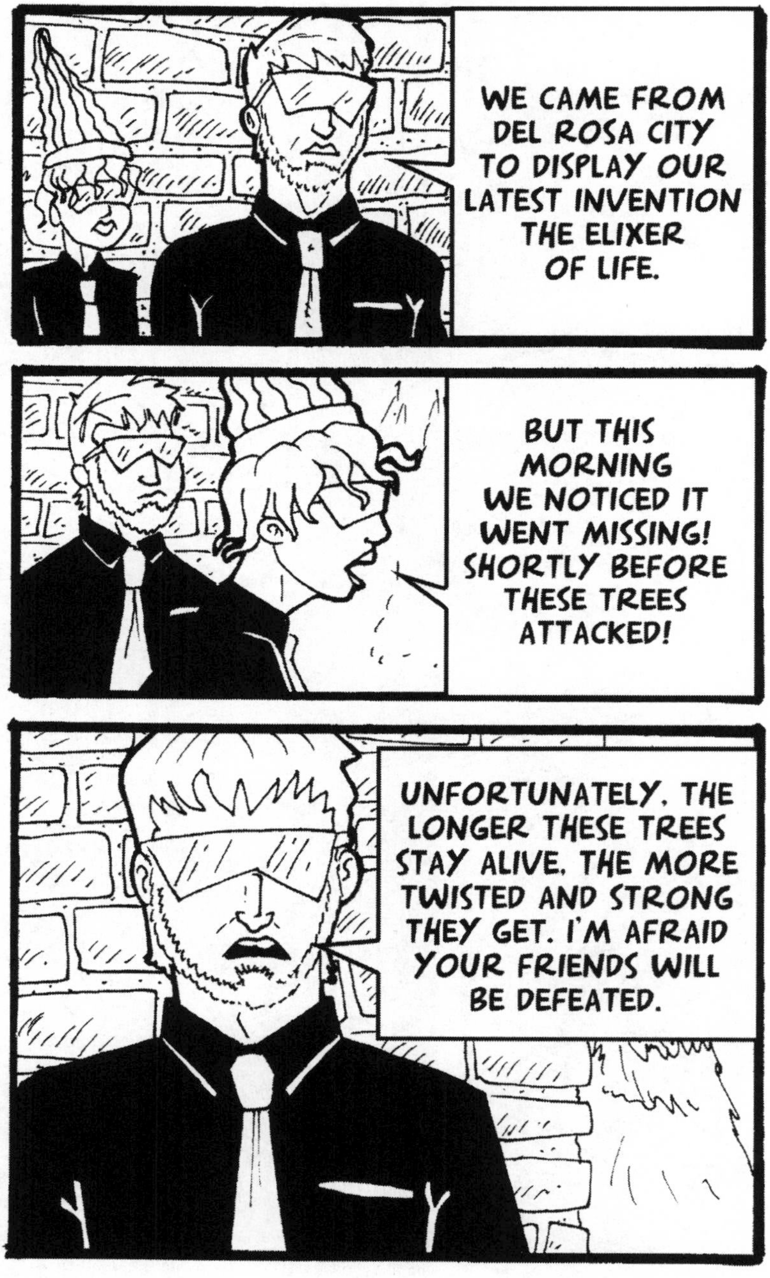
WE CAME FROM DEL ROSA CITY TO DISPLAY OUR LATEST INVENTION THE ELIXER OF LIFE.
BUT THIS MORNING WE NOTICED IT WENT MISSING! SHORTLY BEFORE THESE TREES ATTACKED!
UNFORTUNATELY, THE LONGER THESE TREES STAY ALIVE, THE MORE TWISTED AND STRONG THEY GET. I'M AFRAID YOUR FRIENDS WILL BE DEFEATED.

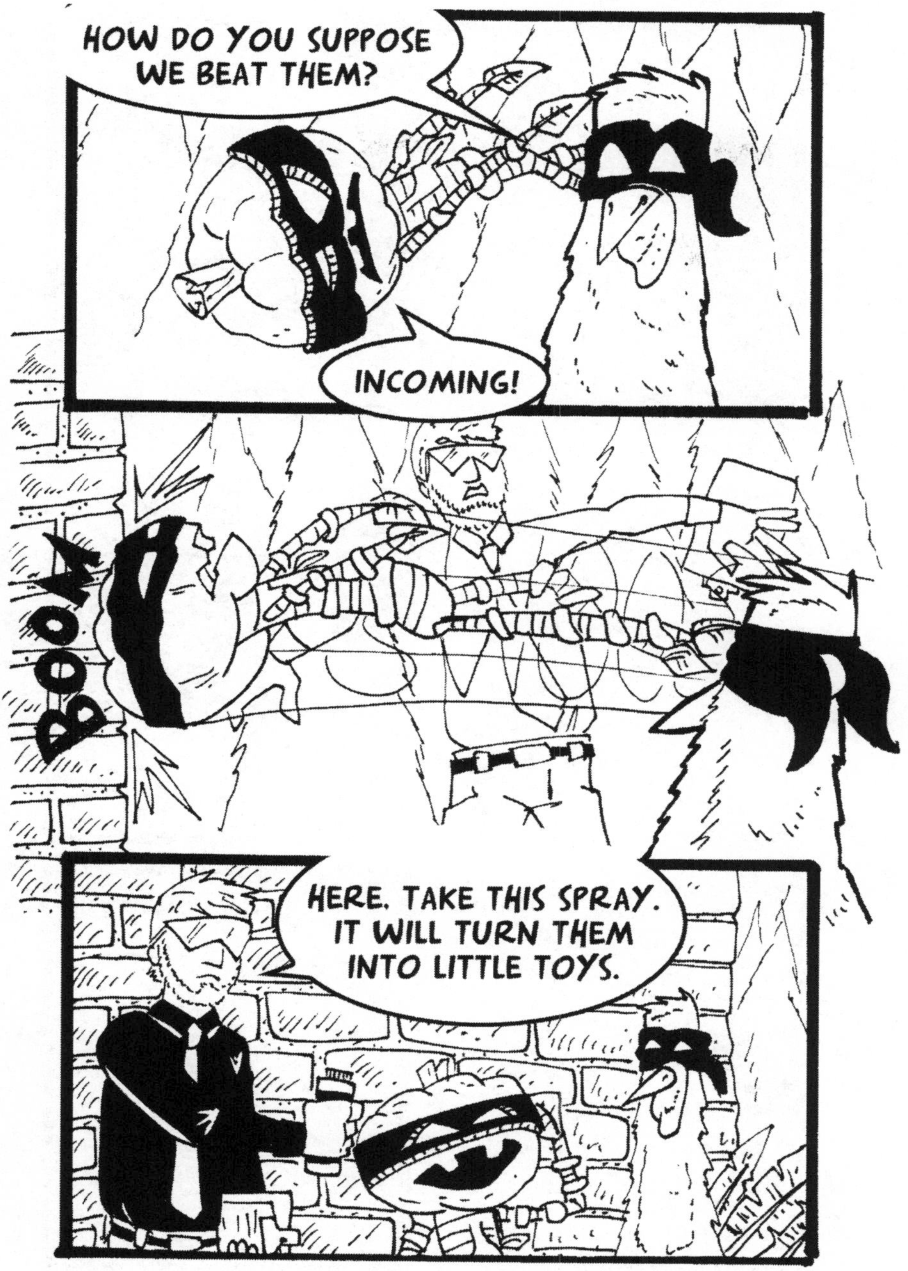
HOW DO YOU SUPPOSE WE BEAT THEM?
INCOMING!
BOOM
HERE. TAKE THIS SPRAY. IT WILL TURN THEM INTO LITTLE TOYS.

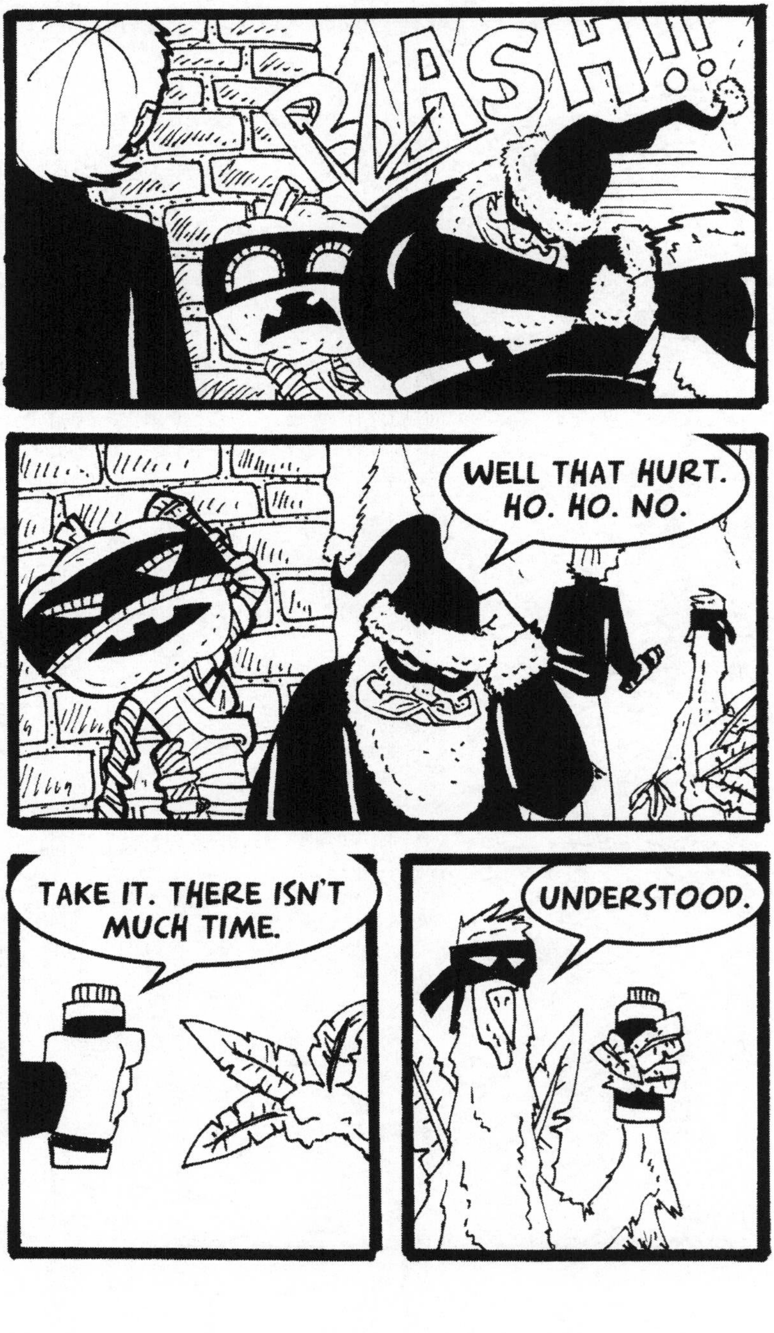
BASH!!!
WELL THAT HURT. HO. HO. NO.
TAKE IT. THERE ISN'T MUCH TIME.
UNDERSTOOD.

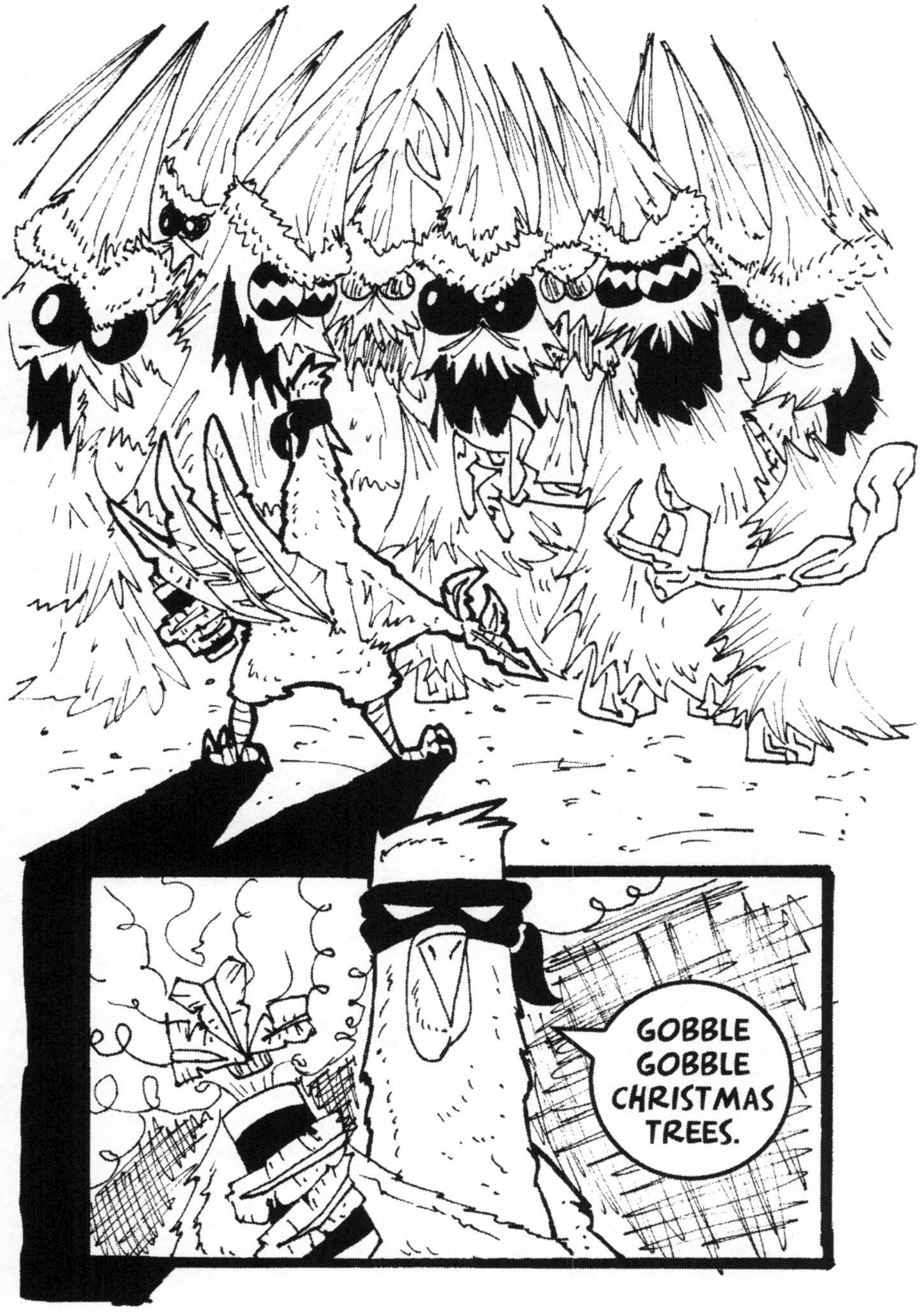
GOBBLE
GOBBLE
CHRISTMAS
TREES.

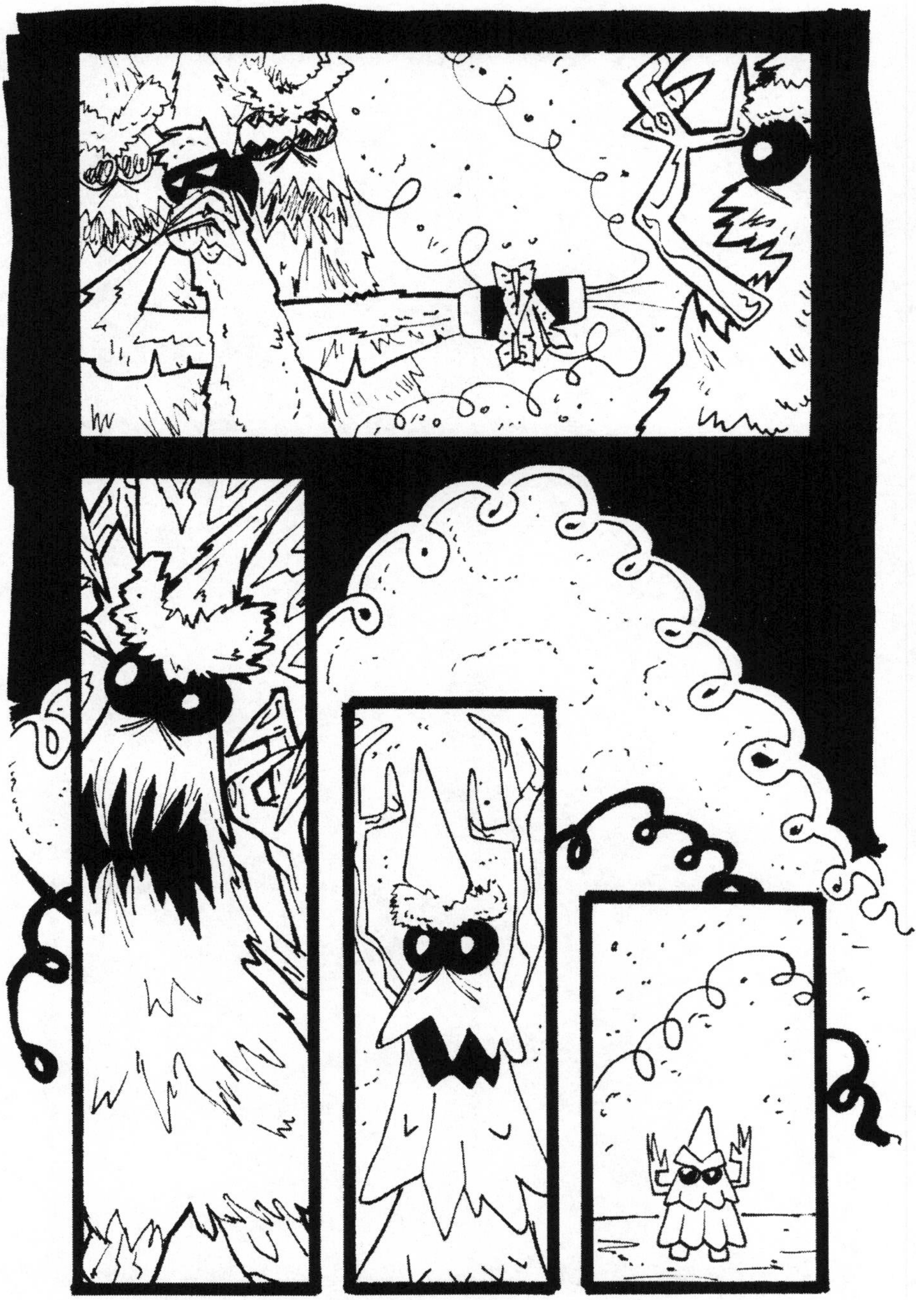

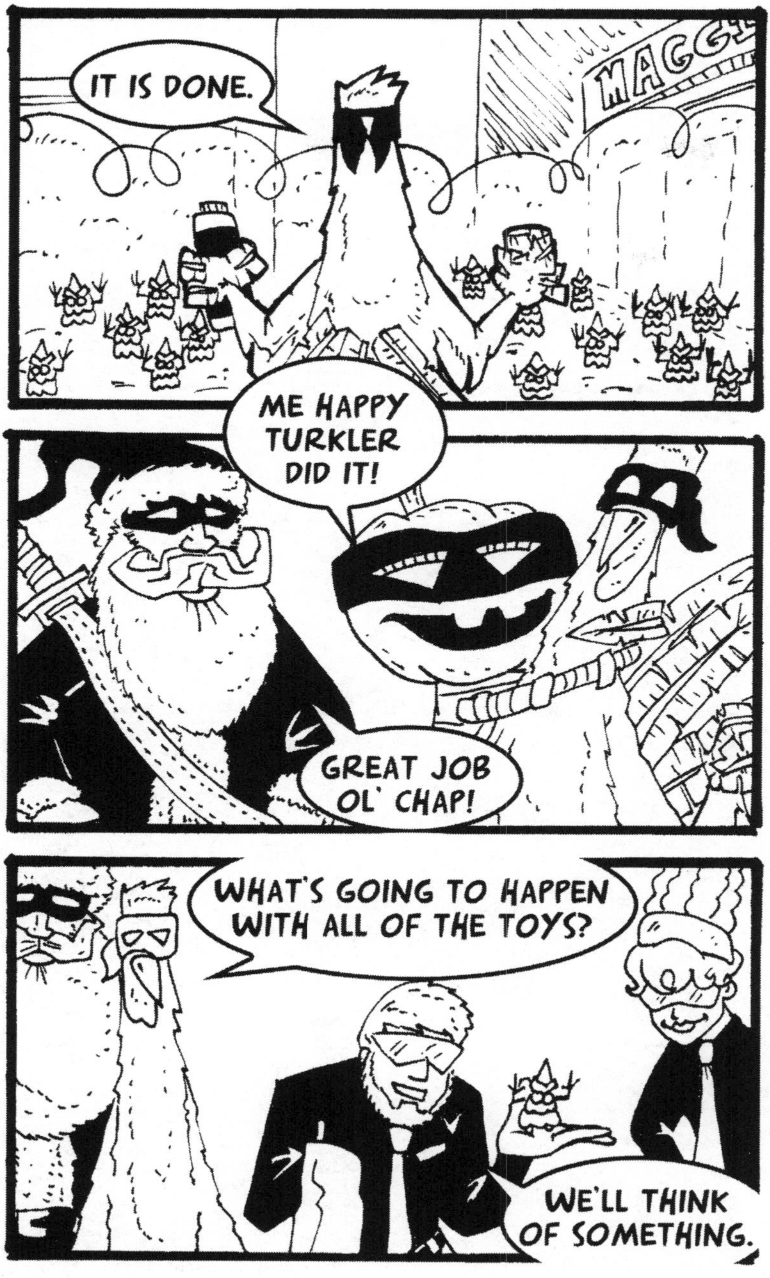
MAGG
IT IS DONE.
ME HAPPY TURKLER DID IT!
GREAT JOB OL' CHAP!
WHAT'S GOING TO HAPPEN WITH ALL OF THE TOYS?
WE'LL THINK OF SOMETHING.

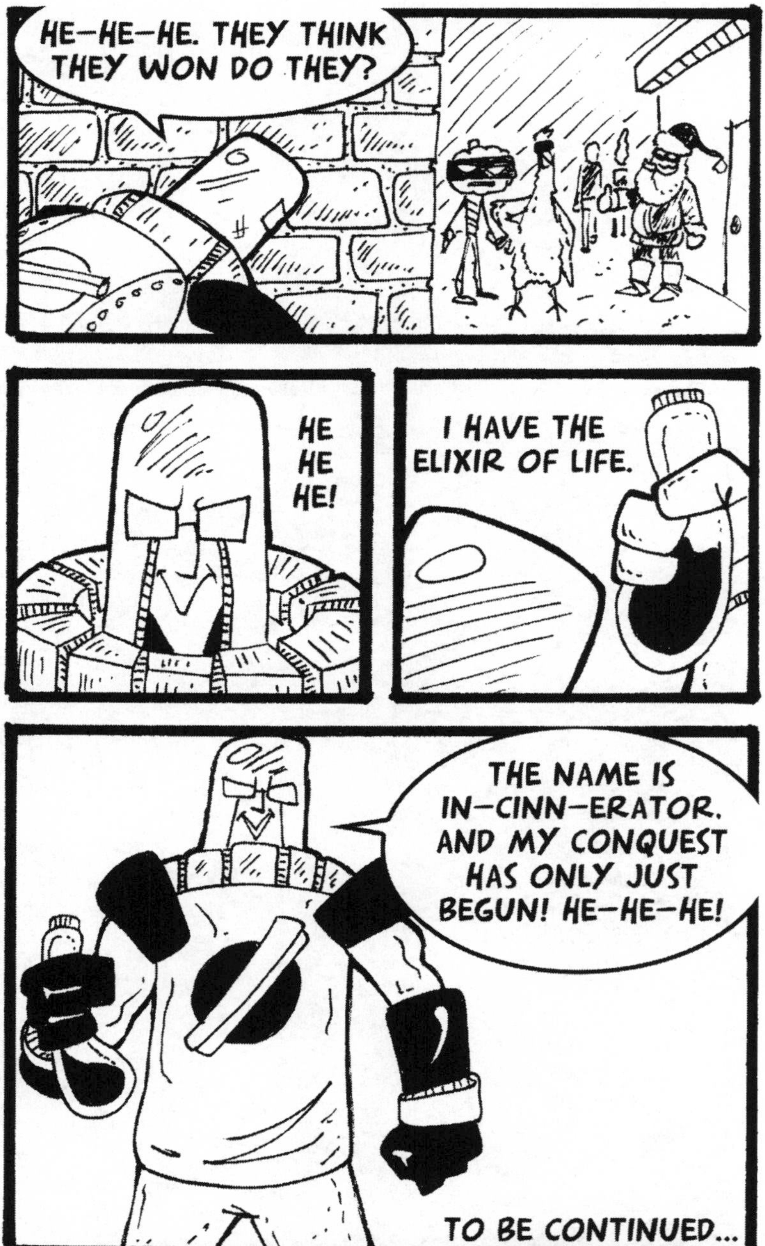
HE-HE-HE. THEY THINK THEY WON DO THEY?
HE HE HE!
I HAVE THE ELIXIR OF LIFE.
THE NAME IS IN-CINN-ERATOR. AND MY CONQUEST HAS ONLY JUST BEGUN! HE-HE-HE!
TO BE CONTINUED...

SOME EXTRAS!

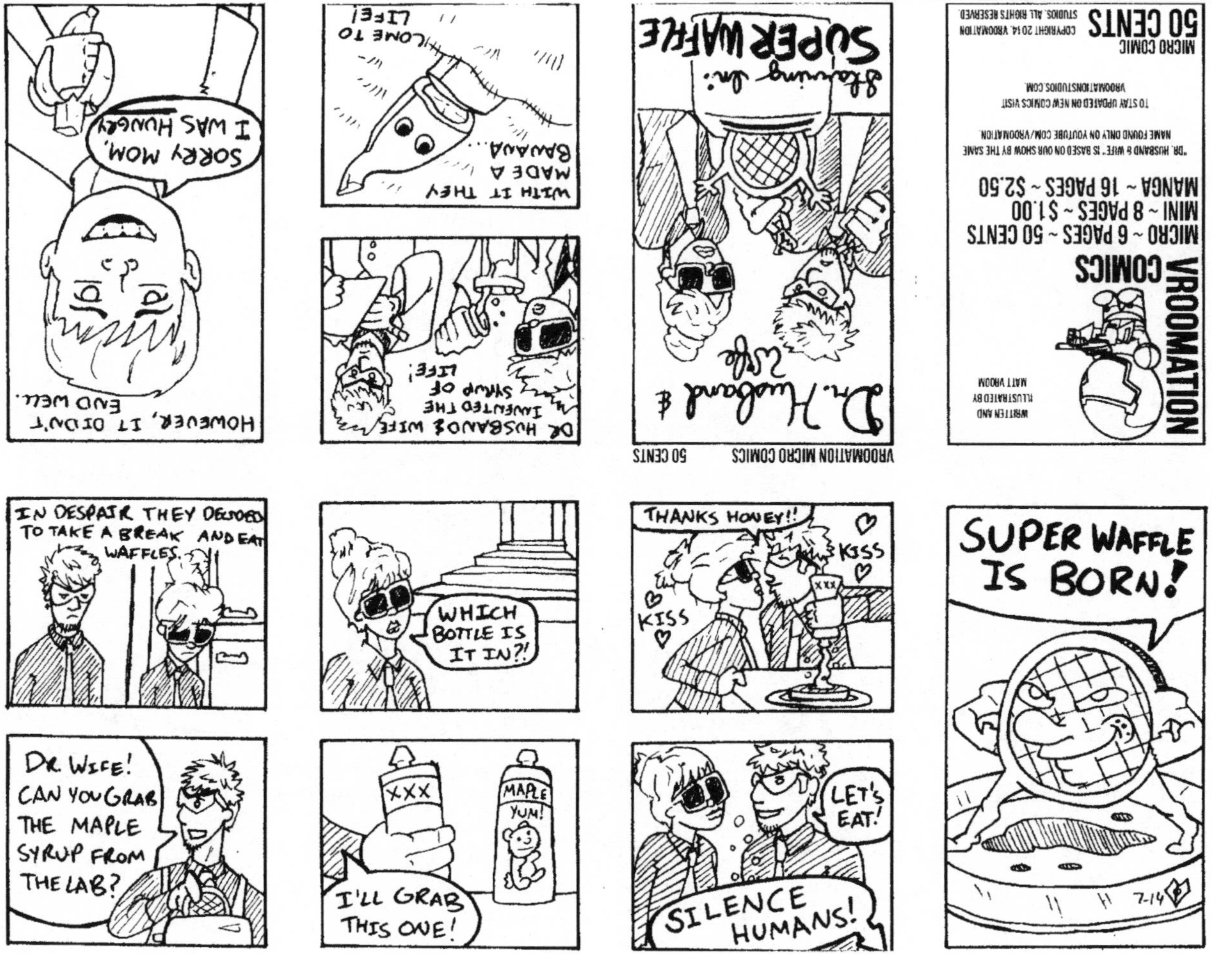
VROOMATION MICRO COMICS
50 CENTS
Dr. Husband & Wife
Starring In: SUPER WAFFLE
DR HUSBAND & WIFE INVENTED THE SYRUP OF LIFE!
WITH IT THEY MADE A BANANA...
COME TO LIFE!
HOWEVER, IT DIDN'T END WELL.
SORRY MOM, I WAS HUNGRY
IN DESPAIR THEY DECIDED TO TAKE A BREAK AND EAT WAFFLES.
DR. WIFE! CAN YOU GRAB THE MAPLE SYRUP FROM THE LAB?
WHICH BOTTLE IS IT IN?!
XXX
MAPLE YUM!
I'LL GRAB THIS ONE!
THANKS HONEY!!
KISS
KISS
XXX
LET'S EAT!
SILENCE HUMANS!
SUPER WAFFLE IS BORN!
7-14
VROOMATION COMICS
WRITTEN AND ILLUSTRATED BY MATT VROOM
MICRO ~ 6 PAGES ~ 50 CENTS
MINI ~ 8 PAGES ~ $1.00
MANGA ~ 16 PAGES ~ $2.50
"DR. HUSBAND & WIFE" IS BASED ON OUR SHOW BY THE SAME NAME FOUND ONLY ON YOUTUBE.COM/VROOMATION.
TO STAY UPDATED ON NEW COMICS VISIT VROOMATIONSTUDIOS.COM.
MICRO COMIC 50 CENTS
COPYRIGHT 2014, VROOMATION STUDIOS. ALL RIGHTS RESERVED.

GRAVITY COMICS 75¢
GUARDIANS OF THE KITCHEN
BY MATT VROOM
#1
BREWING IN THE DARKEST CORNER OF THE KITCHEN WAS A GREAT EVIL OF STINKY PROPORTIONS.
ON ONE FATEFUL DAY, IT HAD AWAKENED AND UNLEASHED A STENCH THAT PLAGUED THE KITCHEN.
NO ONE COULD ESCAPE THE DESTRUCTIVE POWER OF THE STENCH!
PLEASE HELP!
THE SMELL IS TOO STRONG!
WAAAAH!!
DO NOT FEAR DISHES! THE GUARDIANS ARE HERE!
IT'S MOUSE SLAYER, SUPER WAFFLE & THE ONCE LIVING BANANA!
OH YEAH!
AT THAT MOMENT THE STENCH MONSTER AROSE FROM THE TRASH CAN OF DOOM TO FIGHT THEM!
WHOA!
WOOSH
HE'S GOT THE BANANA!
OH NO!
HE'S TOO POWERFUL...
UH... GUYS, A LITTLE HELP?
HA HA HA HA HA HA HA
WHAT IS TO BECOME OF THE ONCE LIVING BANANA? FIND OUT IN OUR NEXT ISSUE OF GUARDIANS OF THE KITCHEN
TO BE CONTINUED...
GRAVITY COMICS
COMICS, CRUISER BOARDS, T-SHIRTS, ANIMATIONS AND MORE.
PLEASE VISIT
WWW.GRAVITYCOMICS.COM
MICRO COMIC ~ 75 CENTS

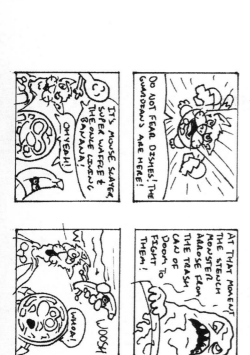

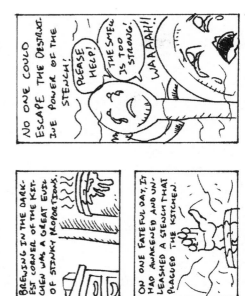

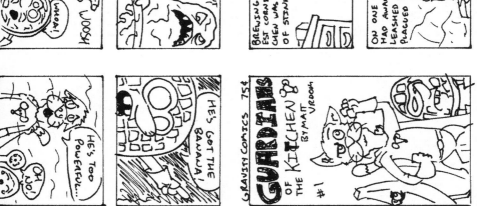

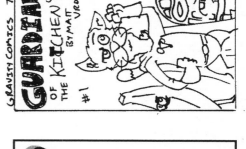

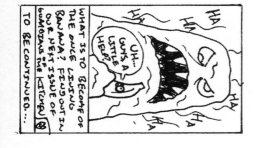

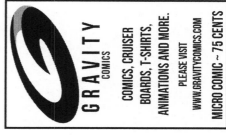

Ultra-Gravity: The Web Series

Bzzz
Bzz
Bzzz
WHAK

MILO!! DID YOU JUST BLOW UP THAT PLANET?!
What planet?
TYRANNUS II!! WE WERE SUPPOSED TO COLONIZE IT, NOT DESTROY IT!!
HOW DO YOU KNOW IT WAS ME?
THANKFULLY NO ONE WAS DOWN ON THAT PLANET.
IT DID SMELL AWFULLY BAD...
SO I DID YOU A FAVOR?
RIGHT YOU DID, SON! NOW I AM GOING TO DO YOU A FAVOR. CONGRATS YOU'RE FIRED!!

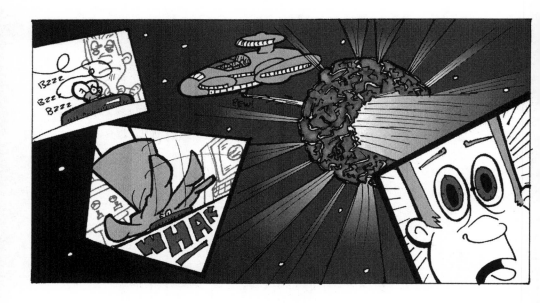

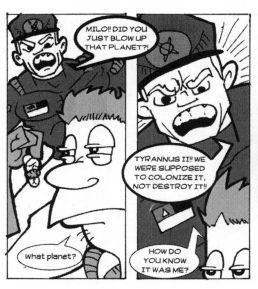

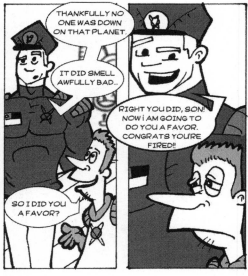

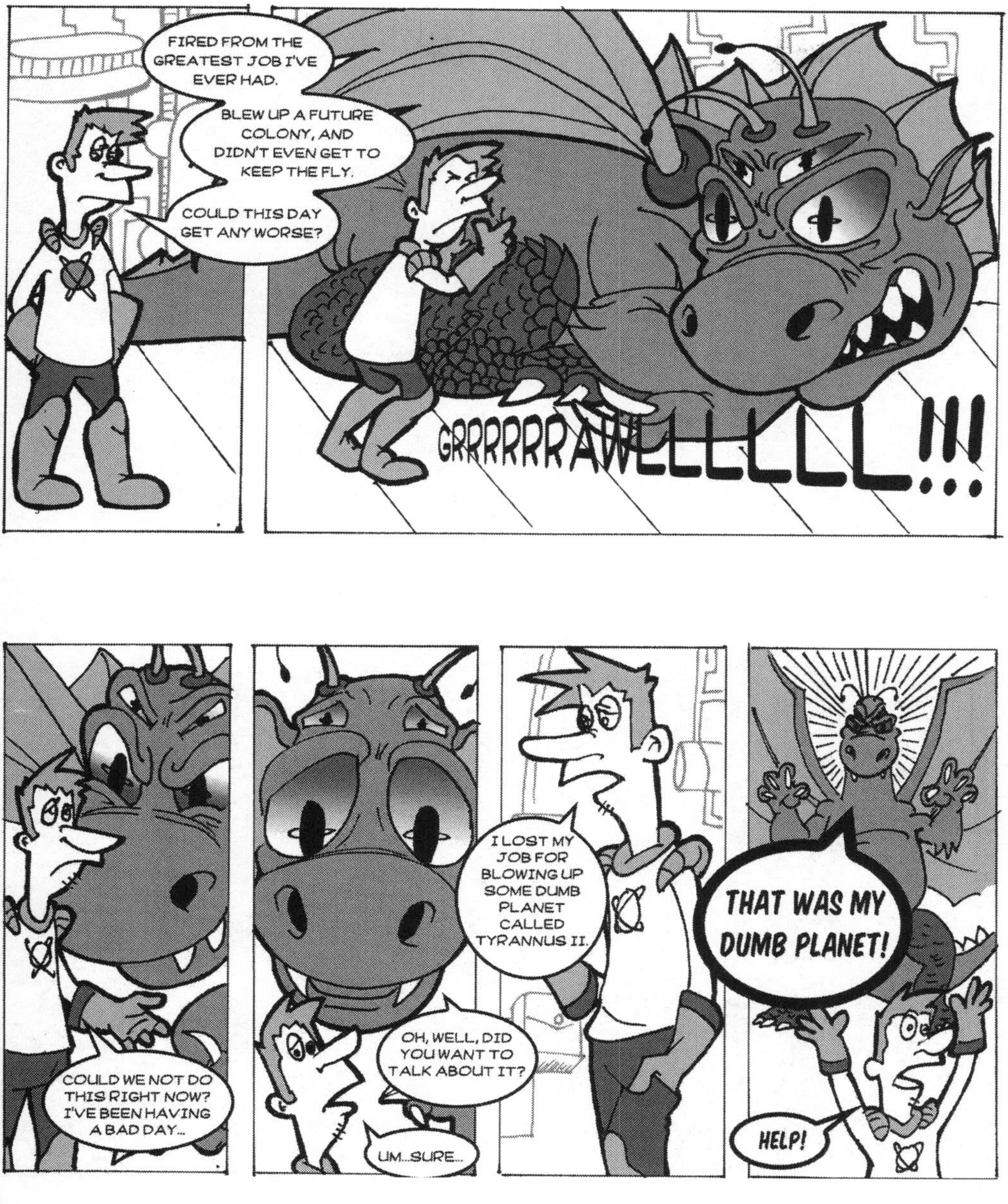
FIRED FROM THE GREATEST JOB I'VE EVER HAD.
BLEW UP A FUTURE COLONY, AND DIDN'T EVEN GET TO KEEP THE FLY.
COULD THIS DAY GET ANY WORSE?
GRRRRRRAWLLLLLLL!!!
COULD WE NOT DO THIS RIGHT NOW? I'VE BEEN HAVING A BAD DAY...
OH, WELL, DID YOU WANT TO TALK ABOUT IT?
UM...SURE...
I LOST MY JOB FOR BLOWING UP SOME DUMB PLANET CALLED TYRANNUS II.
THAT WAS MY DUMB PLANET!
HELP!

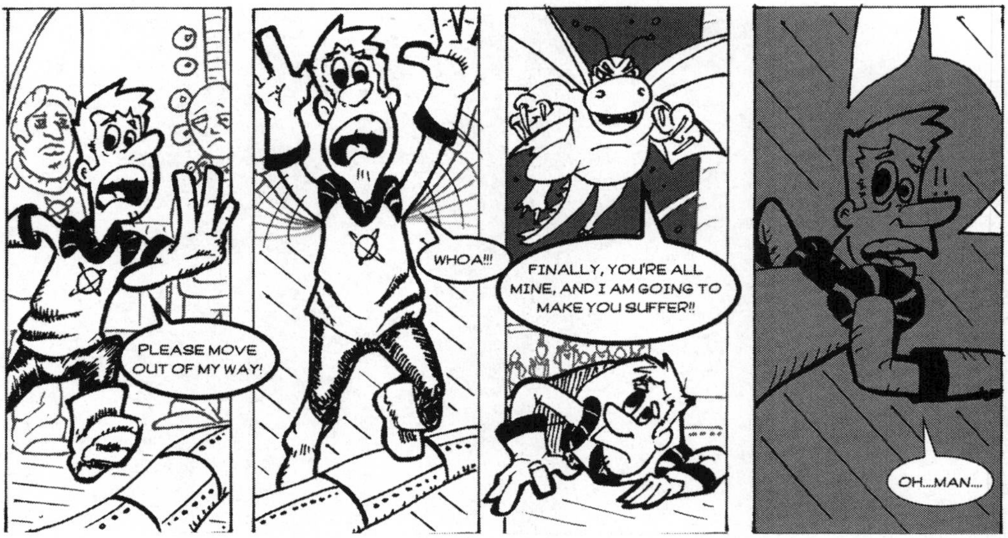
PLEASE MOVE OUT OF MY WAY!
WHOA!!!
FINALLY, YOU'RE ALL MINE, AND I AM GOING TO MAKE YOU SUFFER!!
OH....MAN....

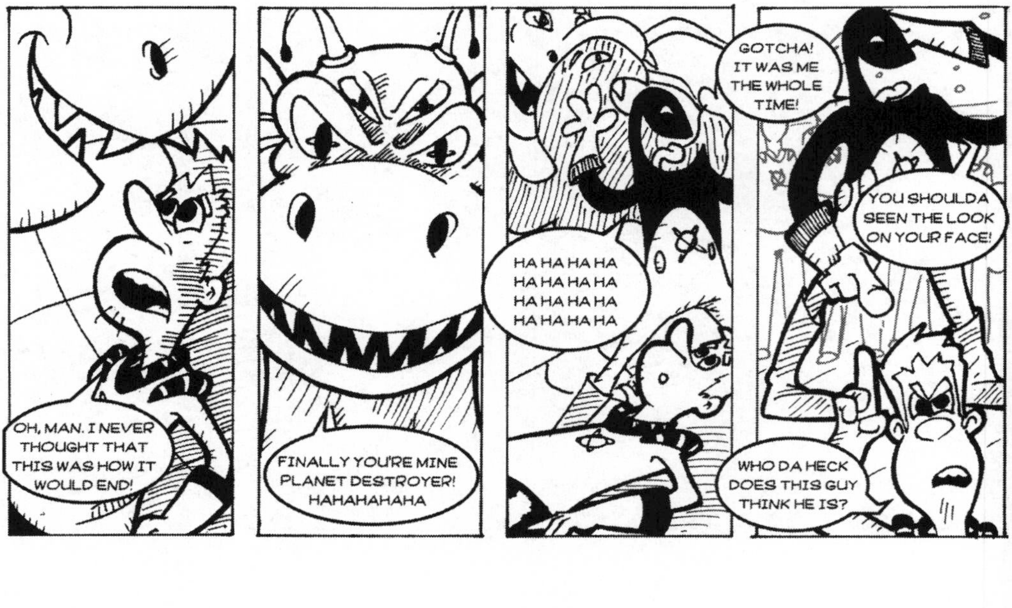
OH, MAN. I NEVER THOUGHT THAT THIS WAS HOW IT WOULD END!
FINALLY YOU'RE MINE PLANET DESTROYER! HAHAHAHAHA
HA HA HA HA HA HA HA HA HA HA HA HA HA HA HA HA
GOTCHA! IT WAS ME THE WHOLE TIME!
YOU SHOULDA SEEN THE LOOK ON YOUR FACE!
WHO DA HECK DOES THIS GUY THINK HE IS?

SO, YOU'RE A SHAPESHIFTER FROM ANOTHER DIMENSION?
YA, AND NOW I'M KINDA STUCK HERE.
AND HERE I THOUGHT I HAD IT ROUGH.
OH IT'S NOT SO BAD! THIS DIMENSION IS SO LESS CROWDED.
SO WHAT ARE YOU DOING HERE?
I CAME TO RECRUIT YOU!
WELCOME YOU TO THE ULTRA-GRAVITY EXPLORATION OPERATION STATION!

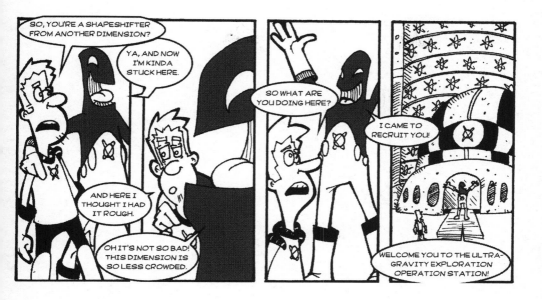

Matt's Notes:

This web comic was my second series to publish online. The first being Super Elders: The Web Comic. Which you can see at superelderscomic.com. The reason that isn't published in this book is because I am working on a big project related to it, and have plans.

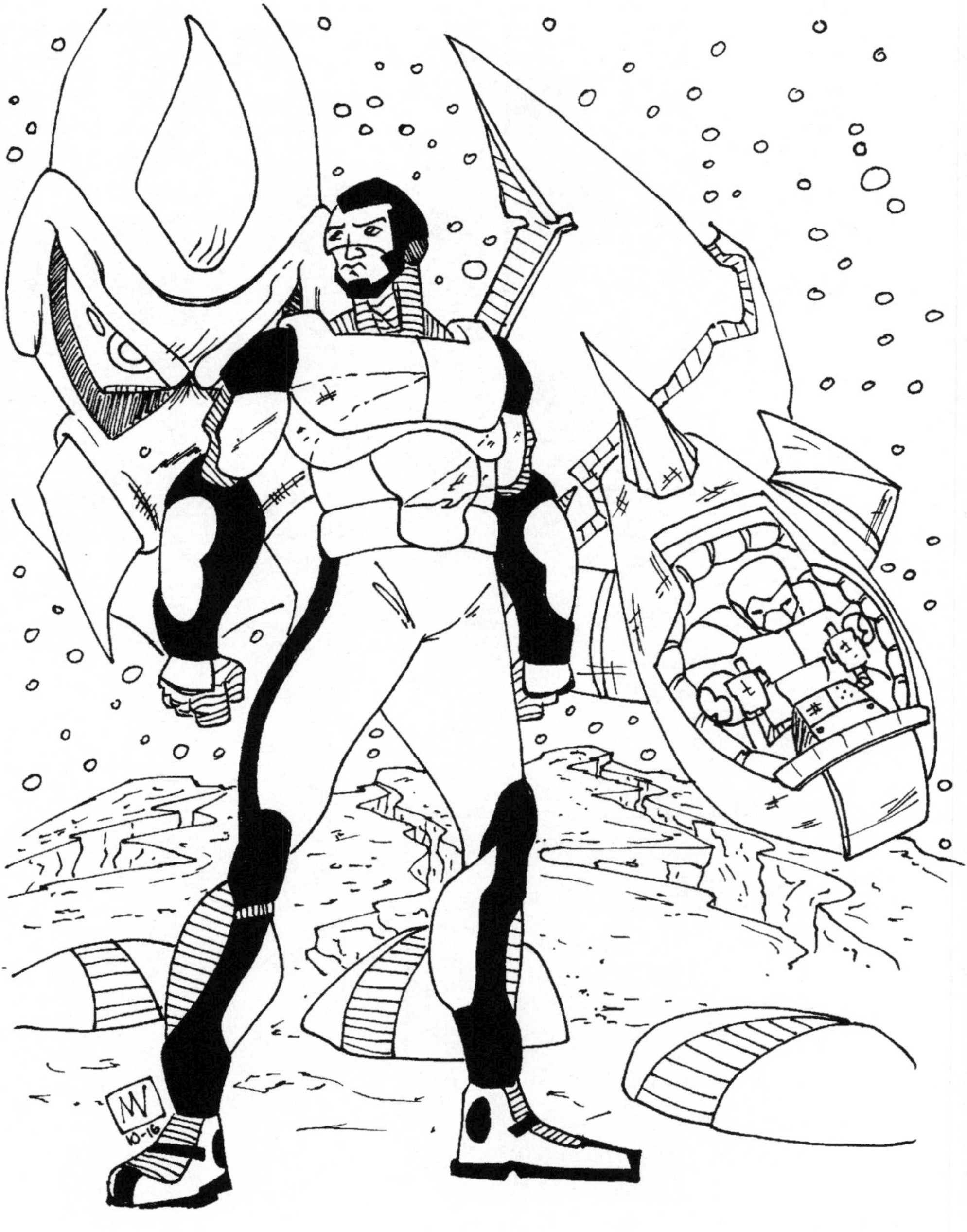

MATT VROOM

Matt Vroom is an avid comic book reader and writer. He and his wife started Vroomation Studios in 2013 as a caricature/party entertainment company in Rexburg, ID. Since then the company has grown into an online entertainment source, and has been a fun project.

Vroom has wrote and illustrated several exciting stories such as *Super Elders*, *Planet Ultra*, and *Holiday Ninjas*.

He has also been the illustrator for the book *I Miss My Daddy*, and independent comic book series *Pi-Guy*.

His personal website is www.mattvroom.com, and his company website is www.vroomation.com.

Thank you for reading!

Made in the USA
Charleston, SC
30 November 2016